JAMES BRYCE.

THE

HOLY ROMAN EMPIRE.

By JAMES BRYCE, D.C.L.,

FELLOW OF ORIEL COLLEGE AND REGIUS PROFESSOR OF CIVIL LAW IN THE
UNIVERSITY OF OXFORD, M.P. FOR ABERDEEN.

Reprinted from the Latest Revised London Edition.

WILDSIDE PRESS

www.wildsidebooks.com

PREFACE.

THE object of this treatise is not so much to give a narrative history of the countries included in the Romano-Germanic Empire — Italy during the Middle Ages, Germany from the ninth century to the nineteenth — as to describe the Holy Empire itself as an institution or system, the wonderful offspring of a body of beliefs and traditions which have almost wholly passed away from the world. Such a description, however, would not be intelligible without some account of the great events which accompanied the growth and decay of Imperial power ; and it has therefore appeared best to give the book the form rather of a narrative than of a dissertation; and to combine with an exposition of what may be called the theory of the Empire an outline of the political history of Germany, as well as some notices of the affairs of mediæval Italy. To make the succession of events clearer, a chronological list of Emperors and Popes has been prefixed.

The great events of 1866 and 1870 reflect back so much light upon the previous history of Germany, and so much need, in order to be properly understood, to be viewed in their relation to the character and influence of the old Empire, that although they do not fall within the original limits of this treatise, some remarks upon them, and the causes which led to them, will not be out of place in it, and will perhaps add to whatever interest or value it may possess. As the Author found that to introduce these remarks into the body of the work would oblige him to take to pieces and rewrite the last three chapters, a task he had no time for, he has preferred to throw them into a new supplementary chapter, which accordingly contains a brief sketch of the rise of Prussia, of the state of Germany under the Confederation which expired in 1866, and of the steps whereby the German nation has regained its political unity in the new Empire.

The book has been revised throughout, and some additions made to it, for most of which the Author has to express his thanks to his learned German translator, Dr. Arthur Winckler, of Brunswick. He also desires to acknowledge the benefit which he derived, in preparing the last chapter, from the suggestions of his friend Mr. A. W. Ward, Professor of History in Owens College, Manchester, whose eminence as a historian is too well known to need any tribute from him.

LINCOLN'S INN, LONDON,
June 28, 1873.

This Edition has been revised, and a number of corrections made, for most of which the Author is indebted to the learning of his friend, the Italian translator of the book, Count Ugo Balzani, himself a distinguished authority on Italian history.

December 22, 1886.

CONTENTS.

CHAPTER V.

EMPIRE AND POLICY OF CHARLES.

CHAPTER VI.

CAROLINGIAN AND ITALIAN EMPERORS.

CHAPTER VII.

THEORY OF THE MEDIÆVAL EMPIRE.

CHAPTER VIII.

THE ROMAN EMPIRE AND THE GERMAN KINGDOM.

CHAPTER IX.

SAXON AND FRANCONIAN EMPERORS.

CHAPTER X.

STRUGGLE OF THE EMPIRE AND THE PAPACY.

CHAPTER XI.

THE EMPERORS IN ITALY: FREDERICK BARBAROSSA.

CHAPTER XII.

IMPERIAL TITLES AND PRETENSIONS.

CHAPTER XVI.

THE CITY OF ROME IN THE MIDDLE AGES.

CHAPTER XVII.

THE RENAISSANCE : CHANGE IN THE CHARACTER OF THE EMPIRE.

CONTENTS.

CHAPTER XVIII.

THE REFORMATION AND ITS EFFECTS UPON THE EMPIRE.

CHAPTER XIX.

THE PEACE OF WESTPHALIA : LAST STAGE IN THE DECLINE OF THE EMPIRE.

CHAPTER XX.

FALL OF THE EMPIRE.

CHAPTER XXI.

CONCLUSION : GENERAL SUMMARY.

SUPPLEMENTARY CHAPTER.

THE NEW GERMAN EMPIRE.

APPENDIX.

DATES OF

SEVERAL IMPORTANT EVENTS

IN THE HISTORY OF THE EMPIRE.

CHRONOLOGICAL TABLE

OF

EMPERORS AND POPES.

Year of Accession	Bishops of Rome.	Emperors.	Year of Accession
A.D.			B.C.
		Augustus.	27
			A.D.
		Tiberius.	14
		Caligula.	37
		Claudius.	41
42	St. Peter, (according to Jerome).		
		Nero.	54
67	Linus, (according to Irenæus, Eusebiuss, Jerome).		
68	Clement, (according to Tertullian and Rufinus).	Galba, Otho, Vitellius, Vespasian.	68
78	Anacletus (?).		
		Titus.	79
		Domitian.	81
91	Clement, (according to some later writers).		
		Nerva.	96
		Trajan.	98
100	Evarestus (?).		
109	Alexander (?).		
		Hadrian.	117
119	Sixtus I.		
129	Telesphorus.		
		Antoninus Pius.	138

Year of Accession	Bishops of Rome.	Emperors.	Year of Accession
A.D.			A.D.
139	Hyginus.		
143	Pius I		
157	Anicetus.		
		Marcus Aurelius.	161
168	Soter.		
177	Eleutherius.		
		Commodus.	180
		Pertinax.	193
		Didius Julianus.	193
		Niger.	193
193	Victor (?).	Septimius Severus.	193
202	Zephyrinus (?).		
		Caracalla, Geta.	211
		Opilius Macrinus, Dia- dumenian.	217
		Elagabalus.	218
219	Calixtus I.		
		Alexander Severus.	222
223	Urban I.		
230	Pontianus.		
235	Anterius or Anteros.	Maximim.	235
236	Fabianus.		
		The two Gordians, Maximus Pupienus, Balbinus.	237
		The third Gordian.	238
		Philip.	244
		Decius.	249
251	Cornelius.	Hostilian, Gallus.	251
252	Lucius I.	Volusian.	252
253	Stephen I.	Æmilian, Valerian, Gallienus.	253
		Gallienus alone.	260
257	Sixtus II.		
259	Dionysius.		
		Claudius II.	268
269	Felix.		
		Aurelian.	270
275	Eutychianus.	Tacitus.	275
		Florian.	276
		Probus.	276
		Carus.	282
283	Caius:		
		Carinus, Numerian.	284
		Diocletian.	284
		Maximian, associated with Diocletian.	286

Year of Accession	Bishops of Rome.	Emperors.	Year of Accession
A.D.			A.D.
296	Marcellinus.		
304	Vacancy.	Constantius, Galerius.	305
		Severus	306
		Constantine (the Great).	306
		Licinius.	307
308	Marcellus I.	Maximin.	308
		Constantine, Galerius, Licinius, Maximin, Maxentius and Maximian reigning jointly.	309
310	Eusebius.		
311	Melchiades.		
314	Sylvester I.		
		Constantine (the Great) alone.	323
336	Marcus I.		
337	Julius I.	Constantine II, Constantius II, Constans.	237
		Magnentius.	
352	Liberius.		
		Constantius alone.	353
356	Felix (Anti-pope).		
		Julian.	361
		Jovian.	363
		Valens and Valentinian I	364
366	Damasus I.		
		Gratian and Valentinian I.	367
		Gratian and Valentinian II.	375
		Theodosius.	379
384	Siricius.		
		Arcadius (in the East), Honorius (in the West).	395
398	Anastasius I.		
402	Innocent I.		
		Theodosius II. (E)	408
417	Zosimus.		
418	Boniface I.		
418	Eulalius (Anti-pope).		
422	Celestine I.		
		Valentinian III. (W)	424
432	Sixtus III.		
440	Leo I (the Great).		
		Marcian. (E)	450
		Maximus, Avitus. (W)	455
		Majorian. (W)	455

Year of Accession	Bishops of Rome.	Emperors.	Year of Accession
A.D.			A.D.
		Leo I. (E)	457
461	Hilarius.	Severus. (W)	461
		Vacancy. (W)	465
		Anthemius. (W)	467
468	Simplicius.		
		Olybrius. (W)	472
		Glycerius. (W)	473
		Julius Nepos. (W)	474
		Leo II, Zeno, Basiliscus. (all E)	474
		Romulus Augustulus. (W)	475
		(End of the Western line in Romulus Augustus.)	476
483	Felix III.*	(*Henceforth, till* A.D. 800, *Emperors reigning at Constantinople*).	
		Anastasius I.	491
492	Gelasius I.		
496	Anastasius II.		
498	Symmachus.		
498	(Laurentius, Anti-pope)		
514	Hormisdas.		
		Justin I.	518
523	John I.		
526	Felix IV.		
		Justinian.	527
530	Boniface II.		
530	(Diocorus, Anti-pope).		
532	John II.		
535	Agapetus I.		
536	Silverius.		
537	Vigilius.		
555	Pelagius I.		
560	John III.		
		Justin II.	565
574	Benedict I.		
278	Pelagius II.	Tiberius II.	578
		Maurice.	582
590	Gregory I (the Great).		
		Phocas.	602
604	Sabinianus.		
607	Boniface III.		
607	Boniface IV.		

* Reckoning the Anti-pope Felix (A.D. 356) as Felix II.

Year of Accession	Popes.	Emperors.	Year of Accession
A.D.			A.D.
		Heraclius.	610
615	Deus dedit.		
618	Boniface V.		
625	Honorius I.		
638	Severinus.		
640	John IV.		
		Constantine III, Heracleonas, Constans II.	641
642	Theodorus I.		
649	Martin I.		
654	Eugenius I.		
657	Vitalianus.		
		Constantine IV (Pogonatus).	668
672	Adeodatus.		
676	Domnus or Donus I.		
678	Agatho.		
682	Leo II.		
683(?)	Benedict II.		
685	John V.	Justinian II.	685
685(?)	Conon.		
687	Sergius I.		
687	(Paschal, Anti-pope).		
687	(Theodorus, Anti-pope).		
		Leontius.	694
		Tiberius III.	697
701	John VI.		
705	John VII.	Justinian II restored.	705
708	Sisinnius.		
708	Constantine.		
		Philippicus Bardanes.	711
		Anastasius II.	713
715	Gregory II.		
		Theodosius III.	716
		Leo III (the Isaurian).	718
731	Gregory III.		
741	Zacharias.	Constantine V (Copronymus).	741
752	Stephen (II).		
752	Stephen II (or III).		
757	Paul I.		
767	Constantine (Anti-pope).		
768	Stephen III (IV).		
772	Hadrian I.		
		Leo IV.	775
		Constantine VI.	780
795	Leo III.		

Year of Accession	Popes.	Emperors.	Year of Accession
A.D.			**A.D.**
		Deposition of Constantine VI by Irene.	797
		Charles I (the Great).	800
		(*Following henceforth the new Western line*).	
		Lewis I (the Pious).	814
816	Stephen IV.		
817	Paschal I.		
824	Eugenius II.		
827	Valentinus.		
827	Gregory IV.		
		Lothar I.	840
844	Sergius II.		
847	Leo IV.		
855	Benedict III.	Lewis II (in Italy).	855
855	(Anastasius, Anti-pope).		
858	Nicholas I.		
867	Hadrian II.		
872	John VIII.		
		Charles II, the Bald (W. Frankish).	875
		Charles III, the Fat (E. Frankish).	881
882	Martin II.		
884	Hadrian III.		
885	Stephen V.		
891	Formosus.	Guido (in Italy).	891
		Lambert (in Italy).	894
896	Boniface VI.	Arnulf (E. Frankish).	896
896	Stephen VI.		
897	Romanus.		
897	Theodore II.		
898	John IX.		
		*Lewis (the Child).**	899
900	Benedict IV.		
		Lewis III of Provence (in Italy).	901
903	Leo V.		
903	Christopher.		
904	Sergius III.		
911	Anastasius III.	*Conrad I.*	911(?)
913	Lando.		
914	John X.		
		Berengar (in Italy).	915
		Henry I (the Fowler).	918
928	Leo VI.		

* The names in italic are those of German kings who never made any claim to the imperial title.

Year of Accession	Popes.	Emperors.	Year of Accession
A.D.			A.D.
929	Stephen VII.		
931	John XI.		
936	Leo VII.	*Otto I (the Great)*	
939	Stephen VIII.	crowned E. Frankish	
941	Martin III.	king at Aachen.	936
946	Agapetus II.		
955	John XII.		
		Otto I, crowned Emperor at Rome.	
963	Leo VIII.		962
964	(Benedict V, Anti-pope?).		
965	John XIII.		
972	Benedict VI.		
		Otto II.	973
974	(Boniface VII, Antipope?).		
974	Domnus II (?).		
974	Benedict VII.		
983	John XIV.	Otto III.	983
985	John XV.		
996	Gregory V.		
996	(John XVI, Anti-pope?).		
999	Sylvester II.		
		Henry II (the Saint).	1002
1003	John XVII.		
1003	John XVIII.		
1009	Sergius IV.		
1012	Benedict VIII.		
1024	John XIX.	Conrad II (the Salic).	1024
1033	Benedict IX.		
		Henry III (the Black).	1039
1044	(Sylvester, Anti-pope).		
1045	Gregory VI.		
1046	Clement II.		
1048	Damasus II.		
1048	Leo IX.		
1054	Victor II.		
		Henry IV.	1056
1057	Stephen IX.		
1058	Benedict X.		
1059	Nicholas II.		
1061	Alexander II.		
1073	Gregory VII (Hildebrand).		
		(Rudolf of Swabia, rival)	1077
1080	(Clement, Anti-pope).		
		(Hermann of Luxemburg, rival).	
1086	Victor III.		1081

Year of Accession	Popes.	Emperors.	Year of Accession
A.D.			A.D.
1087	Urban II.		
		(Conrad of Franconia, rival).	1093
1099	Paschal II.		
1102	(Albert, Anti-pope).		
1105	(Sylvester, Anti-pope).		
		Henry V.	1106
1118	Gelasius II.		
1118	(Gregory, Anti-pope).		
1119	Calixtus II.		
1121	(Celestine, Anti-pope).		
1124	Honorius II.		
		Lothar II.	1125
1130	Innocent II.		
	(Anacletus, Anti-pope).	*Conrad III.	1138
1138	(Victor, Anti-pope).		
1143	Celestine II.		
1144	Eucius II.		
1145	Eugenius III.		
		Frederick I (Barbarossa).	1152
1153	Anastasius IV.		
1154	Hadrian IV.		
1159	Alexander III.		
1159	(Victor, Anti-pope).		
1164	(Paschal, Anti-pope).		
1168	(Calixtus, Anti-pope).		
1181	Lucius III.		
1185	Urban III.		
1187	Gregory VIII.		
1187	Clement III.		
		Henry VI.	1190
1191	Celestine III.		
		*Philip, Otto IV (rivals).	1197
1198	Innocent III.		
		Otto IV.	1208
		Frederick II.	1212
1216	Honorius III.		
1227	Gregory IX.		
1241	Celestine IV.		
1241	Vacancy.		
1243	Innocent IV.	(Henry Raspe, rival).	1246
		(William of Holland, rival).	1246–7
		*Conrad IV.	1250
1254	Alexander IV.	*Interregnum.*	1254

* Those marked with an asterisk were never actually crowned at Rome.

Year of Accession	Popes.	Emperors.	Year of Accession
A.D.			A.D.
		*Richard (earl of Cornwall), *Alfonso (king Castile), (rivals).	
1261	Urban IV.		1257
1265	Clement IV.		
1269	Vacancy.		
1271	Gregory X.		
		*Rudolf I (of Hapsburg)	1273
1276	Innocent V.		
1276	Hadrian V.		
1277	John XX or XXI.		
1277	Nicholas III.		
1281	Martin IV.		
1285	Honorius IV.		
1289	Nicholas IV.		
1292	Vacancy.	*Adolf (of Nassau).	1292
1294	Celestine V.		
1294	Boniface VIII.		
		*Albert I (of Hapsburg).	1298
1303	Benedict XI.		
1305	Clement V.		
		Henry VII (of Luxemburg).	1308
		Lewis IV (of Bavaria).	1314
1314	Vacancy.	(Frederick of Austria, rival).	
1316	John XXI or XXII.		
1334	Benedict XII.		
1342	Clement VI.		
		Charles IV (of Luxemburg).	1347
1352	Innocent VI.	(Günther of Schwartzburg, rival).	
1362	Urban V.		
1370	Gregory XI.		
1378	Urban VI.	* Wenzel (of Luxemburg).	1378
	(Clement VII, Antipope).		
1389	Boniface IX.		
1394	(Benedict, Anti-pope).		
		*Rupert (of the Palatinate).	1400
1404	Innocent VII.		
1406	Gregory XII.		
1409	Alexander V.		
1410	John XXII or XXIII.	Sigismund (of Luxemburg).	1410

* Those marked with an asterisk were never actually crowned at Rome.

Year of Accession	Popes.	Emperors.	Year of Accession
A.D.		(Jobst of Moravia, rival).	A.D.
1417	Martin V.		
1431	Eugene IV.		
		*Albert II (of Hapsburg).†	1438
1439	(Felix V, Anti-pope).		
		Frederick III.	1440
1447	Nicholas V.		
1455	Calixtus IV		
1458	Pius II.		
1464	Paul II.		
1471	Sixtus IV.		
1484	Innocent VIII.		
1493	Alexander VI.	*Maximilian I.	1493
1503	Pius III.		
1503	Julius II.		
1513	Leo X.		
		‡Charles V.	1519
1522	Hadrian VI.		
1523	Clement VII.		
1534	Paul III.		
1550	Julius III.		
1555	Marcellus II.		
1555	Paul IV.		
		*Ferdinand I.	1558
1559	Pius IV.		
		*Maximilian II.	1564
1566	Pius V.		
1572	Gregory XIII.		
		*Rudolf II.	1576
1585	Sixtus V.		
1590	Urban VII.		
1590	Gregory XIV.		
1591	Innocent IX.		
1592	Clement VIII.		
1604	Leo XI.		
1604	Paul V.		
		*Matthias.	1612
		*Ferdinand II.	1619
1621	Gregory XV.		
1623	Urban VIII.		
		*Ferdinand III.	1637
1644	Innocent X.		

* Those marked with an asterisk were never actually crowned at Rome.

† All the succeeding Emperors, except Charles VII and Francis I, belong to the house of Hapsburg.

† Crowned Emperor, but at Bologna, not at Rome.

Year of Accession	Popes.	Emperors.	Year of Accession
A.D.			A.D.
1655	Alexander VII.		
		*Leopold I.	1658
1667	Clement IX.		
1670	Clement X.		
1676	Innocent XI.		
1689	Alexander VIII.		
1691	Innocent XII.		
1700	Clement XI.		
		*Joseph I.	1705
		*Charles VI.	1711
1720	Innocent XIII.		
1724	Benedict XIII.		
1730	Clement XII.		
1740	Benedict XIV.		
		*Charles VII (of Bavaria).	1742
		*Francis I (of Lorraine).	1745
1758	Clement XIII.		
		*Joseph II.	1765
1769	Clement XIV.		
1775	Pius VI.		
		*Leopold II.	1790
		*Francis II.	1792
1800	Pius VII.		
		Abdication of Francis II.	1806
1823	Leo XII.		
1829	Pius VIII.		
1831	Gregory XVI.		
1846	Pius IX.		

* Those marked with an asterisk were never actually crowned at Rome.

THE HOLY ROMAN EMPIRE.

CHAPTER I.

INTRODUCTORY.

OF those who in August, 1806, read in the English news-papers that the Emperor Francis II had announced to the Diet his resignation of the imperial crown, there were probably few who reflected that the oldest political institution in the world had come to an end. Yet it was so. The Empire which a note issued by a diplomatist on the banks of the Danube extinguished, was the same which the crafty nephew of Julius had won for himself, against the powers of the East, beneath the cliffs of Actium; and which had preserved almost unaltered, through eighteen centuries of time, and through the greatest changes in extent, in power, in character, a title and pretensions from which all meaning had long since departed. Nothing else so directly linked the old world to the new—nothing else displayed so many strange contrasts of the present and the past, and summed up in those contrasts so much of European history. From the days of Constantine till far down into the middle ages it was, conjointly with the Papacy, the recognized center and head of Christendom, exercising over the minds of men an influence such as its material strength could never have commanded. It is of this influence and of the causes that gave it power rather than of the external history of the Empire, that the following pages are designed to treat. That history is indeed full of

interest and brilliancy, of grand characters and striking
situations. But it is a subject too vast for any single
canvas. Without a minuteness of detail sufficient to make
its scenes dramatic and give us a lively sympathy with the
actors, a narrative history can have little value and still less
charm. But to trace with any minuteness the career of
the Empire, would be to write the history of Christendom
from the fifth century to the twelfth, of Germany and
Italy from the twelfth to the nineteenth; while even a narrative of more restricted scope, which should attempt to
disengage from a general account of the affairs of those
countries the events that properly belong to imperial history, could hardly be compressed within reasonable limits.
It is therefore better, declining so great a task, to attempt
one simpler and more practicable though not necessarily
inferior in interest ; to speak less of events than of principles, and endeavor to describe the Empire not as a State
but as an Institution, an institution created by and em-
bodying a wonderful system of ideas. In pursuance of
such a plan, the forms which the Empire took in the several stages of its growth and decline must be briefly
sketched. The characters and acts of the great men who
founded, and guided and overthrew it must from time to
time be touched upon. But the chief aim of the treatise
will be to dwell more fully on the inner nature of the Empire, as the most signal instance of the fusion of Roman
and Teutonic elements in modern civilization : to show
such a combination was possible ; how Charles and Otto
were led to revive the imperial title in the West ; how far
during the reigns of their successors it preserved the memory of its origin, and influenced the European commonwealth of nations.

Strictly speaking, it is from the year 800 A.D., when a
King of the Franks was crowned Emperor of the Romans
by Pope Leo III, that the beginning of the Holy Roman

Empire must be dated. But in history there is nothing isolated, and just as to explain a modern Act of Parliament or a modern conveyance of lands we must go back to the feudal customs of the thirteenth century, so among the institutions of the Middle Ages there is scarcely one which can be understood until it is traced up either to classical or to primitive Teutonic antiquity. Such a mode of inquiry is most of all needful in the case of the Holy Empire, itself no more than a tradition, a fancied revival of departed glories. And thus, in order to make it clear out of what elements the imperial system was formed, we might be required to scrutinize the antiquities of the Christian Church; to survey the constitution of Rome in the days when Rome was no more than the first of the Latin cities; nay, to travel back yet further to that Jewish theocratic policy whose influence on the minds of the mediæval priesthood was necessarily so profound. Practically, however, it may suffice to begin by glancing at the condition of the Roman world in the third and fourth centuries of the Christian era. We shall then see the old Empire with its scheme of absolutism fully matured; we shall mark how the new religion, rising in the midst of a hostile power, ends by embracing and transforming it; and we shall be in a position to understand what impression the whole huge fabric of secular and ecclesiastical government which Roman and Christian had piled up made upon the barbarian tribes who pressed into the charmed circle of the ancient civilization.

CHAPTER ›II.

THE ROMAN EMPIRE BEFORE THE INVASIONS OF THE BARBARIANS.

The Roman Empire in the second century. THAT ostentation of humility which the subtle policy of Augustus had conceived, and the jealous hypocrisy of Tiberius maintained, was gradually dropped by their successors, till despotism became at last recognized in principle as the government of the Roman Empire. With an aristocracy decayed, a populace degraded, an army no longer recruited from Italy, the semblance of liberty that yet survived might be swept away with impunity. Republican forms had never been known in the provinces at all, and the aspect which the imperial administration had originally assumed there, soon reacted on its position in the capital. Earlier rulers had disguised their supremacy by making a slavish senate the instrument of their more cruel or arbitrary acts. As time went on, even this veil was withdrawn; and in the age of Septimus Severus, the Emperor stood forth to the whole Roman world as the single center and source of power and political action. The warlike character of the Roman state was preserved in his title of General; his provincial lieutenants were military governors; and a more terrible enforcement of the theory was found in his dependence on the army, at once the origin and support of all authority. But, as he united in himself every function of government, his sovereignty was civil as well as military. Laws emanated from him; all officials acted under his commission; the sanctity of his person bordered on divinity. This increased concentration of power was mainly required by the necessities of frontier defence, for within there was more decay than disaffection. Few troops were quartered through the country: few fortresses checked the march of armies in the struggles which placed Vespasian and Severus on the throne. The distant crash of war from the Rhine or the Euphrates was scarcely heard or heeded in the profound quiet of the Mediterranean coasts, where, with piracy, fleets had disappeared. No quarrels of race or religion disturbed that calm, for all national distinctions were becoming merged in the idea of a common Empire. The gradual extension of Roman citizenship through the *coloniæ,* the working of the equalized and *Obliteration of national distinctions.* equalizing Roman law, the even pressure of the government on all subjects, the movement of population caused by commerce and the slave traffic, were steadily assimilating the various peoples. Emperors who were for the most part natives of the provinces cared little to cherish Italy or conciliate Rome: it was their policy to keep open for every subject a career by whose freedom they had themselves risen to greatness, and to recruit the senate from the most illustrious families in the cities of Gaul, Spain and Asia. The edict by which Caracalla extended to all natives of the Roman world the rights of Roman citizenship, though prompted by no motives of kindness, proved in the end a boon. Annihilating legal distinctions, it completed the work which trade and literature and toleration to all beliefs but one were already performing, and left, so far as we can tell, only one nation still cherishing a national feeling. The Jew was kept apart by his religion: but the Jewish people were already dispersed over the world. Speculative philosophy lent her aid to this general assimi-

lation. Stoicism, with its doctrine of a universal system
of nature, made minor distinctions between man and man
seem insignificant: and by its teachers the idea of cosmo-
politanism was for the first time proclaimed. Alexandrian
Neo-Platonism, uniting the tenets of many schools, first
bringing the mysticism of the East into connection with
the logical philosophies of Greece, had opened up a new
ground of agreement or controversy for the minds of all
the world. Yet Rome's commanding position
The Capital. was scarcely shaken. Her actual power was
indeed confined within narrow limits. Rarely were her
senate and people permitted to choose the sovereign: more
rarely still could they control his policy; neither law nor
custom raised them above other subjects, or accorded to
them any advantage in the career of civil or military ambition. As in time past Rome had sacrificed domestic
freedom that she might be the mistress of others, so now
to be universal, she, the conqueror, had descended to the
level of the conquered. But the sacrifice had not wanted
its reward. From her came the laws and language that had
overspread the world: at her feet the nations laid the offer-
ings of their labor: she was the head of the Empire and of
civilization, and in riches, fame and splendor far outshone
as well the cities of that time as the fabled glories of
Babylon or Persepolis.

Scarcely had these slowly-working influences brought
about this unity, when other influences began
Diocletian to threaten it. New foes assailed the frontiers;
and Con-
stantine. while the loosening of the structure within was
shown by the long struggles for power which
followed the death or deposition of each successive emperor. In the period of anarchy after the fall of Valerian,
generals were raised by their armies in every part of the
Empire, and ruled great provinces as monarchs apart,
owning no allegiance to the possessor of the capital.

The founding of the kingdoms of modern Europe might
have been anticipated by two hundred years, had the barbarians been bolder, or had there not arisen in Diocletian a
prince active and politic enough to bind up the fragments
before they had lost all cohesion, meeting altered conditions by new remedies. By dividing and localizing authority, he confessed that the weaker heart could no longer
make its pulsations felt to the body's extremities. He parcelled out the supreme power among four persons, and then
sought to give it a factitious strength, by surrounding it
with an oriental pomp which his earlier predecessors would
have scorned. The sovereign's person became more sacred,
and was removed further from the subject by the interposition of a host of officials. The prerogative of Rome was
menaced by the rivalry of Nicomedia, and the nearer greatness of Milan. Constantine trod in the same path, extending the system of titles and functionaries, separating the
civil from the military, placing counts and dukes along the
frontiers and in the cities, making the household larger, its
etiquette stricter, its offices more important, though to a
Roman eye degraded by their attachment to the monarch's
person. The crown became, for the first time, the fountain of honor. These changes brought little good.
Heavier taxation depressed the aristocracy:* population
decreased, agriculture withered, serfdom spread : it was
found more difficult to raise native troops and to pay any
troops whatever. The removal of the seat of power to
Byzantium, if it prolonged the life of a part of the Empire,
shook it as a whole, by making the separation of East and
West inevitable. By it Rome's self-abnegation that she
might Romanize the world, was completed; for though the
new capital preserved her name, and followed her customs

---

* According to the vicious financial system that prevailed, the
curiales in each city were required to collect the taxes, and when
there was a deficit, to supply it from their own property.

and precedents, yet now the imperial sway ceased to be
connected with the city which had created it.   Thus
did the idea of Roman monarchy become more universal; for, having lost its local center, it subsisted no
longer historically, but, so to speak, naturally, as a part
of an order of things which a change in external conditions seemed incapable of disturbing.   Henceforth the
Empire would be unaffected by the disasters of the city.
And though, after the   partition   of   the   Empire
had been confirmed by Valentinian, and finally settled
on the death of Theodosius, the seat of the Western
government   was   removed   first   to   Milan   and   then
to Ravenna, neither event destroyed Rome's prestige, nor
the notion of a single imperial nationality common to all
her subjects.   The Syrian, the Pannonian, the Briton, the
Spaniard, still called himself a Roman.*

For that nationality was now beginning to be supported
by a new and vigorous power.   The Emperors
Christianity.   had indeed opposed it as disloyal and revolutionary ; had more than once put forth their whole
strength to root it out.   But the unity of the Empire, and the ease of communication through its parts, had

---

* See the eloquent passage of Claudian, *In secundum consulatum
Stilicbonis*, 129, *sqq.*, from which the following lines are taken
(150–160):

" Hæc est in gremio victos quæ sola recepit,
   Humanumque genus communi nomine fovit,
   Matris, non dominæ, ritu; civesque vocavit
   Quos domuit, nexuque pio longinqua revinxit.
   Hujus pacificis debemus moribus omnes
   Quod veluti patriis re ionibus utitur hospes:
   Quod sedem mutare licet: quod cernere Thulen
   Lusus, et horrendos quondam penetrare recessus:
   Quod bibimus passim Rhodanum, potamus Oronten,
   Quod cuncti gens una sumus.   Nec terminus unquam
   Romanæ ditionis erit."

favored the spread of Christianity: persecution had scattered the seeds more widely had forced on it a firm organization, had given it martyr-heroes and a history. When Constantine, partly perhaps from a genuine moral sympathy, yet doubtless far more in the well-grounded belief that he had more to gain from the zealous sympathy of its professors than he could lose by the aversion of those who still cultivated a languid paganism, took Christianity to be the religion of the Empire; it was already a great political force, able, and not more able than willing, to repay him by aid and submission. Yet the league was struck in no mere mercenary spirit, for the league was inevitable. Of the evils and *Its Alliance with the* dangers incident to the system then founded, *State.* there was as yet no experience: of that antagonism between Church and State which to a modern appears so natural, there was not even an idea. Among the Jews, the State had rested upon religion; among the Romans, religion had been an integral part of the political constitution, a matter far more of national or tribal or family feeling than of personal*. Both in Israel and at Rome the mingling of religious with civic patriotism had been harmonious, giving strength and elasticity to the whole body politic. So perfect a union was now no longer possible in the Roman Empire, for the new faith had already a governing body of her own in those rulers and teachers whom the growth of sacramentalism, and of sacerdotalism its necessary consequence, was making every day more powerful, and marking off more sharply from the mass of the Christian people. Since therefore the ecclesiastical organization could not be identical with the civil, it became its counterpart. Suddenly called from danger and

---

* In the Roman jurisprudence, *ius sacrum* is a branch of *ius publicum*.

ignominy to the seat of power, and finding her inexperi-
ence perplexed by a sphere of action vast and varied, the
Church was compelled to frame herself upon the model
of the secular administration.   Where her own machinery
was defective, as in the case of doctrinal disputes affecting
the whole Christian world, she sought the interposition of
the sovereign; in all else she strove not to sink in, but to
reproduce for herself the imperial system.   And just as
with the extension of the Empire all the independent
rights of districts, towns, or tribes had disappeared, so
now the primitive freedom and diversity of individual
Christians and local Churches, already circumscribed by
the frequent struggles against heresy, was finally over-
borne by the idea of one visible catholic Church, uniform
in faith and ritual; uniform, too, in her relation to the
civil power and the increasingly oligarchical character of
her government.   Thus, under the combined force of
doctrinal theory and practical needs, there shaped itself
a hierarchy of patriarchs, metropolitans and bishops, their
jurisdiction, although still chiefly spiritual, enforced by
the laws of the state, their provinces and dioceses usually
corresponding to the administrative divisions of the
Empire.   As no patriarch yet enjoyed more than an
honorary supremacy, the head of the Church—so far as
she could be said to have a head—was virtually the Emperor himself.   The apparent right to intermeddle in
religious affairs which he derived from the office of Pontifex Maximus was readily admitted; and the clergy, preaching the duty of passive obedience now as it had been
preached in the days of Nero and Diocletian,* were well

---

* Tertullian, writing circ. A.D. 200, says: "Sed quid ego amplius
de religione atque pietate Christiana in imperatorem ‚quem necesse
est suspiciamus ut eum quem Dominus noster elegerit.   Et merito
dixerim, noster est magis Cæsar, ut a nostro Deo constitutus."—
Apologet. cap. 34.

pleased to see him preside in councils, issue edicts against
heresy, and testify even by arbitrary measures his zeal for
the advancement of the faith and the overthrow of pagan
rites. But though the tone of the Church remained
humble, her strength waxed greater, nor were occasions
wanting which revealed the future that was in store for
her. The resistance and final triumph of Athanasius
proved that the new society could put forth a power of
opinion such as had never been known before: the abase-
ment of Theodosius the Emperor before Ambrose the
Archbishop admitted the supremacy of spiritual authority.
In the decreptitude of old institutions, in the barrenness
of literature and the feebleness of art, it was to the Church
that the life and feelings of the people sought more and
more to attach themselves; and when in the fifth century
the horizon grew black with clouds of ruin, those who
watched with despair or apathy the approach of irresistible foes, fled for comfort to the shrine of a religion which
even those foes revered.

But that which we are above all concerned to remark here
is, that this church system, demanding a more rigid uniformity in doctrine and organization, making more
and more vital the notion of a visible body *It embraces*
of worshipers united by participation in *and pre-*
the same sacraments, maintained and propa- *serves the*
gated afresh the feeling of a single Roman *imperial*
people throughout the world. Christianity as *idea.*
well as civilization became conterminous with the Roman
Empire.*

---

* See the book of Optatus, bishop of Milevis, *Contra Donatistas.*
".Non enim respublica est in ecclesia, sed ecclesia in republica, id est,
in imperio Romano, cum super imperatorem non sit nisi solus Deus:"
(p. 999 of vol. ii. of Migne's *Patrologiæ Cursus completus*). The treatise of Optatus is full of interest, as showing the growth of the idea
of the visible Church, and of the primacy of Peter's chair, as consti-
tuting its center and representing its unity.

CHAPTER III.

THE BARBARIAN INVASIONS.

UPON a world so constituted did the barbarians of the
North descend. From the dawn of history they show as
The Barba- a dim background to the warmth and light of
rians. the Mediterranean coast, changing little while
kingdoms rise and fall in the South : only
thought on when some hungry swarm comes down to pillage or to settle. It is always as foes that they are known.
The Romans never forgot the invasion of Brennus ; and
their fears, renewed by the irruption of the Cimbri and
Teutones, could not let them rest till the extention of the
frontier to the Rhine and the Danube removed Italy from
immediate danger. A little more perseverance under
Tiberius, or again under Hadrian, would probably have
reduced all Germany as far as the Baltic and the Oder.
But the politic or jealous advice of Augustus * was followed, and it was only along the frontiers that Roman arts
and culture affected the Teutonic races. Commerce was
brisk ; Roman envoys penetrated the forests to the
courts of rude chieftains ; adventurous barbarians entered
the provinces, sometimes to admire, oftener, like the
brother of Arminius,† to take service under the Roman
flag, and rise to a distinction in the legion which some

---

* " Addiderat consilium coercendi intra terminos imperii."—Tac.
Ann. i. 2.

† Tac. *Ann.* ii. 9.

feud denied them at home. This was found even more convenient by the hirer than by the employed ; till by degrees barbarian mercenaries came to form the largest, or at least the most effective, part of the Roman armies. The body-guard of Augustus had been so composed; the prætorians were generally selected from the bravest frontier troops, most of them German; the practice could not but increase with the extinction of the free peasantry, the growth of villenage, and the effeminacy of all classes. Emperors who were, like Maximin, themselves foreigners, encouraged a system by whose means they had risen, and whose advantages they knew. After Constantine, the barbarians form the majority of the troops; after Theodosius, a Roman is the exception. The soldiers of the Eastern Empire in the time of Arcadius are almost all Goths, vast bodies of *Admitted* whom had been settled in the provinces; while *to Roman* in the West, Stilicho* can oppose Rhodogast *titles and* only by summoning the German auxiliaries *honors.* from the frontiers. Along with this practice there had grown up another, which did still more to make the barbarians feel themselves members of the Roman state. The pride of the old republic had been exclusive, but under the Empire the maxim was accepted that birth and race should exclude no subject from any post which his abilities deserved. This principle, which had removed all obstacles from the path of the Spaniard Trajan, the Pannonian Miximim, the Numidian Philip, was afterward extended to the conferring of the honor and power on persons who did not even profess to have passed through the grades of Roman service, but remained leaders of their own tribes. Ariovistus had been soothed by the title of Friend of the Roman People; in the third century the insignia of the

---

* Stilicho, the bulwark of the Empire, seems to have been himself a Vandal by extraction.

consulship* were conferred on a Herulian chief: Crocus and his Alemanni entered as an independent body into the service of Rome; along the Rhine whole tribes received, under the name of Laeti, lands within the provinces on condition of military service; and the foreign aid which the Sarmatian had proffered to Vespasian against his rival, and Marcus Aurelius had indignantly rejected in the war with Cassius, became the usual, at last the sole support of the Empire, in civil as well as in external strife.

Thus in many ways was the old antagonism broken down —Romans admitting barbarians to rank and office, barbarians catching something of the manners and culture of their neighbors. And thus when the final movement came, and the Teutonic tribes slowly established themselves through the provinces, they entered not as savage strangers, but as colonists knowing something of the system into which they came, and not unwilling to be considered its members; despising the degenerate provincials who struck no blow in their own defence, but full of respect for the majestic power which had for so many centuries confronted and instructed them.

Their feelings toward the Roman Empire. Great during all these ages, but greatest when they were actually traversing and settling in the Empire, must have been the impression which its elaborate machinery of government and mature civilization made upon the minds of the Northern invaders. With arms whose fabrication they had learned from their foes, these dwellers in the forest conquered well-tilled fields, and entered towns whose busy workshops, marts stored with the productions of distant countries, and palaces rich in monuments of art, equally roused their wonder. To the beauty of statuary or painting they might often be blind, but the rudest mind

---

* Of course not the consulship itself, but the *ornamenta consularia.*

must have been awed by the massive piles with which
vanity or devotion, or the passion for amusement, had
adorned Milan and Verona, Arles, Treves and Bordeaux.
A deeper awe would strike them as they gazed on the
crowding worshippers and stately ceremonial of Christianity, most unlike their own rude sacrifices. The exclama-
tion of the Goth Athanaric, when led into the market-place
of Constantinople, may stand for the feelings of his nation:
" Without doubt the Emperor is a God upon earth, and he
who attacks him is guilty of his own blood."*

The social and political system, with its cultivated language and literature, into which they came, would impress
fewer of the conquerors, but by those few would be admired
beyond all else. Its regular organization supplied what
they most needed and could least construct for themselves,
and hence it was that the greatest among them were the
most desirous to preserve it. The Mongol Attila excepted,
there is among these terrible hosts no destroyer ; the wish
of each leader is to maintain the existing order, to spare
life, to respect every work of skill and labor, above all to
perpetuate the methods of Roman administra-
tion, and rule the people as the deputy or suc-   *Their de-
cessor of their Emperor. Titles conferred by   sire to pre-
him were the highest honors they knew : they   serve its in-
were also the only means of acquiring some-   stitution.*
thing like a legal claim to the obedience of the subject,
and of turning a patriarchal or military chieftainship into
the regular sway of an hereditary monarch. Civilis had
long since endeavored to govern his Batavians as a Roman
general.† Alaric became master-general of the armies of
Illyricum. Clovis exulted in the consulship; his son
Theodebert received Provence, the conquest of his own bat-
tle-ax, as the gift of Justinian. Sigismund the Bur-

---

* Jordanes, *De Rebus Geticis*, cap. 28.
† Tac. *Hist.* i. and iv.

gundian king, created count and patrician by the Emperor
Anastasius, professed the deepest gratitude and the firmest faith to that Eastern court which was absolutely powerless to help or to hurt him. "My people is yours," he
writes, "and to rule them delights me less than to serve
you; the hereditary devotion of my race to Rome has made
us account those the highest honors which your military
titles convey ; we have always preferred what an Emperor
gave to all that our ancestors could bequeath. In ruling
our nation we hold ourselves but your lieutenants : you,
whose divinely-appointed sway no barrier bounds, whose
beams shine from the Bosphorus into distant Gaul,
employ us to administer the remoter regions of your
Empire: your world is our fatherland."* A contemporary
historian has recorded the remarkable disclosure of his
own thoughts and purposes, made by one of the ablest
of the barbarian chieftans, Athaulf the Visigoth, the
brother-in-law and successor of Alaric. "It was at first my
wish to destroy the Roman name and erect in its place a

---

* "Vester quidem est populus meus sed me plus servire vobis quam
illi præesse delectat. Traxit istud a proavis generis mei apud vos
decessoresque vestros semper animo Romana devotio, ut illa nobis
magis claritas putaretur, quam vestra per militæ titulos porrigeret
celsitudo : cunctisque auctoribus meis semper magis ambitum est
quod a principibus sumerent quam quod a patribus attulissent.
Cumque gentem nostram videamur regere, non aliud nos quam
milites vestros credimus ordinari. . . . Per nos administratis re-
motarum spatia regionum : patria nostra vester orbis est. Tangit
Galliam suam lumen orientis, et radius qui illis partibus oriri
creditur, hic refulget. Dominationem vobis divinitus præstitam obex
nulla concludit, nec ullis provinciarum terminis diffusio felicium
sceptrorum limitatur. Salvo divinitatis honore sit dictum."—Letter
printed among the works of Avitus, Bishop of Vienne. (Migne's
Patrologia, vol. lix. p. 285). This letter, as its style shows, is the
composition not of Sigismund himself, but of Avitus, writing on
Sigismund's behalf. But this makes it scarcely less valuable evidence of the feelings of the time.

Gothic empire, taking to myself the place and the powers of Cæsar Augustus. But when experience taught me that the untameable barbarism of the Goths would not suffer them to live beneath the sway of law, and that the abolition of the institutions on which the state rested would involve the ruin of the state itself, I chose the glory of renewing and maintaining by Gothic strength the fame of Rome, desiring to go down to posterity as the restorer of that Roman power which it was beyond my power to replace. Wherefore I avoid war and strive for peace."*

Historians have remarked how valuable must have been the skill of Roman officials to princes who from leaders of tribes were become rulers of wide lands; and in particular how indispensable the aid of the Christian bishops, the intellectual aristocracy of their new subjects, whose advice could alone guide their policy and conciliate the vanquished. Not only is this true ; it is but a small part of the truth; one form of that manifold and overpowering influence which the old system exercised over its foes not less than its own children. For it is hardly too much to say that the thought of antagonism to the empire and the wish to extinguish it never crossed the mind of the barbarians.† The conception of that empire was too uni-

---

* " Referre solitus est (*sc.* Ataulphus) se in primis ardenter inhiasse: ut obliterato Romanorum nomine Romanum omne solum Gothorum imperium et faceret et vocaret: essetque, ut vulgariter loquar, Gothia quod Romania fuisset ; fieretque nunc Ataulphus quod quondam Cæsar Augustus. At ubi multa experientia probavisset, neque Gothos ullo modo parere legibus posse propter effrenatam barbariem, neque reipublicæ interdici leges oportet sine quibus respublica non est respublica, elegisse se saltem, ut gloriam sibi de restituendo in integrum augendoque Romano nomine Gothorum viribus quæreret, habereturque apud posteros Romanæ restitutionis auctor postquam esse non potuerat immutator. Ob hoc abstinere a bello, ob hoc inhiare paci nitebatur."—Orosius, vii. 43.

† Athaulf formed only to abandon it.

versal, too august, too enduring. It was everywhere
around them, and they could remember no time when it
had not been so. It had no association of people or place
whose fall could seem to involve that of the whole fabric;
it had that connection with the Christian church which
made it all-embracing and venerable.

The belief in its eternity. There were especially two ideas whereon it
rested, and from which it obtained a peculiar
strength and a peculiar direction. The one was
the belief that as the dominion of Rome was universal, so
must it be eternal. Nothing like it had been seen before.
The empire of Alexander had lasted a short life-time; and
within its wide compass were included many arid wastes,
and many tracts where none but the roving savage had
ever set foot. That of the Italian city had for fourteen
generations embraced all the most wealthy and populous
regions of the civilized world, and had laid the foundations of its power so deep that they seemed destined to last
forever. If Rome moved slowly for a time, her foot was
always planted firmly: the ease and swiftness of her later
conquests proved the solidity of the earlier ; and to her,
more justly than to his own city, might the boast of the
Athenian historian be applied: that she advanced farthest
in prosperity, and in adversity drew back the least. From
the end of the republican period her poets, her orators, her
jurists, ceased not to repeat the claim of world-dominion,
and confidently predict its eternity.* The proud belief of
his countrymen which Virgil had expressed:

> " His ego nec metas rerum, nec tempora pono:
> Imperium sine fine dedi "—

---

* See, among other passages, Varro, *De lingua Latina*, iv. 34; Cic.
Pro Domo, 33; Virg. *Aen.* ix. 448; Hor. *Od.* iii. 30, 8; Tibull. ii. 5,
23; Ovid, *Am.* i. 15, 26; *Trist.* iii. 7, 51; and cf. in the Digest, l. 1,
33; xiv. 2, 9. The phrase " urbs æterna " appears in a constitution
issued by Valentinian III. Tertullian speaks of Rome as " civitas
sacrosancta."

was shared by the early Chritians when they prayed for
the persecuting power whose fall would bring Antichrist
upon earth. Lactantius writes: "When Rome the head
of the world shall have fallen, who can doubt that the end
is come of human things, ay, of the earth itself. She, she
alone is the state by which all things are upheld even until
now; wherefore let us make prayers and supplications to
the God of heaven, if indeed his decrees and his purposes
can be delayed, that that hateful tyrant come not sooner
then we look for, he for whom are reserved fearful deeds,
who shall pluck out that eye in whose extinction the world
itself shall perish."* With the triumph of Christianity
this belief had found a new basis. For as the Empire had
decayed, the Church had grown stronger: and now while

---

* Lact. *Divin. Instit.* vii. 25: "Etiam res ipsa declarat lapsum
ruinamque rerum brevi fore: nisi quod incolumi urbe Roma nihil
istiusmodi videtur esse metuendum. At vero cum caput illud orbis
occiderit, et ῥύμη esse cœperit quod Sibyllæ fore aiunt, quis dubitet
venisse iam finem rebus humanis, orbique terrarum? Illa, illa est
civitas quæ adhuc sustentat omnia, precandusque nobis et adorandus
est Deus cœli si tamen statuta eius et placita differri possunt, ne
citius quam putemus tyrannus ille abominabilis veniat qui tantum
facinus moliatur, ac lumen illud effodiat cuius interitu mundus ipse
lapsurus est." Cf. Tertull. *Apolog.* cap. xxxii: "Est et alia maior
necessitlas nobis orandi pro imperatoribus, etiam pro omni statu
imperii rebusque Romanis, qui vim maximam universo orbi immin-
entem ipsamque clausulam sæculi acerbitates horrendas comminantem
Romani imperii commeatu scimus retardari." Also the same writer,
Ad Scapulam, cap. ii: "Ceristianus sciens imperatorem a Deo suo
constitui, necesse est ut ipsum diligat et revereatur et honoret et
salvum velit cum toto Romano imperio quousque sæculum stabit:
tamdiu enim stabit." So too the author—now usually supposed to
be Hilary the Deacon—of the Commentary on the Pauline Epistles
ascribed to S. Ambrose: "Non prius veniet Dominus quam regni
Romani defectio fiat, et appareat antichristus qui interficiet sanctos,
reddita Romanis libertate, sub suo tamen nomine."—Ad II Thess.
ii. 4, 7.

the one, trembling at the approach of the destroyer, saw province after province torn away, the other, rising in stately youth, prepared to fill her place and govern in her name, and in doing so, to adopt and sanctify and propagate anew the notion of a universal and unending state.

The second chief element in this conception was the association of such a state with one irresponsible governor, the Emperor. The hatred to the name of king, which their earliest political struggles had left in the Romans, by obliging their ruler to take a new and strange title, marked him off from all the other sovereigns of the world. To the provincials especially he became an awful impersonation of the great machine of government which moved above and around them. It was not merely that he was, like a modern king, the center of power and the dispenser of honor: his pre-eminence, broken by no comparison with other princes, by the ascending ranks of no aristocracy, had in it something almost supernatural. The right of legislation had become vested in him alone; the decrees of the people, and resolutions of the senate, and edicts of the magistrates were, during the last three centuries, replaced by imperial constitutions; his domestic council, the consistory, was the supreme court of appeal; his interposition, like that of some terrestrial Providence, was invoked, and legally provided so to be, to reverse or overleap the ordinary rules of law.* From the time of Julius and Augustus his person had been hallowed by the office of chief pontiff† and the tribunician power; to swear by his head was considered the

Sanctity of the imperial name.

---

* For example, by the " restitutio natalium," and the " adrogatio per rescriptum principis," or, as it is expressed, "per sacrum oraculum."

† Even the Christian Emperors took the title of Pontifex Maximus, till Gratian refused it: ἀθέμιστον εἶναι Χριστιάνῳ τὸ σχῆμα νομίσας.—Zosimus, lib. iv. cap. 36.

most solemn of all oaths* his effigy was sacred,† even on a
coin; to him or to his Genius temples were erected and Divine
honors paid while he lived;‡ and when, as it was expressed,
he ceased to be among men, the title of Divus was
accorded to him, after a solemn consecration.§ In the
confused multiplicity of mythologies, the worship of the
Emperor was the only worship common to the whole
Roman world, and was therefore that usually proposed as
a test to the Christians on their trial. Under the new
religion the form of adoration vanished, the sentiment of
reverence remained; and the right to control the Church
as well as the State admitted at Nicæa, and habitually exercised by the sovereigns of Constantinople, made the Emperor hardly less essential to the new conception of a
world-wide Christian monarchy than he had been to the
military despotism of old. These considerations explain
why the men of the fifth century, clinging to preconceived
ideas, refused to believe in that dissolution of the Empire
which they saw with their own eyes. Because it could not
die, it lived. And there was in the slowness of the change
and its external aspect, as well as in the fortunes of the

---

* "Maiore formidine et callidiore timiditate Cæsarem observatis
quam ipsum ex Olympo Iovem, et merito, si sciatis. . . . Citius
denique apud vos per omnes Deos quam per unum genium Cæsaris
peieratur."—Tertull. *Apolog.* c. xxviii. Cf. Zos. v. 51: εἰ μὲν γὰρ
πρὸς τὸν θεὸν ἐτυχήκει διδόμενος ὁρκὸς, ἦν ἂν ὡς εἰκὸς παριδε-
ῖν ἐνδίδοντας τῇ τοῦ θεοῦ φιλανθρωπίᾳ τὴν ἐπὶ τῇ ἀσεβείᾳ
συγγνώμην. ἐπεὶ δὲ κατὰ τὴν τοῦ βασιλέως ὀμωμόκεσαν κεφα-
λῆς, οὐκ εἶναι θεμιτὸν αὐτοῖς εἰς τὸν τοσοῦτον ὅρκον ἐξαμα-
ρτεῖν

† Tac. *Ann.* i. 73; iii. 38, etc.

‡ It is curious that this should have begun in the first years of the
Empire. See, among other passages that might be cited from the
Augustan poets, Virg. *Georg.* i. 24; iv. 560; Hor. *Od.* iii. 3, 11;
Ovid, *Epp. ex Ponto*, iv. 9. 105.

§ Hence Vespasian's dying jest, "Ut puto, Deus fio."

capital, something to favor the illusion. The Roman
name was shared by every subject; the Roman city was no
longer the seat of government, nor did her capture extinguish the imperial power, for the maxim was now
accepted, Where the Emperor is, there is Rome*. But her
continued existence, not permanently occupied by any conqueror, striking the nations with an awe which the history
or the external splendors of Constantinople, Milan, or
Ravenna could nowise inspire, was an ever new assertion
of the endurance of the Roman race and dominion. Dishonored and defenceless, the spell of her name was still
strong enough to arrest the conqueror in the moment of
triumph. The irresistible impulse that drew Alaric was
one of glory or revenge, not of destruction: the Hun
turned back from Aquileia with a vague fear upon him :
the Ostrogoth adorned and protected his splendid prize.

Last Days of the West- ern Empire.   In the history of the last days of the
Western Empire, two points deserve special re-
mark: its continued union with the Eastern
branch, and the way in which its ideal dignity
was respected while its representatives were despised.
After Stilicho's death and Alaric's invasion, its fall was a
question of time. While one by one the provinces were
abandoned by the central government, left either to be
occupied by invading tribes or to maintain a precarious
independence, like Britain and Armorica,† by means
of municipal unions, Italy lay at the mercy of
the barbarian auxiliaries and was governed by
their leaders. The degenerate line of Theodosius might
have seemed to reign by hereditary right, but after their
extinction in Valentinian III each phantom Emperor—
Maximus, Avitus, Majorian, Anthemius, Olybrius — re-

---

* ὅπου ἂν ὁ βασιλεὺς ᾖ, ἐκεῖ ἡ Ῥώμη.—Herodian.

† If the accounts we find of the Armorican republican be trusted.

ceived the purple from the haughty Ricimer, general of
the troops, only to be stripped of it when he presumed to
forget his dependence. Though the division between
Arcadius and Honorius had definitely severed the two
realms for administrative purposes, they were still supposed to constitute a single Empire, and the rulers of the
East interfered more than once to raise to the Western
thrones princes they could not protect upon it. Ricimer's
insolence quailed before the shadowy grandeur of the imperial title : his ambition, and Gundobald his successor's,
were bounded by the name of patrician. The bolder
genius of Odoacer,* general of the barbarian auxiliaries,
resolved to abolish an empty pageant, and extinguish the
title and office of Emperor of the West. Yet over him too
the spell had power; and as the Gaulish warrior had gazed
on the silent majesty of the senate in a deserted city, so
the Herulian revered the power before which the world
had bowed, and though there was no force to check or to
affright him, shrank from grasping in his own barbarian
hand the scepter of the Cæsars. When, at Odoacer's
bidding, Romulus Augustulus, the boy whom a whim
of fate had chosen to be the last native Cæsar of Rome,
had formally announced his resignation to the senate, a
deputation from that body proceeded to the
Eastern court to lay the insignia of royalty at   *Its extinc-
the feet of the reigning Emperor Zeno. The   *tion by*
West, they declared, no longer required an Em-   *Odoacer,*
peror of its own: one monarch sufficed for the   *A.D. 476.*
world; Odoacer was qualified by his wisdom and courage

---

* Odoacer or Odovaker, as it seems his name ought to be written, is
usually, but incorrectly, described as a King of the Heruli, who led
his people into Italy and overthrew the Empire of the West; others
call him King of the Rugii, or Skyrri, or Turcilingi. The truth
seems to be that he was not a king at all, but the son of a Skyrrian
chieftain (Edecon, known as one of the envoys whom Attila sent to

to be the protector of their state, and upon him Zeno was entreated to confer the title of patrician and the administration of the Italian provinces.* The Emperor granted what he could not refuse, and Odoacer, taking the title of King,† continued the consular office, respected the civil and ecclesiastical institutions of his subjects, and ruled for fourteen years as the nominal vicar of the Eastern Emperor. There was thus legally no extinction of the Western Empire at all, but only a reunion of East and West. In form, and to some extent also in the belief of men, things now reverted to their state during the first two centuries of the Empire, save that Byzantium instead of Rome was the center of the civil government. The joint tenancy which had been conceived by Diocletian, carried further by Constantine, renewed under Valentinian, I and again at the death of Theodosius, had come to an end; once more did a single Emperor sway the scepter of the world, and head an undivided Catholic Church.‡ To

---

Constantinople), whose personal merits made him chosen by the barbarian auxiliaries to be their leader. The Skyrri were a small tribe, apparently akin to the more powerful Heruli, whose name is often extended to them.

* Αὔλουστος ὁ Ὀρέστου υἱὸς ἀκούσας Ζήνωνα πάλιν τὴν βασιλείαν ἀνακεκτῆσθαι τῆς ἔω. . . . ἠνάγκασε τὴν βουλὴν ἀποστεῖλαι πρεσβείαν Ζήνωνι σημαίνουσαν ὡς ἰδίας μὲν αὐτοῖς βασιλείας οὐ δέοι, κοινὸς δὲ ἀποχρήσει μόνος ὧν αὐτοκράτωρ ἐπ' ἀμφοτέροις τοῖς πέρασι. τὸν μέντοι Ὀδόαχον ὑπ' αὐτῶν προβεβλῆσθαι ἱκανὸν ὄντα σώζειν τὰ παρ' αὐτοῖς πράγματα πολιτικὴν ἐχὼν νοῦν καὶ σύνεσιν ὁμοῦ καὶ μάχιμον, καὶ δεῖσθαι τοῦ Ζήνωνος πατρικίου τε αὐτῷ ἀποστεῖλαι ἀζίαν καὶ τὴν τῶν Ἰτάλων τουτῷ ἐφεῖναι διοίκησιν.—Malchus ap. Photium in *Corp. Hist. Byzant.*

† Not king of Italy, as is often said. The barbarian kings did not for several centuries employ territorial titles; the title "king of France," for instance, was first used by Henry IV. Jordanes says that Odoacer never so much as assumed the insignia of royalty.

‡ Cf. Sismondi, *Histoire de la Chute de l'Empire Occidentale.*

those who lived at the time, this year (476 A. D.) was no
such epoch as it has since become, nor was any impression
made on men's minds commensurate with the real significance of the event. For though it did not destroy the
Empire in idea, nor wholly even in fact, its consequences
were from the first great. It hastened the development
of a Latin as opposed to Greek and Oriental forms of
Christianity : it emancipated the Popes : it gave a new
character to the projects and government of the Teutonic
rulers of the West. But the importance of remembering
its formal aspects to those who witnessed it will be felt as
we approach the era when the Empire was revived by
Charles the Frank.

Odoacer's monarchy was not more oppressive than those
of his neighbors in Gaul, Spain, and Africa.
But the mercenary *fœderati* who supported it   *Odoacer.*
were a loose swarm of predatory tribes : themselves without cohesion, they could take no firm root in Italy.
During the eighteen years of his reign no progress seems
to have been made toward the reorganization of society ;
and the first real attempt to blend the peoples and
maintain the traditions of Roman wisdom in the hands of
a new and vigorous race was reserved for a more famous
chieftain, the greatest of all the barbarian
conquerors, the forerunner of the first barba-   *Theodoric.*
rian Emperor, Theodoric the Ostrogoth. The aim of his
reign, though he professed deference to the Eastern court
which had favored his invasion,* was the establishment
of a national monarchy in Italy. Brought up as a hos-
tage in the court of Byzantium, he learned to know the
advantages of an orderly and cultivated society and
the principles by which it must be maintained ; called

* "Nil deest nobis imperio vestro famulantibus."—Theodoric to
Zeno: Jordanes, *De Rebus Geticis*, cap. 57.

in early manhood to roam as a warrior-chief over the plains
of the Danube, he acquired along with the arts of command a sense of the superiority of his own people in valor
and energy and truth. When the defeat and death of
Odoacer had left the peninsula at his mercy, he sought no
further conquest, easy as it would have been to tear away
new provinces from the Eastern realm, but strove only to
preserve and strengthen the ancient polity of Rome, to
breathe into her decaying institutions the spirit of a fresh
life, and without endangering the military supremacy of
his own Goths, to conciliate by indulgence and gradually
raise to the level of their masters the degenerate population
of Italy. The Gothic nation appears from the first less
cruel in war and more prudent in council than any of their
Germanic brethren,* all that was most noble among them
shone forth now in the rule of the greatest of the Amali.
From his palace at Verona,† commemorated in the song of

---

* " Unde et pæne omnibus barbaris Gothi sapientiores exstiterunt
Græcisque pæne consimiles."—Jorn. cap. 5.

† Theodoric (Thiodorich) seems to have resided usually at Ravenna,
where he died and was buried; a remarkable building which tradition points out as his tomb stands a little way out of the town, near
the railway station, but the porphyry sarcophagus, in which his
body is supposed to have lain, has been removed thence, and may be
seen built up into the wall of the building called his palace, situated
close to the church of Sant' Apollinare, and not far from the tomb of
Dante. There does not appear to be any sufficient authority for
attributing this building to Ostrogothic times; it is very different
from the representation of Theodoric's palace which we have in the
contemporary mosaics of Sant' Apollinare in urbe. In the German
legends, however, Theodoric is always the prince of Verona (Dietrich
von Berne), no doubt because that city was better known to the
Teutonic nations, and because it was thither that he moved his court
when transalpine affairs required his attention. His castle there
stood in the old town on the left bank of the Adige, on the height
now occupied by the citadel; it is doubtful whether any trace of it

the Nibelungs, he issued equal laws for Roman and Goth, and bade the intruder, if he must occupy part of the lands, at least respect the goods and the person of his fellow subject. Jurisprudence and administration remained in native hands: two annual consuls, one named by Theodoric, the other by the Eastern monarch, presented an image of the ancient state; and while agriculture and the arts revived in the provinces, Rome herself celebrated the visits of a master who provided for the wants of her people, and preserved with care the monuments of her former splendor. With peace and plenty men's minds took hope, and the study of letters revived. The last gleam of classical literature gilds the reign of the barbarian.

By the consolidation of the two races under one wise government, Italy might have been spared six hundred years of gloom and degradation. It was not so to be. Theodoric was tolerant, but toleration was itself a crime in the eyes of his orthodox subjects : the Arian Goths were and remained strangers and enemies among the Catholic Italians. Scarcely had the scepter passed from the hands of Theodoric to his unworthy offspring, when Justinian, who had viewed with jealousy the greatness of his nominal lieutenant, determined to assert his dormant rights over Italy; its people welcomed *Italy reconquered by Justinian.* Belisarius as a deliverer, and in the struggle that followed the race and name of the Ostrogoths perished forever. Thus again reunited in fact, as it had been all the while united in name, to the Roman Empire, the peninsula was divided into counties and dukedoms, and obeyed the exarch of Ravenna, viceroy of the Byzantine court, till the arrival of the Lombards in A.D.

---

remain, for the old foundations which we now see may have belonged to the fortress erected by Gian Galeazzo Visconti in the fourteenth century.

568 drove him from some districts, and left him only a feeble authority in the rest.

Beyond the Alps, though the Roman population had now ceased to seek help from the Eastern court, the Empire's rights still subsisted in theory, and were never legally extinguished. As has been said, they were admitted by the conquerors themselves: by Athaulf, when he reigned in Aquitaine as the vicar of Honorius, and recovered Spain from the Suevi to restore it to its ancient masters: by the Visigothic kings of Spain, when they permitted the Mediterranean cities to send tribute to Byzantium; by Clovis, when, after the representatives of the old government, Syagrius and the Armorican cities, had been overpowered or absorbed, he received with delight from the Eastern emperor Anantasius the grant of a Roman dignity to confirm his possession. Arrayed like a Fabius or Valerius in the consul's embroidered robe, the Sicambrian chieftain rode through the streets of Tours, while the shout of the provincials hailed him Augustus.* They already obeyed him, but his power was now legalized in their eyes, and it was not without a melancholy pride that they saw the terrible conqueror himself yield to the spell of the Roman name, and do homage to the enduring majesty of their legitimate sovereign.†

The Transalpine provinces.

---

* " Igitur Chlodovechus ab imperatore Anastasio codicillos de consulatu accepit, et in basilica beati Martini tunica blatea indutus est et chlamyde, imponens vertici diadema . . . et ab ea die tanquam consul aut (= et) Augustus est vocitatus."—Gregory of Tours, ii, 58.

† Sir F. Palgrave (*English Commonwealth*) considers this grant as equivalent to a formal ratification of Clovis' rule in Gaul. Hallam rates its importance lower (*Middle Ages*, note iii, to chap. i). Taken in connection with the grant of south-eastern Gaul to Theodebert by Justinian, it may fairly be held to show that the influence of the empire was still felt in these distant provinces.

Yet the severed limbs of the Empire forgot by degrees their original unity. As in the breaking up of the old society, which we trace from the sixth to the eighth century, rudeness and ignorance grew *Lingering influences* apace, as language and manners were changed *of Rome.* by the infiltration of Teutonic settlers, as men's thoughts and hopes and interests were narrowed by isolation from their fellows, as the organization of the Roman province and the Germanic tribe alike dissolved into a chaos whence the new order began to shape itself, dimly and doubtfully as yet, the memory of the old Empire, its symmetry, its sway, its civilization, must needs wane and fade. It might have perished altogether but for the two enduring witnesses Rome had left—her Church and her Law. The barbarians had at first *Religion.* associated Christianity with the Romans from whom they learned it: the Romans had used it as their only bulwark against oppression. The hierarchy were the natural leaders of the people, and the necessary councillors of the king. Their power grew with the extinction of civil government and the spread of superstition; and when the Frank found it too valuable to be abandoned to the vanquished people, he insensibly acquired the feelings and policy of the order he entered.

As the Empire fell to pieces, and the new kingdoms which the conquerors had founded themselves began to dissolve, the Church clung more closely to her unity of faith and discipline, the common bond of all Christian men. That unity must have a center, that center was Rome. A succession of able and zealous pontiffs extended her influence (the sanctity and the writings of Gregory the Great were famous through all the West): never occupied by barbarians, she retained her peculiar character and customs: and laid the foundations of a power over men's souls more durable than that which she had lost over their bodies.* Only second in importance to this influence was that which was exercised by the perma-

Jurisprudence. nence of the old law, and of its creature the municipality. The barbarian invaders retained the customs of their ancestors, characteristic memorials of a rude people, as we see them in the Salic law or in the ordinances of Ina and Alfred. But the subject population and the clergy continued to be governed by that elaborate system which the genius and labor of many generations had raised to be the most lasting monument of Roman greatness.

The civil law had maintained itself in Spain and Southern Gaul, nor was it utterly forgotten even in the North, in Britain, on the borders of Germany. Revised editions of the Theodosian code were issued by the Visigothic and Burgundian princes. For some centuries it was the patrimony of the subject population everywhere, and in Aquitaine and Italy has outlived feudalism. The presumption in later times was that all men were to be judged by it who could not be proved to be subject to some other.† Its phrases, its forms, its courts, its subtlety and precision, all recalled the strong and refined society which had produced it. Other motives, as well as those of kindness to their subjects, made the new kings favor it; for it exalted their prerogative, and the submission enjoined by it on one class of

---

* Even so early as the middle of the fifth century, S. Leo the Great could say to the Roman people, " Isti (sc. Petrus et Paulus) sunt qui te ad hanc gloriam provexerunt ut gens sancta, populus electus, civitas sacerdotalis et regia, per sacram B. Petri sedem caput crbis effecta latius præsideres religione divina quam dominatione terrena."—*Sermon on the Feast of SS. Peter and Paul.* (Opp. *ap.* Migne, tom. i. p. 336).

† "Ius Romanum est adhuc in viridi observantia et eo iure præsumitur quilibet vivere nisi adversum probetur."—Maranta, quoted by Marquard Freher.

their subjects soon came to be demanded from the other, by their own laws the equals of the prince. Considering attentively how many of the old institutions continued to subsist, and studying the feelings of that time, as they are faintly preserved in its scanty records, it seems hardly too much to say that in the eighth century the Roman Empire still existed in the West: existed in men's minds as a power weakened, delegated, suspended, but not destroyed.

It is easy for those who read the history of an age in the light of those that followed it, to perceive that in this men erred; that the tendency of events was wholly different; that society had entered on a new phase, wherein every change did more to localize authority and strengthen the aristocratic principle at the expense of the despotic. We can see that other forms of life, more full of promise for the distant future, had already begun to show themselves: they—with no type of power or beauty, but that which had filled the imagination of their forefathers, and now loomed on them grander than ever through the mist of centuries—mistook, as it has been said of Rienzi in later days, memories for hopes, and sighed only for the renewal of its strength. Events were at hand by which these hopes seemed destined to be gratified.

CHAPTER IV.

RESTORATION OF THE WESTERN EMPIRE.

It was toward Rome as their ecclesiastical capital that the thoughts and hopes of the men of the sixth and seventh centuries were constantly directed. Yet not from Rome, feeble and corrupt, nor on the exhausted soil of Italy, was the deliverer to arise. Just when, as we may suppose, the vision of a renewal of imperial authority in the Western provinces was beginning to vanish away, there appeared in the furthest corner of Europe, sprung of a race but lately brought within the pale of civilization, a . line of chieftains devoted to the service of the Holy See, and among them one whose power, good fortune, and heroic character pointed him out as worthy of a dignity to which doctrine and tradition had attached a sanctity almost divine.

Of the new monarchies that had risen on the ruins of *The Franks.* Rome, that of the Franks was by far the greatest. In the third century they appear, with Saxons, Alemanni, and Thuringians, as one of the greatest German tribe leagues. The Sicambri (for it seems probable that this famous race was a chief source of the Frankish nation) had now laid aside their former hostility to Rome, and her future representatives were thenceforth, with few intervals, her faithful allies. Many of their chiefs rose to high place: Malarich receives from Jovian the charge of the Western provinces;

Bauto and Mellobaudes figure in the days of Theodosius
and his sons; Meroveous (if Meroveus be a real name)
fights under Aetius against Attila in the great battle of
Chalons ; his countrymen endeavor in vain to save Gaul.
from the Suevi and Burgundians. Not till the Empire was
evidently helpless did they claim a share of the booty ;
then Clovis, or Chlodovech, chief of the Salian tribe, leaving his kindred the Ripuarians in their seats on the
lower Rhine, advances from Flanders to wrest Gaul
from the barbarian nations which had entered in some
sixty years before. Few conquerors have had
a career of more unbroken success. By the $^{A.D. 486.}$
defeat of the Roman governor Syagrius he was left master
of the northern provinces : the Burgundian kingdom in
the valley of the Rhone was in no long time reduced to dependence: last of all, the Visigothic power was overthrown
in one great battle, and Aquitaine added to the dominions
of Clovis. Nor were the Frankish arms less prosperous
on the other side of the Rhine. The victory of Tolbiac
led to the submission of the Alemanni : their allies the
Bavarians followed, and when the Thuringian power had
been broken by Theodorich I (son of Clovis), the Frankish
league embraced all the tribes of western and southern
Germany. The state thus formed, stretching from the
Bay of Biscay to the Inn and the Ems, was of course in no
sense a French, that is to say, a Gallic monarchy. Nor,
although the widest and strongest empire that had yet
been founded by a Teutonic race, was it, under the Merovingian kings, a united kingdom at all, but rather a con-
geries of principalities, held together by the predominance
of a single tribe and a single family, who ruled in Gaul as
masters over a subject race, and in Germany exercised a
sort of hegemony among kindred and scarcely inferior
tribes. But toward the middle of the eighth century a
change began. Under the rule of Pipin of Herstal and

his son Charles Martel, mayors of the palace to the last feeble Merovingians, the Austrasian Franks in the lower Rhineland became acknowledged heads of the nation, and were able, while establishing a firmer government at home, to direct its whole strength in projects of foreign ambition. The form those projects took arose from a circumstance which has not yet been mentioned. It was not solely or even chiefly to their own valor that the Franks owed their past greatness and the yet loftier future which awaited them, it was to the friendship of the clergy and the favor of the Apostolic See. The other Teutonic nations, Goths, Vandals, Burgundians, Suevians, Lombards, had been most of them converted by Arian missionaries who proceeded from the Roman Empire during the short period when Arian doctrines were in the ascendant. The Franks, who were among the latest converts, were Catholics from the first, and gladly accepted the clergy as their teachers and allies. Thus it was that while the hostility of their orthodox subjects destroyed the Vandal kingdom in Africa and the Ostrogothic kingdom in Italy, the eager sympathy of the priesthood enabled the Franks to vanquish their Burgundian and Visigothic enemies, and made it comparatively easy for them to blend with the Roman population in the provinces. They had done good service against the Saracens of Spain ; they had aided the English Boniface in his mission to the heathen of Germany;* and at length, as the most powerful among Catholic nations, they attracted the eyes of the ecclesiastical head of the West, now sorely bested by domestic foes.

Since the invasion of Alboin, Italy has groaned under a complication of evils. The Lombards who had entered

---

* " Denique gens Francorum multos et fœcundissimos fructus Domino attulit, non solum credendo, set et alios salutifere convertendo," says the emperor Lewis II, in A.D. 871.

along with that chief in A.D. 568 had settled in considerable numbers in the valley of the Po, and founded the duchies of Spoleto and Benevento, leaving the rest of the country to be *Italy: the Lombards.* governed by the exarch of Ravenna as viceroy of the Eastern crown. This subjection was, however, little better than nominal. Although too few to occupy the whole peninsula, the invaders were yet strong enough to harass every part of it by inroads which met with no resistance from a population unused to arms, and without the spirit to use them in self-defence. More cruel and repulsive, if we may believe the evidence of their enemies, than any other of the Northern tribes, the Lombards were certainly singular in their aversion to the clergy, never admitting them to the national councils. Tormented by their repeated attacks, Rome sought help in vain from Byzantium, whose forces, scarce able to repel from their walls the Avars and Saracens, could give no support to the distant exarch of Ravenna. The Popes were the *The Popes.* Emperor's subjects; they awaited his confirmation, like other bishops; they had more than once been the victims of his anger.* But as the city became more accustomed in independence, and the Pope rose to a predominance, real if not yet legal, his tone grew bolder than that of the Eastern patriarchs. In the controversies that had raged in the Church, he had had the wisdom or good fortune to espouse (though not always from the first) the orthodox side: it was now by another quarrel of religion that his deliverance from an unwelcome yoke was accomplished.†

---

* Martin, as Sylverius earlier.

† A singular account of the origin of the separation of the Greeks and Latins occurs in the treatise of Landulfus de Columna (Landolfo Colonna), *De translatione Imperii Romani* (circa 1320). "The tyranny of Heraclius," says he, "provoked a revolt of the Eastern nations. They could not be reduced, because the Greeks at the

The Emperor Leo, born among the Isaurian mountains,
where a purer faith may yet have lingered, and
Iconoclastic stung by the Mohammedan taunt of idolatry,
controversy. determined to abolish the worship of images,
which seemed fast obscuring the more spiritual part of
Christianity. An attempt sufficient to cause tumults
among the submissive Greeks, excited in Italy a fiercer
commotion. The populace rose with one heart in defence
of what had become to them more than a symbol: the
exarch was slain: the Pope, though unwilling to sever himself from the lawful head and protector of the Church,
must yet excommunicate the prince whom he could not
reclaim from so hateful a heresy. Liudprand, king of the
Lombards, improved his opportunity: falling on the exarchate as the champion of images, on Rome as the minister of the Greek Emperor, he overran the one, and
all but succeeded in capturing the other. The Pope
escaped for the moment, but saw his peril ; placed
between a heretic and a robber, he turned his gaze
beyond the Alps, to a Catholic chief who had just
achieved a signal deliverance for Christendom on the
field of Poitiers. Gregory II had already opened com-
munications with Charles Martel, mayor of the palace, and
virtual ruler of the Frankish realm.* As the crisis becomes

---

same time began to disobey the Roman pontiff, receding, like Jero-
boam, from the true faith. Others among these schismatics (apparently with the view of strengthening their political revolt) carried
their heresy further and founded Mohammedanism." Similarly, the
Franciscan Marsilius of Padua (cira 1324) says that Mohammed, "a
rich Persian," invented his religion to keep the East from returning
to allegiance to Rome. It is worth remarking that few, if any, of
the earlier historians (from the tenth to the fifteenth century) refer
to the emperors of the West from Constantine to Augustulus : the
very existence of this Western line seems to have been even in the
eighth or ninth century altogether forgotten.

* Anastasius, *Vitæ Pontificum Romanorum*, i, *ap.* Muratori

more pressing, Gregory III finds in the same quarter his only hope, and appeals to him, in urgent letters, to haste to the succor of the Holy Church.* Some accounts add that Charles was offered, in the name of the Roman people, the office of consul and patrician. It is at least *The Popes Appeal to the Franks.* certain that here begins the connection of the old imperial seat with the rising german power: here first the pontiff leads a political movement, and shakes off the ties that bound him to his legitimate sovereign. Charles died before he could obey the call; but his son Pipin (surnamed the Short) made good use of the new friendship with Rome. He was the third of his family who had ruled the Franks with a monarch's full power: it seemed time to abolish the pageant of Merovingian royalty; yet a departure from the ancient line might shock the feelings of the people. A course was taken whose dangers no one then foresaw: the Holy See, now for the first time invoked as an international power, pronounced the deposition of Childeric, and gave to the royal office of his successor, Pipin, a sanctity hitherto unknown; adding to the old Frankish election, which consisted in raising the chief on a shield amid the clash of arms, the Roman diadem and the Hebrew rite of anointing. The compact between the chair of Peter and the Teutonic throne was hardly sealed, when the latter was summoned to discharge its share of the duties. Twice did Aistulf, the Lombard, assail Rome, twice did Pipin descend to the rescue: the second time at the bidding of a letter written in the name of St. Peter himself.† Aistulf could make no resistance;

---

* Letters in *Codex Carolinus,* in Muratori's *Scriptores Rerum Italicarum,* vol. iii. (part 2d), addressed " Subregulo Carolo."

† Letter in *Cod. Carol.* (Mur. *R. S. I.* iii. [2.] p. 96), a strange mixture of earnest adjurations, dexterous appeals to Frankish pride,

and the Frank bestowed on the Papal chair all that
belonged to the exarchate in North Italy,
Pipin patri- receiving as the meed of his services the title
cian of the of Patrician.*
Romans,
A.D. 754.   As a foreshadowing of the higher dignity that
was to follow, this title requires a passing notice.
Introduced by Constantine at a time when its original
Import of meaning had been long forgotten, it was
this title. designed to be and for awhile remained, the
name not of an office but of a rank, the highest after those of emperor and consul.   As such, it was
usually conferred upon provincial governors of the first
class, and in time also upon barbarian potentates whose
vanity the Roman court might wish to flatter.   Thus
Odoacer, Theodoric, the Burgundian king Sigismund,
Clovis himself, had all received it from the Eastern emperor; so too in still later times it was given to Saracenic
and Bulgarian prince.†   In the sixth and seventh centuries an invariable practice seems to have attached it to
the Byzantine viceroys of Italy, and thus, as we may con-

---

and long scriptural quotations: " Declaratum quippe est quod super
omnes gentes vestra Francorum geus prona mihi Apostolo Dei Petro
exstitit, et ideo ecclesiam quam mihi Dominus tradidit vobis per
manus Vicarii mei commendavi."

* The exact date when Pipin received the title cannot be made out.
Pope Stephen's next letter (p. 96 of Mur. iii.) is addressed " Pipino,
Carolo et Carolomanno patriciis."   And so the *Chronicon Casinense*
(Mur. iv. 273) says it was first given to Pipin.   Gibbon can hardly be
right in attributing it to Charles Martel, although one or two documents may be quoted in which it is used of him.   As one of these is
a letter of Pope Gregory II's, the explanation may be that the title
was offered or intended to be offered to him, although never accepted
by him.

† The title of Patrician appears even in the remote West: it stands
in a charter of Ina the West Saxon king, and in one given by Richard
of Normandy in A.D. 1015.   Ducange, *s. v.*

jecture, a natural confusion of ideas had made men take
it to be, in some sense, an official title, conveying an extensive though undefined authority, and implying in particular the duty of overseeing the Church and promoting her
temporal interests. It was doubtless with such a meaning that the Romans and their bishop bestowed it upon
the Frankish kings, acting quite without legal right, for
it could emanate from the emperor alone, but choosing it
as the title which bound its possessor to render to the
Church support and defence against her Lombard foes.
Hence the phrase is always "*Patricius Romanorum;*" not
as in former times, "*Patricius*" alone: hence it is usually
associated with the terms "*defensor*" and "*protector.*" And
since "defence" implies a corresponding measure of obedience on the part of those who profit by it, there must have
been conceded to the new patrician more or less of positive
authority in Rome, although not such as to extinguish the
supremacy of the emperor.

So long indeed as the Franks were separated by a hostile
kingdom from their new allies, this control remained
little better than nominal. But when on
Pipin's death the restless Lombards again took
up arms and menaced the possessions of the
Church, Pipin's son Charles or Charlemagne
swept down like a whirlwind from the Alps at
the call of Pope Hadrian, seized King Desiderius in his capital, himself assumed the Lombard crown, and made northern Italy thenceforward an
integral part of the Frankish Empire. Proceeding to Rome
at the head of his victorious army, the first of a long line of
Teutonic kings who were to find her love more deadly than
her hate, he was received by Hadrian with distinguished
honors, and welcomed by the people as their leader and deliverer. Yet even then, whether out of policy or from that sentiment of reverence to which his ambitious mind did not

Extinction of the Lombard kingdom by Charles king of the Franks.

refuse to bow, he was moderate in claims of jurisdiction, he yielded to the pontiff the place of honor in processions, and renewed, although in the guise of a Lord and conqueror, the gift of the Exarchate and Pentapolis, which Pipin had made to the Roman Church twenty years before.

A.D. 774.

It is with a strange sense, half of sadness, half of amusement, that in watching the progress of this grand historical drama, we recognize the meaner motives by which its chief actors were influenced. The Frankish and the Roman pontiff were for the time the two most powerful forces that urged the movement of the world, leading it on by swift steps to a mighty crisis of its fate, themselves guided, as it might well seem, by the purest zeal for its spiritual welfare. Their words and acts, their whole character and bearing in the sight of expectant Christendom, were worthy men destined to leave an indelible impress on their own and many succeeding ages. Nevertheless in them too appears the undercurrent of vulgar human desires and passions. The lofty and fervent mind of Charles was not free from the stirrings of personal ambition: yet these may be excused, if not defended, as almost inseparable from an intense and restless genius, which, be it never so unselfish in its ends, must in pursuing them fix upon everything its grasp and raise out of everything its monument. The policy of the Popes was prompted by motives less noble. Ever since the extinction of the Western Empire had emancipated the ecclesiastical potentate from secular control, the first and most abiding object of his schemes and prayers had been the aquisition of territorial wealth in the neighborhood of his capital. He had indeed a sort of justification —for Rome, a city with neither trade nor industry, was crowded with poor, for whom it devolved on the bishop to provide. Yet the pursuit was one which could not fail to

Charles and Hadrian.

pervert the purpose of the Popes and give a sinister character to all they did. It was this fear for the lands of the
Church far more than for religion or the safety of the
city—neither of which were really endangered by the Lombard attacks—that had prompted their passionate appeals
to Charles Martel and Pipin; it was now the well-grounded
hope of having these possessions confirmed and extended
by Pipin's greater son that made the Roman ecclesiastics
so forward in his cause. And it was the same lust after
worldly wealth and pomp, mingled with the dawning
prospect of an independent principality, that now began to
seduce them into a long course of guile and intrigue. For
this is probably the very time, although the exact date
cannot be established, to which must be assigned the
extraordinary forgery of the Donation of Constantine,
whereby it was pretended that power over Italy and the
whole West had been granted by the first Christian Emperor to Pope Sylvester and his successors in the Chair of
the Apostle.

For the next twenty-four years Italy remained quiet.
The government of Rome was carried on in the name of
the Patrician Charles, although it does not appear that he
sent thither any official representative ; while at the same
time both the city and the exarchate continued to admit
the nominal supremacy of the Eastern Emperor, employ-
ing the years of his reign to date documents. In A.D. 796
Leo III succeeded Pope Hadrian, and signal-
ized his devotion to the Frankish throne   *Accession*
by sending to Charles the banner of the city   *of Pope*
and the keys of the holiest of all Rome's   *Leo III.*
shrines, the confession of St. Peter, asking that   *A.D. 796.*
some officer should be deputed to the city to receive from
the people their oath of allegiance to the Patrician. He
had soon need to seek the Patrician's help for himself. In
A.D. 798 a sedition broke out : the Pope, going in solemn

procession from the Lateran to the church of S. Lorenzo
in Lucina, was attacked by a band of armed men, headed
by two officials of his court, nephews of his predecessor;
was wounded and left for dead, and with difficulty succeeded in escaping to Spoleto, whence he fled northward
into the Frankish lands. Charles had led his army against
the revolted Saxons: thither Leo following overtook him
at Paderborn in Westphalia. The king received with respect his spiritual father, entertained and conferred with
him for some time, and at length sent him back to Rome
under the escort of Angilbert, one of his trustiest ministers; promising to follow ere long in person. After some
months peace was restored in Saxony, and in the autumn
of 799 Charles descended from the Alps once more, while
Leo revolved deeply the great scheme for whose accomplishment the time was now ripe.

Three hundred and twenty-four years had passed since
the last Cæsar of the West resigned his power into the
hands of the senate, and left to his Eastern
Belief in the brother the sole headship of the Roman world.
Roman Em- To the latter Italy had from that time been
pire not ex-
tinct. nominally subject; but it was only during one
brief interval between the death of Teia the
last Ostrogothic king and the descent of Alboin the
first Lombard, that his power had been really effective.
In the further provinces, Gaul, Spain, Britain, it was
only a memory. But the idea of a Roman Empire as a
necessary part of the world's order had not vanished: it had
been admitted by those who seemed to be destroying it; it
had been cherished by the church; was still recalled
by laws and customs; was dear to the subject population,
who fondly looked back to the days when slavery was at
least mitigated by peace and order. We have seen the
Teuton endeavoring everywhere to identify himself
with the system he overthrew. As Goths, Burgundians

and Franks, sought the title of consul or patrician, as the
Lombard kings when they renounced their Arianism styled
themselves Flavii, so even in distant England the fierce
Saxon and Anglian conquerors used the names of Roman
dignities, and before long began to call themselves *imperatores* and *basileis* of Britain.   Within the last century
and a half the rise of Mohammedanism * had brought out
the common Christianity of Europe into a fuller relief.
The false prophet had left one religion, one Empire, one
Commander of the faithful: the Christian commonwealth
needed more than ever an efficient head and center.   Such
leadership it could nowise find in the Court of the Bosphorus, growing ever feebler and more alien to the West.
The name of " respublica," permanent at the elder Rome,
had never been applied to the Eastern Empire.   Its government was from the first half Greek, half Asiatic ; and
had now drifted away from its ancient traditions into the
forms of an Oriental despotism.   Claudian had already
sneered at " Greek Quirites:" † the general use, since
Heraclius' reign, of the Greek tongue, and the difference
of manners and usages, made the taunt now
more deserved.   The Pope had no reason to   *Motives of*
wish well to the Bazantine princes, who while   *the Pope.*
insulting his weakness had given him no help against the
savage Lombards, and who for nearly seventy years ‡ had
been contaminated by a heresy the more odious that it
touched not speculative points of doctrine the most famil-

---

* After the *translatio ad Francos* of A.D. 800, the two empires cor-
respond exactly to the two Khalifates of Bagdad and Cordova.
　　　　　　　† " Plaudentem cerne senatum
　　Et Byzantinos proceres, Graiosque Quirites."
　　　　　　　　　　　　　　In Eutrop. ii, 135.
　‡ Several emperors during this period had been patrons of images,
as was Irene at the moment of which I write : the stain nevertheless
adhered to their government as a whole.

iar usages of worship. In North Italy their power was extinct; no pontiff since Zacharias had asked their confirmation of his election: nay, the appointment of the intruding Frank to the patriciate, an office which it belonged to the Emperor to confer, was of itself an act of rebellion. Nevertheless their rights subsisted : they were still, and while they retained the imperial name, must so long continue, titular sovereigns of the Roman city. Nor could the spiritual head of Christendom dispense with the temporal; without the Roman Empire there could not be a Roman, nor by necessary consequence (as men thought) a Catholic and Apostolic Church.* For as will be shown more fully hereafter, men could not separate in fact what was indissoluble in thought : Christianity must stand or fall along with the great Christian state : they were but two names for the same thing. Thus urged, the Pope took a step which some among his predecessors are said to have already contemplated,† and toward which the events of the last fifty years had pointed. The moment was opportune. The widowed empress Irene, equally famous for her beauty, her talents and her crimes, had deposed and blinded her son Constantine VI : a woman, an usurper, almost a parricide, sullied the throne of the world. By what right, it might well be asked, did the factions of Byzantium impose a master on the original

---

* To a modern eye there is, of course, no necessary connection between the Roman empire and a Catholic and Apostolic Church ; in fact, the two things seem rather, such has been the impression made on us by the long struggle of church and state, in their nature mutually antagonistic. The interest of history lies not least in this, that it shows us how men have at different times entertained wholly different notions respecting the relation to one another of the same ideas or the same institutions.

† Monachus Sangallensis, *De Gestis Karoli ;* in Pertz, *Monumenta Germaniæ Historica.*

seat of empire? It was time to provide better for the most august of human offices: an election at Rome was as valid as at Constantinople—the possessor of the real power should also be clothed with the outward dignity. Nor could it be doubted where that possessor was to be found. The Frank had been always faithful to Rome: his baptism was the enlistment of a new barbarian auxiliary. His services against Arian heretics and Lombard marauders, against the Saracen of Spain and the Avar of Pannonia, had earned him the title of Champion of the Faith and Defender of the Holy See. He was now unquestioned lord of Western Europe, whose subject nations, Keltic and Teutonic, were eager to be called by his name and to imitate his customs.* In Charles, the hero who united under one scepter so many races, who ruled all as the vicegerent of God, the pontiff might well see, as later ages saw, the new golden head of a second image,† erected on the ruins of that whose mingled iron and clay seemed crumbling to nothingness behind the impregnable bulwarks of Constantinople.

At length the Frankish host entered Rome. The Pope's cause was heard; his innocence, already vindicated by a miracle, was pronounced by the Patrician in full synod; his accusers condemned in his stead. Charles remained in the city for some weeks; and on Christmas-day, A.D. 800,‡ he heard mass in the basilica of St. Peter. On the spot where now the gigantic dome of Bramante and Michael Angelo towers over the buildings of the modern city, the

Coronation of Charles at Rome, A.D. 800.

---

* Monachus Sangallensis; *ut supra.* So Pope Gregory the Great two centuries earlier: "Quanto cæteros homines regia dignitas antecedit, tanto cæterarum gentium regna regni Francorum culmen excellit." Ep. v. 6.

† Alciatus, *De Formula imperii Romani.*

‡ Or rather, according to the then prevailing practice of beginning the year from Christmas-day, A.D. 801.

spot which tradition had hallowed as that of the Apostle's
martyrdom, Constantine the Great had erected the oldest
and stateliest temple of Christian Rome. Nothing could
be less like than was this basilica to those northern cathe
drals, shadowy, fantastic, irregular, crowded with pillars,
fringed all round by clustering shrines and chapels, which
are to most of us the types of mediæval architecture. In
its plan and decorations, in the spacious sunny hall, the
roof plain as that of a Greek temple, the long row of
Corinthian columns, the vivid mosaics on its walls, in its
brightness, its sternness, its simplicity, it had preserved
every feature of Roman art, and had remained a perfect
expression of Roman character.* Out of the transept, a
flight of steps led up to the high altar underneath and just
beyond the great arch, the arch of triumph as it was
called: behind in the semicircular apse sat the clergy, rising tier above tier around its walls; in the midst, high
above the rest, and looking down past the altar over the
multitude, was placed the bishop's throne,† itself the curule
chair of some forgotten magistrate.‡ From that chair the

---

* An elaborate description of old St. Peter's may be found in Bunsen's and Platner's *Beschreibung der Stadt Rom;* with which compare
Bunsen's work on the Basilicas of Rome.

† The primitive custom was for the bishop to sit in the center of
the apse, at the central point of the east end of the church (or, as it
would be more correct to say, the end furthest from the door), just as
the judge had done in those law courts on the model of which the
first basilicas were constructed. This arrangement may still be seen
in some of the churches of Rome, as well as elsewhere in Italy; nowhere better than in the churches of Ravenna, particularly the beautiful one of Sant' Apollinare in Classe, and in the cathedral of Torcello, near Venice.

‡ On this chair were represented the labors of Hercules and the
signs of the zodiac. It is believed at Rome to be the veritable chair
of the Apostle himself, and whatever may be thought of such an
antiquity as this, it can be satisfactorily traced back to the third or

Pope now rose, as the reading of the Gospel ended, advanced to where Charles—who had exchanged his simple Frankish dress for the sandals and the chlamys of a Roman patrician*—knelt in prayer by the high altar, and as in the sight of all he placed upon the brow of the barbarian chieftain the diadem of the Cæsars, then bent in obeisance before him, the church rang to the shout of the multitude, again free, again the lords and center of the world, " Karolo Augusto a Deo coronato magno et pacifico imperatori vita et victoria."† In that shout, echoed by the Franks without, was pronounced the union, so long in preparation, so mighty in its consequences, of the Roman and the Teuton, of the memories and the civilization of the South with the fresh energy of the North, and from that moment modern history begins.

---

fourth century of Christianity. (The story that it is inscribed with verses from the Koran is, I believe, without foundation.) It is of oak and acacia wood, and is now inclosed in a gorgeous casing of bronze, and placed aloft at the extremity of St. Peter's, just over the spot where a bishop's chair would in the old arrangement of the basilica have stood. The sarcophagus in which Charles himself lay, till the French scattered his bones abroad, had carved on it the rape of Proserpine. It may still be seen in the gallery of the basilica at Aachen.

* Eginhard, *Vita Karoli.*

† The coronation scene is described in all the annals of the time, to which it is therefore needless to refer more particularly

CHAPTER V.

EMPIRE AND POLICY OF CHARLES.

THE coronation of Charles is not only the central event of the Middle Ages, it is also one of those very few events of which, taking them singly, it may be said that if they had not happened, the history of the world would have been different. In one sense indeed it has scarcely a parallel. The assassins of Julius Cæsar thought that they had saved Rome from monarchy, but monarchy came inevitable in the next generation. The conversion of Constantine 'changed the face of the world, but Christianity was spreading fast, and its ultimate triumph was only a question of time. Had Columbus never spread his sails, the secret of the western sea would yet have been pierced by some later voyager: had Charles V broken his safe-conduct to Luther, the voice silenced at Wittenberg would have been taken up by echoes elsewhere. But if the Roman Empire had not been restored in the West in the person of Charles, it would never have been restored at all, and the inexhaustible train of consequences for good and for evil that followed could not have been. Why this was so may be seen by examining the history of the next two centuries. In that day, as through all the Dark and Middle Ages, two forces were striving for the mastery. The one was the instinct of separation, disorder, anarchy, caused by the ungoverned impulses and barbarous ignorance of the great bulk of mankind; the other was that passionate longing of the better minds for a formal unity of governments, which had his historical basis in the memories of the old Roman Empire, and its most constant expression in the devotion to a visible and Catholic Church. The former tendency, as everything shows, was, in politics at least, the stronger, but the latter, used and stimulated by an extraordinary genius like Charles, achieved in the year 800 a victory whose results were never to be lost. When the hero was gone, the returning wave of anarchy and barbarism swept up violent as ever, yet it could not wholly obliterate the past : the Empire, maimed and shattered though it was, had struck its roots too deep to be overthrown by force, and when it perished at last, perished from inner decay. It was just because men felt that no one less than Charles could have won such a triumph over the evils of the time, by framing and establishing a gigantic scheme of government, that the excitement and hope and joy which the coronation evoked were so intense. Their best evidence is perhaps to be found not in the records of that time itself, but in the cries of lamentation that broke forth when the Empire began to dissolve toward the close of the ninth century, in the marvelous legends which attached themselves to the name of Charles the Emperor, a hero of whom any exploit was credible,* in the devout admiration wherewith his German successors looked back to, and strove in all things to imitate, their all but superhuman prototype.

As the event of A.D. 800 made an unparalleled impres-

---

* Before the end of the tenth century we find the monk Benedict of Soracte ascribing to Charles an expedition to Palestine, and other marvelous exploits. The romance which passes under the name of Archbishop Turpin is well known. All the best stories about Charles — and some of them are very good — may be found in the book of the Monk of St. Gall. Many refer to his dealings with the bishops, toward whom he is described as acting like a good-humored school-master.

sion on those who lived at the time, so has it engaged
the attention of men in succeeding ages, has

Import of the corona-tion.

been viewed in the most opposite lights, and
become the theme of interminable controversies. It is better to look at it simply as it appeared to the men who witnessed it. Here, as in so many
other cases, may be seen the errors into which jurists have
been led by the want of historical feeling. In rude and
unsettled states of society men respect forms and obey
facts, while careless of rules and principles. In England,
for example, in the eleventh and twelfth centuries, it signified very little whether an aspirant to the throne was
next lawful heir, but it signified a great deal whether he
had been duly crowned and was supported by a strong
party. Regarding the matter thus, it is not hard to see
why those who judged the actors of A.D. 800 as they would
have judged their contemporaries should have misunderstood the nature of that which then came to pass.
Baronius and Bellarmine, Spanheim and Conring, are advocates bound to prove a thesis, and therefore believing it;
nor does either party find any lack of plausible arguments.*
But civilian and canonist alike proceed upon strict legal
principles, and no such principles can be found in the
case, or applied to it. Neither the instances cited by the
Cardinal from the Old Testament of the power of priests
to set up and pull down princes, nor those which show the
earlier Emperors controlling the bishops of Rome, really
meet the question. Leo acted not as having alone the
right to transfer the crown; the practice of hereditary succession and the theory of popular election would have
equally excluded such a claim ; he was the spokesman of
the popular will, which, identifying itself with the sacer-

---

* Baronius, *Ann.*, ad ann. 800 ; Bellarminus, *De translatione imperii Romani adversus Illyricum;* Spanhemius, *De ficta translatione
imperii ;* Conringius, *De imperio Romano Germanico.*

dotal power, hated the Easterns and was grateful to the
Franks. Yet he was also something more. The act, as
it specially affected his interests, was mainly his work, and
without him would never have been brought about at all.
It was natural that a confusion of his secular functions
as leader, and his spiritual as consecrating priest, should
lay the foundation of the right claimed afterward of raising and deposing monarchs at the will of Christ's vicar.
The Emperor was passive throughout; he did not, as in
Lombardy, appear as a conqueror, but was received by the
Pope and the people as a friend and ally. Rome no doubt
became his capital, but it had already obeyed him as
Patrician, and the greatest fact that stood out to posterity
from the whole transaction was that the crown was bestowed, was at least imposed, by the hands of the pontiff.
He seemed the trustee and depositary of the imperial
authority.*

The best way of showing the thoughts and motives of
those concerned in the transaction is to transcribe the narratives of three contemporary, or almost com-
temporary annalists, two of them German and
one Italian. The annals of Lauresheim say:
*Contempo-
rary ac-
counts.*
"And because the name of the Emperor had
now ceased among the Greeks, and their Empire was possessed by a woman, it then seemed both to Leo the Pope
himself, and to all the holy fathers who were present in
the self-same council, as well as to the rest of the Christian
people, that they ought to take to be Emperor Charles,
king of the Franks, who held Rome herself, where the
Cæsars had always been wont to sit, and all the other regions
which he ruled through Italy and Gaul and Germany; and
inasmuch as God had given all these lands into his hand,
it seemed right that with the help of God and at the

---

* See especially Greenwood, *Cathedra Petri,* vol. iii. p. 109.

prayer of the whole Christian people he should have the name of Emperor also. Whose petition King Charles willed not to refuse, but submitting himself with all humility to God, and of the prayer of the priests and of the whole Christian people, on the day of the nativity of our Lord Jesus Christ he took on himself the name of Emperor, being consecrated by the lord Pope Leo."*

Very similar in substance is the account of the Chronicle of Moissac (ad ann. 801):

" Now when the king upon the most holy day of the Lord's birth was rising to the mass after praying before the confession of the blessed Peter the Apostle, Leo the Pope, with the consent of all the bishops and priests and of the senate of the Franks and likewise of the Romans, set a golden crown upon his head, the Roman people also shouting aloud. And when the people had made an end of chanting the Laudes, he was adored by the Pope after the manner of the emperors of old. For this also was done by the will of God. For while the said Emperor abode at Rome certain men were brought unto him, who said that the name of Emperor had ceased among the Greeks, and that among them the Empire was held by a woman called Irene, who had by guile laid hold on her son the Emperor, and put out his eyes, and taken the Empire to herself, as it is written of Athaliah in the Book of the Kings; which when Leo the Pope and all the assembly of the bishops and priests and abbots heard, and the senate of the Franks and all the elders of the Romans they took counsel with the rest of the Christian people, that they should name Charles king of the Franks to be Emperor, seeing that he held Rome the mother of empire where the Cæsars and Emperors were always used to sit; and that the heathen might not mock the Christians if

---

* *Ann. Lauṛesb.*, ap. Pertz, *M. G. H.* i.

the name of Emperor should have ceased among the Christians."*

These two accounts are both from a German source: that which follows is Roman, written probably within some fifty or sixty years of the event. It is taken from the life of Leo III in the *Vitæ Pontificum Romanorum*, compiled by Anastasius the papal librarian.

"After these things came the day of the birth of our Lord Jesus Christ, and all men were again gathered to-gether in the aforesaid basilica of the blessed Peter the Apostle, and then the gracious and venerable pontiff did with his own hands crown Charles with a very precious crown. Then all the faithful people of Rome, seeing the defence that he gave and the love that he bare to the holy Roman Church and her vicar, did by the will of God and of the blessed Peter, the keeper of the keys of the king-dom of Heaven, cry with one accord with a loud voice 'To Charles, the most pious Augustus, crowned of God, the great and peace-giving Emperor, be iife and victory.' While he, before the holy confession of the blessed Peter the Apostle, was invoking divers saints, it was proclaimed thrice, and he was chosen by all to be Emperor of the Romans. Thereon the most holy pontiff anointed Charles with holy oil, and likewise his most excellent son to be king, upon the very day of the birth of our Lord Jesus Christ; and when the mass was finished, then after the mass the most serene Lord Emperor offered gifts."†

In these three accounts there is no serious discrepancy as to the facts, although the Italian priest, as is natural, heightens the importance of the part played by the Pope,

---

* *Apud* Pertz, *M. G. H.* i.

† *Vitæ Pontif.* in Mur. *S. R. I.* Anastasius in reporting the shout of the people omits the word "Romanorum," which the other annalists insert after "imperatori."

while the Germans are too anxious to rationalize the event,
talking of a synod of the clergy, a consultation of the
people, and a formal request to Charles, which the silence
of Eginhard, as well as the other circumstances of the
case, forbid us to accept as literally true. Similarly
Anastasius passes over the adoration rendered by the
Pope to the Emperor, upon which most of the Frankish
records insist in a way which puts it beyond doubt. But
the impression which the three narratives
Impression leave is essentially the same. They all show
which they how little the transaction can be made to wear
convey. a strictly legal character. The Frankish king
does not of his own might seize the crown, but rather
receives it as coming naturally to him, as the legitimate
consequence of the authority he already enjoyed. The
Pope bestows the crown, not in virtue of any right of
his own as head of the Church: he is merely the instrument of God's providence, which has unmistakably
pointed out Charles as the proper person to defend and
lead the Christian commonwealth. The Roman people
do not formally elect and appoint, but by their applause
accept the chief who is presented to them. The act is
conceived of as directly ordered by the Divine Providence
which has brought about a state of things that admits
of but one issue, an issue which king, priest, and
people have only to recognize and obey; their personal
ambitions, passions, intrigues, sinking and vanishing in
reverential awe at what seems the immediate interposition
of Heaven. And as the result is desired by all parties
alike, they do not think of inquiring into one another's
rights, but take their momentary harmony to be natural
and necessary, never dreaming of the difficulties and con-
flicts which were to arise out of what seemed then so
simple. And it was just because everything was thus left
undetermined, resting not on express stipulation but rather

on a sort of mutual understanding, a sympathy of beliefs and wishes which augured no evil, that the event admitted of being afterward represented in so many different lights. For centuries later, when *Later theories respecting the coronation.* Papacy and Empire had been forced into the mortal struggle by which the fate of both was decided, three distinct theories regarding the coronation of Charles will be found advocated by three different parties, all of them plausible, all of them to some extent misleading. The Swabian Emperors held the crown to have been won by their great predecessor as the prize of conquest, and drew the conclusion that the citizens and bishop of Rome had no rights as against themselves. The patriotic party among the Romans, appealing to the early history of the Empire, declared that by nothing but the voice of their senate and people could an Emperor be lawfully created, he being only their chief magistrate, the temporary depositary of their authority. The Popes pointed to the indisputable fact that Leo imposed the crown, and argued that as God's earthly vicar it was then his, and must always continue to be their right to give to whomsoever they would an office which was created to be the handmaid of their own. Of these three it was the last view that eventually prevailed, yet to an impartial eye it cannot claim, any more than do the two others, to contain the whole truth. Charles did not conquer, nor the Pope give, nor the people elect. As the act was unprecedented, so was it illegal; it was a revolt of the ancient Western capital against a daughter who had become a mistress; an exercise of the sacred right of insurrection, justified by the weakness and wickedness of the Byzantine princes, hallowed to the eyes of the world by the sanction of Christ's representative, but founded upon no law, nor competent to create any for the future.

It is an interesting and somewhat perplexing question,

how far the coronation scene, an act as imposing in
its circumstances as it was momentous in its
Was the results, was prearranged among the parties.
coronation Eginhard tells us that Charles was accustomed
a surprise? to declare that he would not, even on so high
a festival, have entered the church had he known of the
Pope's intention.　Even if the monarch had uttered, the
secretary would hardly have recorded a falsehood long after
the motive that might have·prompted it had disappeared.
Of the existence of that motive which has been most commonly assumed, a fear of the discontent of the Franks
who might think their liberties endangered, little or no
proof can be brought from the records of the time, wherein
the nation is represented as exulting in the new dignity of
their chief as an accession of grandeur to themselves.　Nor
can we suppose that Charles' disavowal was meant to
soothe the offended pride of the Byzantine princes, from
whom he had nothing to fear, and who were none the more
likely to recognize his dignity, if they should believe it to
be not of his own seeking.　Yet it is hard to suppose the
whole affair a surprise ; for it was the goal toward
which the policy of the Frankish kings had for many
years pointed, and Charles himself, in sending before
him to Rome many of the spiritual and temporal
magnates of his realm, in summoning thither his
son Pipin from the war against the Lombards of
Benevento, had shown that he expected some more
than ordinary result from this journey to the imperial city.　Alcuin moreover, Alcuin of York, the prime
minister of Charles in matters religious and literary,
appears from one of his extant letters to have sent as a
Christmas gift to his royal pupil a carefully corrected and
superbly adorned copy of the Scriptures, with the words
"ad splendorem imperialis potentiæ."　This has commonly been taken for conclusive evidence that the plan

had been settled beforehand, and such it would be were there not some reasons for giving the letter an earlier date, and looking upon the word "imperialis" as a mere magniloquent flourish.* More weight is therefore to be laid upon the arguments supplied by the nature of the case itself. The Pope, whatever his confidence in the sympathy of the people, would never have ventured on so momentous a step until previous conferences had assured him of the feelings of the king, nor could an act for which the assembly were evidently prepared have been kept a secret. Nevertheless, the declaration of Charles himself can neither be evaded nor set down to mere dissimulation. It is more just to him, and on the whole more reasonable, to suppose that Leo, having satisfied himself of the wishes of the Roman clergy and people as well as of the Frankish magnates, resolved to seize an occasion and place so eminently favorable to his long-cherished plan, while Charles, carried away by the enthusiasm of the moment and seeing in the pontiff the prophet and instrument of the divine will, accepted a dignity which he might have wished to receive at some later time or in some other way. If, therefore, any positive conclusion be adopted, it would seem to be that Charles, although he had probably given a more or less vague consent to the project, was surprised and disconcerted by a sudden fulfillment which interrupted his own carefully studied designs. And although a deed which changed the history of the world was in any case no accident, it may well have worn to the Frankish and Roman spectators the air of a surprise. For there were no preparations apparent in the church; the king was not, like his Teutonic successors in the aftertime, led in procession to the pontifical throne: suddenly, at the very moment when

---

* Lorentz, *Leben Alcuins.* And cf. Döllinger, *Das Kaiserthum Karls des Grossen und seiner Nachfolger.*

he rose from the sacred hollow where he had knelt among the ever-burning lamps before the holiest of Christian relics —the body of the prince of the Apostles—the hands of that Apostle's representative placed upon his head the crown of glory and poured upon him the oil of sanctification. There was something in this to thrill the beholders with the awe of a divine presence, and make them hail him whom that presence seemed almost visibly to consecrate, the "pious and peace-giving Emperor, crowned of God."

The reluctance of Charles to assume the imperial title is ascribed by Eginhard to a fear of the jealous hostility of the Easterns, who could not only deny his claim to it, but might disturb by their intrigues his dominions in Italy. Accepting this statement, the problem remains, how is this reluctance to be reconciled with those acts of his which clearly show him aiming at the Roman crown? An ingenious and probable, if not certain solution, is suggested by a recent historian,* who argues from a minute examination of the previous policy of Charles, that while it was the great object of his reign to obtain the crown of the world, he foresaw at the same time the opposition of the Eastern Court, and the want of legality from which his title would in consequence suffer. He was therefore bent on getting from the Byzantines, if possible, a transference of their crown; if not, at least a recognition of his own: and he appears to have hoped to win this by the negotiations which had been for some time kept on foot with the Empress Irene. Just at this moment came the coronation by Pope Leo, interrupting these deep-laid schemes, irritating the Eastern Court, and forcing Charles into the position of a rival who could not with dignity adopt a soothing or submissive tone. Nevertheless, he seems not even then to have abandoned

Theories of the motives of Charles.

---

* See a very learned and interesting tract entitled *Das Kaiserthum Karls des Grossen und seiner Nachfolger*, by Dr. v. Döllinger.

the hope of obtaining a peaceful recognition. Irene's crimes did not prevent him, if we may credit Theophanes,* from seeking her hand in marriage. And when the project of thus uniting the East and West in a single Empire, baffled for a time by the opposition of her minister Ætius, was rendered impossible by her subsequent dethronement and exile, he did not abandon the policy of conciliation until a surly acquiescence in rather than admission of his dignity had been won from the Byzantine sovereigns Michael and Nicephorus.†

Whether, supposing Leo to have been less precipitate, a cession of the crown, or an acknowledgement of the right of the Romans to confer it, could ever have been obtained by Charles is perhaps more than doubtful. But it is clear that he judged rightly in rating its importance high, for the want of it was the great blemish in his own and his successors' dignity. To show how this was so, reference must be made to the events of A.D. 476. Both the extinction of the Western Empire in that year and its revival in A.D. 800 have been very generally misunderstood in modern times, and although the mistake is not, in a certain sense, of practical importance, yet it tends to confuse history and to blind us to the ideas of the people who acted on both occasions. When Odoacer compelled the abdication of Romulus Augustulus, he did not abolish the Western Empire as a separate power, but caused it to be reunited with or sink into the Eastern, so that from that time there was, as there had been before Diocletian, a single

Defect in the title of the Teutonic Emperors.

---

* Ἀποκρισιάριοι παρὰ Καρούλλου καὶ Λέοντος αἰτούμενοι ξευχθῆναι αὐτὴν τῷ Καρούλλῳ πρὸς γάμον καὶ ἐνῶσαι τὰ Ἑωά καὶ τὰ Ἑσπερία.—Theoph. *Chron.* in *Corp. Scriptt. Hist. Byz.*

† Their ambassadors at last saluted him by the desired title "Laudes ei dixerunt imperatorem eum et basileum appellantes." Eginh. *Ann.*, ad ann. 812.

undivided Roman Empire. In A.D. 800 the very memory
of the separate Western Empire, as it had stood from the
death of Theodosius till Odoacer, had, so far as appears,
been long since lost, and neither Leo nor Charles nor any
one among their advisers dreamed of reviving it. They,
too, like their predecessors, held the Roman Empire to be
one and indivisible, and proposed by the coronation of the
Frankish king not to proclaim a severance of the East and
West, but to reverse the act of Constantine, and make Old
Rome again the civil as well as the ecclesiastical capital of
the Empire that bore her name. Their deed was in its
essence illegal, but they sought to give it every semblance
of legality: they professed and partly believed that they
were not revolting against a reigning sovereign, but
legitimately filling up the place of the deposed Constantine VI; the people of the imperial city exercising their
ancient right of choice, their bishop his right of consecration.

Their purpose was but half accomplished. They could
create, but they could not destroy: they set up an Emperor
of their own, whose representatives thenceforward ruled
the West, but Constantinople retained her sovereigns as of
yore; and Christendom saw henceforth two imperial lines,
not as in the time before A.D. 476, the conjoint heads of a
single realm, but rivals and enemies, each denouncing the
other as an impostor, each professing to be the only true
and lawful head of the Christian Church and people. Although therefore we must in practice speak during the
next seven centuries (down till A.D. 1453, when Constantinople fell before the Mohammedan) of an Eastern and a
Western Empire, the phrase is in strictness incorrect, and
was one which either court ought to have repudiated.
The Byzantines always did repudiate it;* the Latins usually;

---

* Although they occasionally conceded the title of Emperor to the
Teutonic sovereign: as in the instances cited.

although, yielding to facts, they sometimes condescended
to employ it themselves. But their theory was always the
same. Charles was held to be the legitimate successor,
not of Romulus Augustulus, but of Leo IV, Heraclius,
Justinian, Arcadius and the whole Eastern line; and hence
it is that in all the annals of the time and of many succeeding centuries, the name of Constantine VI, the sixty-
seventh in order from Augustus, is followed without a
break by that of Charles, the sixty-eighth.

The maintenance of an imperial line among the Easterns was a continuing protest against the validity of
Charles' title. But from their enmity he had
little to fear, and in the eyes of the world he   *Government*
seemed to step into their place, adding the tra-   *of Charles*
ditional dignity which had been theirs to the   *as Emperor.*
power that he already enjoyed. North Italy and Rome
ceased forever to own the supremacy of Byzantium ; and
while the Eastern princes paid a shameful tribute to the
Mussulman, the Frankish Emperor—as the recognized
head of Christendom—received from the patriarch of Jerusalem the keys of the Holy Sepulcher and the banner of
Calvary; the gift of the Sephulcher itself, says Eginhard,
from Aaron king of the Persians.* Out of this peaceful intercourse with the great Khalif the romancers
created a crusade. Within his own dominions his sway assumed a more sacred character. Already had his unwearied
and comprehensive activity made him through-
out his reign an ecclesiastical no less than   *His author-*
a civil ruler, summoning and sitting in coun-   *ity in mat-*
                                                ters eccle-
cils, examining and appointing bishops, settling *siastical.*
by capitularies the smallest points of church
discipline and polity. A synod held at Frankfort in A.D.
794 condemned the decrees of the second council of Nicæa,

---

* Harun er Rashid; Eginh. *Vita Karoli*, cap. 16.

which has been approved by Pope Hadrian, censured in
violent terms the conduct of the Byzantine rulers in suggesting them, and without excluding images from churches,
altogether forbade them to be worshiped or even venerated.
Not only did Charles preside in and direct the deliberations of this synod, although legates from the Pope were
present—he also caused a treatise to be drawn up stating
and urging its conclusions; he pressed Hadrian to declare
Constantine VI a heretic for enouncing doctrines to which
Hadrian had himself consented.   There are letters·of his
extant in which he lectures Pope Leo in a tone of easy
superiority, admonishes him to obey the holy canons, and
bids him pray earnestly for the success of the efforts which
it is the monarch's duty to make for the subjugation of
pagans and the establishment of sound doctrine throughout the Church.   Nay, subsequent Popes themselves* admitted and applauded the despotic superintendence of
matters spiritual which he was wont to exercise, and which
led some one to give him playfully a title that had once
been applied to the Pope himself, "Episcopus epis-
coporum."

Acting and speaking thus when merely king, it may be
thought that Charles needed no further title
The imperi-   to justify his power.   The inference is in truth
al office in   rather the converse of this.   Upon what he
its ecclesi-
astical re-   had done already the imperial title must nec-
lations.   essarily follow: the attitude of protection and
control which he held toward the Church and
the Holy See belonged, according to the ideas of the time,
especially and only to an Emperor.   Therefore his coronation was the fitting completion and legitimation of his authority, sanctifying rather than increasing it.   We have,

---

* So Pope John VIII in a document quoted by Waitz, *Deutsche
Verfassungsgeschichte,* iii.

however, one remarkable witness to the importance that
was attached to the imperial name, and the enhancement
which he conceived his office to have received from it.
In a great assembly held at Aachen, A.D. 802,
the lately-crowned Emperor revised the laws of
the races that obeyed him, endeavoring to har-
monize and correct them, and issued a capitulary singular
*Capitulary
of A.D. 802.*
in subject and tone.* All persons within his dominions,
as well ecclesiastical as civil, who have already sworn allegiance to him as king, are thereby commanded to swear
to him afresh as Cæsar; and all who have never yet sworn,
down to the age of twelve, shall now take the same oath.
"At the same time it shall be publicly explained to all
what is the force and meaning of this oath, and how much
more it includes than a mere promise of fidelity to the
monarch's person. Firstly, it binds those who swear it to
live, each and every one of them, according to his strength
and knowledge, in the holy service of God; since the Lord
Emperor cannot extend over all his care and discipline.
Secondly, it binds them neither by force nor fraud to seize
or molest any of the goods or servants of his crown.
Thirdly, to do no violence nor treason towards the holy
Church, or to widows, or orphans, or strangers, seeing that
the Lord Emperor has been appointed after the Lord and
his saints, the protector and defender of all such." Then
in similar fashion purity of life is prescribed to the monks;
homicide, the neglect of hospitality, and other offences
are denounced, the notions of sin and crime being inter-
mingled and almost identified in a way to which no
parallel can be found, unless it be in the mosaic code.
There God, the invisible object of worship, is also, though
almost incidentally, the judge and political ruler of Israel;
here the whole cycle of social and moral duty is deduced

---

* Pertz, *M. G. H.* iii. (legg. I).

from the obligation of obedience to the visible autocratic head of the Christian state.

In most of Charles' words and deeds, nor less distinctly in the writings of his adviser Alcuin, may be discerned the working of the same theocratic ideas. Among his intimate friends he chose to be called by the name of David, exercising in reality all the powers of the Jewish king; presiding over this kingdom of God upon earth rather as a second Constantine or Theodosius than in the spirit and traditions of the Julii or the Flavii. Among his measures there are two which in particular recall the first Christian Emperor. As Constantine founds so Charles erects on a firmer basis the connection of Church and State. Bishops and abbots are as essential a part of rising feudalism as counts and dukes. Their benifices are held under the same conditions of fealty and the service in war of their vassal tenants, not of the spiritual person himself: they have similar rights of jurisdiction, and are subject alike to the imperial *missi*. The monarch tries often to restrict the clergy, as persons, to spiritual duties; quells the insubordination of the monasteries; endeavors to bring the seculars into a monastic life by instituting and regulating chapters. But after granting wealth and power, the attempt was vain; his strong hand withdrawn, they laughed at control. Again, it was by him first that the payment of tithes, for which the priesthood had long been pleading, was made compulsory in Western Europe, and the support of the ministers of religion entrusted to the laws of the state.

In civil affairs also Charles acquired, with the imperial title, a new position. Later jurists labor to distinguish his power as Roman Emperor from that which he held already as king of the Franks and their subject allies : they insist that his coronation gave him the capital only, that it is absurd to talk of a Roman Empire in regions whither the

Influence of the imperial title in Germany and Gaul.

eagles had never flown.* In such expressions there
seems to lurk either confusion or misconception. It
was not the actual government of the city that Charles obtained in A.D. 800 ; that his father had already held as
Patrician and he had constantly exercised in the same
capacity: it was far more than the titular sovereignty of
Rome which had hitherto been supposed to be vested in the
Byzantine princes: it was nothing less than the headship
of the world, believed to appertain of right to the lawful
Roman Emperor, whether he reigned on the Bosphorus,
the Tiber, or the Rhine. As that headship, although
never denied, had been in abeyance in the West for several centuries, its bestowal on the king of so vast a realm
was a change of the first moment, for it made the coronation not merely a transference of the seat of Empire, but
a renewal of the Empire itself, a bringing back of it from
faith to sight, from the world of belief and theory to the
world of fact and reality. And since the powers it gave
were autocratic and unlimited, it must swallow up all
minor claims and dignities : the rights of Charles the
Frankish king were merged in those of Charles the successor of Augustus, the lord of the world. That his imperial
authority was theoretically irrespective of place is clear
from his own words and acts, and from all the monuments
of that time. He would not, indeed, have dreamed of
treating the free Franks as Justinian had treated his half-
Oriental subjects, nor would the warriors who followed his
standard have brooked such an attempt. Yet even to
German eyes his position must have been altered by the
halo of vague splendor which now surrounded him ; for
all, even the Saxon and the Slave, had heard of Rome's
glories, and revered the name of Cæsar. And in his

---

* Putter, *Historical Development of the German Constitution;* so too
Conring, and esp. David Blondel, *Adv. Chiffletium.*

effort to wield discordant elements into one body, to
introduce regular gradations of authority, to

*Action of
Charles on
Europe.*

contol the Teutonic tendency to localization by
his *missi*—officials commissioned to traverse each
some part of his dominions, reporting on and re-
dressing the evils they found—and by his own oft-repeated
personal progresses, Charles was guided by the traditions of
the old Empire. His sway is the revival of order and
culture, fusing the West into a compact whole, whose
parts are never thenceforward to lose the marks of their
connection and their half-Roman character, gathering up
all that is left in Europe of spirit and wealth and knowledge, and hurling it with the new force of Christianity on
the infidel of the South and the masses of untamed barbarism to the North and East. Ruling the world by the gift
of God, and the transmitted rights of the Romans and
their Cæsar whom God had chosen to conquer it, he re-
news the original aggressive movement of the Empire :
the civilized world has subdued her invader,* and now
arms him against savagery and heathendom. Hence the
wars, not more of the sword than of the cross, against
Saxons, Avars, Slaves, Danes, Spanish Arabs, where monasteries are fortresses and baptism the badge of submission. The overthrow of the Irminsûl,† in the first Saxon

---

* "Græcia capta ferum victorem cepit," is repeated in this conquest
of the Teuton by the Roman.

† The notion that once prevailed that the Irminsûl was the "pillar
of Hermann," set up on the spot of the defeat of Varus, is, however,
now generally discredited. Some German antiquaries take the pillar
to be a rude figure of the native god or hero Irmin, who, as Grimm
(*Deutsche Mythologie*, i, 325) thinks, may be an eponym of the Her-
minones, and was probably worshiped by the Saxons as a warlike
representation of Wodan. The omission of their ancestors to commemorate the victory that saved them from Rome has been at last
supplied by the modern Germans, who in 1875 set up a colossal
statue of Arminius or Hermann in the Teutoburger Wald, not far

ᴄampaign,* sums up the changes of seven centuries.   The
Romanized Teuton destroys the monument of his country's
freedom, for it is also the emblem of paganism and barbarism.   The work of Arminius is undone by his successor.

This, however, is not the only side from which Charles'
policy and character may be regarded.   If the unity of the
Church and the shadow of imperial prerogative
was one pillar of his power, the other was the *His position
as Frankish*
Frankish nation.   The Empire was still mili- *king.*
tary, though in a sense strangely different from
that of Julius or Severus.   The warlike Franks had per-
meated Western Europe; their primacy was admitted by
the kindred tribes of Lombards, Bavarians, Thuringians,
Alemannians and Burgundians; the Slavic peoples on the
borders trembled and paid tribute; Alfonso of Asturius
found in the Emperor a protector against the infidel foe.
His influence, if not his exerted power, crossed the ocean:
the kings of the Scots sent gifts and called him lord:†
the restoration of Eardulf to Northumbria, still more of
Egbert to Wessex, might furnish a better ground for the

---

from the reputed scene of the battle.   He has in fact become the
earliest national hero.   A rude ditty, apparently referring to the destruction of the pillar by Charles, still lives in the memory of the
Westphalians round Paderborn, and runs thus :

" Hermen sla dermen
Sla pipen, sla trummen
De Kaiser wil kummen
Met hammer un stangen
Wil Hermen uphangen."

Mommsen (*Die Oertlichkeit der Varus-schlacht*) places the scene of
the battle eight or ten miles N. of Osnabrück, near a spot called
Barenau.   (Note to edition of 1887.)

* Eginhard, *Ann.*

† Most probably the Scots of Ireland.—Eginhard, *Vita Karoli,*
cap. 16.

claim of suzerainty than many to which his successors had
afterward recourse.　As it was by Frankish arms that this
predominance in Europe which the imperial title adorned
and legalized had been won, so was the government of
Charles Roman in semblance rather than in fact.　It was
not by restoring the effete mechanism of the old Empire,
but by his own vigorous personal action and that of his
great officers, that he strove to administer and reform.
With every effort of a strong central government, there is
no despotism; each nation retains its laws, its hereditary
chiefs, its free popular assemblies.　The conditions granted
to the Saxons after such cruel warfare, conditions so favorable that in the next century their dukes hold the foremost place in Germany, show how little he desired to make
the Franks a dominant caste.

He repeats the attempt of Theodoric to breathe a Teutonic spirit into Roman forms.　The conception was magnificent; great results followed its partial execu-
General re-
sults of his　tion.　Two causes forbade success.　The one
Empire.　was the ecclesiastical, especially the Papal
power, apparently subject to the temporal, but
with a strong and undefined prerogative which only waited
the occasion to trample on what it had helped to raise.
The Pope might take away the crown he had bestowed,
and turn against the Emperor the Church which now
obeyed him.　The other was to be found in the discord-
ance of the component parts of the Empire.　The nations
were not ripe for settled life or extensive schemes of polity;
the differences of race, language, manners, over vast and
thinly peopled lands baffled every attempt to maintain
their connnection : and when once the spell of the great
mind was withdrawn, the mutually repellent forces began
to work, and the mass dissolved into that chaos out of
which it had been formed.　Nevertheless, the parts separated not as they met, but having all of them undergone

influences which continued to act when political connection had ceased. For the work of Charles—a genius preeminently creative—was not lost in the anarchy that followed: rather are we to regard his reign as the beginning of a new era, or as laying the foundations whereon men continued for many generations to build.

It is no longer necessary to show how little the modern French, the sons of the Latinized Kelt, have to do with the Teutonic Charles. At Rome he might assume the chlamys and the sandals, but at the *Personal habits and sympathies.* head of his Frankish host he strictly adhered to the customs of his country, and was beloved by his people as the very ideal of their own character and habits.* Of strength and stature almost superhuman, in swimming and hunting unsurpassed, steadfast and terrible in fight, to his friends gentle and condescending, he was a Roman, much less a Gaul, in nothing but his culture and his schemes of government, otherwise a Teuton. The center of his realm was the Rhine ; his capitals Aachen † and Engilenheim ;‡ his army Frankish ; his sympathies— as they are shown in the gathering of the old hero-lays,§ the composition of a German grammar, the ordinance against confining prayer to the three languages, Hebrew, Greek and Latin — were all for the race from which he sprang, and whose advance, represented by the victory of

---

* Eginhard, *Vita Karoli*, cap. 23.

† Aix-la-Chapelle (called by English writers of the seventeenth century, Aken). See the lines given in Pertz's edition of Eginhard, beginning:

> "Urbs Aquensis, urbs regalis,
> Sedes regni principalis,
> Prima regum curia."

‡ Engilenheim, or Ingelheim, lies near the left shore of the Rhine between Mentz and Bingen.

§ Eginhard, *Vita Karoli*, cap. 29.

Austrasia, the true Frankish fatherland, over Neustria
and Aquitaine, spread a second Germanic wave over the
conquered countries.

There were in his Empire, as in his own mind, two elements; those two from the union and mutual action and
His Empire and character generally. reaction of which modern civilization has
arisen. These vast domains, reaching from
the Ebro to the Carpathian mountains, from
the Eyder to the Liris, were all the conquests
of the Frankish sword, and were still governed
almost exclusively by viceroys and officers of Frankish
blood. But the conception of the Empire, that which
made it a State and not a mere mass of subject tribes like
those great Eastern dominions which rise and perish in a
life-time, the realms of Sesostris, or Attila, or Timur, was
inherited from an older and a grander system, was not
Teutonic but Roman—Roman in its ordered rule, in its
uniformity and precision, in its endeavor to subject the
individual to the system—Roman in its effort to realize a
certain limited and human perfection, whose very completeness shall exclude the hope of further progress. And
the bond, too, by which the Empire was held together was
Roman in its origin, although Roman in a sense which
would have surprised Trajan or Severus, could it have
been foretold them. The ecclesiastical body was already
organized and centralized, and it was in his rule over the
ecclesiastical body that the secret of Charles' power lay.
Every Christian—Frank, Gaul, or Italian—owed loyalty
to the head and defender of his religion: the unity of the
Empire was a reflection of the unity of the Church.

Into a general view of the government and policy of
Charles it is not possible here to enter. Yet his legislation,
his assemblies, his administrative system, his magnificent
works, recalling the projects of Alexander and Cæsar,* the

---

* Eginhard, *Vita Karoli*, cap. 17.

zeal for education and literature which he showed in the collection of manuscripts, the founding of schools, the gathering of eminent men from all quarters around him, cannot be appreciated apart from his position as restorer of the Roman Empire. Like all the foremost men of our race, Charles was all great things in one, and was so great just because the workings of his genius were so harmonious. He was not a mere barbarian warrior any more than he was an astute diplomatist; there is none of all his qualities which would not be forced out of its place were we to characterize him chiefly by it. Comparisons between famous men of different ages are generally as worthless as they are easy: the circumstances among which Charles lived do not permit us to institute a minute parallel between his greatness and that of those two to whom it is the modern fashion to compare him, nor to say whether he was or could have become as profound a politician as Cæsar, as skillful a commander as Napoleon.* But neither to the Roman nor to the Corsican was he inferior in that one quality by which both he and they chiefly impress our imaginations—that intense, vivid, unresting energy which swept him over Europe in campaign after campaign, which sought a field for its workings in theology, science, literature, no less than in politics and war. As it was this wondrous activity that made him the conqueror of Europe, so was it by the variety of his culture that he became her civilizer. From him, in whose wide deep mind the whole mediæval theory of the world and human life mirrored itself, did mediæval society take the form and impress which it retained for centuries, and the traces whereof are among us and upon us to this day.

---

* It is not a little curious that of the three whom certain Bonapartists sought to represent as French national heroes all should have been foreigners, and two foreign conquerors.

The great Emperor was buried at Aachen, in that basilica
which it had been the delight of his later years to erect and
adorn with the treasures of ancient art. His tomb under
the dome—where now we see an enormous slab, with the
words *" Carolo Magno"*—was inscribed, *" Magnus atque
Orthodoxus Imperator."** Poets, fostered by his own zeal,
sang of him who had given to the Franks the sway of
Romulus.† The gorgeous mists of romance gradually rose
and wreathed themselves round his name, till by canonization as a saint he received the highest glory the world or
the Church could confer.‡ For the Roman Church claimed

---

* This basilica was built upon the model of the church of the Holy
Sepulcher at Jerusalem, and as it was the first church of any size
that had been erected in those regions for centuries past, it excited
extraordinary interest among the Franks and Gauls. In many of its
features it greatly resembles the beautiful church of San Vitale, at
Ravenna (also modeled upon that of the Holy Sepulcher), which was
begun by Theodoric, and completed under Justinian. Probably San
Vitale was used as a pattern by Charles' architects: we know that he
caused marble columns to be brought from Ravenna to deck the
church at Aachen. Over the tomb of Charles, below the central
dome (to which the Gothic choir we now see was added some centuries later), there hangs a huge chandelier, the gift of Frederick
Barbarossa.

† " Romuleum Francis præstitit imperium."—Elegy of Ermoldus
Nigellus, in Pertz, *M. G. H.* t. i. So too Florus the Deacon :

" Huic etenim cessit etiam gens Romula genti,
Regnorumque simul mater Roma inclyta cessit ;
Huius ibi princeps regni diademata sumpsit
Munere apostolico, Christi munimine fretus."

‡ A curious illustration of the influence of the name and fame of
Charles, even on remote nations, is supplied by a story in the Heimskringla. Alfhild, a concubine of St. Olaf, had given birth to a child
at night, while Olaf was asleep ; and Sigvat his favorite skald, seeing
it to be weak, and fearing it might die, caused it to be baptized at
once, and gave it the name of Magnus. When the king awoke
and heard what had been done, he was angry, and calling Sigvat,
asked : " Why hast thou called the child Magnus, which is not a

then, as she claims still, the privilege which humanity in one form or another seems scarce able to deny itself, of raising to honors almost divine its great departed; and as in pagan times temples had risen to a deified Emperor, so churches were dedicated to St. Charlemagne. Between Sanctus Carolus and Divus Julius how strange an analogy and how strange a contrast!

---

name of our race ?" The skeld answered : " I called him after King Karl Magnus, who I knew had been the best man in the world." The child grew up to be King Magnus the Good, the most popular and one of the greatest of all the Norwegian kings ; and from him the name became a common one over all the North.

CHAPTER VI.

CAROLINGIAN AND ITALIAN EMPERORS.

LEWIS the Pious,* left by Charles' death sole heir, had been some years before associated with his father in the Empire, and had been crowned by his own hands in a way which, intentionally or not, appeared to deny the need of Papal sanction. But it was soon seen that the strength to grasp the scepter had not passed with it. Too mild to restrain his turbulent nobles, and thrown by over-conscientiousness into the hands of the clergy, he had reigned few years when dis. sensions broke out on all side. Charles had wished the Empire to continue one, under the supremacy of a single Emperor, but with its several parts, Lombardy, Aquitaine, Austrasia, Bavaria, each a kingdom held by a scion of the reigning house. A scheme dangerous in itself, and rendered more so by the absence or neglect of regular rules of succession, could with difficulty have been managed by a wise and firm monarch. Lewis tried in vain to satisfy his sons (Lothar, Lewis and Charles) by dividing and redividing: they rebelled; he was deposed, and forced by the bishops to do penance: again restored, but without power, a tool in the hands of contending factions. On his death the sons flew to arms, and the first of the

Lewis the Pious.

---

* Usage has established this translation of "Hludowicus Pius," but "gentle" or "kind-hearted" would better express the meaning of the epithet.

dynastic quarrels of modern Europe was fought out on the field of Fontenay. In the partition treaty of Verdun which followed, the Teutonic principle of equal division among heirs triumphed over the Roman one of the transmission of an *Partition of Verdun, A.D. 843.* indivisible Empire: the practical sovereignty of all three brothers was admitted in their respective territories, a barren precedence only reserved to Lothar, with the imperial title which he, as the eldest, already enjoyed. *Lothar I.* A more important result was the separation of the Gaulish and German nationalities. Their difference of feeling, shown already in the support of Lewis the pious by the Germans against the Gallo-Franks and the Church,* took now a permanent shape: modern Germany proclaims the era of A.D. 843 the beginning of her national existence, and celebrated its thousandth anniversary thirty-two years ago. To Charles the Bald was given Francia Occidentalis, that is to say, Neustria and Aquitaine; to Lothar, who as Emperor must possess the two capitals, Rome and Aachen, a long and narrow kingdom stretching from the North Sea to the Mediterranean, and including the northern half of Italy; Lewis (surnamed, from his kingdom, the German) received all east of the Rhine, Franks, Saxons, Bavarians, Austria, Carinthia, with possible supremacies over Czechs and Moravians beyond. Throughout these regions German was spoken; through Charles' kingdom a corrupt tongue, equally removed from Latin and from modern French. Lothar's, being mixed and having no national basis, was the weakest of the three, and soon dissolved into the separate sovereignties of Italy, Burgundy, and Lotharingia, or, as we call it, Lorraine.

---

* Von Ranke discovers in this early traces of the aversion of the Germans to the pretensions of the spiritual power.—*History of Germany during the Reformation:* Introduction.

On the tangled history of the period that follows it is not possible to do more than ˙touch. After passing from one branch of the Carolingian line to another,* the imperial scepter was at last possessed and disgraced by Charles the Fat, who united all the dominions of his great-grandfather. This unworthy heir could not avail himself of recovered territory to strengthen or defend the expiring monarchy. He was driven out of Italy in A.D. 887, and his death in 888 has been usually taken as the date of the extinction of the Carolingian Empire of the West. The Germans, still attached to the ancient line, chose Arnulf, an illegitimate Carolingian for their king: he entered Italy and was crowned Emperor by his partisan Pope Formosus, in 896. But Germany, divided and helpless, was in no condition to maintain her power over the Southern lands: Arnulf retreated in haste, leaving Rome and Italy to sixty years of stormy independence.

Lewis II.
Charles II.
Charles III.

End of the Carolingian Empire of the West
A.D. 888.

That time was indeed the nadir of order and civilization. From all sides the torrent of barbarism which Charles the Great had stemmed was rushing down upon his empire. The Saracen wasted the Mediterranean coasts, and sacked Rome herself. The Dane and Norseman swept the Atlantic and the North Sea, pierced France and Germany by their rivers, burning, slaying, carrying off into captivity: pouring through the Straits of Gibraltar, they fell upon Provence and Italy. By land, while Wends and Czechs and Obotrites threw off the German yoke and threatened the borders, the wild Hungarian bands, pressing in from the steppes of the Caspian, dashed over Germany like the

---

* Singularly enough, when one thinks of modern claims, the dynasty of France (Francia occidentalis) had the least share of it. Charles the Bald was the only West Frankish Emperor, and reigned a very short time.

flying spray of a new wave of barbarism, and carried the terror of their battle-axes to the Apennines and the ocean. Under such strokes the already loosened fabric swiftly dissolved. No one thought of common defence or wide organization: the strong built castles, the weak became their bondsmen, or took shelter under the cowl: the governor—count, abbot, or bishop—tightened his grasp, turned a delegated into an independent, a personal into a territorial authority, and hardly owned a distant and feeble suzerain. The grand vision of a universal Christian empire was utterly lost in the isolation, the antagonism, the increasing localization of all powers: it might seem to have been but a passing gleam from an older and better world.

In Germany, the greatness of the evil worked at last its cure. When the male line of the eastern branch of the Carolingians had ended in Lewis (surnamed the Child), son of Arnulf, the chieftains chose and the people accepted Conrad the Franconian, and after him Henry the Saxon duke, *The German Kingdom.* both representing the female line of Charles. Henry laid the foundations of a firm monarchy, driving back the Magyars and Wends, recovering Lotharingia, founding towns to be centers of orderly *Henry the Fowler.* life and strongholds against Hungarian irruptions. He had meant to claim at Rome his kingdom's rights, rights which Conrad's weakness had at least asserted by the demand of tribute ; but death overtook him, and the plan was left to be fulfilled by Otto his son.

The Holy Roman Empire, taking the name in the sense which it commonly bore in later centuries, as denoting the sovereignty of Germany and Italy vested in a Germanic prince, is the creation of Otto the *Otto the Great.* Great. Substantially, it is true, as well as technically, it was a prolongation of the Empire of

Charles; and it rested (as will be shown in the sequel)
upon ideas essentially the same as those which brought
about the coronation of A.D. 800. But a revival is always
more or less a revolution: the one hundred and fifty years
that had passed since the death of Charles had brought
with them changes which made Otto's position in Germany and Europe less commanding and less autocratic
than his predecessor's. With narrower geographical limits,
his Empire had a less plausible claim to be the heir of
Rome's universal dominion ; and there were also differences in its inner character and structure sufficient to justify us in considering Otto (as he is usually considered by
his countrymen) not a mere successor after an interregnum,
but rather a second founder of the imperial throne in the
West.

Before Otto's descent into Italy is described, something
must be said of the condition of that country, where circumstances had again made possible the plan of Theodoric,
permitted it to become an independent kingdom, and
attached the imperial title to its sovereign.

The bestowal of the purple on Charles the Great was not
really that " translation of the Empire from the Greeks to
Italian Em- the Franks," which it was afterward described
perors. as having been. It was not meant to settle
the office in one nation or one dynasty :
there was but an extension of that principle of
the equality of all Romans which had made Trajan
and Maximin Emperors. The "*arcanum imperii,*"
whereof Tacitus speaks, "*posse principem alibi quam
Romæ fieri,*"* had long before become *alium quam
Romanum ;* and now, the names of Roman and Christian
having grown co-extensive, a barbarian chieftain was, as a
Roman citizen, eligible to the office of Roman Emperor.

---

* Tac. *Hist.* i. 4.

Treating him as such, the people and pontiff of the capital had in the vacancy of the Eastern throne asserted their ancient rights of election, and while attempting to reverse the act of Constantine, had re-established the division of Valentinian. The dignity was therefore in strictness personal to Charles; in point of fact, and by consent, hereditarily transmissible, just as it had formerly become in the families of Constantine and Theodosius. To the Frankish crown or nation it was by no means legally attached, though they might think it so; it had passed to their king only because he was the greatest European potentate, and might equally well pass to some stronger race, if any such appeared. Hence, when the line of Carolingian Emperors ended in Charles the Fat, the rights of Rome and Italy might be taken to revive, and there was nothing to prevent the citizens from choosing whom they would. At that memorable era (A.D. 888) the four kingdoms which this prince had united fell asunder; West France, where Odo or Eudes then began to reign, was never again united in Germany; East France (Germany) chose Arnulf; Burgundy* split up into two principalities, in one of which (Transjurane) Rudolf proclaimed himself king, while the other (Cisjurane with Provence) submitted to Boso;† while Italy was divided between the parties of Berengar of Friuli

---

* For an account of the various applications of the name Burgundy, see Appendix, Note A.

† The accession of Boso took place in A.D. 877, eleven years before Charles the Fat's death. But the new kingdom could not be considered legally settled until the latter date, and its establishment is at any rate a part of that general break-up of the great Carolingian Empire whereof A.D. 888 marks the crisis. See Appendix A at the end. It is a curious mark of the reverence paid to the Carolingian blood, that Boso, a powerful and ambitious prince, seems to have chiefly rested his claims on the fact that he was husband of Irmingard, daughter of the Emperor Lewis II. Baron de Gingins la Sarraz quotes a charter of his (drawn up when he seems to have doubted whether to call himself king), which begins, "Ego Boso Dei gratia id quod sum, et coniux mea Irmingardis proles imperialis."

and Guido of Spoleto. The former was chosen king by
the estates of Lombardy; the latter, and on his speedy
death his son Lambert, was crowned Emperor by the
Pope. Arnulf's descent chased them away and vindicated
the claims of the Franks, but on his flight Italy and the
anti-German faction at Rome became again free. Berengar was made king of Italy, and afterward Emperor.
Lewis of Burgundy, son of Boso, renounced his fealty to
Berengar, and procured the imperial dignity, whose vain
title he retained through years of misery and exile, till
A.D. 928.* None of the Emperors were strong enough to
rule well even in Italy; beyond it they were not so much
as recognized. The crown had become a bauble with
which unscrupulous Popes dazzled the vanity of princes
whom they summoned to their aid, and soothed the credu-
lity of their more honest supporters. The demoralization
and confusion of Italy, the shameless profligacy of Rome
and her pontiffs during this period, were enough to prevent a true Italian kingdom from being built up on the
basis of Roman choice and national unity. Italian indeed
it can scarcely be called, for these Emperors were still in
blood and manners Teutonic, and akin rather to their
Transalpine enemies than their Romanic subjects. But
Italian it might soon have become under a vigorous rule
which would have organized it within and knit it together
to resist attacks from without. And therefore the attempt
to establish such a kingdom is remarkable, for it might
have had great consequences; might, if it had prospered,
have spared Italy much suffering and Germany endless
waste of strength and blood. He who from the summit
of Milan cathedral sees across the misty plain the gleaming
turrets of its icy wall sweep in a great arc from North to
West, may well wonder that a land which nature has so

---

* Lewis had been surprised by Berengar at Verona, blinded, and
forced to take refuge in his own kingdom of Provence.

severed from its neighbors should, since history begins, have been always the victim of their intrusive tyranny.

In A.D. 924 died Berengar, the last of these phantom Emperors. After him Hugh of Burgundy, and Lothar his son, reigned as kings of Italy, if puppets in the hands of a riotous aristocracy can be so called. Rome was meanwhile ruled by the consul or senator Alberic,* who had renewed her never quite extinct republican institutions, and in the degradation of the papacy was almost absolute in the city. Lothar dying, his widow Adelheid† was sought in marriage by Adalbert son of Berengar II, the new Italian monarch. A gleam of romance is shed on the Empire's revival by her beauty and her adventures. Rejecting the odious alliance, she was seized by Berengar, escaped with difficulty from the loathsome prison where his barbarity had confined her, and appealed to Otto the German king, the model of that knightly virtue which was beginning to show itself after the fierce brutality of the last age. He listened, descended into Lombardy by the Adige valley, espoused the injured queen, and forced Berengar to hold his kingdom as a vassal of the East Frankish crown. That prince was turbulent and faithless; new complaints reached ere long his liege lord, and envoys from the Pope offered Otto the imperial title if he would revisit and pacify Italy. The proposal was well-timed. Men still thought, as they had thought in the centuries before the Carolingians, that the Empire was suspended, not extinct; and the desire to see its effective power restored, the belief that

Marginal notes: *Adelheid Queen of Italy.* *Otto's first expedition into Italy, A.D. 951.* *Invitation sent by the Pope to Otto.*

---

* Alberic is called variously senator, consul, patrician and prince of the Romans.

† Adelheid was daughter of Rudolf, king of Transjurane Burgundy. She was at this time in her nineteenth year.

without it the world could never be right, might seem better grounded than it had been before the coro-

Motives for reviving the Empire.
nation of Charles. Then the imperial name
had recalled only the faint memories of Roman
majesty and order; now it was also associated
with the golden age of the first Frankish Emperor, when a
single firm and just hand had guided the state, reformed
the church, repressed the excesses of local power: when
Christianity had advanced against heathendom, civilizing
as she went, fearing neither Hun nor Saracen. One annalist tells us that Charles was elected " lest the pagans should
insult the Christians, if the name of Emperor should have
ceased among the Christians.* The motive would be bitterly enforced by the calamities of the last fifty years. In
a time of disintegration, confusion, strife, all the longings
of every wiser and better soul for unity, for peace and
law, for some bond to bring Christian men and Christian
states together against the common enemy of the faith,
were but so many cries for the restoration of the Roman
Empire.† These were the feelings that on the field of
Merseberg broke forth in the shout of " Henry the Emperor:" these the hopes of the Teutonic host when after
the great deliverance of the Lechfeld they greeted Otto,
conqueror of the Magyars, as " Imperator Augustus, Pater
Patriæ."‡

---

* *Chron. Moiss.*, in Pertz; *M. G. H.* i. 305.

† See especially the poem of Florus the Deacon (printed in the
Benedictine collection and in Migne), a bitter lament over the dissolution of the Carolingian empire. It is too long for quotation. I give
four lines here :
"Quid faciant populi quos ingens alluit Hister,
    Quos Rhenus Rhodanusque rigant, Ligerisve, Padusve,
    Quos omnes dudum tenuit concordia nexos,
    Foedere nunc rupto divortia moesta fatigant."

‡ Witukind, *Annales*, in Pertz. It may, however, be doubted
whether the annalist is not here giving a very free rendering of the
triumphant cries of the German army.

The anarchy which an Emperor was needed to heal was at its worst in Italy, desolated by the feuds of a crowd of petty princes. A succession of infamous Popes, raised by means yet more infamous, the lovers and sons of Theodora and Marozia, had *Condition of Italy.* disgraced the chair of the Apostle, and though Rome herself might be lost to decency, Western Christendom was roused to anger and alarm. Men had not yet learned to satisfy their consciences by separating the person from the office. The rule of Alberic had been succeeded by the wildest confusion, and demands were raised for the renewal of that imperial authority which all admitted in theory,* and which nothing but the resolute opposition of Alberic himself had prevented Otto from claiming in 951. From the Byzantine Empire, whither Italy was more than once tempted to turn, nothing could be hoped; its dangers from foreign enemies were aggravated by the plots of the court and the seditions of the capital; it was becoming more and more alienated from the West by the Photian schism and the question regarding the Procession of the Holy Ghost, which that quarrel had started. Germany was extending and consolidating herself, had escaped domestic perils, and might think of reviving ancient claims. No one could be more willing to revive them than Otto the Great. His ardent spirit, after waging a bold and successful struggle against the turbulent magnates of his German realm, had engaged him in wars with the surrounding nations; and was now captivated by the vision of a wider sway and a loftier world-embracing dignity. Nor was the prospect which the papal offer opened up less welcome to his people. Aachen, their capital, was the ancestral home of the house of Pipin: their sovereign, although himself a

---

* Cf. esp. the " *Libellus de imperatoria potestate iu urbe Roma,*" in Pertz.

Saxon by race, titled himself king of the Franks, in opposition to the Frankish rulers of the Western branch,
whose Teutonic character was disappearing among the Romans of Gaul ; they held themselves in every way the true
representatives of the Carolingian power, and accounted
the period since Arnulf's death nothing but an interregnum
which had suspended but not impaired their rights over
Rome. "For so long," says a writer of the time, "as
there remain kings of the Franks, so long will the dignity
of the Roman Empire not wholly perish, seeing that it
will abide in its kings." * The recovery of Italy was therefore to German eyes a righteous as well as a glorious
design : approved by the Teutonic Church which had
lately been negotiating with Rome on the subject of mis-
sions to the heathen; embraced by the people, who saw in
it an accession of strength to their young kingdom.
Everything smiled on Otto's enterprise, and the connection which was destined to bring so much strife and woe
to Germany and to Italy was welcomed by the wisest of
both countries as the beginning of a better era.

Whatever were Otto's own feelings, whether or not he
felt that he was sacrificing, as modern writers have thought
that he did sacrifice, the greatness of his
German kingdom to the lust of universal dominion, he showed no hesitation in his acts.
Descending from the Alps with an overpowering force, he was acknowledged as king of
Italy at Pavia ;† and, having first taken an oath to pro-

Descent of
Otto the
Great into
Italy.

---

* " Licet videamus Romanorum regnum in maxima parte jam de-
structum, tamen quamdiu reges Francorum duraverint qui Romanum
imperium tenere debent, dignitas Romani imperii ex toto non peribit,
quia stabit in regibus suis."—*Liber de Antichristo*, adressed by Adso,
abbot of Moutieren-Der, to Queen Gerberga (circa A.D. 950).

† From the money which Otto struck in Italy, it seems probable
that he did occasionally use the title of king of Italy or of the Lombards. That he was crowned can hardly be considered quite certain.

tect the Holy See and respect the liberties of the city, advanced to Rome. There, with Adelheid his queen, he was crowned by John XII, on the day of the Purification, the second of February, A.D. 962. *His coronation at Rome, A.D. 962.* The details of his election and coronation are unfortunately still more scanty than in the case of his great predecessor. Most of our authorities represent the act as of the Pope's favor,* yet it is plain that the consent of the people was still thought an essential part of the ceremony, and that Otto rested after all on his host of conquering Saxons. Be this as it may, there was neither question raised nor opposition made in Rome ; the usual courtesies and promises were exchanged between Emperor and Pope, the latter owning himself a subject, and the citizens swore for the future to elect no pontiff without Otto's consent.

---

* "A papa imperator ordinatur," says Hermannus Contractus. " Dominum Ottonem, ad hoc usque vocatum regem, non solum Romano sed et pœne totius Europæ populo acclamante imperatorem consecravit Augustum."—*Annal. Quedlinb.*, ad ann. 962. " Benedictionem a domno apostolico Iohanne, cuius rogatione huc venit, cum sua coniuge promeruit imperialem ac patronus Romanæ effectus est ecclesiæ."—Thietmar. "Acclamatione totius Romani populi ab apostolico Iohanne, filio Alberici, imperator et Augustus vocatur et ordinatur."—Continuator Reginonis. And similarly the other annalists.

CHAPTER VII.

THEORY OF THE MEDIÆVAL EMPIRE.

THESE were the events and circumstances of the time:
let us now look at the causes. The restoration of the
Empire by Charles may seem to be sufficiently
Why the accounted for by the width of his conquests,
revival of by the peculiar connection which already sub-
the Empire sisted between him and the Roman Church, by
was desired. his commanding personal character, by the
temporary vacancy of the Byzantine throne. The causes of
its revival under Otto must be sought deeper. Making every
allowance for the favoring incidents which have already
been dwelt upon, there must have been some further influence at work to draw him and his successors, Saxon and
Frankish kings, so far from home in pursuit of a barren
crown, to lead the Italians to accept the dominion of a
stranger and a barbarian, to make the Empire itself appear
through the whole Middle Age not what it seems now, a
gorgeous anachronism, but an institution divine and necessary, having its foundations in the very nature and order
of things. The empire of the elder Rome had been splendid in its life, yet its judgment was written in the misery
to which it had brought the provinces, and the helplessness that had invited the attacks of the barbarian. Now,
as we at least can see, it had long been dead, and the
course of events was adverse to its revival. Its actual
representatives, the Roman people, were a turbulent rabble,

sunk in a profligacy notorious even in that guilty age.
Yet not the less for all this did men cling to the idea, and
strive through long ages to stem the irresistible time-cur-
rent, fondly believing that they were breasting it even
while it was sweeping them ever faster and faster away from
the old order into a region of new thoughts, new feelings,
new forms of life. Not till the days of the Reformation
was the illusion dispelled.

The explanation is to be found in the state of the
human mind during these centuries. The Middle Ages
were essentially unpolitical. Ideas as familiar
to the commonwealths of antiquity as to ourselves, ideas of the common good as the object

Mediæval theories.

of the State, of the rights of the people, of the comparative merits of different forms of government, were to
them, though sometimes carried out in fact, in their speculative form unknown, perhaps incomprehensible. Feudalism was the one great institution to which those times gave
birth, and feudalism was a social and a legal system,
only indirectly and by consequence a political one. Yet
the human mind, so far from being idle, was in certain
directions never more active; nor was it possible for it to
remain without general conceptions regarding the relation
of men to each other in this world. Such conceptions
were neither made an expression of the actual present condition of things nor drawn from an induction of the past;
they were partly inherited from the system that had preceded, partly evolved from the principles of that metaphysical theology which was ripening into scholasticism.*

---

* I do not mean to say that the system of ideas which it is endeavored to set forth in the following pages was complete in this particular form, either in the days of Charles, or those of Otto, or those of
Frederick Barbarossa. It seems to have been constantly growing
and decaying from the fourth century to the sixteenth, the relative

Now the two great ideas which expiring antiquity bequeathed to the ages that followed were those of a World-Monarchy and a World-Religion.

Before the conquests of Rome, men, with little knowledge of each other, with no experience of wide political union,* had held differences of race to be natural

The World-Religion. and irremovable barriers. Similarly, religion appeared to them a matter purely local and national; and as there were gods of the hills and gods of the valleys, of the land and of the sea, so each tribe rejoiced in its peculiar deities, looking on the natives of another country who worshiped other gods as Gentiles, natural foes, unclean beings. Such feelings, if keenest in the East, frequently show themselves in the early records of Greece and Italy: in Homer the hero who wanders over the unfruitful sea glories in sacking the cities of the

---

prominence of its cardinal doctrines varying from age to age. But, just as the painter who sees the ever-shifting lights and shades play over the face of a wide landscape faster than his brush can place them on the canvas, in despair at representing their exact position at any single moment, contents himself with painting the effects that are broadest and most permanent, and at giving rather the impression which the scene makes on him than every detail of the scene itself, so here the best and indeed the only practicable course seems to be that of setting forth in its most self-consistent form the body of ideas and beliefs on which the empire rested, although this form may not be exactly that which they can be asserted to have worn in any one century, and although the illustrations adduced may have to be taken sometimes from earlier, sometimes from later writers. As the doctrine of the empire was in its essence the same during the whole Middle Age, such a general description as is attempted here may, I venture to hope, be found substantially true for the tenth as well as for the fourteenth century.

* Empires like the Persian did nothing to assimilate the subject races, who retained their own laws and customs, sometimes their own princes, and were bound only to serve in the armies and fill the treasury of the Great King.

stranger;* the primitive Latins have the same word for a foreigner and an enemy; the exclusive systems of Egypt, Hindostan, China, are only more vehement expressions of the belief which made Athenian philosophers look on a state of war between Greeks and Barbarians as natural,† and defend slavery on the same ground of the original diversity of the races that rule and the races that serve. The Roman dominion giving to many nations a common speech and law, smote this feeling on its political side ; Christianity more effectually banished it from the soul by substituting for the variety of local pantheons the belief in one God, before whom all men are equal.‡

It is on the religious life that nations repose. Because divinity was divided, humanity had been divided likewise ; the doctrine of the unity of God now enforced the unity of man, who had been created in His *Coincides* image.§ The first lesson of Christianity was *with the* love, a love that was to join in one body those *World Em-* whom suspicion and prejudice and pride of race *pire.* had hitherto kept apart. There was thus formed by the new religion a community of the faithful, a Holy Empire, designed to gather all men into its bosom, and standing opposed to the manifold polytheisms of the older world

---

* Od. iii. 72 :

. . . . *ἦ μαψιδίως ἀλάλησθε,*
οἷά τε ληϊστῆρες, ὑπεὶρ ἅλα, τοίτ᾽ ἀλόωνται
ψυχὰς παρθέμενοι, κακὸν ἀλλοδαποῖσι φέροντες;

Cf. Od. ix, 39 : and the Hymn to the Pythian Apollo, l. 274. So in Il. v. 214. *ἀλλότριος φώς.*

† Plato, in the beginning of the Laws, represents it as natural between all states *πόλεμος φύσει ὑπάρχει πρὸς ἁπάσας τὰς πόλεις.*

‡ See especially Acts xvii, 26 ; Gal. iii, 28 ; Eph. ii, 11 sqq., iv, 3–6 ; Col. iii, 11.

§ This is drawn out bv Laurent, *Histoire du Droit des Gens;* and Ægidi, *Der Fürstenrath nach dem Luneviller Frieden.*

exactly as the universal sway of the Cæsars was contrasted
with the innumerable kingdoms and republics that had
gone before it. The analogy of the two made them appear
parts of one great world-movement toward unity : the coincidence of their boundaries, which had begun before
Constantine, lasted long enough after him to associate
them indissolubly together, and make the names of Roman
and Christian convertible.* Œcumenical councils, where
the whole spiritual body gathered itself from every part of
the temporal realm under the presidency of the temporal
head, presented the most visible and impressive examples
of their connection.† The language of civil government
was, throughout the West, that of the sacred writings and
of worship; the greatest mind of his generation consoled
the faithful for the fall of their earthly commonwealth
Rome, by describing to them its successor and representa-

---

* "Romanos enim vocitant homines nostræ religionis."—Gregory of
Tours, quoted by Ægidi, from A. F. Pott, *Essay on the Words " Rö-
misch," " Romanisch," " Roman," " Romantisch."* So in the Middle
Ages, 'Ρωμαῖοι is used to mean Christians, as opposed to Ἕλληνες,
heathens. Cf. Ducange, " Romani olim dicti qui alias Christiani vel
etiam Catholici."

† As a reviewer of a former edition has understood this passage as
meaning that " people imagined the Christian religion was to last forever because the Holy Roman Empire was never to decay," it may be
worth while to say that this is far from being the purport of the
argument which this chapter was designed to state. The converse
would be nearer the truth:—" people imagined the Holy Roman Empire was never to decay, because the Christian religion was to last forever." The phenomenon may perhaps be stated thus: Men who
were already disposed to believe the Roman Empire to be eternal for
one set of reasons, came to believe the Christian Church to be eternal
for another and to them more impressive set of reasons. Seeing the two
institutions allied in fact, they took their alliance and connection to
be eternal also; and went on for centuries believing in the necessary
existence of the Roman Empire because they believed in its necessary
union with the Catholic Church.

tive the "city which hath foundations, whose builder and maker is God." *

Of these two parallel unities, that of the political and that of the religious society, meeting in the higher unity of all Christians, which may be indifferently called Catholicity or Romanism (since in that day those words would have had the same meaning), that only which had been entrusted to the keeping of the Church survived the storms of the fifth century. Many reasons may be assigned for the firmness with which she clung to it. Seeing one institution after another falling to pieces around her, seeing how countries and cities were being severed from each other by the irruption of strange tribes and the increasing difficulty of communication, she strove to save religious fellowship by strengthening the ecclesiastical organization, by drawing tighter every bond of outward union. Necessities of faith were still more powerful. Truth, it was said, is one, and as it must bind into one body all who hold it, so it is only by continuing in that body that they can preserve it. Thus with the growing rigidity of dogma, which may be traced from the council of Jerusalem to the council of Trent, there had arisen the idea of supplementing revelation by tradition as a source of doctrine, of exalting the universal conscience and belief above the individual: and allowing the soul to approach God only through the universal consciousness, represented by the sacerdotal order: principles still maintained by one branch of the Church, and for some at least of which far weightier reasons could be assigned then, in the paucity

Preserva-tion of the unity of the Church.

Mediæval Theology requires One Visible Catholic Church.

---

* Augustine, in the *De Civitate Dei.* His influence, great through all the Middle Ages, was greater on no one than on Charles. "Delectabatur et libris sancti Augustini, præcipueque his qui De Civitate Dei prætitulati sunt."—Eginhard, *Vita Karoli,* cap. 24.

of written records and the blind ignorance of the mass of
the people than any to which their modern advocates have
recourse. There was another cause yet more deeply seated,
and which it is hard adequately to describe. It was not exactly a want of faith in the unseen, nor a shrinking fear
which dared not look forth on the universe alone: it was
rather the powerlessness of the untrained mind to realize
the idea as an idea and live in it; it was the tendency to
see everything in the concrete, to turn the parable into a
fact, the doctrine into its most literal application, the
symbol into the essential ceremony; the tendency which
intruded earthly Madonnas and saints between the worshiper and the spiritual Deity, and could satisfy its
devotional feelings only by visible images even of these:
which conceived of man's aspirations and temptations as
the result of the direct actions of angels and devils;
which expressed the strivings of the soul after purity by
the search for the Holy Grail: which in the Crusades sent
myriads to win at Jerusalem by earthly arms the sepulcher
of Him whom they could not serve in their own spirit nor
approach by their own prayers. And therefore it was
that the whole fabric of mediæval Christianity rested upon
the idea of the Visible Church. Such a Church could be
in nowise local or limited. To acquiesce in the establishment of National Churches would have appeared to those
men, as it must always appear when scrutinized, contra-
dictory to the nature of a religious body, opposed to the
genius of Christianity, defensible, when capable of defence
at all, only as a temporary resource in the presence of
insuperable difficulties. Had this plan, on which so many
have dwelt with complacency in later times, been proposed
either to the primitive Church in its adversity or to the
dominant Church of the ninth century, it would have been
rejected with horror; but since there were as yet no nations;
the plan was one which did not and could not present it-

self.   The Visible Church was therefore the Church Universal, the whole congregation of Christian men dispersed throughout the world.

Now of the Visible Church the emblem and stay was the priesthood; and it was by them, in whom dwelt whatever of learning and thought was *Idea of po-* left in Europe, that the second great idea *litical unity* whereof mention has been made—the belief in *upheld by* one universal temporal state—was preserved. *the clergy.*
As a matter of fact, that state had perished out of the West, and it might seem their interest to let its memory be lost.   They, however, did not so calculate their interest. So far from feeling themselves opposed to the civil authority in the seventh and eighth centuries, as they came to do in the twelfth and thirteenth, the clergy were fully persuaded that its maintenance was indispensable to their own welfare.   They were, be it remembered, at first Romans themselves, living by the Roman law, using Latin as their proper tongue and imbued with the idea of the historical connection of the two powers.   And by them chiefly was that idea expounded and enforced for many generations, by none more earnestly than by Alcuin of York, the adviser of Charles.*   The limits of those two powers had become confounded in practice; bishops were princes, the chief ministers of the sovereign, sometimes even the leaders of their flocks in war; kings were accustomed to summon ecclesiastical councils and appoint to ecclesiastical offices.

---

* "Quapropter universorum precibus fidelium optandum est, ut in omnem gloriam vestram extendatur imperium, ut silicet catholica fides . . . veraciter in una confessione cunctorum cordibus infigatur, quatenus summi Regis donante pietate eadem sanctæ pacis et perfectæ caritatis omnes ubique regat et custodiat unitas." Quoted by Waitz (*Deutsche Verfassungsgeschichte*, ii. 182) from an unprinted letter of Alcuin.

But, like the unity of the Church, the doctrine of a universal monarchy had a theoretical as well as an histori- *Influence of the meta- physics of the time upon the theory of a World- State.* cal basis, and may be traced up to those metaphysical ideas out of which the system we call Realism developed itself. The beginnings of philosophy in those times were logical, and its first efforts were to distribute and classify: system, subordination, uniformity, appeared to be that which was most desirable in thought as in life. The search after causes became a search after principles of classification ; since simplicity and truth were held to consist not in an analysis of thought into its elements, nor in an observation of the process of its growth, but rather in a sort of genealogy of notions, a statement of the relations of classes as containing or excluding each other. These classes, genera or species, were not themselves held to be conceptions formed by the mind from phenomena, nor mere accidental aggregates of objects grouped under and called by some common name; they were real things, existing independently of the individuals who composed them, recognized rather than created by the human mind. In this view, Humanity is an essential quality present in all men, and making them what they are : as regards it they are therefore not many but one, the differences between individuals being no more than accidents. . The whole truth of their being lies in the universal property, which alone has a permanent and independent existence. The common nature of the individuals thus gathered into one Being is typified in its two aspects, the spiritual and the secular, by two persons, the World-Priest and the World-Monarch, who present on earth a similitude of the Divine unity. For, as we have seen, it was only through its concrete and symbolic expression that a thought could then be apprehended.* Although it was to unity in re-

---

* A curious illustration of this tendency of mind is afforded by the

ligion that the clerical body was both by doctrine and by practice attached, they found this inseparable from the corresponding unity in politics. They saw that every act of man has a social and public as well as a moral and personal bearing, and concluded that the rules which directed and the powers which rewarded or punished must be parallel and similar, not so much two powers as different manifestations of one and the same. That the souls of all Christian men should be guided by one hierarchy, rising through successive grades to a supreme head, while for their deeds they were answerable to a multitude of local, unconnected, mutually irresponsible potentates, appeared to them necessarily opposed to the Divine order. As they could not imagine, nor value if they had imagined, a communion of the saints without its expression in a visible church, so in matters temporal they recognized no brotherhood of spirit without the bonds of form, no universal humanity save in the image of a universal state.*

descriptions we meet with of Learning or Theology (*Studium*) as a concrete existence, having a visible dwelling in the University of Paris. The three great powers which rule human life, says one writer, the Popedom, the Empire and Learning, have been severally entrusted to the three foremost nations of Europe: Italians, Germans, French. "His siquidem tribus, scilicet sacerdotio imperio et studio, tanquam tribus virtutibus, videlicet naturali vitali et scientiali, catholica ecclesia spiritualiter mirificatur, augmentatur et regitur. His itaque tribus, tanquam fundamento, pariete et tecto, eadem ecclesia tanquam materialiter proficit. Et sicut ecclesia materialis uno tantum fundamento et uno tecto eget, parietibus vero quatuor, ita imperium quatuor habet parietes, hoc est, quatuor imperii sedes, Aquisgranum, Arelatum, Mediolanum, Romam."—*Jordanis Chronica;* *ap.* Schardius, *Sylloge Tractatuum.* And see Döllinger, *Die Vergangenheit und Gegenwart der katholischen Theologie*, p. 8.

* "Una est sola respublica totius populi Christiani, ergo de necessitate erit et unus solus princeps et rex illius reipublicæ, statutus et stabilitus ad ipsius fidei et populi Christiani dilatationem et defensionem. Ex qua ratione concludit etiam Augustinus (*De Civitate Dei*,

In this, as in so much else, the men of the Middle Ages were the slaves of the letter, unable, with all their aspirations, to rise out of the concrete, and prevented by the very grandeur and boldness of their conceptions from carrying them out in practice against the enormous obstacles that met them.

Deep as this belief had struck its roots, it might never have risen to maturity nor sensibly affected the progress of events, had it not gained in the pre-existence of the monarchy of Rome a definite shape and a definite purpose. It was chiefly by means of the Papacy that this came to pass. When under Constantine the Christian Church was framing her organization on the model of the state which protected her, the bishop of the metropolis perceived and improved the analogy between himself and the head of the civil government. The notion that the chair of Peter was the imperial throne of the Church had dawned upon the Popes very early in their history, and grew stronger every century under the operation of causes already specified. Even before the Empire of the West had fallen, St. Leo the Great could boast that to Rome, exalted by the preaching of the chief of the Apostles to be a holy nation, a chosen people, a priestly and royal city, there had been appointed a spiritual dominion wider than her earthly sway.* In A.D. 476 Rome ceased to be the political capital of the Western countries, and the Papacy, inheriting no small part of the

The ideal state supposed to be embodied in the Roman Empire.

---

lib xix.) quod extra ecclesiam nunquam fuit nec potuit nec poterit esse verum imperium, etsi fuerint imperatores qualitercumque et secundum quid, non simpliciter, qui fuerunt extra fidem Catholicam et ecclesiam."—Engelbert (abbot of Admont in Upper Austria), *De Ortu et Fine Imperii Romani* (circa 1310). In this "de necessitate" everything is included.

* See note *, p. 30.

Emperor's power, drew to herself the reverence which the
name of the city still commanded, until by the middle of
the eighth, or, at least, of the ninth century she had per-
fected in theory a scheme which made her the exact counterpart of the departed despotism, the center of the hierarchy, absolute mistress of the Christian world.   The
character of that scheme is best set forth in the singulai
document, most stupendous of all the mediæval forgeries,
which under the name of the Donation of
Constantine commanded for seven centuries
the unquestioning belief of mankind.*   Itself
a portentous falsehood, it is the most unim-

*Constan-
tine's Do-
nation.*

peachable evidence of the thoughts and beliefs of the
priesthood which framed it, some time between the middle
of the eighth and the middle of the tenth century.   It
tells how Constantine the Great, cured of his leprosy by
the prayers of Sylvester, resolved, on the fourth day from
his baptism, to forsake the ancient seat for a new capital
on the Bosphorus, lest the continuance of the secular government should cramp the freedom of the spiritual, and
how he bestowed therewith upon the Pope and his successors the sovereignty over Italy and the countries of the
West.   But this is not all, although this is what historians,
in admiration of its splendid audacity, have chiefly dwelt
upon.   The edict proceeds to grant to the Roman pontiff
and his clergy a series of dignities and privileges, all of
them enjoyed by the Emperor and his senate, all of them
showing the same desire to make the pontifical a copy of
the imperial office.   The Pope is to inhabit the Lateran
palace, to wear the diadem, the collar, the purple cloak, to
carry the scepter, and to be attended by a body of cham-
berlains.   Similarly his clergy are to ride on white horses

---

* This is admirably brought out by Ægidi, *Der Fürstenrath nach
dem Luneviller Frieden.*

and receive the honors and immunities of the senate and patricians.*

The notion which prevails throughout, that the chief of the religious society must be in every point conformed to his prototype the chief of the civil, is the key *Interdepen-* to all the thoughts and acts of the Roman *dence of* clergy; not less plainly seen in the details of *Papacy and* papal ceremonial than it is in the gigantic *Empire.* scheme of papal legislation. The Canon law was intended by its authors to reproduce and rival the

---

*See the original forgery (or rather the extracts which Gratian gives from it) in the *Corpus Iuris Canonici, Dist.* xcvi, cc. 13, 14 : "Et sicut nostram terrenam imperialem potentiam, sic sacrosanctam Romanam ecclesiam decrevimus veneranter honorari, et amplius quam nostrum imperium et terrenum thronum sedem beati Petri gloriose exaltari, tribuentes ei potestatem et gloriæ dignitatem atque vigorem et honorificentiam imperialem. . . . Beato Sylvestro patri nostro summo pontifici et universali urbis Romæ papæ, et omnibus eius successoribus pontificibus, qui usque in finem mundi in sede beati Petri erunt sessuri, de præsenti contradimus palatium imperii nostri Lateranese, deinde diadema, videlicet coronam capitis nostri, simulque phrygium, necnon et superhumerale, verum etiam et chlamydem purpuream et tunicam coccineam, et omnia imperialia indumenta, sed et dignitatem imperialem præsidentium equitum, conferentes etiam et imperialia sceptra, simulque cuncta signa atque banda et diversa ornamenta imperialia et omnem processionem imperialis culminis et gloriam potestatis nostrae. . . . Et sicut imperialis militia ornatur ita et clerum sanctæ Romanæ ecclesiæ ornari decernimus. . . Unde ut pontificalis apex non vilescat sed magis quam terreni imperii dignitas gloria et potentia pecoretur, ecce tam palatium nostrum quam Romanam umbem et omnes Italæ seu occidentalium regionum provincias loca et civitates beatissimo papæ Sylvestro universali papæ contradimus atque relinquimus. . . . Ubi enim principatis sacerdotum et Christianæ religionis caput ab imperatore cœlesti constitutem est, iustum non est ut illic imperatator terrenus habeat potestatem." The practice of kissing the pope's foot was adopted in imitation of the old imperial court. It was afterward revived by the German emperors.

imperial jurisprudence; a correspondence was traced between its divisions and those of the Corpus Juris Civilis, and Gregory IX, who was the first to consolidate it into a code, sought the fame and received the title of the Justinian of the Church. But the wish of the clergy was always, even in the weakness or hostility of the temporal power, to imitate and rival, not to supersede it; since they held It the necessary compliment of their own, and thought the Christian people equally imperilled by the fall of either. Hence the reluctance of Gregory II to break with the Byzantine princes,* and the maintenance of their titular sovereignty till A.D. 800: hence the part which the Holy See played in transferring the crown to Charles, the first sovereign of the West capable of fulfilling his duties; hence the grief with which its weakness under his successors was seen, the gladness when it descended to Otto as representative of the Frankish kingdom.

Up to the era of A.D. 800 there had been at Constantinople a legitimate historical prolongation of the Roman Empire. Technically, as we have seen, the election of Charles, after the deposition of *The Roman Empire revived in a new character.* Constantine VI, was itself a prolongation, and maintained the old rights and forms in their integrity. But the Pope, though he knew it not, did far more than effect a change of dynasty when he rejected Irene and crowned the barbarian chief. Restorations are always delusive. As well might one hope to stop the earth's course in her orbit as to arrest that ceaseless change and movement in human affairs which forbids an

---

* Döllinger has shown in a recent work (*Die Papst-Fabeln des Mittelalters*) that the common belief that Gregory II excited the revolt against Leo the Iconoclast is unfounded. So Anastasius, " Ammonebat (*sc.* Gregorius Secundus) ne a fide vel amore Romani imperii desisterent."—*Vitæ Pontif. Rom.*

old institution, suddenly transplanted into a new order of
things, from filling its ancient place and serving its former
end. The dictatorship at Rome in the second Punic war
was not more unlike the dictatorships of Sulla and Cæsar,
nor the States general of Louis XIII to the assembly which
his unhappy descendant convoked in 1789, than was the
imperial office of Theodosius to that of Charles the Frank;
and the seal, ascribed to A.D. 800, which bears the legend
"Renovatio Romani Imperii,"* expresses, more justly perhaps than was intended by its author, a second birth of the
Roman Empire.

It is not, however, from Carolingian time that a proper
view of this new creation can be formed. That period
was one of transition, of fluctuation and uncertainty, in
which the office, passing from one dynasty and country to
another, had not time to acquire a settled character and
claims, and was without the power that would have enabled
it to support them. From the coronation of Otto the
Great a new period begins, in which the ideas that have
been described as floating in men's minds took clearer
shape, and attached to the imperial title a body of definite
rights and definite duties. It is this new phase, the
Holy Empire, that we have now to consider.

The realistic philosophy, and the needs of a time when

---

* Of this curious seal, a leaden one, preserved at Paris, the figure was
given upon the cover of an ancient book.   There are very few monuments of that age whose genuineness can be considered altogether
beyond doubt; but this seal has many respectable authorities in its
favor. See, among others, Le Blanc, *Dissertation historique sur
quelques Monnoies de Charlemagne*, Paris, 1689; J. M. Heineccius, *De
Veteribus Germanorum aliarumque nationum sigillis*, Lips. 1709;
Anastasius, *Vitæ Pontificum Romanorum*, ed. Vignoli, Romæ, 1752;
Götz, *Deutschlands Kayser-Münzen des Mittelalters*, Dresden, 1827;
and the authorities cited by Waitz, *Deutsche Verfassungsgeschichte*,
iii. 179, n. 4.

the only notion of civil or religious order was submission to authority, required the World-State to be a monarchy; tradition, as well as the continuance of certain institutions, gave the monarch the name of Roman Emperor. A king could not be universal sovereign, for there were many *Position and functions of the Emperor.* kings: the Emperor must be, for there had never been but one Emperor; he had in older and brighter days been the actual lord of the civilized world; the seat of his power was placed beside that of the spiritual autocrat of Christendom.* His functions will be seen most clearly if we deduce them from the leading principle of mediæval mythology, the exact correspondence of earth and heaven. As God, in the midst of the celestial hierarchy, ruled blessed spirits in paradise, so the Pope, His vicar, raised above priests, bishops, metropolitans, reigned over the souls of mortal men below. But as God is Lord of earth as well as of heaven, so must he (the *Imperator cœlestis*)† be represented by a second earthly viceroy, the Emperor (*Imperator terrenus*), whose authority shall be of and for this present life. And as in this present world the soul cannot act save through the body, while yet the body is no more than an instrument

---

* " Præterea mirari se dilecta fraternitas tua quod non Francorum set Romanorum imperatores nos appellemus; set scire te convenit quia nisi Romanorum imperatores essemus, utique nec Francorum. A Romanis enim hoc nomen et dignitatem assumpsimus, apud quos profecto primum tantæ culmen sublimitatis effulsit," etc.— *Letter of the Emperor Lewis II to Basil the Emperor at Constantinople,* from *Chron. Salernit.,* ap. Murat. *S. R. I.*

† " lllam (*sc.* Romanam ecclesiam) solus ille fundavit, et super petram fidei mox nascentis erexit, qui beato æternæ vitæ clavigero terreni simul et cœlestis imperii iura commisit."—*Corpus Iuris Canonici,* Dist. xxii. c. 1. The expression is not uncommon in mediæval writers. So " unum est imperium Patris et Filii et Spiritus Sancti, cuius est pars ecclesia constituta in terris," in Lewis II's letter.

and means for the soul's manifestation, so must there be a
rule and care of men's bodies as well as of their souls, yet
subordinated always to the well-being of that which is the
purer and the more enduring. It is under the emblem of
soul and body that the relation of the papal and imperial
power is presented to us throughout the Middle Ages.*
The Pope, as God's vicar in matters spiritual, is to lead
men to eternal life; the Emperor, as vicar in matters temporal, must so control them in their dealings with one another that they may be able to pursue undisturbed the
spiritual life, and thereby attain the same supreme and
common end of everlasting happiness. In the view of
this object his chief duty is to maintain peace in the world,
whil toward the Church his position is that of Advocate,
a title borrowed from the practice adopted by churches
and monasteries of choosing some powerful baron to protect their lands and lead their tenants in war.† The

---

* "Merito summus Pontifex Romanus episcopus dici potest rex et
sacerdos. Si enim dominus noster Iesus Christus sic appellatur, non
videtur incongruum suum vocare successorem. Corporale et temporale ex spirituali et perpetuo dependet, sicut corporis operatio ex
virtute animæ. Sicut ergo corpus per animam habet esse virtutem
et operationem, ita et temporalis iurisdictio principum per spiritualem
Petri et successorum eius." — St. Thomas Aquinas, *De Regimine
Principum.*

† "Nonne Romana ecclesia tenetur imperatori tanquam suo pa-
trono, et imperator ecclesiam fovere et defensare tanquam suus vere
patronus? certe sic. . . . Patronis vero concessum est ut prælatos in ecclesiis sui patronatus eligant. Cum ergo imperator onus sen-
tiat patronatus, ut qui tenetur eam defendere, sentire debet honorem
et emolumentum." I quote this from a curious document in Goldast's collection of tracts (*Monarchia Imperii*), entitled "*Letter of the
four Universities, Paris, Oxford, Prague, and the 'Romana gen-
eralitas,' to the Emperor Wenzel and Pope Urban*," A.D. 1380. The
title can scarcely be right, but if the document is, as in all probability it is, not later than the fifteenth century, its being misde-
scribed, or even its being a forgery, does not make it less valuable as
an evidence of men's ideas.

functions of Advocacy are twofold : at home to make the
Christian people obedient to the priesthood, and to execute
their decrees upon heretics and sinners ; abroad to propo-
gate the faith among the heathen, not sparing to use
carnal weapons.* Thus does the Emperor answer in
every point to his antitype the Pope, his power being yet
of a lower rank, created on the analogy of the papal, as
the papal itself had been modeled after the elder Empire.
The parallel holds good even in its details ; for just as we
have seen the churchman assuming the crown and robes
of the secular prince, so now did he array the Emperor in
his own ecclesiastical vestments, the stole and the dalmatic,
gave him a clerical as well as a sacred character, removed
his office from all narrowing associations of birth or
country, inaugurated him by rites every one of
which was meant to symbolize and enjoin duties *Correspondence and*
in their essence religious. Thus the Holy *harmony of*
Roman Church and the Holy Roman Empire *the spiritual*
are one and the same thing, in two aspects ; *and tem-*
and Catholicism, the principle of the universal *poral*
Christian society, is also Romanism ; that is, *powers.*
rests upon Rome as the origin and type of its universality;
manifesting itself in a mystic dualism which corresponds

---

* So Leo III in a charter issued on the day of Charles' coronation :
". . . actum in præsentia gloriosi atque excellentissimi filii nostri
Caroli quem auctore Deo in defensionem et provectionem sanctæ uni-
versalis ecclesiæ hodie Augustum sacravimus."—Jaffé, *Regesta Pontificum Romanorum*, ad ann. 800. So, indeed, Theodulf of Orleans,
a contemporary of Charles, ascribes to the emperor an almost papal
authority over the church itself :

"Cœli habet hic (*sc.* Papa) claves, proprias te iussit habere ;
Tu regis ecclesiæ, nam regit ille poli ;
Tu regis eius opes, clerum populumque gubernas,
Hic te cœlicolas ducet ad usque choros."
In D. Bouquet, v, 415.

to the two natures of its Founder. As divine and eternal, its head is the Pope, to whom souls have been entrusted ; as human and temporal, the Emperor, commissioned to rule men's bodies and acts.

In nature and compass the government of these two potentates is the same, differing only in the sphere of its working ; and it matters not whether we call the Pope a spiritual Emperor or the Emperor a secular Pope. Nor though the one office is below the other as far as man's life on earth is less precious than his life hereafter, is therefore, on the older and truer theory, the imperial authority, delegated by the papal. For, as has been said already, God is represented by the Pope not in every capacity, but only as the ruler of spirits in heaven: as sovereign of earth, He issues His commission directly to the Emperor. Opposition between two servants of the same King is inconceivable, each being bound to aid and foster the other: the co-operation of both being needed in all that concerns the welfare of Christendom at large. *Union of Church and State.* This is the one perfect and self-consistent scheme of the union of Church and State; for, taking the absolute coincidence of their limits to be self-evident, it assumes the infallibility of their joint government, and derives, as a corollary from that infallibility, the duty of the civil magistrate to root out heresy and schism no less than to punish treason and rebellion. It is also the scheme which, granting the possibility of their harmonious action, places the two powers in that relation which gives each of them its maximum of strength. But by a law to which it would be hard to find exceptions, in proportion as the State became more Christian, the Church, who to work out her purposes had assumed worldly forms, became by the contact worldlier, meaner, spiritually weaker; and the system which Constantine founded amid such rejoicings, which culminated so tri-

umphantly in the Empire Church of the Middle Ages, has
in each succeeding generation been slowly losing ground,
has seen its brightness dimmed and its completeness
marred, and sees now those who are most zealous on behalf of its surviving institutions feebly defend or silently
desert the principle upon which all must rest.

The complete accord of the papal and imperial powers
which this theory, as sublime as it is impracticable, requires, was attained only at a few points in their history.*
It was finally supplanted by another view of their relation,
which, professing to be a development of a principle recognized as fundamental, the superior importance of the religious life, found increasing favor in the eyes of fervent
churchmen.† Declaring the Pope sole representative on
earth of the Deity, it concluded that from him, and not
directly from God, must the Empire be held—held feud-
ally, it was said by many—and it thereby thrust down the
temporal power to be the slave instead of the sister of the
spiritual.‡ Nevertheless, the Papacy in her meridian, and
under the guidance of her greatest minds, of Hildebrend,
of Alexander, of Innocent, not seeking to abolish or ab-

---

* Perhaps at no more than three: in the time of Charles and Leo;
again under Otto III and his two Popes, Gregory V and Sylvester II;
thirdly, under Henry III; certainly never thenceforth.

† The *Sachsenspiegel* (*Speculum Saxonicum*, circ. A.D. 1240), the
great North-German law book, says, "The Empire is held from God
alone, not from the Pope. Emperor and Pope are supreme each in
what has been entrusted to him: the Pope in what concerns the soul;
the Emperor in all that belongs to the body and to knighthood."
The *Schwabenspiegel*, compiled half a century later, subordinates the
prince to the pontiff: "Daz weltliche Schwert des Gerichtes daz lihet
der Babest dem Chaiser; daz geistlich ist dem Babest gesetzt daz er
damit richte."

‡ So Boniface VIII in the bull *Unam Sanctam*, will have but one
head for the Christian people: "Igitur ecclesiæ unius et unicæ unum
corpus, unum caput, non duo capita quasi monstrum."

sorb the civil government, required only its obedience, and exalted its dignity against all save herself.* It was reserved for Boniface VIII, whose extravagant pretensions betrayed the decay that was already at work within, to show himself to the crowding pilgrims at the jubilee of A.D. 1300, seated on the throne of Constantine, arrayed with sword and crown, and scepter, shouting aloud, "I am Cæsar—I am Emperor."†

The theory of an Emperor's place and functions thus sketched cannot be definitely assigned to any point of time; for it was growing and changing from the fifth century to the fifteenth.

Proofs from mediæval documents.

Nor need it surprise us that we do not find in any one author a statement of the grounds whereon it

---

* St. Bernard writes to Conrad III : "Non veniat anima mea in consilium eorum qui dicunt vel imperio pacem et libertatem ecclesiæ vel ecclesiæ prosperitatem et exaltationem imperii nocituram." So in the *De Consideratione:* "Si utrumque simul habere velis, perdes utrumque," of the papal claim to temperal and spiritual authority, quoted by Gieseler.

† "Sedens in solio armatus et cinctus ensem, habensque in capite Constantini diadema, stricto dextra capulo ensis accincti, ait: 'Numquid ego summus sum pontifex? nonne ista est cathedra Petri? Nonne possum imperii iura tutari? ego ego sum imperator.'"—Fr. Pipinus (*ap.* Murat. *S. R. I.* ix.) l. iv. c. 41. These words, however, are by this writer ascribed to Boniface when receiving the envoys of the Emperor Albert I, in A.D. 1299. I have not been able to find authority for their use at the jubilee, but give the current story for what it is worth. It has been suggested that Dante may be alluding to this sword scene in a well-known passage of the Purgatorio (xvi. l. 106):

> "Soleva Roma, che 'l buon mondo feo
>   Duo Soli aver, che l' una e l' altra strada
>   Facean vedere, e del mondo e di Deo.
> L' un l' altro ha spento, ed è giunta la spada
>   Col pastorale: e l' un coll, altro insieme
>   Per viva forza mal convien che vada."

rested, since much of what seems strangest to us was then too obvious to be formally explained. No one, however, who examines mediæval writings can fail to perceive, sometimes from direct words, oftener from allusions or assumptions, that such ideas as these are present to the minds of the authors.* That which it is easiest to prove is the connection of the Empire with religion. From every record, from chronicles and treatises, proclamations, laws and sermons, passages may be adduced wherein the defence and spread of the faith, and the maintenance of concord among the Christian people, are represented as the function to which the Empire has been set apart. The belief expressed by Lewis II, "Imperii dignitas non in vocabuli voce sed in gloriosæ pietatis culmine consistit,"† appears again in the address of the Archbishop of Mentz to Conrad II,‡ as Vicar of God ; is reiterated by Frederick I,§ when he writes to the prelates of Germany, " On earth God has placed no more than two powers, and as there is in heaven but one God, so is there here one Pope and one Emperor. Divine providence has specially appointed the Roman Empire to prevent the continuance of schism in

---

* See especially Peter de Andlo (*De Imperio Romano*); Landolfo Colonna (*De translatione Imperii Romani*); Dante (*De Monarchia*); Engelbert (*De Ortu et Fine Imperii Romani*); Marsilius Patavius (*De translatione Imperii Romani*); Æneas Sylvius Piccolomini (*De Ortu et Authoritate Imperii Romani*); Zoannetus (*De Imperio Romano atque ejus Iurisdictione*); and the writers in Schardius' *Sylloge*, and in Goldast's Collection of Tracts, entitled *Monarchia Imperii*.

† Letter of Lewis II to Basil the Macedonian, in *Chron. Salernit.* in Mur. *S. R. I.;* also given by Baronius, *Ann. Eccl.* ad ann. 871.

‡ "Ad summum dignitatis pervenisti: Vicarius es Christi."—Wippo, *Vita Chuonradi* (*ap.* Pertz), c. 3.

§ Letter in Radewic, *ap.* Murat. *S.R.I.* [The name is now usually written Rahewin: so Wtzai in new e*d* ⌐f Mon. Germ.]

the Church;"* is echoed by jurists and divines down to
the days of Charles V.† It was a doctrine which we shall
find the friends and foes of the Holy See equally concerned
to insist on, the one to make the transference (*translatio*)
from the Greeks to the Germans appear entirely the Pope's
work, and so establish his right of overseeing or cancelling
his rival's election, the others by setting the Emperor at
the head of the Church to reduce the Pope to the place of
chief bishop of his realm.‡ His headship was dwelt upon
chiefly in the two duties already noticed. As the counterpart of the Mussulman Commander of the Faithful, he
was leader of the Church militant against her infidel foes,
was in this capacity summoned to conduct crusades, and in
later times recognized chief of the confederacies against
the conquering Ottomans. As representative of the whole
Christian people, it belonged to him to convoke General
Councils, a right not without importance even when exercised concurrently with the Pope, but far more weighty
when the object of the Council was to settle a disputed
election, or, as at Constance, to depose the reigning pontiff
himself.

No better illustrations can be desired than those to be

---

* Lewis IV is styled in one of his proclamations, " Gentis humanæ,
orbis Christiani custos, urbi et orbi a Deo electus præesse."—Pfeffinger, *Vitriarius Illustratus.*

† In a document issued by the Diet of Speyer (A.D. 1529) the emperor is called " Oberst, Vogt und Haupt der Christenheit." Hier-
onymus Balbus, writing about the same time, puts the question
whether all Christians are subject to the emperor in temporal things,
as they are to the pope in spiritual, and answers it by saying : " Cum
ambo ex eodem fonte perfluxerint et eadem semita incedant, de
utroque idem puto sentiendum."

‡ " Non magis ad Papam depositio seu remotio pertinet quam ad
quoslibet regum prælatos, qui reges suos prout assolent, consecrant
et inungunt."—*Letter of Frederick II* (lib. i, c. 3).

found in the office for the imperial coronation at Rome, too long to be transcribed here, but well worthy of an attentive study.* The rights prescribed in it are rights of consecration to a religious office: the Emperor, beside the sword, globe and *The Coronation ceremonies.* scepter of temporal power, receives a ring as the symbol of his faith, is ordained a subdeacon, assists the Pope in celebrating mass, partakes as a clerical person of the communion in both kinds, is admitted a canon of St. Peter and St. John Lateran. The oath to be taken by an elector begins, " Ego N. volo regem Romanorum in Cæsarem promovendum, temporale caput populo Christiano eligere." The Emperor swears to cherish and defend the Holy Roman Church and her bishop: the Pope prays after the reading of the Gospel, " Deus qui ad prædicandum æterni regni evangelium Imperium Romanum præparasti, prætende famulo tuo Imperatori nostro arma cœlestia." Among the Emperor's official titles there occur these : " Head of Christendom," " Defender and Advocate of the Christian Church," " Temporal Head of the Faithful," " Protector of Palestine and of the Catholic Faith."†

Very singular are the reasonings used by which the necessity and divine right of the Empire are proved out of the Bible. The mediæval theory of the relation of the civil power to the priestly was profoundly influenced by the account in the Old Testament of the Jewish theocracy, in which the king, though the institution of his office *The rights of the Empire proved from the Bible.* was a derogation from the purity of the older system appears divinely chosen and commissioned, and stood in

---

* *Liber Ceremonialis Romanus,* lib. i, sect 5 ; with which compare the *Coronatio Romana* of Henry VII, in Pertz, and Muratori's Dissertation in vol. i, of the *Antiquitates Italiæ Medii Ævi.*

† See Goldast, *Collection of Imperial Constitutions ;* and Moser, *Römische Kayser.*

a peculiarly intimate relation to the national religion.
From the New Testament the authority and eternity of
Rome herself was established. Every passage was seized
on where submission to the powers that be is enjoined,
every instance cited where obedience had actually been
rendered to imperial officials, a special emphasis being laid
on the sanction which Christ Himself had given to Roman
dominion by pacifying the world through Augustus, by
being born at the time of the taxing, by paying tribute
to Cæsar, by saying to Pilate, " Thou couldest have no
power at all against Me except it were given thee from
above."

More attractive to the mystical spirit than these direct
arguments were those drawn from prophecy, or based
on the allegorical interpretation of Scripture. Very early
in Christian history had the belief formed itself that the
Roman Empire—as the fourth beast of Daniel's vision,
as the iron legs and feet of Nebuchadnezzar's image—
was to be the world's last and universal kingdom. From
Origen and Jerome downward it found unquestioned
acceptance,* and that not unnaturally. For no new
power had arisen to extinguish the Roman, as the Persian
monarchy had been blotted out by Alexander, as the
realms of his successors had fallen before the conquering republic herself. Every Northern conqueror, Goth,
Lombard, Burgundian, had cherished her memory and
preserved her laws; Germany had adopted even the

---

* The abbot Engelbert (*De Ortu et Fine Imperii Romani*) quotes
Origen and Jerome to this effect, and proceeds himself to explain,
from 2 Thess. ii, how the falling away will precede the coming of
Antichrist. There will be a triple " discessio," of the kingdoms of the
earth from the Roman empire, of the Church from the Apostolic
See, of the faithful from the faith. Of these, the first causes the
second ; the temporal sword to punish heretics and schismatics being
no longer ready to work the will of the rulers of the Church.

name of the Empire "dreadful and terrible and strong exceedingly, and diverse from all that were before it." To these predictions, and to many others from the Apocalypse, were added those which in the Gospels and Epistles foretold the advent of Antichrist.* He was to succeed the Roman dominion, and the Popes are more than once warned that by weakening the Empire they are hastening the coming of the enemy and the end of the world.† It is not only when groping in the dark labyrinths of prophecy that mediæval authors are quick in detecting emblems, imaginative in explaining them. Men were wont in those days to interpret Scripture in a singular fashion. Not only did it not occur to them to ask what meaning words had to those to whom they were

---

* A full statement of the views that prevailed in the earlier Middle Age regarding Antichrist—as well as of the singular prophecy of the Frankish emperor who shall appear in the latter days, conquer the world, and then going to Jerusalem shall lay down his crown on the Mount of Olives and deliver over the kingdom to Christ—may be found in the little treatise, *Vita Antichristi*, which Adso, monk and afterward abbot of Moutier-en-Der, compiled (circa 950) for the information of Queen Gerberga, wife of Lois d'Outremer. Antichrist is to be born a Jew of the tribe of Dan (Gen. xlix, 17), "non de episcopo et monacha, sicut alii delirando dogmatizant, sed de immundissima meretrice et crudelissimo nebulone. Totus in peccato concipietur, in peccato generabitur, in peccato nascetur." His birthplace is Babylon : he is to be brought up in Bethsaida and Chorazin. Adso's book may be found printed in Migne, t. ci, p. 1290.

† S. Thomas explains the prophecy in a remarkable manner, showing how the decline of the empire is no argument against its fulfillment. " Dicendum quod nondum cessavit, sed est commutatum de temporali in spirituale, ut dicit Leo Papa in sermone de Apostolis : et ideo discessio a Romano imperio debet intelligi non solum a temporali sed etiam a spirituali, scilicet a fide Catholica Romanæ Ecclesiæ. Est autem hoc conveniens signum nam Christus venit, quando Romanum imperium omnibus dominabatur : ita e contra signum adventus Antichristi est discessio ab eo."—*Comment, ad 2 Thess.* ii.

originally addressed; they were quite as careless whether
the sense they discovered was one which the language
used would naturally and rationally bear to any reader at
any time. No analogy was too faint, no allegory too fanciful, to be drawn out of a simple text; and, once propounded, the interpretation acquired in argument all the
authority of the text itself. Thus the two swords of which
Christ said, "It is enough," became the spiritual and temporal powers, and the grant of the spiritual to Peter in-
volves the supremacy of the Papacy.* Thus one writer
proves the eternity of Rome from the seventy-second Psalm,
"They shall fear thee as long as the sun and moon endure,
throughout all generations;" the moon being of course,
since Gregory VII, the Roman Empire, as the sun, or
greater light, is the Popedom. Another quoting, "Qui
tenet teneat donec auferatur,"† with Augustine's explanation thereof,‡ says, that when "he who letteth" is removed, tribes and provinces will rise in rebellion, and the
Empire to which God has committed the government of
the human race will be dissolved. From the miseries of
his own time (he wrote under Frederick III) he predicts
that the end is near. The same spirit of symbolism seized
on the number of the electors: "the seven lamps burning
in the unity of the sevenfold spirit which illume the Holy
Empire."§ Strange legends told how Romans and Ger-

* See note †, page 116. The papal party sometimes insisted that
both swords were given to Peter, while the imperialists assigned the
temporal sword to John. Thus a gloss to the *Sachsenspiegel* says,
"Dat eine svert hadde Sinte Peter, dat het nu de paves: dat andere
hadde Johannes, dat het nu de keyser."

† 2 Thess. ii. 7.

‡ St. Augustine, however, though he states the view (applying the
passage to the Roman Empire) which was generally received in the
Middle Ages, is careful not to commit himself positively to it.

§ *Jordanis Chronica* (written toward the close of the thirteenth
century.

mans were of one lineage; how Peter's staff had been found
on the banks of the Rhine, the miracle signifying that a
commission was issued to the Germans to reclaim wandering sheep to the one fold. So complete does the scriptural
proof appear in the hands of mediæval churchmen, many
holding it a mortal sin to resist the power ordained of God,
that we forget they were all the while only adapting to an
existing institution what they found written already; we
begin to fancy that the Empire was maintained, obeyed,
exalted for centuries, on the strength of words to which we
attach in almost every case a wholly different meaning.

It would be a task both pleasant and profitable to pass
on from the theologians to the poets and artists of the
Middle Ages, and endeavor to trace through
their works the influence of the ideas which *Illustrations
from Mediæ-
val Art.*
have been expounded above. But it is one far
too wide for the scope of the present treatise;
and one which would demand an acquaintance with those
works themselves such as only minute and long-continued
study could give. For even a slight knowledge enables
any one to see how much still remains to be interpreted in
the imaginative literature and in the paintings of those
times, and how apt we are in glancing over a piece of work
to miss those seemingly trifling indications of the artist's
thought or belief which are all the more precious that they
are indirect or unconscious. Therefore a history of mediæval art which shall evolve its philosophy from its concrete
forms, if it is to have any value at all, must be minute in
description as well as subtle in method. But lest this
class of illustrations should appear to have been wholly forgotten, it may be well to mention here two paintings in
which the theory of the mediæval empire is unmistakably
set forth. One of them is in Rome, the other in Florence;
every traveler in Italy may examine both for himself.

The first of these is the famous mosaic of the Lateran

triclinium, constructed by Pope Leo III about A.D. 800, and which, afterward restored and moved to its present site, may still be seen over against the façade of St. John Lateran. Originally meant to adorn the state banqueting hall of the Popes, it is now placed in the open air, in the finest situation in Rome, looking from the brow of a hill across the green ridges of the Campagna to the olive groves of Tivoli and the glistening crags and snow-capped summits of the Umbrian and Sabine Apennine. It represents in the center Christ surrounded by the Apostles, whom He is sending forth to preach the Gospel; one hand is extended to bless, the other holds a books with the words " Pax Vobis." Below and to the right Christ is depicted again, and this time sitting: on his right hand kneels Pope Sylvester, on his left the Emperor Constantine; to the one he gives the keys of heaven and hell, to the other a banner surmounted by a cross. In the group on the opposite, that is, on the left side of the arch, we see the Apostle Peter seated, before whom in like manner kneel Pope Leo III and Charles the Emperor; the latter wearing, like Constantine, his crown. Peter, himself grasping the keys, gives to Leo the pallium of an archbishop, to Charles the banner of the Christian army. The inscription is, " Beate Petre donas vitam Leoni PP et bictoriam Carulo regi donas ;" while round the arch is written, " Gloria in excelsis Deo, et in terra pax omnibus bonæ voluntatis."

Mosaic of the Lateran Palace at Rome.

The order and nature of the idea here symbolized is sufficiently clear. First comes the revelation of the Gospel, and the divine commission to gather all men into its fold. Next, the institution, at the memorable era of Constantine's conversion, of the two powers by which the Christian people is to be respectively taught and governed. Thirdly, we are shown the permanent Vicar of God, the Apostle who keeps the keys of heaven and hell, re-establish-

ing these same powers on a new and firmer basis.* The
badge of ecclesiastical supremacy he gives to Leo as the
spiritual head of the faithful on earth, the banner of the
Church Militant to Charles, who is to maintain her cause
against heretics and infidels.

The second painting is of greatly later date. It is a
fresco in the chapter-house of the Dominican convent of
Santa Maria Novella† at Florence, usually
known as the Capellone degli Spagnuoli. It *Fresco in*
has been commonly ascribed, on Vasari's au- *S. Maria*
thority, to Simone Martini of Siena, but an *Novella at*
examination of the dates of his life seems to *Florence.*
discredit this view.‡ Most probably it was executed between A.D. 1340 and 1350. It is a huge work, covering

---

* Compare with this the words which Pope Hadrian I had used,
some twenty-three years before, of Charles as representative of Constantine: " Et sicut temporibus Beati Sylvestri, Romani pontificis, a
sanctæ recordationis piissimo Constantino magno imperatore, per eius
largitatem sancta Dei catholica et apostolica Romana ecclesia elevata
atque exaltata est, et potestatem in his Hesperiæ patribus largiri dignatus est, ita et in his vestris felicissimis temporibus atque nostris,
sancta Dei ecclesia, id est, beati Petri apostoli germinet atque exsultet,
ut omnes gentes quæ hæc audierint edicere valeant, ' Domine salvum
fac regem, et exaudi nos in die in qua invocaverimus te;' quia ecce
novus Christianissimus Dei Constantinus imperator his temporibus
surrexit, per quem omnia Deus sanctæ suæ ecclesiæ beati apostolorum
principis Petri largiri dignatus est."—*Letter XLIX of Cod. Carol,*
A.D. 777 (in Mur. *Scriptores Rerum Italicarum*). This letter is
memorable as containing the first allusion, or what seems an allusion,
to Constantine's Donation. The phrase " sancta Dei ecclesia, id est,
B. Petri apostoli," is worth noting.

† The church in which the opening scene of Boccaccio's *Decameron*
is laid.

‡ So Kugler (Eastlake's ed. vol. i. p. 144), and so also Messrs. Crowe
and Cavalcaselle, in their *New History of Painting in Italy*, vol. ii.
pp. 85 sqq.

one whole wall of the chapter-house, and filled with figures, some of which, but seemingly on no sufficient authority, have been taken to represent eminent persons of the time —Cimabue, Arnolfo, Boccaccio, Petrarch, Laura and others. In it is represented the whole scheme of man's life here and hereafter—the Church on earth and the Church in heaven. Full in front are seated side by side the Pope and the Emperor: on their right and left, in a descending row, minor spiritual and temporal officials; next to the Pope a cardinal, bishops and doctors; next to the Emperor, the King of France and a line of nobles and knights. Behind them appears the Duomo of Florence as an emblem of the Visible Church, while at their feet is a flock of sheep (the faithful) attacked by ravening wolves (heretics and schismatics), whom a pack of spotted dogs (the Dominicans)* combat and chase away. From this, the central foreground of the picture, a path winds round and up a height to a great gate where the Apostle sits on guard to admit true believers: they passing through it are met by choirs of seraphs, who lead them on through the delicious groves of Paradise. Above all, at the top of the painting and just over the spot where his two lieutenants, Pope and Emperor, are placed below, is the Saviour enthroned amid saints and angels.†

Here, too, there needs no comment. The Church Militant is the perfect counterpart of the Church Triumphant:

---

* Domini canes.   Spotted because of their black-and-white raiment.

† There is, of course, a great deal more detail in the picture, which it does not appear necessary to describe.   St. Dominic is a conspicuous figure.   It is worth remarking that the emperor, who is on the pope's left hand, and so made slightly inferior to him while superior to every one else, holds in his hand, instead of the usual imperial globe, a death's head, typifying the transitory nature of his power.

her chief danger is from those who would rend the unity of
her visible body, the seamless garment of her *Anti-nation-*
heavenly Lord; and that devotion to His person *al character*
which is the sum of her faith and the essence *of the Em-*
of her being, must on earth be rendered to *pire.*
those two lieutenants whom He has chosen to govern in His
name.

A theory such as that which it has been attempted to
explain and illustrate, is utterly opposed to restrictions of
place or person. The idea of the Christian people, all
whose members are equal in the sight of God—an idea so
forcibly expressed in the unity of the priesthood, where
no barrier separated the successor of the Apostle from the
humblest curate—and in the prevalence of one language
for worship and government, made the post of Emperor
independent of the race, or rank, or actual resources of its
occupant. The Emperor was entitled to the obedience of
Christendom, not as hereditary chief of a victorious tribe,
or feudal lord of a portion of the earth's surface, but as
solemnly invested with an office. Not only did he excel
in dignity the kings of the earth, his power was different in its nature; and, so far from supplanting or rivaling
theirs, rose above them to become the source and needful
condition of their authority in their several territories,
the bond which joined them in one harmonious body.
The vast dominions and vigorous personal action of Charles
the Great had concealed this distinction while he reigned;
under his successors the imperial crown appeared disconnected from the direct government of the kingdoms they
had established, existing only in the form of an undefined
suzerainty, as the type of that unity without which men's
minds could not rest. It was characteristic of the Middle
Ages, that demanding the existence of an Emperor, they
were careless who he was or how he was chosen, so he had
been duly inaugurated ; and that they were not shocked

by the contrast between unbounded rights and actual helplessness. At no time in the world's history has theory,
pretending all the while to control practice, been so utterly
divorced from it. Ferocious and sensual, that age worshiped humility and asceticism : there has never been a
purer ideal of love, nor a grosser profligacy of life.

The power of the Roman Emperor cannot as yet be
called international; though this, as we shall see, became
in later times its most important aspect; for in the tenth
century national distinctions had scarcely begun to exist.
But its genius was clerical and old Roman, in no wise territorial or Teutonic : it rested not on armed hosts or wide
lands, but upon the duty, the awe, the love of its subject.

CHAPTER VIII.

THE ROMAN EMPIRE AND THE GERMAN KINGDOM.

THIS was the office which Otto the Great assumed in
A.D. 962. But it was not his only office. He was already a
German king; and the new dignity by no means superseded
the old. This union in one person of two
characters, a union at first personal, then official, and which became at last a fusion of the
two into something different from either, is
the key to the whole subsequent history of
Germany and the Empire.

*Union of
the Roman
Empire
with the
German
kingdom.*

Of the German kingdom little need be said, since it differs in no essential respect from the other kingdoms of
Western Europe as they stood in the tenth century. The
five or six great tribes or tribe-leagues which
composed the German nation had been first
brought together under the scepter of the
Carolingians; and though still retaining marks

*Germany
and its
monarchy.*

of their independent origin, were prevented from separating by community of speech and a common pride in the
great Frankish Empire. When the line of Charles the
Great ended in A.D. 911, by the death of Lewis the Child
(son of Arnulf), Conrad, duke of the Franconians, and
after him Henry (the Fowler), duke of the Saxon, was
chosen to fill the vacant throne. By his vigorous yet con-
ciliatory action, his upright character, his courage and
good fortune in repelling the Hungarians, Henry laid
deep the foundations of royal power; under his more

famous son it rose into a stable edifice. Otto's coronation
feast at Aachen, where the great nobles of the realm did
him menial service, where Franks, Bavarians, Suabians,
Thuringians and Lorrainers, gathered round the Saxon
monarch, is the inauguration of a true Teutonic realm,
which, though it called itself not German but East Frankish, and claimed to be the lawful representative of the
Carolingian monarchy, had a constitution and a tendency
in many respects different.

There had been under those princes a singular mixture
of the old German organization by tribes or districts (the
so-called Gauverfassung), such as we find in
the earliest records, with the method introduced by Charles of maintaining by means of officials,
some fixed, others moving from place to place, the control
of the central government. In the suspension of that government which followed his days, there grew up a system
whose seeds had been sown as far back as the time
of Clovis, a system whose essence was the combination of
the tenure of land by military service with a peculiar personal relation between the landlord and his tenant, whereby
the one was bound to render fatherly protection, the other
aid and obedience. This is not the place for tracing the
origin of feudality on Roman soil, nor for showing how, by
a sort of contagion, it spread into Germany, how it struck
firm root in the period of comparative quiet under Pipin
and Charles, how from the hands of the latter it took the
impress which determined its ultimate form, how the weakness of his successors allowed it to triumph everywhere.
Still less would it be possible here to examine its social
and moral influence. Politically it might be defined as the
system which made the owner of a piece of land, whether
large or small, the sovereign of those who dwelt thereon :
an annexation of personal to territorial authority more
familiar to Eastern despotism than to the free races

Feudalism.

of primitive Europe. On this principle were founded, and by it are explained, feudal law and justice, feudal finance, feudal legislation, each tenant holding toward his lord the position which his own tenants held toward himself. And it is just because the relation was so uniform, the principle so comprehensive, the ruling class so firmly bound to its support, that feudalism has been able to lay upon society that grasp which the struggles of more than twenty generations have scarcely shaken off.

Now by the middle of the tenth century, Germany, less fully committed than France to feudalism's worst feature, the hopeless bondage of the peasantry, was otherwise thoroughly feudalized. As for that equality of all the freeborn save the sacred line *The feudal king.* which we find in the Germany of Tacitus, there had been substituted a gradation of ranks and a concentration of power in the hands of a landholding caste, so had the monarch lost his ancient character as leader and judge of the people, to become the head of a tyrannical oligarchy. He was titular lord of the soil, could exact from his vassals service and aid in arms and money, could dispose of vacant fiefs, could at pleasure declare war or make peace. But all these rights he exercised far less as sovereign of the nation than as standing in a peculiar relation to the feudal tenants, a relation in its origin strictly personal, and whose prominence obscured the political duties of prince and subject. And great as these rights might become in the hands of an ambitious and politic ruler, they were in practice limited by the corresponding duties he owed to his vassals, and by the difficulty of enforcing them against a powerful offender. The king was not permitted to retain in his own hands escheated fiefs, must even grant away those he had held before coming to the throne; he could not interfere with the jurisdiction of his tenants in their own lands, nor pre-

vent them from waging war or forming leagues with each
other like independent princes. Chief among
The no-
bility.
the nobles stood the dukes, who, although their
authority was now delegated, theoretically at
least, instead of independent, territorial instead of personal, retained nevertheless much of that hold on the
exclusive loyalty of their subjects which had belonged to
them as hereditary leaders of the tribe under the ancient
system. They were, with the three Rhenish archbishops, by
far the greatest subjects, often aspiring to the crown,
sometimes not unable to resist its wearer. The constant
encroachments which Otto made upon their privileges,
especially through the institution of the Counts Palatine,
destroyed their ascendancy, but not their importance. It
was not till the thirteenth century that they disappeared
with the rise of the second order of nobility. That order,
at this period far less powerful, included the counts margraves or marquises and landgraves, originally officers of
the crown, now feudal tenants ; holding their lands of
the dukes, and maintaining against them the same contest
which they in turn waged with the crown. Below these
came the barons and simple knights, then the diminishing
class of freeman, the increasing one of serfs. The institutions of primitive Germany were almost all
The Ger-
manic
feudal
polity
generally.
gone; supplanted by a new system, partly the
natural result of a formation of a settled from
a half-nomad society, partly imitated from that
which had arisen upon Roman soil, west of the
Rhine and south of the Alps. The army was
no longer the Heerban of the whole nation, which had
been wont to follow the king on foot in distant expeditions,
but a cavalry militia of barons and their retainers, bound
to service for a short period, and rendering it unwillingly
where their own interest was not concerned. The fre-

quent popular assemblies, whereof under the names of the
Mallum, the Placitum, the Mayfield, we hear so much
under Clovis and Charles, were now never summoned, and
the laws that had been promulgated there were, if not
abrogated, practically obsolete. No national council
existed, save the Diet in which the higher nobility, lay and
clerical, met their sovereign, sometimes to decide on foreign war, oftener to concur in the grant of a fief or the
proscription of a rebel. Every district had its own rude
local customs administered by the court of the local lord:
other law there was none, for imperial jurisprudence had
in these lately civilized countries not yet filled the place
left empty by the disuse of the barbarian codes.

This condition of things was indeed better than that
utter confusion which had gone before, for a principle of
order had began to group and bind the tossing atoms ;
and though the union into which it drove men was a hard
and narrow one, it was something that they should have
learned to unite themselves at all. Yet nascent feudality
was but one remove from anarchy; and the tendency to
isolation and diversity continued, despite the efforts of the
Church and the Carolingian princes, to be all-powerful in
Western Europe. The German kingdom was already a
bond between the German races, and appears strong
and united when we compare it with the France of Hugh
Capet, or the England of Ethelred II; yet its history to
the twelfth century is little else than a record of disorders,
revolts, civil wars, of a ceaseless struggle on the part of
the monarch to enforce his feudal rights, a resistance by
his vassals equally obstinate and more frequently successful. What the issue of the contest might have been if
Germany had been left to take her own course is matter
of speculation, though the example of every European
state except England and Poland may incline the balance

in favor of the crown.   But the strife had scarcely begun
when a new influence was interposed; the Ger-
The Roman man king became Roman Emperor.   No two
Empire and systems can be more unlike than those whose
the German headship became thus vested in one person:
kingdom. the one centralized, the other local; the one resting on a sublime theory, the other the rude offspring
of anarchy; the one gathering all power into the
hands of an irresponsible monarch, the other limiting his
rights and authorizing resistance to his commands;
the one demanding the equality of all citizens as
creatures equal before Heaven, the other bound up
with an aristocracy the proudest, and in its gradations of
rank the most exact that Europe had ever seen.   Characters so repugnant could not, it might be thought, meet in
one person, or if they met must strive till one swallowed
up the other.   It was not so.   In the fusion which began
from the first, though it was for a time imperceptible, each
of the two characters gave and each lost some of its attributes: the king became more than German, the Emperor
less than Roman, till at the end of six centuries, the monarch in whom two "persons" had been united, appeared
as a third different from either of the former, and might
not inappropriately be entitled " German Emperor."* The
nature and progress of this change will appear in the
after history of Germany, and cannot be described here
without in some measure anticipating subsequent events.
A word or two may indicate how the process of fusion
began.

   It was natural that the great mass of Otto's subjects, to
whom the imperial title, dimly associated with Rome and

---

* Although this was, of course, never his legal title.   Till 1806 he
was "Romanorum Imperator semper Augustus;" "Römischer
Kaiser."

the Pope, sounded grander than the regal, without being
known as otherwise different, should in thought and speech
confound them. The sovereign and his ecclesiastical advisers, with far clearer views of the new office and of the
mutual relation of the two, found it impossible to separate
them in practice, and were glad to merge the lesser in the
greater. For as lord of the world, Otto was Emperor
north as well as south of the Alps. When he
issued an edict, he claimed the obedience of *Results of*
his Teutonic subjects in both capacities; when *this union*
as Emperor he led the armies of the gospel *in one per-*
against the heathen, it was the standard of *son.*
their feudal superior that his armed vassals followed; when
he founded churches and appointed bishops, he acted
partly as suzerain of feudal lands, partly as protector of
the faith, charged to guide the Church in matters temporal. Thus the assumption of the imperial crown
brought to Otto as its first result an apparent increase of
domestic authority; it made his position by its historical
associations more dignified, by its religious more hallowed;
it raised him higher above his vassals and above other sovereigns; it enlarged his prerogative in ecclesiastical affairs,
and by necessary consequence gave to ecclesiastics a more
important place at court and in the administration of government than they had enjoyed before. Great as was the
power of the bishops and abbots in all the feudal kingdoms, it stood nowhere so high as in Germany. There
the Emperor's double position, as head ɔoth of Church
and State, required the two organizations to be exactly
parallel. In the eleventh century a full half of the land
and wealth of the country, and no small part of its military strength, was in the hands of Churchmen; their
influence predominated in the Diet; the archchancellor-
ship of the Empire, highest of all offices, was held by,
and eventually came to belong of right to, the Archbishop

of Mentz as primate of Germany.   It was by Otto, who in
resuming the attitude must repeat the policy of Charles,
that the greatness of the clergy was thus advanced.   He
is commonly said to have wished to weaken the aristocracy
by raising up rivals to them in the hierarchy.   It may
have been so, and the measure was at any rate a disastrous one,
for the clergy soon approved themselves not less rebellious
than those whom they were to restrain.   But in accusing
Otto's judgment, historians have often forgotten in what
position he stood to the Church, and how it behoved him,
according to the doctrine received, to establish in her an
order like in all things to that which he found already subsisting in the State.

The style which Otto adopted showed his desire thus to
merge the king in the Emperor.*   Charles had called himself "Imperator Cæsar Carolus rex Franco-
Changes in title. rum invictissimus;" and again, "Carolus serenissimus Augustus, Pius, Felix, Romanorum
gubernans Imperium, qui et per misericordiam Dei rex
Francorum atque Langobardorum."   Otto and his first
successors, who until their coronation at Rome had used
the titles of " Rex Francorum," or " Rex Francorum Orientalium," or oftener still " Rex " alone, discarded after it
all titles save the highest of " Imperator Augustus;" seeming thereby, though they too had been crowned at Aachen
and Milan, to claim the authority of Cæsar through all
their dominions.   Tracing as we are the history of a title,
it is needless to dwell on the significance of the change.†

---

* Pütter, *Dissertationes de Instauratione Imperii Romani ;* cf.
Goldast's *Collection of Constitutions ;* and the proclamations and
other documents collected in Pertz, *M. G. H.* (legg. I.)

† Pütter (*De Instauratione Imperii Romani*) will have it that upon
this mistake, as he calls it, of Otto's, the whole subsequent history of
the empire turned ; that if Otto had but continued to style himself
"Francorum Rex," Germany would have been spared all her Italian
wars.

Charles, son of the Ripuarian allies of Probus, had been a Frankish chieftain on the Rhine ; Otto, the Saxon, successor of the Cheruscan Arminius, would rule his native Elbe with a power borrowed from the Tiber.

Nevertheless, the imperial element did not in every respect predominate over the royal. The monarch might desire to make good against his turbulent barons the boundless prerogative which he acquired *Imperial power* with his new crown, but he lacked the power *feudalized.* to do so ; and they, disputing neither the supremacy of that crown nor his right to wear it, refused with good reason to let their own freedom be infringed upon by any act of which they had not been the authors. So far was Otto from embarking on so vain an enterprise, that his rule was even more direct and more personal than that of Charles had been. There was no scheme of mechanical government, no claim of absolutism; there was only the resolve to make the energetic assertion of the king's feudal rights subserve the further aims of the Emperor. What Otto demanded he demanded as Emperor, what he received he received as king; the singular result was that in Germany the imperial office was itself pervaded and transformed by feudal ideas. Feudality needing, to make its theory complete, a lord paramount of the world, from whose grant all ownership in land must be supposed to have emanated, and finding such a suzerain in the Emperor, constituted him liege lord of all kings and potentates, keystone of the feudal arch, himself, as it was expressed, " holding " the world from God. There were not wanting Roman institutions to which these notions could attach themselves. Constantine, imitating the courts of of the East, had made the dignitaries of his household great officials of the State : these were now reproduced in the cup-bearer, the seneschal, the marshal, the chamberlain of the Empire, so soon to become its electoral princes.

The holding of land on condition of military service was Roman in its origin : the divided ownership of feudal law found its analogies in the Roman tenure of emphyteusis. Thus while Germany was Romanized the Empire was feudalized, and came to be considered not the antagonist but the perfection of an aristocratic system. And it was this adaption to existing political facts that enabled it afterward to assume an international character. Nevertheless, even while they seemed to blend, there remained between the genius of imperialism (if one may use a now preverted word) and that of feudalism a deep and lasting hostility. And so the rule of Otto and his successors was in a measure adverse to feudal polity, not from knowledge of what Roman government had been, but from the necessities of their position, raised as they were to an unapproachable height above their subjects, surrounded with a halo of sanctity as protectors of the Church. Thus were they driven to reduce local independence, and assimilate the various races through their vast territories. It was Otto who made the Germans, hitherto an aggregate of tribes, a single people, and welding them into a strong political body taught them to rise through its collective greatness to the consciousness of national life, never thenceforth to be extinguished.

One expedient against the land-holding oligarchy which Roman traditions as well as present needs might have suggested, it was scarcely possible for Otto to use.
The Commons. He could not invoke the friendship of the Third Estate, for as yet none existed. The Teutonic order of freemen, which two centuries earlier had formed the bulk of the population, was now fast disappearing, just as in England all who did not become thanes were classed as ceorls, and from ceorls sank for the most part, after the Conquest, into villeins. It was only in the Alpine valleys and along the shores of the ocean that free democratic communities maintained themselves. Town-

life there was none, till Henry the Fowler forced his
forest-loving people to dwell in fortresses that might repel
the Hungarian invaders; and the burgher class thus beginning to form was too small to be a power in the state.
But popular freedom, as it expired, bequeathed to the
monarch such of its rights as could be saved from the
grasp of the nobles; and the crown thus became what it
has been wherever an aristocracy presses upon both, the
ally, though as yet the tacit ally, of the people. More,
too, than the royal could have done, did the imperial
name invite the sympathy of the commons. For in all,
however ignorant of its history, however unable to comprehend its functions, there yet lived a feeling that it was in
some mysterious way consecrated to Christian brotherhood
and equality, to peace and law, to the restraint of the
strong and the defense of the helpless.

CHAPTER IX.

SAXON AND FRANCONIAN EMPERORS.

HE who begins to read the history of the Middle Ages is
alternately amused and provoked by the seeming absurdi-
ties that meet him at every step.   He finds writers proclaiming amid universal assent magnificent theories which
no one attempts to carry out.   He sees men who are stained
with every vice full of sincere devotion to a religion which,
even when its doctrines were most obscured, never sullied
the purity of its moral teaching.   He is disposed to conclude that such people must have been either fools or hyp-
ocrites.   Yet such a conclusion would be wholly erroneous.
Every one knows how little a man's actions conform to the
general maxims which he would lay down for himself, and
how many things there are which he believes without real-
izing: believes sufficiently to be influenced, yet not sufficiently to be governed by them.   Now in the Middle Ages
this perpetual opposition of theory and practice was peculiarly abrupt.   Men's impulses were more violent and their
conduct more reckless than is often witnessed in modern
society; while the absence of a criticizing and measuring
spirit made them surrender their minds more unreservedly
than they would now do to a complete and imposing theory.
Therefore it was, that while everyone believed in the rights
of the Empire as a part of divine truth, no one would yield
to them where his own passions or interests interfered.
Resistance to God's Vicar might be and indeed was admitted to be a deadly sin, but it was one which nobody hesi-

tated to commit. Hence, in order to give this unbounded imperial prerogative any practical efficiency, it was found necessary to prop it up by the limited but tangible authority of a feudal king. And the one spot in Otto's empire on which feudality had never fixed its grasp, and where therefore he was forced to rule merely as Emperor, and not also as king, was that in which he and his successors were never safe from insult and revolt. That spot was his capital. Accordingly an account of what befel the first Saxon Emperor in Rome is a not unfitting comment on the theory expounded above, as well as a curious episode in the history of the Apostolic Chair.

After his coronation Otto had returned to North Italy, where the partisans of Berengar and his son Adalbert still maintained themselves in arms. Scarcely was he gone when the restless John XII, who found too late that in seeking an ally he had given himself a master, renounced his allegiance, opened negotiations with Berengar, and even scrupled not to send envoys pressing the heathen Magyars to invade Germany. The Emperor was soon informed of these plots, as well as of the flagitious life of the pontiff, a youth of twenty-five, the most profligate if not the most guilty of all who have worn the tiara. But he affected to despise them, saying, with a sort of unconscious irony, "He is a boy, the example of good men may reform him." When, however, Otto returned with a strong force, he found the city gates shut, and a party within furious against him. John XII was not only Pope, but as the heir of Alberic, the head of a strong faction among the nobles, and a sort of temporal prince in the city. But neither he nor they had courage enough to stand a siege: John fled into the Campagna to join Adalbert, and Otto entering convoked a synod in St. Peter's. Himself presiding as temporal head

Otto the Great in Rome.

of the Church, he began by inquiring into the character
and manners of the Pope. At once a tempest of accusa-
tions burst forth from the assembled clergy. Liudprand,
a credible although a hostile witness, gives us a long list
of them:—"Peter, cardinal-priest, rose and witnessed that
he had seen the Pope celebrate mass and not himself communicate. John, bishop of Narnia, and John, cardinal-
deacon, declared that they had seen him ordain a deacon
in a stable, neglecting the proper formalities. They said
further that he had defiled by shameless acts of vice the
pontifical palace; that he had openly diverted himself with
hunting; had put out the eyes of his spiritual father Benedict; had set fire to houses; had girt himself with a sword,
and put on a helmet and hauberk. All present, laymen
as well as priests, cried out that he had drunk to the devil's
health; that in throwing the dice he had invoked the help
of Jupiter, Venus, and other demons; that he had celebrated matins at uncanonical hours, and had not fortified
himself by making the sign of the cross." After these
things the Emperor, who could not speak Latin, since the
Romans could not understand his native, that is to say, the
Saxon tongue, bade Liudprand bishop of Cremona interpret for him, and adjured the council to declare whether
the charges they had brought were true, or sprang only of
malice and envy. Then all the clergy and people cried
with a loud voice, " If John the Pope hath not committed
all the crimes which Benedict the deacon hath read over,
and even greater crimes than these, then may the chief of
the Apostles, the blessed Peter, who by his word closes
heaven to the unworthy and opens it to the just, never
absolve us from our sins, but may we be bound by the
chain of anathema, and on the last day may we stand on
the left hand along with those who have said to the Lord
God, ' Depart from us, for we will not know Thy ways.' "
The solemnity of this answer seems to have satisfied

Otto and the council : a letter was despatched to John, couched in respectful terms, recounting the charges brought against him, and asking him to appear to clear himself by his own oath and that of a sufficient number of compurgators. John's reply was short and pithy.

"John the bishop, the servant of the servants of God, to all the bishops. We have heard tell that you wish to set up another Pope; if you do this, by Almighty God I excommunicate you, so that you may not have power to perform mass or to ordain no one." *

To this Otto and the synod replied by a letter of humorous expostulation, begging the Pope to reform both his morals and his Latin. But the messenger who bore it could not find John: he had repeated what seems to have been thought his most heinous sin, by going into the country with his bow and arrows; and after a search had been made in vain, the synod resolved to take a decisive step. Otto, who still led their deliberations, demanded the condemnation of the Pope; the assembly deposed him by acclamation, "because of his reprobate life," and having obtained the Emperor's consent, proceeded in an equally hasty manner to *Deposition of John XII.* raise Leo, the chief secretary and a layman, to the chair of the Apostle.

Otto might seem to have now reached a position loftier and firmer than that of any of his predecessors. Within little more than a year from his arrival in Rome, he had exercised powers greater than those of Charles himself,

---

* "Iohannes episcopus, servus servorum Dei, omnibus episcopis. Nos audivimus dicere quia vos vultis alium papam facere si hoc facitis, da Deum omnipotentem excommunico vos, ut non habeatis licentiam missam celebrare aut nullum ordinare."—Liudprand, *ut supra.* The "da" is curious, as showing the progress of the change from Latin to Italian. The answer sent by Otto and the council takes exception to the double negative.

ordering the dethronement of one pontiff and the installation of another, forcing a reluctant people to bend themselves to his will. The submission involved in his oath to protect the Holy See was more than compensated by the oath of allegiance to his crown which the Pope and the Romans had taken, and by their solemn engagement not to elect nor ordain any future pontiff without the Emperor's consent.* But he had yet to learn what this obedience and these oaths were worth. The Romans had eagerly joined in the expulsion of John; they soon began to regret him. They were mortified to see their streets filled by a foreign soldiery, the habitual license of their manners sternly repressed, their most cherished privilege, the right of choosing the universal bishop, grasped by the strong hand of a master who used it for purposes in which they did not sympathize. In a fickle and turbulent people, disaffection quickly turned to rebellion. One night, Otto's troops being most of them dispersed in their quarters at a *Revolt of the Romans.* distance, the Romans rose in arms, blocked up the Tiber bridges, and fell furiously upon the Emperor and his creature the new Pope. Superior valor and constancy triumphed over numbers, and the Romans were overthrown with terrible slaughter; yet this lesson did not prevent them from revolting a second time, after Otto's departure in pursuit of Adalbert. John XII returned to the city, and when his pontifical career was speedily closed by the sword of an injured husband,† the people chose a new Pope in defiance of the

---

* " Cives fidelitatem promittunt hæc addentes et firmiter iurantes nunquam se papam electuros aut ordinaturos præter consensum atque electionem domini imperatoris Ottonis Cæsaris Augusti filiique ipsius Ottonis."—Liudprand, *Gesta Ottonis*, lib. vi.

† " In timporibus adeo a dyabulo est percussus ut infra dierum octo spacium eodem sit in vulnere mortuus," says the chronicler, crediting with but little of his wonted cleverness the supposed

Emperor and his nominee. Otto again subdued and again forgave them, but when they rebelled for a third time, in A.D. 966, he resolved to show them what imperial supremacy meant. Thirteen leaders, among them the twelve tribunes, were executed, the consuls were banished, republican forms entirely suppressed, the government of the city entrusted to Pope Leo as viceroy. He, too, must not presume on the sacredness of his person to set up any claims to independence. Otto regarded the pontiff as no more than the first of his subjects, the creature of his own will, the depositary of an authority which must be exercised according to the discretion of his sovereign. The citizens had yielded to the Emperor an absolute veto on papal elections in A.D. 963. Otto obtained from his nominee, Leo VIII, a confirmation of this privilege, which it was afterward supposed that Hadrian I had granted to Charles, in a decree which may yet be read in the collections of the canon law.* The vigorous exercise of such a power might be expected to reform as well as to restrain the apostolic see; and it was for this purpose, and in noble honesty, that the Teutonic sovereigns employed it. But the fortunes of Otto in the city are a type of those which his successors are destined to experience. Notwithstanding their clear rights and the momentary enthusiasm with which they were greeted in Rome, not all the efforts of Emperor after Emperor could gain any firm hold on the capital they were so proud of. Visiting it only once or twice in their reigns, they must be supported among a

---

author of John's death, who well might have desired a long life for so useful a servant. He adds a detail too characteristic of the time to be omitted : " Sed eucharistiæ viaticum, ipsius instinctu qui eum percusserat, non percepit."

* *Corpus Iuris Canonici*, Dist. lxiii., " *In synodo.*" A decree which is probably substantially genuine, although the form in which we have it is evidently of later date.

fickle populace by a large army of strangers, which melted
away with terrible rapidity under the sun of Italy amid
the deadly hollows of the Campagna.* Rome soon resumed
her turbulent independence.

Causes partly the same prevented the Saxon princes
from gaining a firm footing throughout Italy.
Otto's rule in Italy. Since Charles the Bald had bartered away for
the crown all that made it worth having, no
Emperor had exercised substantial authority there.   The
missi dominici had ceased to traverse the country; the
local governors had thrown off control, a crowd of petty potentates had established principalities by aggressions on their
weaker neighbors.   Only in the dominions of great nobles,
like the Marquis of Tuscany and Duke of Spoleto, and in
some of the cities where the supremacy of the bishop was
paving the way for a republican system, could traces of
political order be found, or the arts of peace flourish.
Otto, who, though he came as a conqueror, ruled legitimately
as Italian king, found his feudal vassals less submissive
than in Germany.   While actually present he succeeded
by progresses and edicts, and stern justice, in doing something to still the turmoil; on his departure Italy relapsed
into that disorganization for which her natural features
are not less answerable than the mixture of her races.
Yet it was at this era, when the confusion was wildest
that there appeared the first rudiments of an Italian
nationality, based partly on geographical position, partly
on the use of a common language and the slow growth
of peculiar customs and modes of thought.   But though
already jealous of the Tedescan, national feeling was still
very far from disputing his sway.   Pope, princes and

---

* Cf. St. Peter Damiani's lines—
    "Roma vorax hominum domat ardua colla virorum,
    Roma ferax febrium necis est uberrima frugum,
    Romanæ febres stabili sunt iure fideles."

cities bowed to Otto as King and Emperor; nor did he
bethink himself of crushing while it was weak a sentiment
whose development threatened the existence of his empire.
Holding Italy equally for his own with Germany, and ruling both on the same principles, he was content to keep it
a separate kingdom, neither changing its institutions, nor
sending Saxons, as Charles had sent Franks, to represent
his government.*

The lofty claims which Otto acquired with the Roman
crown urged him to resume the plans of
foreign conquest which had lain neglected   *Otto's
since the days of Charles: the growing vigor   foreign
of the Teutonic people, now definitely   *policy.*
separating themselves from surrounding races (this is the
era of the Marks—Brandenburg, Meissen, Schleswig),
placed in his hands a force to execute those plans which
his predecessors had wanted. In this, as in his other en-
terprises, the great Emperor was active, wise, successful.
Retaining the extreme south of Italy, and unwilling to
confess the loss of Rome, the Greeks had not ceased to
annoy her German masters by intrigue, and might now,
under the vigorous leadership of Nicephorus and Tzimiskes, hope again to menace them in arms. Policy, and
the fascination which an ostentatiously legitimate court exercised over the Saxon stranger,   *Toward
made Otto, as Napoleon wooed Maria Louisa,   Byzantium.*
seek for his heir the hand of the princess Theophano.
Liudprand's account of his embassy represents in an
amusing manner the rival pretensions of the old and new
Empires.† The Greeks, who fancied that with the name
they preserved the character and rights of Rome, held it

---

* There was a separate chancellor for Italy, as afterward for the
kingdom of Burgundy.

† Liudprand, *Legatio Constantinopolitana.*

almost as absurd as it was wicked that a Frank should
insult their prerogative by reigning in Italy as Emperor.
They refused him that title altogether ; and when the
Pope had, in a letter addressed *"Imperatori Græcorum,"*
asked Nicephorus to gratify the wishes of the Emperor of
the Romans, the Eastern was furious. " You are no
Romans," said he, " but wretched Lombards: what means
this insolent Pope ? with Constantine all Rome migrated
hither." The wily bishop appeased him by abusing the
Romans, while he insinuated that Byzantium could lay no
claim to their name, and proceeded to vindicate the Francia
and Saxonia of his master. " 'Roman' is the most contemptuous name we can use—it conveys the reproach of
every vice, cowardice, falsehood, avarice. But what can
be expected from the descendants of the fratricide Romulus ? to his asylum were gathered the offscourings of the
nations : thence came these κοσμοκράτορες." Nicephorus
demanded the "theme" or province of Rome as the price
of compliance;* Tzimiskes was more moderate, and Theophano became the bride of Otto II.

Holding the two capitals of Charles the Great, Otto
might vindicate the suzerainty over the West
Toward the West Franks. Frankish kingdom which it had been meant
that the imperial title should carry with it.
Arnulf had asserted it by making Eudes, the
first Capetian king, receive the crown as his feudatory:
Henry the Fowler had been less successful. Otto pursued
the same course, intriguing with the discontented nobles
of Louis d'Outremer, and receiving their fealty as Superior
of Roman Gaul. These pretensions, however, could have
been made effective only by arms, and the feudal militia
of the tenth century was no such instrument of conquest

---

* " Sancti imperii nostri olim servos principes, Beneventanum silicet,
tradat," etc.   The epithet is worth noticing.

as the hosts of Clovis and Charles had been. The star of the Carolingian of Laon was paling before the rising great-ness of the Parisian Capets : a Romano-Keltic nation had formed itself, distinct in tongue from the Franks, whom it was fast absorbing, and still less willing to submit to a Saxon stranger. Modern France* dates from the acces-sion of Hugh Capet, A.D. 987, and the claims of the Roman Empire were never afterward formally admitted.

Of that France, however, Aquitaine was virtually inde-pendent. Lotharingia and Burgundy belonged to it as little as did England. The former of these kingdoms had adhered to the West Frankish king, Charles the Simple, against the East Frankish Conrad: *Lorraine* but now, as mostly German in blood and speech, *and Bur-gundy.* threw itself into the arms of Otto, and was thenceforth an integral part of the Empire. Burgundy, a separate kingdom, had, by seeking from Charles the Fat a ratification of Boso's election, by admitting, in the person of Rudolph the first Transjurane king, the feudal superiority of Arnulf, acknowledged itself to be dependent on the German crown. Otto governed it for thirty years, nominally as the guardian of the young king Conrad (son of Rudolf II).

Otto's conquests to the North and East approved him a worthy successor of the first Emperor. He penetrated far into Jutland, annexed Schleswig, made Harold the Blue-toothed his vassal. The Slavic tribes were obliged to submit, to follow the German host in war, to allow the

---

* Liudprand calls the Eastern Franks, " Franci Teutonici " to dis-tinguish them from the Romanized Franks of Gaul or " Francigenæ " as they were frequently called. The name " Frank " seems even so early as the tenth century to have been used in the East as a general name for the Western peoples of Europe. Liudprand says that the Greek Emperor included " sub Francorum nomine tam Latinos quam Teutonicos." Probably this use dates from the time of Charles.

free preaching of the Gospel in their borders. The Hungarians he forced to forsake their nomad life, and
Denmark and the Slaves. delivered Europe from the fear of Asiatic invasions by strengthening the frontier of Austria.
Over more distant lands, Spain and England,
it was not possible to recover the commanding position of
Charles. Henry, as head of the Saxon name,
England. may have wished to unite its branches on both
sides the sea,* and it was perhaps partly with this intent
that he gained for Otto the hand of Edith, sister of the
English Athelstan. But the claim of supremacy, if any
there was, was repudiated by Edgar, when, exaggerating
the lofty style assumed by some of his predecessors, he
called himself "Basileus and imperator of Britain," †
thereby seeming to pretend to a sovereignty over all the
nations of the island similar to that which the Roman
Emperor claimed over the states of Christendom.

This restored Empire, which professed itself a continuation of the Carolingian, was in many respects different. It
was less wide, including, if we reckon strictly,
Extent of Otto's Em- pire. only Germany proper and two-thirds of Italy ;
or counting in subject but separate kingdoms,
Burgundy, Bohemia, Moravia, Poland, Den-
mark, perhaps Hungary. Its character was less ecclesias-

---

* Conring, *De Finibus Imperii.*

† Basileus was a favorite title of the English kings before the Conquest. Titles like this used in these early English charters prove, it
need hardly be said, absolutely nothing as to the real existence of
any rights or powers of the English king beyond his own borders.
What they do prove (over and above the taste for florid rhetoric in
the royal clerks) is the impression produced by the imperial style,
and by the idea of the Emperor's throne as supported by the thrones
of kings and other lesser potentates. See hereon Freeman, *Hist.
of Norm. Conqest,* vol. i. ch. 3, § 4; who however surely draws from
the use of such titles in England conclusions graver than they
warrant.

tical. Otto exalted indeed the spiritual potentates of his realm, and was earnest in spreading Christianity among the heathen : he was master of the Pope and Defender of the Holy Roman Church. But religion held a less important place in his mind and his administration: he *Comparison between it and that of Charles.* made fewer wars for its sake, held no councils, and did not, like his predecessor, criticize the discourses of bishops. It was also less Roman. We do not know whether Otto associated with that name anything more than right to universal dominion and a certain oversight of matters spiritual, nor how far he believed himself to be treading in the steps of the Cæsars. He could not speak Latin, he had few learned men around him, he cannot have possessed the varied cultivation which had been so fruitful in the mind of Charles. Moreover, the conditions of his time were different, and did not permit similar attempts at wide organization. The local potentates would have submitted to no *missi dominici ;* separate laws and jurisdictions would not have yielded to imperial capitularies ; the *placita* at which those laws were frámed or published would not have been crowded, as of yore, by armed freemen. But what Otto could he did, and did it to good purpose. Constantly traversing his dominions, he introduced a peace and prosperity before unknown, and left everywhere the impress of an heroic character. Under him the Germans became not only a united nation, but were at once raised on a pinnacle among European peoples as the imperial race, the possessors of Rome and Rome's authority. While the political connection with Italy stirred their spirit, it brought with it a knowledge and culture hitherto unknown, and gave the newly-kindled energy an object. Germany became in her turn the instructress of the neighboring tribes, who trembled at Otto's scepter; Poland and Bohemia received from her their arts and their learning with their religion. If the revived Romano-Germanic Empire was less splendid than the Empire of the West had been under Charles, it was, within narrower limits, firmer and more lasting, since based on a social force which the other had wanted. It perpetuated the name, the language, the literature, such as it then was, of Rome ; it extended her spiritual sway ; it strove to represent that concentration for which men cried, and became a power to unite and civilize Europe.

The time of Otto the Great has required a fuller treatment, as the era of the Holy Empire's foundation: succeeding rulers may be more quickly dismissed. Yet Otto III's reign cannot pass unnoticed: short, sad, full of bright promise never fulfilled. His mother was the Greek princess Theophano; his preceptor, the illustrious Gerbert; through the one he felt himself connected with the old Empire, and had imbibed the absolutism of Byzantium: by the other he had been reared in the dream of a renovated Rome, with her memories turned to realities. To accomplish that renovation, who so fit as he who with the vigorous blood of the Teutonic conqueror inherited the venerable rights of Constantinople? It was his design, now that the solemn millennial era of the founding of Christianity had arrived, to renew the majesty of the city and make her again the capital of a world-embracing Empire, victorious as Trajan's, despotic as Justinian's, holy as Constantine's. His young and visionary mind was too much dazzled by the gorgeous fancies it created to see the world as it was: Germany rude, Italy unquiet, Rome corrupt and faithless. In A.D. 995, at the age of fifteen, he took from his grandmother's hands the reins of government, and entered Italy to receive his crown, and quell the turbu-

Otto II,
A.D. 973-
983.

Otto III,
A.D. 983-
1002.

His Ideas.
Fascination
exercised
over him by
the name of
Rome.

lence of Rome. There he put to death the rebel Crescentius, in whom modern enthusiasm has seen a patriotic
republican, who, reviving the institutions of Alberic, had
ruled as consul or senator, sometimes entitling himself
Emperor. The young monarch reclaimed, perhaps extended, the privilege of Charles and Otto the Great, by
nominating successive pontiffs : first Bruno his cousin
(Gregory V), then Gerbert, whose name of
Sylvester II recalled significantly the ally of *Pope Sylvester II, A.D. 1000.*
Constantine: Gerbert, to his contemporaries a
marvel of piety and learning, in later legend
the magician who, at the price of his own soul, purchased
preferment from the Enemy, and by him was at last carried off in the body. With the substitution of these men
for the profligate priests of Italy, began that Teutonic
reform of the Papacy which raised it from the abyss of the
tenth century to the point where Hildebrand found it.
The Emperors were working the ruin of their power by
their most disinterested acts.

With his tutor on Peter's chair to second or direct
him, Otto labored on his great project in a spirit almost
mystic. He had an intense religious belief in
the Emperor's duties to the world—in his proclamations he calls himself " Servant of the
Apostles," "Servant of Jesus Christ "*—to-
gether with the ambitious antiquarianism of *Schemes of Otto III. Changes of style and usage.*
a fiery imagination, kindled by the memorials
of the glory and power he represented. Even the wording
of his laws witnesses to the strange mixture of notions that
filled his eager brain. " We have ordained this," says an
edict, " in order that, the Church of God being freely and
firmly stablished, our Empire may be advanced and the
crown of our knighthood triumph; that the power of the

---

* Proclamation in Pertz, *M. G. H.* ii.

Roman people may be extended and the commonwealth be restored ; so may we be found worthy after living righteously in the tabernacle of this world, to fly away from the prison of this life and reign most righteously with the Lord." To exclude the claims of the Greeks he used the title " *Romanorum Imperator* " instead of the simple "*Imperator* " of his predecessors. His seals bear a legend resembling that used by Charles, " *Renovatio Imperii Romanorum;*" even the "commonwealth," despite the results that name had produced under Alberic and Crescentius, was to be re-established. He built a palace on the Aventine, then the most healthy and beautiful quarter of the city; he devised a regular administrative system of government for his capital—naming a patrician, a prefect and a body of judges, who were commanded to recognize no law but Justinian's. The formula of their appointment has been preserved to us: in it the Emperor delivering to the judge a copy of the code bids him " with this code judge Rome and the Leonine city and the whole world." He introduced into the simple German court the ceremonious magnificence of Byzantium, not without giving offence to many of his followers.* His father's wish to draw Italy and Germany more closely together, he followed up by giving the chancellorship of both countries to the same churchman, by maintaining a strong force of Germans in Italy, and by taking his Italian retinue with him through the Transalpine lands. How far these brilliant and far-reaching plans were capable of realization, had their author lived to attempt it, can be but guessed at. It is reasonable to suppose that whatever power he might have gained in the South he would have lost in the North. Dwelling

---

* " Imperator antiquam Romanorum consuetudinem iam ex magna parte delatam suis cupiens renovare temporibus multa faciebat quæ diversi diverse sentiebant."—Thietmar, *Chron.* ix. ap. Pertz, *M. G. H.* iii.

rarely in Germany, and in sympathies more a Greek than a Teuton, he reined in the fierce barons with no such tight hand as his grandfather had been wont to do; he neglected the schemes of northern conquest; he released the Polish dukes from the obligation of tribute. But all, save that those plans were his, is now no more than conjecture, for Otto III, "the wonder of the world," as his own generation called him, died childless on the threshold of manhood; the victim, if we may trust a story of the time, of the revenge of Stephania, widow of Cresentius, who ensnared him by her beauty, and slew him by a lingering poison. They carried him across the Alps with laments whose echoes sound faintly yet from the pages of monkish chroniclers, and buried him in the choir of the basilica at Aachen some fifty paces from the tomb of Charles beneath the central dome. Two years had not passed since, setting out on his last journey to Rome, he had opened that tomb, had gazed on the great Emperor sitting on a marble throne, robed and crowned, with the Gospel book open before him; and there, touching the dead hand, unclasping from the neck its golden cross, had taken, as it were, an investiture of Empire from his Frankish forerunner. Short as was his life and few his acts, Otto III is in one respect more memorable than any who went before or came after him. None save he desired to make the seven-hilled city again the seat of dominion, reducing Germany and Lombardy and Greece to their rightful place of subject provinces. No one else so forgot the present to live in the light of the ancient order; no other soul was so possessed by that fervid mysticism and that reverence for the glories of the past, whereon rested the idea of the mediæval Empire.

The direct line of Otto the Great had now ended, and though the Franks might elect and the Saxons accept Henry II,* Italy was nowise affected by their acts.

* *Annales Quedlinb.*, ad ann. 1002.

Neither the Empire nor the Lombard kingdom could as
yet be of right claimed by the German king.

*Italy inde-
pendent.* Her princes placed Ardoin, marquis of Ivrea,
on the vacant throne of Pavia, moved partly by
the growing aversion to a Transalpine power, still more by
the desire of impunity under a monarch feebler than any
since Berengar. But the selfishness that had exalted
Ardoin soon overthrew him. Ere long a party among the
nobles, seconded by the Pope, invited Henry;* his strong
army made opposition hopeless, and at Rome he received
the imperial crown, A.D. 1014. It is, perhaps,

*Henry II
Emperor.* more singular that the Transalpine kings
should have clung so pertinaciously to Italian
sovereignty than that the Lombards should have so frequently attempted to recover their independence. For the
form r had often little or no hereditary claim, they were
not secure in their seat at home, they crossed a huge
mountain barrier into a land of treachery and hatred.
But Rome's glittering lure was irresistible, and the disunion of Italy promised an easy conquest. Surrounded by
martial vassals, these Emperors were generally for the moment supreme: once their pennons had disappeared in the
gorges of Tyrol, things reverted to their former condition,
and Tuscany was little more dependent than

*Southern
Italy.* France. In Southern Italy the Greek viceroy
ruled from Bari, and Rome was an outpost instead of the center of Teutonic power. A curious evidence
of the wavering politics of the time is furnished by the
Annals of Benevento, the Lombard town which on the
confines of the Greek and Roman realms gave steady obedience to neither. They usually date by and recognize the
princes of Constantinople,† seldom mentioning the Franks,

---

* Henry had already entered Italy in 1004.

† *Annales Beneventani,* in Pertz, *M. G. H.*

till the reign of Conrad II; after him the Western becomes *Imperator*, the Greek, appearing more rarely, is *Imperator Constantinopolitanus.* Assailed by the Saracens, masters already of Sicily, these regions seemed on the eve of being lost to Christendom, and the Romans sometimes bethought themselves of returning under the Byzantine scepter. As the weakness of the Greeks in the South favored the rise of the Norman kingdom, so did the liberties of the northern cities shoot up in the absence of the Emperors and the feuds of the princes. Milan, Pavia, Cremona, were only the foremost among many populous centers of industry, some of them self-governing, all quickly absorbing or repelling the rural nobility, and not afraid to display by tumults their aversion to the Germans.

The reign of Conrad II, the first monarch of the great Franconian line, is remarkable for the accession to the Empire of Burgundy, or, as it is after this time more often called, the kingdom of Arles.* *Conrad II.* Rudolf III, the last king, had proposed to bequeath it to Henry II, and the states were at length persuaded to consent to its reunion to the crown from which it had been separated, though to some extent dependent, since the death of Lothar I (son of Lewis the Pious). On Rudolf's death in 1032, Eudes, count of Champagne, endeavored to seize it, and entered the north-western districts, from which he was dislodged by Conrad with some difficulty. Unlike Italy, it became an integral member of the Germanic realm: its prelates and nobles sat in imperial diets, and retained till recently the style and title of Princes of the Holy Empire. The central government was, however, seldom effective in these outlying territories, exposed always to the intrigues, finally to the aggressions, of Capetian France.

Under Conrad's son, Henry III, the Empire attained the

---

* See Appendix, note A.

meridian of its power.   At home Otto the Great's prerogative had not stood so high.   The duchies,
Henry III.   always the chief source of fear, were allowed to
remain vacant or filled by the relatives of the monarch,
who himself retained, contrary to usual practice, those
of Franconia and (for some years) Swabia.   Abbeys and
sees lay entirely in his gift.   Intestine feuds were repressed
by the proclamation of a public peace.   Abroad, the feudal
superiority over Hungary, which Henry II had gained by
conferring the title of king with the hand of his sister
Gisela, was enforced by war, the country made almost a
province, and compelled to pay tribute.   In
His reform   Rome no German sovereign had ever been so
of the Pope-   absolute.   A disgraceful contest between three
dom.   claimants of the papal chair had shocked even
the reckless apathy of Italy.   Henry deposed them all
and appointed their successor: he became hereditary
patrician, and wore constantly the green mantle and circlet
of gold which were the badges of that office, seeming, one
might think, to find in it some further authority than that
which the imperial name conferred.   The synod passed a
decree granting to Henry the right of nominating the
supreme pontiff; and the Roman priesthood, who had forfeited the respect of the world even more by habitual
simony than by the flagrant corruption of their manners,
were forced to receive German after German as their bishop,
at the bidding of a ruler so powerful, so severe and so
pious.   But Henry's encroachments alarmed his own
nobles no less than the Italians, and the reaction, which
might have been dangerous to himself, was fatal to his
successor.   A mere chance, as some might call
Henry IV,   it, determined the course of history.   The great
A.D. 1056-   Emperor died suddenly in A.D. 1056, and a
1106.   child was left at the helm, while storms were
gathering that might have demanded the wisest hand.

CHAPTER X.

STRUGGLE OF THE EMPIRE AND THE PAPACY.

REFORMED by the Emperors and their Teutonic nominees, the papacy had resumed in the middle of the eleventh
century the schemes of polity shadowed forth by Nicholas
I, and which the degradation of the last age had only suspended. Under the guidance of her greatest mind, Hildebrand, the archdeacon of Rome, she now advanced to
their completion, and proclaimed that war of the ecclesiastical power against the civil power in the person of the
Emperor, which became the center of the subsequent history of both. While the nature of the struggle cannot be
understood without a glance at their previous connection,
the vastness of the subject warns one from the attempt to
draw even its outlines, and restricts our view to those relations of Popedom and Empire which arise directly out
of their respective positions as heads spiritual and temporal of the universal Christian state.

The eagerness of Christianity in the age immediately
following her political establishment to purchase by submission the support of the civil   *Growth of*
power, has been already remarked. The   *the papal*
change from independence to supremacy was   *power.*
gradual. The tale we smile at, how Constantine, healed
of his leprosy, granted the West to Bishop Sylvester, and
retired to Byzantium that no secular prince might interfere with the jurisdiction or profane the neighborhood of
Peter's chair, worked great effects through the belief it
commanded for many centuries. Nay more, its ground-

work was true. It was the removal of the seat of government from the Tiber to the Bosphorous that made the Pope the greatest personage in the city, and in the prostration after Alaric's invasion he was seen to be so. Henceforth he alone was a permanent and effective, though still unacknowledged power, as truly superior to the revived senate and consuls of the phantom republic as Augustus and Tiberius had been to the faint continuance of their earlier prototypes. Pope Leo the First asserted the universal jurisdiction of his see,* and his persevering successors slowly enthralled Italy, Illyricum, Gaul, Spain, Africa, dextriously confounding their undoubted metropolitan and patriarchal rights with those of œcumenical bishop, in which they were finally merged. By his writings and the fame of his personal sanctity, by the conversion of England and the introduction of an impressive ritual, Gregory the Great did more than any other pontiff to advance Rome's ecclesiastical authority. Yet his tone to Maurice of Constantinople was deferential, to Phocas adulatory; his successors were not consecrated till confirmed by the Emperor or the Exarch; one of them was dragged in chains to the Bosphorus, and banished thence to Scythia. When the iconoclastic controversy and the intervention of Pipin broke the allegiance of the Popes to the East, the Franks, as patricians and Emperors, seemed to step into the position which Byzantium had lost.† At Charles' coronation, says the Saxon poet,

> " Et summus eundem
> Præsul adoravit, sicut mos debitus olim
> Principibus fuit antiquis."

---

* " Roma per sedem Beati Petri caput orbis effecta."—See note *, p. 30.

† " Claves tibi *ad regnum* dimisimus."—Pope Stephen to Charles Martel, in *Codex Carolinus*, ap. Muratori, *S. R. I.* iii. Some, however, prefer to read " ad rogum."

Their relations were, however, no longer the same. If
the Frank vaunted conquest, the priest spoke
only of free gift. What Christendom saw   *Relations of*
was that Charles was crowned by the Pope's   *the Papacy*
hands, and undertook as his principal duty   *Empire.*
the protection and advancement of the
Holy Roman Church. The circumstances of Otto
the Great's coronation gave an even more favorable
opening to sacerdotal claims, for it was a Pope who
summoned him to Rome and a Pope who received
from him an oath of fidelity and aid. In the conflict of three powers, the Emperor, the Pontiff and the
people—represented by their senate and consuls, or by the
demagogue of the hour—the most steady, prudent and far-
sighted was sure eventually to prevail. The Popedom had
no minorities, as yet few disputed successions, few revolts
within its own army—the host of churchmen through
Europe. Boniface's conversion of Germany under its
direct sanction, gave it a hold on the rising hierarchy of
the greatest European state; the extension of the rule of
Charles and Otto diffused in the same measure its emis-
saries and pretensions. The first disputes turned on the
right of the prince to confirm the elected Pontiff, which
was afterward supposed to have been granted by Hadrian
I to Charles, in the decree quoted as " *Hadrianus Papa.*"*
This " *ius eligendi et ordinandi summum pantificem,*"
which Lewis I appears as yielding by the " *Ego Ludovi-
cus,*"† was claimed by the Carolingians whenever they felt
themselves strong enough, and having fallen into desue-
tude in the troublous times of the Italian Emperors, was
formally renewed to Otto the Great by his nominee Leo
VIII. We have seen it used, and used in the purest spirit,

---

* *Corpus Iuris Canonici,* Dist. lxiii. c. 22.

† Dist. lxiii. c. 30. This decree is, however, in all probability
spurious.

by Otto himself, by his grandson Otto III, last of all, and most despotically by Henry III. Along with it there had grown up a bold counter-assumption of the Papal chair to be itself the source of the imperial dignity. In submitting to a fresh coronation, Lewis the Pious admitted the invalidity of his former self-performed one: Charles the Bald did not scout the arrogant declaration of John VIII,* that to him alone the Emperor owed his crown; and the council of Pavia,† when it chose him King of Italy, repeated the assertion. Subsequent Popes knew better than to apply to the chiefs of Saxon and Franconian chivalry language which the feeble Nuestrian had not resented; but the precedent remained, the weapon was only hid behind the pontifical robe to be flashed out with effect when the moment should come. There were also two other great steps which Papal power had taken. By the invention and adoption of the False Decretals it had provided itself with a legal system suited to any emergency, and which gave it unlimited authority through the Christian world in causes spiritual and over persons ecclesiastical. Canonistical ingenuity found it easy in one way or another to make this include all causes and persons whatsoever: for crime is always and wrong is often sin, nor can aught be anywhere done which may not affect the clergy.

Temporal power of the Popes. On the gift of Pipin and Charles, repeated and confirmed by Lewis I, Charles II, Otto I and III, and now made to rest on the more venerable authority of the first Christian Emperor, it could

---

* "Nos elegimus merito et approbavimus una cum annisu et voto patrum amplique senatus et gentis togatæ," etc., ap. Baron. *Ann. Eccl.* ad ann. 876.

† "Divina vos pietas B. principum apostolorum Petri et Pauli interventione per vicarium ipsorum dominum Ioannem summum pontificem . . . ad imperiale culmen S. Spiritus iudicio provexit." *Concil. Ticinense,* in Mur. *S. R. I.* ii.

found claims to the sovereignty of Rome, Tuscany and all else that had belonged to the exarchate. Indefinite in their terms, these grants were never meant by the donors to convey full dominion over the districts that belonged to the head of the Empire—but only as in the case of other church estates, a sort of perpetual usufruct, a beneficial enjoyment which had nothing to do with sovereignty. They were, in fact, mere endowments. Nor had the gifts been ever actually reduced into possession; the Pope had been hitherto the victim, not the lord of the neighboring barons. They were not, however, denied, and might be made a formidable engine of attack; appealing to them, the Pope could brand his opponents as unjust and impious ; and could summon nobles and cities to defend him as their liege lord, just as, with no better original right, he invoked the help of the Norman conquerors of Naples and Sicily.

The attitude of the Roman Church to the imperial power at Henry III's death was externally respectful. The right of a German king to the crown of the city was undoubted, and the Pope was his lawful subject. Hitherto the initiative in reform had come from the civil magistrate. But the secret of the pontiff's strength lay in this: he, and he alone, could confer the crown, and had therefore the right of imposing conditions on the recipient. Frequent interregna had weakened the claim of the Transalpine monarch and prevented his power from taking firm root; his title was never by law hereditary: the holy Church had before sought and might again seek a defender elsewhere. And since the need of such defence had originated this transference of the Empire from the Greeks to the Franks, since to render it was the Emperor's chief function, it was surely the Pope's duty as well as his right to see that the candidate was capable of fulfilling his task, to degrade him if he rejected or misperformed it.

The first step was to remove a blemish in the constitution of the Church, by fixing a regular body to choose the
supreme pontiff.   This Nicholas II did in A.D.
Hildebran- 1059, feebly reserving the rights of Henry IV
dine re- and his successors.   Then the reforming spirit,
forms. kindled by the abuses and depravity of the
last century, advanced apace.   It had two main objects—
the enforcement of celibacy, especially on the secular
clergy, who enjoyed in this respect considerable freedom,
and the extinction of simony.   In the former, the Emperors and a large part of the laity were not unwilling to
join : the latter no one dared to defend in theory.   But
when Gregory VII declared that it was sin for the eccle-
siastic to receive his benefice under conditions from a
layman, and so condemned the whole system of feudal investitures to the clergy, he aimed a deadly blow at all
secular authority.   Half of the land and wealth of Germany was in the hands of bishops and abbots, who would
now be freed from the monarch's control to pass under
that of the Pope.   In such a state of things government
itself would be impossible.

Henry and Gregory already mistrusted each other: after
this decree war was inevitable.   The Pope cited his opponent to appear and be judged at Rome for his
Henry IV vices and misgovernment.   The Emperor* re-
and Gre- plied by convoking a synod, which deposed and
gory VII. insulted Gregory.   At once the dauntless monk
pronounced Henry excommunicate, and fixed a day on
which, if still unrepentant, he should cease to reign.
Supported by his own princes, the monarch might have
defied a command backed by no external force; but the
Saxons, never contented since the first place had passed

* Strictly speaking, Henry was at this time only king of the
Romans: he was not crowned Emperor at Rome till 1084.

from their own dukes to the Franconians, only waited the
signal to burst into a new revolt, while through all Germany the Emperor's tyranny and irregularities of life had
sown the seeds of disaffection. Shunned, betrayed,
threatened, he rushed into what seemed the only course
left, and Canosa saw Europe's mightiest prince, titular
lord of the world, a suppliant before the successor of the Apostle. Henry soon found that   *A.D. 1077.*
his humiliation had not served him; driven back into opposition, he defied Gregory anew, set up an anti-pope,
overthrew the rival whom his rebellious subjects had
raised, and maintained to the end of his sad and checkered
life a power often depressed but never destroyed. Nevertheless had all other humiliation been spared, that one
scene in the yard of the Countess Matilda's castle, an imperial penitent standing barefoot and woollen-frocked on
the snow three days and nights, till the priest who sat
within should admit and absolve him, was enough to mark
a decisive change, and inflict an irretrievable disgrace on
the crown so abased. Its wearer could no more, with the
same lofty confidence, claim to be the highest power on
earth, created by and answerable to God alone. Gregory
had extorted the recognition of that absolute superiority
of the spiritual dominion which he was wont to assert so
sternly; proclaiming that to the Pope, as God's Vicar, all
mankind are subject, and all rulers responsible: so that he,
the giver of the crown, may also excommunicate and depose. Writing to William the Conqueror, he says:* " For
as for the beauty of this world, that it may be at different
seasons perceived by fleshly eyes, God hath disposed the
sun and the moon, lights that outshine all others; so lest
the creature whom His goodness hath formed after His

---

* Letter of Gregory VII to William I, A.D. 1080. I quote from
Migne, cxlviii. p. 568. [Jaffé, *Monumenta Gregoriana*, p. 419.]

own image in this world should be drawn astray into fatal dangers, He hath provided in the apostolic and royal dignities the means of ruling it through divers offices. . . . If I, therefore, am to answer for thee on the dreadful day of judgment before the just Judge who cannot lie, the creator of every creature, bethink thee whether I must not very diligently provide for thy salvation, and whether, for thine own safety, thou oughtest not without delay to obey me, that so thou mayest possess the land of the living."

Gregory was not the inventor nor the first propounder of these doctrines; they had been long before a part of mediæval Christianity, interwoven with its most vital doctrines. But he was the first who dared to apply them to the world as he found it. His was that rarest and grandest of gifts, an intellectual courage and power of imaginative belief which, when it has convinced itself of aught, accepts it fully with all its consequences, and shrinks not from acting at once upon it. A perilous gift, as the melancholy end of his own career proved, for men were found less ready than he had thought them to follow out with unswerving consistency like his the principles which all acknowledged. But it was the very suddenness and boldness of his policy that secured the ultimate triumph of his cause, awing men's minds and making that seem realized which had been till then a vague theory. His premises once admitted—and no one dreamed of denying them—the reasonings by which he established the superiority of spiritual to temporal jurisdiction were unassailable. With his authority, in whose hands are the keys of heaven and hell, whose word can bestow eternal bliss or plunge in everlasting misery, no other earthly authority can compete or interfere: if his power extends into the infinite, how much more must he be supreme over things finite? It was thus that Gregory and his successors were wont to argue: the wonder is, not that they were obeyed, but that they were not obeyed more implicitly. In the second sentence of excommunication which Gregory passed upon Henry IV are these words:

"Come now, I beseech you, O most holy and blessed Fathers and Princes, Peter and Paul, that all the world may understand and know that if ye are able to bind and to loose in heaven, ye are likewise able on earth, according to the merits of each man, to give and to take away empires, kingdoms, princedoms, marquisates, duchies, countships and the possessions of all men. For if ye judge spiritual things, what must we believe to be your power over worldly thing? and if ye judge the angels who rule over all proud princes, what can ye not do to their slaves?"

Doctrines such as these do indeed strike equally at all temporal governments, nor were the innocents and Bonifaces of later days slow to apply them so. On the Empire, however, the blow fell first and heaviest. As when Alaric entered Rome, the *Results of the struggle.* spell of ages was broken, Christendom saw her greatest and most venerable institution dishonored and helpless; allegiance was no longer undivided, for who could presume to fix in each case the limits of the civil and ecclesiastical jurisdictions The potentates of Europe beheld in the Papacy a force which, if dangerous to themselves, could be made to repel the pretentions and baffle the designs of the strongest and haughtiest among them. Italy learned how to meet the Teutonic conqueror by gaining the papal sanction for the leagues of her cities. The German princes, anxious to narrow the prerogative of their head, were the natural allies of his enemy, whose spiritual thunders, more terrible than their own lances, could enable them to depose an aspiring monarch, or extort from him any concessions they desired. Their altered tone is marked by the promise they required from Rudolf of Swabia, whom they set up as a rival to Henry, that he would not endeavor to make the throne hereditary.

It is not possible here to dwell on the details of the great struggle of the Investitures, rich as it is in the interest of adventure and character, momentous as were its results for the future. A word or two must suffice to describe the conclusion, not indeed of the whole drama, which was to extend over centuries, but of what may be called its first act. Even that act lasted beyond the lives of the original performers. Gregory VII passed away at Salerno in A.D. 1085, exclaiming with his last breath, "I have loved justice and hated iniquity, therefore I die in exile." Twenty-one years later, in A.D. 1106, Henry IV died, dethroned by an unnatural son whom the hatred of a relentless pontiff had raised in rebellion against him. But that son, the Emperor Henry V, so far from conceding the points in dispute, proved an antagonist more ruthless and not less able than his father. He claimed for his crown all the rights over ecclesiastics that his predecessors had ever enjoyed, and when at his coronation in Rome, A.D. 1111, Pope Paschal II refused to complete the rite until he should have yielded, Henry seized both Pope and cardinals and compelled them by a rigorous imprisonment to consent to a treaty which he dictated. Once set free, the Pope, as was natural, disavowed his extorted concessions, and the struggle was protracted for ten years longer, until nearly half a century had elapsed from the first quarrel between Gregory VII and Henry IV.

Concordat of Worms, A.D. 1122. The Concordat of Worms, concluded in A.D. 1122, was in form a compromise, designed to spare either party the humiliation of defeat. Yet the Papacy remained master of the field. The Emperor retained but one-half of those rights of investiture which had formerly been his. He could never resume the position of Henry III ; his wishes or intrigues might influence the proceedings of a chapter, his oath bound him from open interference. He had entered the strife in the fullness of dignity; he came out of it with tarnished glory and shattered power. His wars had been hitherto carried on with foreign foes, or at worst with a single rebel noble; now his former ally was turned into his fiercest assailant, and had enlisted against him half his court, half the magnates of his realm. At any moment his scepter might be shivered in his hand by the bolt of anathema, and a host of enemies spring up from every convent and cathedral.

Two other results of this great conflict ought not to pass unnoticed. The Emperor was alienated from the Church at the most unfortunate of all moments, the era of the Crusades. To conduct a great religious war against the enemies of the faith, to head the church militant in her carnal as the Popes were accustomed to do in her spiritual strife, this was the very *The Crusades.* purpose for which an Emperor had been called into being; and it was indeed in these wars, more particularly in the first three of them, that the ideal of a Christian commonwealth which the theory of the mediæval Empire proclaimed, was once for all and never again realized by the combined action of the great nations of Europe. Had such an opportunity fallen to the lot of Henry III, he might have used it to win back a supremacy hardly inferior to that which had belonged to the first Carolingians. But Henry IV's proscription excluded him from all share in an enterprise which he must otherwise have led—nay more, committed it to the guidance of his foes. The religious feeling which the Crusades evoked—a feeling which became the origin of the great orders of chivalry, and somewhat later of the two great orders of mendicant friars—turned wholly against the opponent of ecclesiastical claims, and was made to work the will of the Holy See, which had blessed and organized the project. A century and a half later the Pope did not scruple to preach a crusade against the Emperor himself.

Again, it was now that the first seeds were sown of that fear and hatred wherewith the German people never thenceforth ceased to regard the encroaching Romish court. Branded by the Church and forsaken by the nobles, Henry IV retained the affections of the faithful burghers of Worms and Liége. It soon became the test of Teutonic patriotism to resist Italian priestcraft.

The changes in the internal constitution of Germany which the long anarchy of Henry IV's reign had produced are seen when the nature of the prerogative as it stood at the accession of Conrad II, the first Franconian *Limitations* Emperor, is compared with its state at Henry *of imperial* V's death. All fiefs are now hereditary, and *prerogative.* when vacant can be granted afresh only by consent of the States; the jurisdiction of the crown is less wide; the idea is beginning to make progress that the most essential part of the Empire is not its supreme head but the commonwealth of princes and barons. The greatest triumph of these feudal magnates is in the establishment of the elective principle, which when confirmed by the three free elections of Lothar II, Conrad III and Frederick I, passes into an undoubted law. The Prince-Electors are mentioned in A.D. 1156 as a distinct and important body.* The clergy, too, whom the policy of Otto the Great and Henry II had raised, are now not less dangerous than the dukes, whose power it was hoped they would balance ; possibly more so, since protected by their sacred character and their allegiance to the Pope, while able at the same time to command the arms of their countless vassals. Nor

---

* "Gradum statim post Principes Electores."—Frederick I's Privilege of Austria, in Pertz, *M. G. H.* legg. ii.

were the two succeeding Emperors the men to retrieve those disasters. The Saxon Lothar II is the willing minion of the Pope; performs at his coronation a menial service unknown before, and takes a more stringent oath to defend the Holy See, that he may purchase its support against the Swabian faction in his own dominions. Conrad III, the first Emperor of the great house of Hohenstaufen,* represents the anti-papal party; but domestic troubles and an unfortunate crusade prevented him from effecting anything in Italy. He never even entered Rome to receive the crown.

Lothar II, 1125-1138.

Conrad III, 1138-1152.

---

* Hohenstaufen is a castle in what is now the kingdom of Würtemberg, about four miles from the Göppingen station of the railway from Stuttgart to Ulm. It stands, or rather stood, on the summit of a steep and lofty conical hill (visible from several points on the line of railway), commanding a boundless view over the great limestone plateau of the Rauhe Alp, the eastern declivities of the Schwartzwald, and the bare and tedious plains of western Bavaria. Of the castle itself, destroyed in the Peasants' War, there remain only fragments of the wall-foundations: in a rude chapel lying on the hill slope below are some strange half-obliterated frescoes; over the arch of the door is inscribed "Hic transibat Cæsar." Frederick Barbarossa had another famous palace at Kasierslautern, a small town in the Palatinate, on the railway from Mannheim to Treves, lying in a wide valley at the western foot of the Hardt mountains. It was destroyed by the French: and a house of correction has been built upon its site; but in a brewery hard by may be seen some of the huge low-browed arches of its lower story.

CHAPTER XI.

THE EMPERORS IN ITALY: FREDERICK BARBAROSSA.

THE reign of Frederick I, better known under his Italian surname Barbarossa, is the most brilliant in the annals of the Empire. Its territory had been wider under Charles, its strength perhaps greater under Henry III, but it never appeared in such pervading vivid activity, never shone with such luster of chivalry, as under the prince whom his countrymen have taken to be one of their national heroes, and who is still, as the half-mythic type of Teutonic character, honored by picture and statue, in song and in legend, through the breadth of the German lands. The reverential fondness of his annalists and the whole tenor of his life go far to justify this admiration, and dispose one to believe that nobler motives were joined with personal ambition in urging him to assert so haughtily and carry out so harshly those imperial rights in which he had such unbounded confidence. Under his guidance the Transalpine power made its greatest effort to subdue the two antagonists which then threatened and were fated in the end to destroy it—Italian nationality and the Papacy.

Frederick of Hohen-staufen, 1152–1189.

Even before Gregory VII's time it might have been predicted that two such potentates as the Emperor and the Pope, closely bound together, yet each with pretensions wide and undefined, must ere long come into collision. The boldness of that great pontiff in enforcing, the unflinching firm-

His rela-tions to the Popedom.

ness of his successors in maintaining, the supremacy of clerical authority, inspired their supporters with a zeal and courage which more than compensated the advantages· of the Emperor in defending rights he had long enjoyed. On both sides the hatred was soon very bitter. But even had men's passions permitted a reconciliation, it would have been found difficult to bring into harmony adverse principles, each irresistible, mutually destructive. As the spiritual power, in itself purer, since exercised over the soul and directed to the highest of all ends, eternal felicity, was entitled to the obedience of all, laymen as well as clergy; so the spiritual person, to whom, according to the view then universally accepted, there had been imparted by ordination a mysterious sanctity, could not without sin be subject to the lay magistrate, be installed by him in office, be judged in his court, and render to him any compulsory service. Yet it was no less true that civil government was indispensable to the peace and advancement of society; and while it continued to subsist, another jurisdiction could not be suffered to interfere with its workings, nor one-half of the people be altogether removed from its control. Thus the Emperor and the Pope were forced into hostility as champions of opposite systems, however fully each might admit the strength of his adversary's position, however bitterly he might bewail the violence of his own partisans. There had also arisen other causes of quarrel, less respectable but not less dangerous. The pontiff demanded and the monarch refused the lands which the Countess Matilda of Tuscany had bequeathed to the Holy See ; Frederick claiming them as feudal suzerain, the Pope eager by their means to carry out those schemes of temporal dominion which Constantine's donation sanctioned, and Lothar's seeming renunciation of the sovereignty of Rome had done much to encourage. As feudal superior of the Norman kings of Naples and Sicily, as protector of the towns and barons of North Italy who feared the German yoke, the successor of Peter wore already the air of an independent potentate.

No man was less likely than Frederick to submit to these encroachments. He was a sort of imperialist Hildebrand, strenuously proclaiming the immediate depend-

Contest with Hadrian IV. ence of his office on God's gift, and holding it every whit as sacred as his rival's. Of his first journey to Rome he refused to hold the Pope's stirrup,* as Lothar had done, till Pope Hadrian IV's threat that he would withhold the crown enforced compliance. Complaints arising not long after on some other ground, the Pope exhorted Frederick by letter to show himself worthy of the kindness of his mother the Roman Church, who had given him the imperial crown, and would confer on him, if dutiful, benefits still greater. This word benefits—*beneficia*—understood in its usual legal sense of "fief," and taken in connection with the picture which had been set up at Rome to commemorate Lothar's homage, provoked angry shouts from the nobles assembled in diet at Besançon ; and when the legate answered, "From whom, then, if not from our Lord the Pope, does your king hold the Empire?" his life was not safe from their fury. On this occasion Frederick's vigor and the remonstrances of the Transalpine prelates obliged Hadrian to explain away the obnoxious word, and remove the picture. Soon after the quarrel was renewed by other causes, and came to center itself round the Pope's demand that Rome should be left entirely to his government. Frederick, in reply, appeals to the civil law, and closes with the words,

---

* A great deal of importance seems to have been attached to this symbolic act of courtesy. See Art. I of the *Sachsenspiegel.* "Deme pavese is ok gesat to ridene to bescedener tiet up eneme blanken perde, unde de keiser sal ime den stegerip halden dur de sadel nicht ne winde."

"Since by the ordination of God I both am called and am Emperor of the Romans, in nothing but name shall I appear to be ruler if the control of the Roman city be wrested from my hands." That such a claim should need assertion marks the change since Henry III ; how much more that it could not be enforced. Hadrian's ● rises into defiance; he mingles the threat of excommunication with references to the time when the Germans had not yet the Empire. "What were the Franks till Zacharias welcomed Pipin? What is the Teutonic king now till consecrated at Rome by holy hands? The chair of Peter has given and can withdraw its gifts."

The schism that followed Hadrian's death produced a second and more momentous conflict. Frederick, as head of Christendom, proposed to summon the bishops of Europe to a general council, over which *With Pope* he should preside, like Justinian or Heraclius. *Alexander III.* Quoting the favorite text of the two swords, "On earth," he continues, "God has placed no more than two powers: above there is but one God, so here one Pope and one Emperor. The Divine Providence has specially appointed the Roman Empire as a remedy against continued schism."* The plan failed; and Frederick adopted the candidate whom his own faction had chosen, while the rival claimant, Alexander III, appealed, with a confidence which the issue justified, to the support of sound churchmen throughout Europe. The keen and long doubtful strife of twenty years that followed, while apparently a dispute between rival Popes, was in substance an effort by the secular monarch to recover his command of the priesthood; not less truly so than that contemporaneous conflict of the English Henry II and St. Thomas

* Letter to the German bishops in Radewic; Mur., *S. R. I.*, t. vi. p. 833.

of Canterbury, with which it was constantly involved. Unsupported, not all Alexander's genius and resolution could have saved him: by the aid of the Lombard cities, whose league he had counselled and hallowed, and of the fevers of Rome, by which the conquering German host was suddenly annihilated, he won a triumph the more signal that it was over a prince so wise and so pious as Frederick. At Venice, who, inaccessible by her position, maintained a sedulous neutrality, claiming to be independent of the Empire, yet seldom led into war by sympathy with the Popes, the two powers whoes strife had roused all Europe were induced to meet by the mediation of the doge Sebastian Ziani. Three slabs of red marble in the porch of St. Mark's point out the spot where Frederick knelt in sudden awe, and the Pope with tears of joy raised him, and gave the kiss of peace. A later legend, to which poetry and painting have given an undeserved currency,* tells how the pontiff set his foot on the neck of the prostrate king, with the words, "The young lion and the dragon shalt thou trample under feet."† It needed not this exaggeration to enhance the significance of that scene, even more full of meaning for the future than it was solemn and affecting to the Venetian crowd that thronged the church and the piazza. For it was the renunciation by the mightiest prince of his time of the project to which his life had been devoted; it was the abandonment by the secular power of a contest in which it had twice been vanquished, and which it could not renew under more favorable conditions.

Authority maintained so long against the successor of Peter would be far from indulgent to rebellious subjects.

---

* A picture in the great hall of the ducal palace (the Sala del Maggior Consiglio) represents the scene. See the description in Rogers' Italy.

† Psalm xci.

For it was in this light that the Lombard cities appeared
to a monarch bent on reviving all the rights his predecessors had enjoyed : nay, all that the law of
ancient Rome gave her absolute ruler, It *Revival of the study of the civil law.*
would be wrong to speak of a rediscovery of
the civil law. That system had never perished from Gaul and Italy, had been the groundwork of
some codes, and the whole substance, modified only by
the changes in society, of many others. The Church excepted, no agent did so much to keep alive the memory
of Roman institutions. The twelfth century now beheld
the study cultivated with a surprising increase of knowledge
and ardor, expended chiefly upon the Pandects. First
in Italy and the schools of the South, then in Paris and
Oxford, they were expounded, commented on, extolled as
the perfection of human wisdom, the sole, true and
eternal law. Vast as has been the labor and thought
expended from that time to this in the elucidation of the
civil law, the most competent authorities declare that in
acuteness, in subtlety, in all those branches of learning
which can subsist without help from historical criticism,
these so-called Glossatores have been seldom equalled
and never surpassed by their successors. The teachers
of the canon law, who had not as yet become the rivals of
the civilian, and were accustomed to recur to his books
where their own were silent, spread through Europe the
fame and influence of the Roman jurisprudence; while its
own professors were led both by their feeling and their interest to give to all its maxims the greatest weight and the
fullest application. Men just emerging from barbarism,
with minds unaccustomed to create and blindly submissive
to authority, viewed written texts with an awe to us incomprehensible. All that the most servile jurists of Rome
had ever ascribed to their despotic princes was directly
transferred to the Cæsarean majesty who inherited their

name. He was " Lord of the world," absolute master of
the lives and property of all his subjects, that is, of all
men; the sole fountain of legislation, the embodiment of
right and justice. These doctrines, which the great
Bolognese jurists, Bulgarus, Martinus, Hugolinus and
others who constantly surrounded Frederick, taught and
applied, as matter of course, to a Teutonic, a feudal king,
were by the rest of the world not denied, were accepted in
fervent faith by his German and Italian partisans. " To
the Emperor belongs the protection of the whole world,"
says Bishop Otto of Freysing. " The Emperor is a living
law upon earth."* To Frederick, atRoncaglia, the archbishop of Milan speaks for the assembled magnates of
Lombardy: " Do and ordain whatsoever thou wilt, thy will
is law; as it is written, ' Quicquid principi placuit legis
habet vigorem, cum populus ei et in eum omne suum imperium et potestatem concesserit.' "† The Hohenstaufen
himself was not slow to accept these magnificent ascrip-
tions of dignity, and though modestly professing his wish
to govern according to law rather than override the law,
was doubtless roused by them to a more vehement assertion of a prerogative so hallowed by age and by what seemed
a divine ordinance.

That assertion was most loudly called for in Italy. The
Emperors might appear to consider it a conquered country
Frederick in Italy. without privileges to be respected, for they
did not summon its princes to the German
diets, and overawed its own assemblies at Pavia
or Roncaglia by the Transalpine host that followed them.
Its crown, too, was theirs whenever they crossed the Alps
to claim it, while the elections on the banks of the Rhine
might be adorned but could not be influenced by the

---

* Document of 1230, quoted by Von Raumer, v. p. 81.
† Speech of archbishop of Milan, in Radewic; Mur., *S. R. I.*, vi.

presence of barons from the southern kingdom.* In practice, however, the imperial power stood lower in Italy than
in Germany, for it had been from the first intermittent,
depending on the personal vigor and present armed support of each invader. The theoretic sovereignty of the
Emperor-king was nowise disputed: in the cities toll and
tax were of right his : he could issue edicts at the Diet,
and require the tenants in chief to appear with their
vassals. But the revival of a control never exercised since
Henry IV's time, was felt as an intolerable hardship by
the great Lombard cities, proud of riches and population
equal to that of the duchies of Germany or the kingdoms
of the North, and accustomed for more than a century to
a turbulent independence. For republicanism and popular
freedom Frederick had little sympathy. At Rome the fervent Arnold of Brescia had repeated, but with far different
thoughts and hopes, the part of Crescentius.†
The city had thrown off the yoke of its bishop, *Rome under*
and a commonwealth under consuls and senate *Arnold of*
professed to emulate the spirit while it renewed *Brescia.*
the forms of the primitive republic. Its leaders had
written to Conrad III,‡ asking him to help them
to restore the Empire to its position under Constantine and Justinian ; but the German, warned by St.
Bernard, had preferred the friendship of the Pope. Filled
with a vain conceit of their own importance, they repeated
their offers to Frederick when he sought the crown from
Hadrian IV. A deputation, after dwelling in high-flown
language on the dignity of the Roman people, and their

---

* Frederick's election (at Frankfort) was made " non sine quibus-
dam Italiæ baronibus."—Otto Fris. i. But this was the exception.

† See also *post*, Chapter XVI.

‡ "Senatus Populusque Romanus urbis et orbis totius domino
Conrado."

kindness in bestowing the scepter on him, a Swabian and
a stranger, proceeded, in a manner hardly consistent, to
demand a largess ere he should enter the city.   Frederick's
anger did not hear them to the end : " Is this your
Roman wisdom?   Who are ye that usurp the name of
Roman dignities?   Your honors and your authority are
yours no longer; with us are consuls, senate, soldiers.   It
was not you who chose us, but Charles and Otto that rescued you from the Greek and the Lombard, and conquered
by their own might the imperial crown.   That Frankish
might is still the same: wrench, if you can, the club from
Hercules.   It is not for the people to give laws to the
prince, but to obey his command."*   This was Frederick's
version of the " Translation of the Empire."†

He who had been so stern to his own capital was not
likely to deal more gently with the rebels of Milan and
Tortona.   In the contest by which Frederick is
chiefly known to history, he is commonly
painted as the foreign tyrant, the forerunner
of the Austrian oppressor,‡ crushing under the hoofs of
his cavalry the home of freedom and industry.   Such
a view is unjust to a great man and his cause.   To the
despot liberty is always license; yet Frederick was the
advocate of admitted claims; the aggressions of Milan
threatened her neighbors ; the refusal, where no actual
oppression was alleged, to admit his officers and allow his
regalian rights, seemed a wanton breach of oaths and en-

The Lom-
bard cities.

---

* Otto of Freysing.

† Later in his reign, Frederick condescended to negotiate with
these Roman magistrates against a hostile Pope, and entered into a
sort of treaty by which they were declared exempt from all jurisdiction but his own.

‡ See the first note to Shelley's *Hellas*.   Sismondi is mainly answerable for this conception of Barbarossa's position.

gagements, treason against God no less than himself.*
Nevertheless our sympathy must go with the cities, in
whose victory we recognize the triumph of freedom and
civilization. Their resistance was at first probably a mere
aversion to unused control, and to the enforcement of
imposts less offensive in former days than now, and by
long dereliction apparently obsolete.† Republican principles were not avowed, nor Italian nationality appealed
to. But the progress of the conflict developed new
motives and feelings, and gave them clearer notions of
what they fought for. As the Emperor's antagonist, the
Pope was their natural ally: he blessed their arms, and
called on the barons of Romagna and Tuscany for aid; he
made "The Church," ere long their watchword, and
helped them to conclude that league of mutual support by
means whereof the party of the Italian Guelfs was formed.
Another cry, too, began to be heard, hardly less inspiriting
than the last, the cry of freedom and municipal self-government—freedom little understood and terribly abused,
self-government which the cities who claimed it for themselves refused to their subject allies, yet both of them,
through their divine power of stimulating effort and quickening sympathy, as much nobler than the harsh and
sterile system of a feudal monarchy as the citizen of republican Athens rose above the slavish Asiatic or the brutal
Macedonian. Nor was the fact that Italians were resisting

---

* They say rebelliously, says Frederick, " Nolumus hunc regnare
super nos . . . at nos maluimus honestam mortem quam ut,"
etc.—Letter in Pertz, *M. G. H.*, legg. ii.

† " De tributo Cæsaris nemo cogitabat;
    Omnes erant Cæsares, nemo censum dabat;
    Civitas Ambrosii, velut Troia, stabat,
    Deos parum, homines minus formidabat."
Poems relating to the Emperor Frederick of Hohenstaufen, published
by Grimm.

a Transalpine invader without its effect; there was as yet
no distinct national feeling, for half Lombardy, towns as
well as rural nobles, fought under Frederick; but events
made the cause of liberty always more clearly the
cause of patriotism, and increased that fear and hate
of the Tedescan for which Italy has had such bitter
justification.

The Emperor was for a time successful : Tortona was
taken, Milan razed to the ground, her name apparently
lost: greater obstacles had been overcome, and
Temporary success of Frederick. a fuller authority was now exercised than in
the days of the Ottos or the Henrys. The
glories of the first Frankish conqueror were
triumphantly recalled, and Frederick was compared by his
admirers to the hero whose canonization he had procured
and whom he strove in all things to imitate.* " He was
esteemed," says one, " second only to Charles in piety and
justice." " We ordain this," says a decree: " Ut ad Caroli
imitationem ius ecclesiarum statum reipublicæ incolumen
et legum integritatem per totem imperium nostrum serva-
remus."† But the hold the name of Charles had on the
minds of the people, and the way in which he had become,
so to speak, an eponym of Empire, has better witnesses
than grave documents.   A rhyming poet sings:‡

> " Quanta sit potentia vel laus Friderici
> Cum sit patens omnibus, non est opus dici;
> Qui rebelles lancea fodiens ultrici
> Repræsentat Karolum dextera victrici."

The diet at Roncaglia was a chorus of gratulations over
the re-establishment of order by the destruction of the
dens of unruly burghers.

---

* Charles the Great was canonized by Frederick's anti-pope and
confirmed afterward.

† *Acta Concil. Hartzhem.* iii., quoted by Von Raumer, ii. 6.

‡ Poems relating to Frederick I, *ut supra.*

This fair sky was soon clouded. From her quenchless ashes uprose Milan ; Cremona, scorning old jealousies, helped to rebuild what she had destroyed, and the confederates, committed to an all but hope- *Victory of the Lombard* less strife, clung faithfully together till on the *League.* field of Legnano the Empire's banner went down before the carroccio * of the free city. Times were changed since Aistulf and Desiderius trembled at the distant tramp of the Frankish hosts. A new nation had arisen, slowly reared through suffering into strength, now at last by heroic deeds conscious of itself. The power of Charles had overleaped boundaries of nature and language that were too strong for his successor, and that grew henceforth ever firmer, till they made the Empire itself a delusive name. Frederick, though harsh in war, and now balked of his most cherished hopes, could honestly accept a state of things it was beyond his power to change : he signed cheerfully and kept dutifully the peace of Constance, which left him little but a titular supremacy over the Lombard towns.

At home no Emperor since Henry III had been so much respected and so generally prosperous. Uniting in his person the Saxon and Swabian families, he healed the long feud of Welf and Waiblingen: *Frederick* his prelates were faithful to him, even against *as German* Rome: no turbulent rebel disturbed the public *king.* peace. Germany was proud of a hero who maintained her dignity so well abroad, and he crowned a glorious life with a happy death, leading the van of Christian chivalry against the Mussulman. Frederick, the greatest of the Crusaders, is the noblest type of mediæval character in many of its shadows, in all its lights.

---

* The carroccio was a wagon with a flagstaff planted on it, which served the Lombards for a rallying-point in battle.

Legal in form, in practice sometimes almost absolute, the government of Germany was, like that of other feudal kingdoms, restrained chiefly by the difficulty of coercing refractory vassals. All depended on the monarch's character, and one so vigorous and popular as Frederick could generally lead the majority with him and terrify the rest. A false impression of the real strength of his prerogative might be formed from the readiness with which he was obeyed. He repaired the finances of the kingdom, controlled the dukes, introduced a more splendid ceremonial, endeavored to exalt the central power by multiplying the nobles of the second rank, afterward the "college of princes," and by trying to substitute the civil law and Lombard feudal code for the old Teutonic customs, different in every province. If not successful in this project, he fared better with another. Since Henry the Fowler's day towns had been growing up through Southern and Western Germany, especially where rivers offered facilities for trade. Cologne, Treves, Mentz, Worms, Speyer, Nürnberg, Ulm, Regensburg, Augsburg, were already considerable cities, not afraid to beard their lord or their bishop, and promising before long to counterbalance the power of the territorial oligarchy. Policy or instinct led Frederick to attach them to the throne, enfranchising many, granting, with municipal institutions, an independent jurisdiction, conferring various exemptions and privileges; while receiving in turn their good-will and loyal aid, in money always, in men when need should come. His immediate successors trod in his steps, and thus there arose in the state a third order, the firmest bulwark, had it been rightly used, of imperial authority; an order whose members, the Free Cities, were through many ages the centers of German intellect and freedom, the only haven from the storms of civil war, the

The German cities.

surest hope of future peace and union. In them* national congresses to this day sometimes meet: from them aspiring spirits strove to diffuse those ideas of Germanic unity and self-government, which they alone had kept alive. Out of so many flourishing commonwealths, four only were spared by foreign conquerors and faithless princes till the day came which made them again the members of a great and real German state. To the primitive order of German freemen, scarcely existing out of the towns, except in Swabia and Switzerland, Frederick further commended himself by allowing them to be admitted to knighthood, by restraining the license of the nobles, imposing a public peace, making justice in every way more accessible and impartial. To the south-west of the green plain that girdles in the rock of Salzburg, the gigantic mass of the Untersberg frowns over the road which winds up a long defile to the glen and lake of Berchtesgaden. There, far up among its limestone crags, in a spot scarcely accessible to human foot, the peasants of the valley point out to the traveler the black mouth of a cavern, and tell him that within Barbarossa lies amid his knights in an enchanted sleep,† waiting the hour when the ravens shall cease to hover round the peak, and the pear-tree blossom in the valley, to descend with his Crusaders and bring back to Germany the golden age of peace and strength and unity. Often in the evil days that followed the fall of Frederick's house, often when tyranny seemed unendurable and

---

* Lübeck, Hamburg, Bremen and Frankfort. [Since this was first written Frankfort has been annexed by Prussia, and her three surviving sisters have, by their entrance first into the North German confederation, now into the German Empire, lost something of their independence.]

† The legend is one which appears under various forms in many countries.

anarchy endless, men thought on that cavern, and sighed for the day when the long sleep of the just Emperor should be broken, and his shield be hung aloft again as of old in the camp's midst, a sign of help to the poor and the oppressed.

CHAPTER XII.

IMPERIAL TITLES AND PRETENSIONS.

THE era of the Hohenstaufen is perhaps the fittest point at which to turn aside from the narrative history of the Empire to speak shortly of the legal position which it professed to hold to the rest of Europe, as well as of certain duties and observances which throw a light upon the system it embodied. This is not indeed the era of its greatest power: that was already past. Nor is it conspicuously the era when its ideal dignity stood highest; for that remained scarcely impaired till three centuries had passed away. But it was under the Hohenstaufen, owing partly to the splendid abilities of the princes of that famous line, partly to the suddenly gained ascendancy of the Roman law, that the actual power and the theoretical influence of the Empire most fully coincided. There can therefore be no better opportunity for noticing the titles and claims by which it announced itself the representative of Rome's universal dominion, and for collecting the various instances in which they were (either before or after Frederick's time) more or less admitted by the other states of Europe.

The territories over which Barbarossa would have declared his jurisdiction to extend may be classed under four heads:

First, the German lands, in which, and in which alone, the Emperor was, up till the death of Frederick II, effective sovereign.

Second, the non-German districts of the Holy Empire,

where the Emperor was acknowledged as sole monarch, but in practice little regarded.

Third, certain outlying countries, owing allegiance to the Empire, but governed by kings of their own.

Fourth, the other states of Europe, whose rulers, while in most cases admitting the superior rank of the Emperor, were virtually independent of him.

Thus within the actual boundaries of the Holy Empire were included only districts coming under the first and second of the above classes, *i.e.*, Germany, the *Limits of the Empire.* northern half of Italy, and the kingdom of Burgundy or Arles—that is to say, Provence, Dauphiné, the Free County of Burgundy (Franche Comté) and Western Switzerland. Lorraine, Alsace and a portion of Flanders were, of course, parts of Germany. To the north-east, Bohemia and the Slavic principalities in Mecklenburg and Pomerania were as yet not integral parts of its body, but rather dependent outliers. Beyond the march of Brandenburg, from the Oder to the Vistula, dwelt pagan Lithuanians or Prussians,* free till the establishment among them of the Teutonic knights.

Hungary had owed a doubtful allegiance since the days of Otto I. Gregory VII had claimed it as a fief of the *Hungary.* Holy See; Frederick wished to reduce it completely to subjection, but could not overcome the reluctance of his nobles. After Frederick II, by whom it was recovered from the Mongol hordes, no imperial claims were made for so many years that at last they became obsolete, and were confessed to be so by the constitution of Augsburg, A.D. 1566.†

---

* "Pruzzi," says the biographer of St. Adalbert, "quorum Deus est venter et avaritia iuncta cum morte."—*M. G. H.* t. iv. It is curious that this non-Teutonic people should have given their name to the great German kingdom of the present.

† Conring, *De Finibus Imperii.* It is hardly necessary to observe

Under Duke Misico, Poland had submitted to Otto the Great, and continued, with occasional revolts, to obey the Empire, till the beginning of the Great Interregnum (as it is called) in 1254. Its duke was *Poland.* present at the election of Richard, A.D. 1257. Thereafter, in 1295, Duke Primislas had himself crowned king in token of emancipation (for the title of king which Otto III had granted to Boleslas I had become disused) and the country became independent, though some of its provinces were long afterward reunited to the German state. Silesia, originally Polish, was attached to Bohemia by Charles IV, and so became part of the Empire; Posen and Galicia were seized by Prussia and Austria, A.D. 1772.* Down to her partition in that year, the constitution of Poland remained a copy of that which had existed in the German kingdom in the twelfth century.

Lewis the Pious had received the homage of the Danish King Harold, on his baptism at Mentz, A.D. 826; Otto the Great's victories over Harold Blue Tooth made the country regularly subject, and added *Denmark.* the march of Schleswig to the immediate territory of the Empire: but the boundary soon receded to the Eyder, on whose banks might be seen the inscription:

" Eidora Romani terminus imperii."

King Peter † attended at the Diet held at Merseburg shortly after Frederick I's coronation, and received from

---

that the connection of Hungary with the Hapsburgs is of comparatively recent origin, and of a purely dynastic nature. The position of the archdukes of Austria as kings of Hungary had nothing to do legally with the fact that many of them were also chosen Emperors, although practically their possession of the imperial crown had greatly aided them in grasping and retaining the thrones of Hungary and Bohemia.

* They however remained extra-imperial.

† Letter of Frederick I to Otto of Freysing, prefixed to the latter's History. The king is also called Svend.

the Emperor, who as suzerain had been required to decide
a disputed question of succession to the Danish throne,
his own crown ; he did homage, and bore the sword before
the Emperor.   Since the Interregnum Denmark has been
always free.*

Otto the Great was the last Emperor whose suzerainty
the French kings had admitted ; nor were Henry VI and
Otto IV successful in their attempts to enforce it.

France.   Boniface VIII, in his quarrel with Philip the
Fair, offered the French throne, which he had pronounced
vacant, to Albert I ; but the wary Hapsburg declined the
dangerous prize.   The precedence, however, which the
Germans continued to assert, irritated Gallic pride, and
led to more than one contest.   Blondel denies the Empire
any claim to the Roman name ; and in A.D. 1648 the
French envoys at Münster refused for some time to admit
what no other European state disputed.   Till recent times
the title of the Archbishop of Treves, "Archicancellarius
per Galliam atque regnum Arelatense," preserved the
memory of an obsolete supremacy which the constant aggressions of France might seem to have reversed.

No reliance can be placed on the author who tells us
that Sweden was granted by Frederick I to Waldemar the
Dane; †   the fact is improbable, and we do not

Sweden.   hear that such pretensions were ever put forth
before or after.   Norway, too, seems to have been left untouched—the Emperors had no fleets—and Iceland, which
had remained undiscovered ‡ till long after the days of
Charles, was down till the year 1262 the only absolutely
free Republic in the world.

---

* See Appendix, Note B.

† Albertus Stadensis apud Conringium, *De Finibus Imperii.*

‡ The Irish however are said to have occasionally visited it; and
some few Irish hermits appear to have been found there by the
Norwegian colonists in 874.

Nor does it appear that authority was ever exercised by any Emperor in Spain. Nevertheless the choice of Alfonso X by a section of the German electors, in A.D. 1258, may be construed to imply that the *Spain.* Spanish kings were members of the Empire. And when, A.D. 1053, Ferdinand the Great of Castile had, in the pride of his victories over the Moors, assumed the title of "Hispaniæ Imperator," the remonstrance of Henry III declared the rights of Rome over the Western provinces indelible, and the Spaniard, though protesting his independence, was forced to resign the usurped dignity.*

No act of sovereignty is recorded to have been done by any of the Emperors in England, though as heirs of Rome they might be thought to have better rights over it than over Poland or Denmark.† There *England.* was, however, a vague notion that the English, like other kingdoms, must depend on the Empire: a notion which appears in Conrad III's letter to John of Constantinople;‡ and which was countenanced by the submissive tone in which Frederick I was addressed by the Plantagenet Henry

---

* There is an allusion to this in the poems of the Cid. Arthur Duck, *De Usu et Authoritate Iuris Civilis*, quotes the view of some among the older jurists, that Spain having been, as far as the Romans were concerned, a *res derelicta*, recovered by the Spaniards themselves from the Moors, and thus acquired by *occupatio*, ought not to be subject to the Emperors.

† One of the greatest of English kings appears performing an act of courtesy to the Emperor which was probably construed into an acknowledgment of his own inferior position. Describing the Roman coronation of the Emperor Conrad II, Wippo (c. 16), tells us, "His ita peractis in duorum regum præsentia Rudolfi regis Burgundiæ et Chnutonis regis Anglorum divino officio finito imperator duorum regum medius ad cubiculum suum honorifice ductus est."

‡ Letter in Otto Fris. i.: "Nobis submittuntur Francia et Hispania, Anglia et Dania."

II.*   English independence was still more compromised
in the next reign, when Richard I, according to Hoveden,
" Consilio matris suæ deposuit se de regno Angliæ et tradidit illud imperatori (Henrico VI) sicut universorum
domino." But as Richard was at the same time invested
with the kingdom of Arles by Henry VI, his homage may
have been for that fief only ; and it was probably in that
capacity that he voted, as a prince of the Empire, at the
election of Frederick II.   The case finds a parallel in the
claims of England over the Scottish king, doubtful, to say
the least, as regards the domestic realm of the latter, certain as regards Cumbria, which he had long held from the
Southern Crown.†   But Germany had no Edward I.
Henry VI is said at his death to have released Richard
from his submission (this too may be compared with Richard's release to the Scottish William the Lion), and Edward II declared, "regnum Angliæ ab omni subiectione
imperiali esse liberrimum." ‡   Yet the idea survived: the
Emperor Lewis the Bavarian, when he named Edward
III his vicar in the great French war, demanded, though
in vain, that the English monarch should kiss his feet.§
Sigismund,‖ visiting Henry V at London, before the meeting of the council of Constance, was met by the Duke of
Gloucester, who, riding into the water to the ship where

---

* Letter in Radewic says, " Regnum nostrum vobis exponimus.
. . . . Vobis imperandi cedat auctoritas, no bis non deeritvoluntas
obsequendi."

† The alleged instances of homage by the Scots to the Saxon and
early Norman kings are almost all complicated in some such way. They
had once held also the earldom of Huntingdon from the English
crown, and some have supposed (but on no sufficient grounds) that
homage was also done by them for Lothian.

‡ Selden, *Titles of Honor*, part i. chap. ii.

§ Edward refused upon the ground that he was " *rex inunctus*."

‖ Sigismund had shortly before given great offence in France by
dubbing knights.

the Emperor sat, required him, at the sword's point, to declare that he did not come purposing to infringe on the king's authority in the realm of England.* One curious pretension of the imperial crown called forth many protests. It was declared by civilians and canonists that no notary public could have any standing, or attach any legality to the documents he drew, unless he had received his diploma from the Emperor or the Pope. A strenuous denial of a doctrine so injurious was issued by the parliament of Scotland under James III. †

The kingdom of Naples and Sicily, although of course claimed as a part of the Empire, was under the Norman dynasty (A.D. 1060–1189) not merely independent, but the most dangerous enemy of the German power in Italy. Henry VI, the son and successor of Barbarossa, obtained possession of it by marrying Constantia the last heiress of the Norman kings. But both he and Frederick II treated it as a separate patrimonial state, instead of incorporating it with their more northerly dominions. After the death of Conradin, the last of the Hohenstaufen, it passed away to an Angevin, then to an Arragonese dynasty, continuing under both to maintain itself independent of the Empire, nor ever again, except under Charles V, united to the Germanic crown. *Naples.*

One spot in Italy there was whose singular felicity of situation enabled her through long centuries of obscurity and weakness, slowly ripening into strength, to maintain her freedom unstained by any submission to the Frankish and Germanic Emperors. Venice glories in deducing her origin from the fugitives who *Venice.*

---

* Sigismund answered, " Nihil se contra superioritatem regis prætexere."

† Selden, *Titles of Honor*, part. i. chap. ii. Nevertheless, notaries in Scotland, as elsewhere, continued for a long time to style themselves " Ego M. auctoritate imperiali (or papali) notarius."

escaped from Aquileia in the days of Attila: it is at least probable that her population never received an intermixture of Teutonic settlers, and continued during the ages of Lombard and Frankish rule in Italy to regard the Byzantine sovereigns as the representatives of their ancient masters. In the tenth century, when summoned to submit to Otto II, they had said, " We wish to be the servants of the Emperors of the Romans " (the Constantinopolitan), and though they overthrew this very Eastern throne in A.D. 1204, the pretext had served its turn, and had aided them in defying or evading the demands of obedience made by the Teutonic princes. Alone of all the Italian republics, Venice never, down to her extinction by France and Austria in A.D. 1796, recognized within her walls any secular Western authority save her own.

The kings of Cyprus and Armenia sent to Henry VI to confess themselves his vassals and ask his help. Over *The East.* remote Eastern lands, where Frankish foot had never trod, Frederick Barbarossa asserted the indestructible rights of Rome, mistress of the world. A letter to Saladin, amusing from its absolute identification of his own Empire with that which had sent Crassus to perish in Parthia, and had blushed to see Mark Antony " consulum nostrum "* at the feet of Cleopatra, is preserved by Hoveden: it bids the Soldan withdraw at once from the dominions of Rome, else will she, with her new Teutonic defenders, of whom a pompous list follows, drive him from them with all her ancient might.

---

* It is not necessary to prove this letter to have been the composition of Frederick or his ministers. If it be (as it doubtless is) contemporary, it is equally to the purpose as an evidence of the feelings and ideas of the age. As a reviewer of a former edition of this book has questioned its authenticity, I may mention that it is to be found not only in Hoveden, but also in the " Itinerarium regis Ricardi," in Ralph de Diceto, and in the " Chronicon Terrae Sanctae." [See Mr. Stubbs' edition of Hoveden, vol. ii. p. 356.]

Unwilling as were the great kingdoms of Western Europe to admit the territorial supremacy of the Emperor, the proudest among them never refused, until the end of the Middle Ages, to recognize his precedence and address him in a tone of respectful deference. *The Byzantine Emperors.* Very different was the attitude of the Byzantine princes, who denied his claim to be an Emperor at all. The separate existence of the Eastern Church and Empire was not only, as has been said above, a blemish in the title of the Teutonic sovereigns; it was a continuing and successful protest against the whole system of an Empire Church of Christendom, centering in Rome, ruled by the successor of Peter and the successor of Augustus. Instead of the one Pope and one Emperor whom mediæval theory presented as the sole earthly representatives of the invisible head of the Church, the world saw itself distracted by the interminable feud of rivals, each of whom had much to allege on his behalf. It was easy for the Latins to call the Easterns schismatics and their Emperor an usurper, but practically it was impossible to dethrone him or reduce them to obedience: while even in controversy no one could treat the pretensions of communities, who had been the first to embrace Christianity and retained so many of its most ancient forms, with the contempt which would have been felt for any Western sectaries. Seriously, however, as the hostile position of the Easterns seems to us to affect the claims of the Teutonic Empire, calling in question its legitimacy and marring its pretended universality, those who lived at the time seem to have troubled themselves little about it, finding themselves in practice seldom confronted by the difficulties it raised. The great mass of the people knew of the Easterns not even by name; of those who did, the most thought of them only as perverse rebels, Samaritans who refused to worship at Jerusalem, and were little better than infidels. The few ecclesiastics of superior knowledge and insight had their minds preoccupied by the established theory, and accepted it with too intense a belief to suffer anything else to come into collision with it : they do not seem to have even apprehended all that was involved in this one defect. Nor, what is still stranger, in all the attacks made upon the claims of the Teutonic Empire, whether by its Papal or its French antagonists, do we find the rival title of the Byzantine sovereigns adduced in argument against it. Nevertheless, the Eastern Church was then, as she is to this day, a thorn in the side of Papacy; and the Eastern Emperors, so far from uniting for the good of Christendom with their Western breth-

Rivalry of the two Empires. ren, felt toward them a bitter though not unnatural jealousy, lost no opportunity of intriguing for their evil, and never ceased to deny their right to the imperial name. The coronation of Charles was in their eyes an act of unholy rebellion; his successors were barbarian intruders, ignorant of the laws and usages of the ancient state, and with no claim to the Roman name except that which the favor of an insolent pontiff might confer. The Easterns had themselves long since ceased to use the Latin tongue, and were indeed become more than half Orientals in character and manners. But they still continued to call themselves Romans, and preserved most of the titles and ceremonies which had existed in the time of Constantine or Justinian. They were weak, although by no means so weak as modern historians have been till lately wont to paint them, and the weaker they grew the higher rose their conceit, and the more did they plume themselves upon the uninterrupted legitimacy of their crown, and the ceremonial splendor wherewith custom had surrounded its wearer. It gratified their spite to pervert insultingly the titles of Frankish princes. Basil the Macedonian reproached Lewis II with presuming to

use the name of " Basileus," to which Lewis retorted that
he was as good an emperor as Basil himself, but that,
anyhow, *Basileus* was only the Greek for *rex*, and need
not mean "Emperor" at all. Nicephorus would not call
Otto I anything but " King of the Lombards,"* Conrad
III was addressed by Calo-Johannes as "amice imperii
mei Rex ;"† Isaac Angelus had the impudence to style
Frederick I "chief prince of Alemannia."‡ The great

---

* Liutprand, *Legatio Constantinopolitana*, Nicephorus says, " Vis
maius scandalum quam quod se imperatorem vocat."

† Otto of Freysing, i. c. 30.

‡ " Isaachius a Deo constitutus Imperator, sacratissimus, excellen-
tissimus, potentissimus, moderator Romanorum, Angelus totius orbis,
heres coronæ magni Constantini, dilecto fratri imperii sui, maximo
principi Alemanniæ." A remarkable speech of Frederick's to the
envoys of Isaac, who had addressed a letter to him as " Rex Alemaniæ," is preserved by Ansbert (*Historia de Expeditione Friderici
Imperatoris*): " Dominus Imperator divina se illustrante gratia
ulterius dissimulare non valens temerarium fastum regis (*sc.* Græcorum) et usurpantem vocabulum falsi imperatoris Romanorum, hæc
inter cætera exorsus est: ' Omnibus qui sanæ mentis sunt constat,
quia unus est Monarchus Imperator Romanorum, sicut et unus est
pater universitatis, pontifex videlicet Romanus ; ideoque cum ego
Romani imperii sceptrum plusquam per annos XXX absque omnium
regum vel principum contradictione tranquille tenuerim et in Romana
urbe a summo pontifice imperiali benedictione unctus sim et subli-
matus, quia denique Monarchiam prædecessores mei imperatores
Romanorum plusquam per CCCC annos etiam gloriose transmiserint
utpote a Constantinopolitana urbe ad pristinam sedem imperii, caput
orbis Romam, acclamatione Romanorum et principum imperii, auctoritate quoque summi pontificis et S. catholicæ ecclesiæ translatam,
propter tardum et infructuosum Constantinopolitani imperatoris
auxilium contra tyrannos ecclesiæ, mirandum est admodum cur frater
meus dominus vester Constantinopolitanus imperator usurpet inef-
ficax sibi idem vocabulum et glorietur stulte alieno sibi prorsus
honore, cum liquido noverit me et nomine dici et re esse Fridericum
Romanorum · imperatorem semper Augustum.' " Isaac was so far
moved by Frederick's indignation that in his next letter he addressed
him as " generosissimum imperatorem Alemaniæ," and in a third

Emperor, half-resentful, half-contemptuous, told the envoys that he was "Romanorum imperator," and bade the master call himself "Romaniorum" from his Thracian province. · Though these ebullitions were the most conclusive proof of their weakness, the Byzantine rulers sometimes planned the recovery of their former capital, and seemed not unlikely to succeed under the leadership of the conquering Manuel Comnenus. He invited Alexander III, then in the heat of his strife with Frederick, to return to the embrace of his rightful sovereign, but the prudent pontiff and his synod courteously declined.* The Byzantines were, however, too unstable and too much alieniated from Latin feeling to have held Rome, could they even have seduced her allegiance. A few years later they were themselves the victims of the French and Venetian crusaders.

Though Otto the Great and his successors had dropped all titles save the highest (the tedious lists of imperial dignities were happily not yet in being), they did not therefore endeavor to unite their several kingdoms, but continued to go through four distinct coronations at the four capitals of their Empire.† These are concisely given in the verses of Godfrey of Viterbo, a notary of Frederick's household:‡

Dignities and titles.

The four crowns.

"Primus Aquisgrani locus est, post hæc Arelati,
Inde Modoetiæ regali sede locari

---

thus : "Isaakius in Christo fidelis divinitus coronatus, sublimis, potens, excelsus, hæres coronæ magni Constantini et Moderator Romeon Angelus nobilissimo Imperatori antiquæ Romæ, regi Alemaniæ et dilecto fratri imperii sui, salutem," etc., etc. (Ansbert, *ut supra*).

* Baronius, ad ann.
† See Appendix, Note C.
‡ Godefr. Viterb., *Pantheon*, in Mur., *S. R. I.*, tom. vii.

Post solet Italiæ summa corona dari:
Cæsar Romano cum vult diademate fungi
Debet apostolicis manibus reverentur inungi."

By the crowning at Aachen, the old Frankish capital, the
monarch became "king;" formerly "king of the Franks,"
or, "king of the Eastern Franks;" now since Henry II's
time, "king of the Romans, always Augustus." At Monza
(or, more rarely, at Milan) in later times, at Pavia in earlier
times, he became king of Italy, or of the Lombards;* at
Rome he received the double crown of the Roman Empire,
"double," says Godfrey, as "urbis et orbis:"

"Hoc quicunque tenet, summus in orbe sedet ;"

though others hold that, uniting the miter to the crown,
it typifies spiritual as well as secular authority. The crown
of Burgundy† or the kingdom of Arles, first gained by
Conrad II, was a much less splendid matter, and carried
with it little effective power. Most Emperors never assumed
it at all, Frederick I not till late in life, when an interval
of leisure left him nothing better to do. These four
crowns‡ furnish matter of endless discussion to the old
writers ; they tell us that the Roman was golden, the
German silver, the Italian iron, the metal corresponding to
the dignity of each realm.§ Others say that that of Aachen

---

* Dönninges, *Deutsches Staatsrecht*, thinks that the crown of
Italy, neglected by the Ottos, and taken by Henry II, was a recognition of the separate nationality of Italy. But Otto I seems to have
been crowned king of Italy, and Muratori (*Ant. It.* Dissert. iii.)
believes that Otto II and Otto III were likewise.

† See Appendix, Note A.

‡ Some add a fifth crown, of Germany (making that of Aachen
Frankish), which they say belonged to Regensburg.—Marquardus
Freherus.

§ "Dy erste ist tho Aken: dar kronet men mit der Yseren Krone,
so is he Konig over alle Dudesche Ryke. Dy andere tho Meylan, de
is Sulvern, so is he Here der Walen. Dy drüdde is tho Rome; dy is
guldin, so is he Keyser over alle dy Werlt."—Gloss to the *Sachsenspiegel*, quoted by Pfeffinger. Similarly Peter de Andlo.

is iron, and the Italian silver, and give elaborate reasons why it should be so.* There seems to be no doubt that the allegory created the fact, and that all three crowns were of gold (or gilded silver), though in that of Italy there was and is inserted a piece of iron, a nail, it was believed, of the true Cross.

Why, it may well be asked, seeing that the Roman crown made the Emperor ruler of the whole habitable globe, was it thought necessary for him to add to it minor dignities which might be supposed to have been already included in this supreme one? The reason seems to be that the imperial office was conceived of as something different in kind from the regal, and as carrying with it not the immediate government of any particular kingdom, but a general suzerainty over and right of controlling all. Of this a pertinent illustration is afforded by an anecdote told of Frederick Barbarossa. Happening once to inquire of the famous jurists who surrounded him whether it was really true that he was "lord of the world," one of them simply assented, another, Bulgarus, answered, "Not as respects ownership." In this dictum, which is evidently comfortable to the philosophical theory of the Empire, we have a pointed distinction drawn between feudal sovereignty, which supposes the prince original owner of the soil of his whole kingdom, and imperial sovereignty which is irrespective of place, and exercised not over things but over men, as God's rational creatures. But the Emperor, as has been said already, was also the East Frankish king, uniting in himself, to use the legal phrase, two wholly distinct " per-

Meaning of the four coronations.

---

*Cf. Gewoldus, *De Septemviratu imperii Romani.* One would expect some ingenious allegorizer to have discovered that the crown of Burgundy must be, and therefore is, of copper or bronze, making the series complete, like the four ages of men in Hesiod. But I have not been able to find any such.

sons," and hence he might acquire more direct and practically useful rights over a portion of his dominions by being crowned king of that portion, just as a feudal monarch was often duke or count of lordships whereof he was already feudal superior; or, to take a better illustration, just as a bishop may hold livings in his own diocese. That the Emperors, while continuing to be crowned at Milan and Aachen, did not call themselves kings of the Lombards and of the Franks, was probably merely because these titles seemed insignificant compared to that of Roman Emperor.

In this supreme title, as has been said, all lesser honors were blent and lost, but custom or prejudice forbade the German king to assume it till actually crowned at Rome by the Pope.* Matters of phrase and *"Emperor"* title are never unimportant, least of all in an *not assumed* age ignorant and superstitiously antiquarian: *till the* and this restriction had the most important *Roman* consequences. The first barbarian kings had *coronation.* been tribe-chiefs ; and when they claimed a dominion which was universal, yet in a sense territorial, they could not separate their title from the spot which it was their boast to possess, and by virtue of whose name they ruled. "Rome," says the biographer of St. Adalbert, "seeing that she both is and is called the head of the world and the mistress of cities, is alone able to give to kings imperial power, and since she cherishes in her bosom the body of the Prince of the Apostles, she ought of right to appoint

---

* Hence the numbers attached to the names of the Emperors are often different in German and Italian writers, the latter not reckoning Henry the Fowler nor Conrad I. So Henry III (of Germany) calls himself "Imperator Henricus Secundus;" and all distinguish the years of their *regnum* from those of the *imperium.* Cardinal Baronius will not call Henry V anything but Henry III, not recognizing Henry IV's coronation, because it was performed by an anti-pope.

the Prince of the whole earth."* The crown was therefore too sacred to be conferred by any one but the supreme
Origin and results of this practice. Pontiff, or in any city less august than the
ancient capital. Had it become hereditary in
any family, Lothar I's, for instance, or Otto's,
this feeling might have worn off; as it was,
each successive transfer to a new dynasty, to Guido,
to Otto, to Henry II, to Conrad the Salic, strengthened it. The force of custom, tradition, precedent, is in-
calculable, when checked neither by written rules nor free
discussion. What sheer assertion will do is shown by the
success of a forgery so gross as the Isidorian decretals. No
arguments are needed to discredit the alleged decree of
Pope Benedict VIII,† which prohibited the German prince
from taking the name or office of Emperor till approved
and consecrated by the Pontiff, but a doctrine so favorable to papal pretensions was sure not to want advocacy;
Hadrian IV proclaims it in the broadest terms, and
through the efforts of the clergy and the spell of reverence in the Teutonic princes, it passed into an unquestioned belief.‡ That none ventured to use the title till
the Pope conferred it, made it seem in some manner to

---

* Life of S. Adalbert (written at Rome early in the eleventh century, probably by a brother of the monastery of SS. Boniface and
Alexius) in Pertz, *M. G. H.* iv.

† Given by Glaber Rudolphus. It is on the face of it a most im-
pudent forgery: "Ne quisquam audacter Romani Imperii sceptrum
præpostere gestare princeps appetat neve Imperator dici aut esse
valeat nisi quem Papa Romanus morum probitate aptum elegerit,
eique commiserit insigne imperiale."

‡ The *Sachsenspiegel* says, "Die düdeschen solen durch recht den
koning kiesen. Svenne die gewiet wert von den bischopen die dar
to gesat sin, unde uppe den stul to Aken kumt, so hevet he koning-
like walt unde koningliken namen. Svenne yn die paues wiet, so
heute he des rikes gewalt unde keiserliken namen."

depend on his will, enabled him to exact conditions from every candidate, and gave a color to his pretended suzerainty. Since by feudal theory every honor and estate is held from some superior, and since the divine commission has been without doubt issued directly to the Pope, must not the whole earth be his fief, and he the lord paramount, to whom even the Emperor is a vassal? This argument, which derived considerable plausibility from the rivalry between the Emperor and other monarchs, as compared with the universal and undisputed* authority of the Pope, was a favorite with the high sacerdotal party: first distinctly advanced by Hadrian IV, when he set up the picture† representing Lothar's homage, which had so irritated the followers of Barbarossa, though it had already been hinted at in Gregory VII's gift of the crown to Rudolf of Swabia, with the line,—

"Petra dedit Petro, Petrus diadema Rudolfo."

Nor was it only by putting him at the pontiff's mercy that this dependence of the imperial name on a coronation in the city injured the German sovereign.‡ With strange

---

* Universal and undisputed in the West, which, for practical purposes, meant the world. The denial of the supreme jurisdiction of Peter's chair by the Eastern churches affected very slightly the belief of Latin Christendom, just as the existence of a rival emperor at Constantinople with at least as good a legal title as the Teutonic Cæsar, was readily forgotten or ignored by the German and Italian subjects of the latter.

† Odious especially for the inscription:

"Rex venit ante fores nullo prius urbis honore;
Post homo fit Papæ, sumit quo dante coronam."—Radewic.

Another version of the first line is:

"Rex stetit ante fores iurans prius urbis honores."

‡ Mediæval history is full of instances of the superstitious venera-
tion attached to the rite of coronation (made by the Church almost a

inconsistency it was not pretended that the Emperor's rights were any narrower before he received the rite: he could summon synods, confirm papal elections, exercise jurisdiction over the citizens: his claim of the crown itself could not, at least till the times of the Gregorys and the Innocents, be positively denied. For no one thought of contesting the right of the German nation to the Empire, or the authority of the electoral princes, strangers though they were, to give Rome and Italy a master. The republican followers of Arnold of Brescia might murmur, but they could not dispute the truth of the proud lines in which the poet who sang the glories of Barbarossa,* describes the result of the conquest of Charles the Great:

> " Ex quo Romanum nostra virtute redemptum
> Hostibus expulsis, ad nos iustissimus ordo
> Transtulit imperium, Romani gloria regni
> Nos penes est.   Quemcunque sibi Germania regem
> Præficit, hunc dives summisso vertice Roma
> Suscipit, et verso Tiberim regit ordine Rhenus."

But the real strength of the Teutonic kingdom was

---

sacrament), and to the special places where, or even utensils with which it was performed.   Every one knows the importance in France of Rheims and its sacred *ampulla ;* so the Scottish king must be crowned at Scone, an old seat of Pictish royalty—Robert Bruce risked a great deal to receive his crown there; so no Hungarian coronation was valid unless made with the crown of St. Stephen; the possession whereof is still accounted so valuable by the Austrian court.   Great importance seems to have been attached to the imperial globe (Reichsapfel) which the Pope delivered to the Emperor at his coronation.

* Whether the poem which passes under the name of Gunther Ligurinus be his work or that of some scholar in a later age, Conrad Celtes as is commonly supposed, is for the present purpose indifferent. [At present (1886) the view prevails that the poem belongs to the age of Frederick, that " Ligurinus" is its title, and that the name of Gunther for the author is probably wrong.]

wasted in the pursuit of a glittering toy: once in his reign each Emperor undertook a long and dangerous expedition, and dissipated in an inglorious and ever to be repeated strife the forces that might have achieved conquest elsewhere, or made him feared and obeyed at home.

At this epoch appears another title, of which more must be said. To the accustomed "Roman Empire" Frederick Barbarossa adds the epithet of "Holy." Of its earlier origin, under Conrad II (the Salic), which some have supposed,* there is no documentary trace, though there is also no proof to the contrary.† So far as is known it occurs first in the famous Privilege of Austria, granted by Frederick in the fourth year of his reign, the second of his empire, "terram Austriæ quæ clypeus et cor sacri imperii esse dinoscitur;"‡ then afterward, in other manifestoes of his reign; for example, in a letter to Isaac Angelus of Byzantium,§ and in the summons to the princes to help him against Milan : "Quia . . . . urbis et orbis gubernacula tenemus . . . sacro imperio et divæ reipublicæ consulere debemus;"‖ where the second phrase is a synonym explanatory of the first. Used occasionally by Henry VI and Frederick II, it is more frequent under their successors, William, Richard, Rudolf, till after Charles IV's time it becomes habitual, for the last few centuries indispensable. Regarding the origin of so singular a title many theories

The title "Holy Empire."

---

* Zedler, *Universal Lexicon.* s. v. *Reich.*

† It does not occur before Frederick I's time in any of the documents printed by Pertz; and this is the date which Boeclerus also assigns in his treatise, *De Sacro Imperio Romano,* vindicating the terms "sacrum" and "Romanum" against the aspersions of Blondel

‡ Pertz, *M. G. H.,* tom. iv. (legum ii.)

§ Ibid. iv.

‖ Radewic, *ap.* Pertz.

have been advanced. Some declared it a perpetuation of
the court style of Rome and Byzantium, which attached
sanctity to the person of the monarch: thus David
Blondel, contending for the honor of France, calls it a
mere epithet of the Emperor, applied by confusion to
his government.* Others saw in it a religious meaning
referring to Daniel's prophecy, or to the fact that the
Empire was contemporary with Christianity, or to Christ's
birth under it.† Strong churchmen derived it from the
dependence of the imperial crown on the Pope. There
were not wanting persons to maintain that it meant nothing more than great or splendid. We need not, however,
be in any great doubt as to its true meaning and purport.
The ascription of sacredness to the person, the palace, the
letters and so forth, of the sovereign, so common in the
later ages of Rome, had been partly retained in the German
court. Liudprand calls Otto " imperator sanctissimus."‡
Still this sanctity, which the Greeks above all others
lavished on their princes, is something personal, is nothing more than the divinity that always hedges a king.
Far more intimate and peculiar was the relation of the
revived Roman Empire to the church and religion. As
has been said already, it was neither more nor less than the
visible Church, seen on its secular side, the Christian
society organized as a state under a form divinely appointed, and therefore the name " Holy Roman Empire"

---

* Blondellus adv. Chiffletium. Most of these theories are stated by
Boeclerus. Jordanes (*Chronica*) says, " Sacri imperii quod non est
dubium sancti Spiritus ordinatione, secundum qualitatem ipsam et
exigentiam meritorum humanorum disponi."

† Marquard Freher's notes to Peter de Andlo, book i. chap. vii.

‡ So in the song on the capture of the Emperor Lewis II by Adal-
gisus of Benevento, we find the words, " Ludhuicum comprenderunt
sancto, pio, Augusto." (Quoted by Gregorovius, *Geschichte der
Stadt Rom im Mittelalter*, iii. p. 185).

was the needful and rightful counterpart to that of " Holy Catholic Church." Such had long been the belief, and so the title might have had its origin as far back as the tenth or ninth century, might even have emanated from Charles himself. Alcuin in one of his letters uses the phrase " imperium Christianum." But there was a further reason for its introduction at this particular epoch. Ever since Hildebrand had claimed for the priesthood exclusive sanctity and supreme jurisdiction, the papal party had not ceased to speak of the civil power as being, compared with that of their own chief, merely secular, earthly, profane. It may be conjectured that to meet this reproach, no less injurious than insulting, Frederick or his advisers began to use in public documents the expression " Holy Empire;" thereby wishing to assert the divine institution and religious duties of the office he held. Previous Emperors had called themselves " Catholici," " Christiani," " ecclesiæ defensores;"* now their State itself is consecrated an earthly theocracy. " Deus Romanum imperium adversus schisma ecclesiæ præparavit,"† writes Frederick to the English Henry II. The theory was one which the best and greatest Emperors, Charles, Otto the Great, Henry III, had most striven to carry out; it continued to be zealously upheld when it had long ceased to be practicable. In the proclamations of mediæval kings there is a constant dwelling on their Divine commission. Power in an age of violence sought to justify while it enforced its commands, to make brute force less brutal by appeals to a higher sanction. This is seen nowhere more than in the style of the German sovereigns: they delight in the phrases " maiestas sacrosancta,"‡ " imperator divina ordinante providentia,"

---

* Goldast, *Constitutiones.*

† Pertz, *M. G. H.*, legg. ii.

‡ "Apostolic majesty" was the proper title of the king of Hungary. The Austrian court has recently revived it.

"divina pietate," "per misericordiam Dei;" many of which were preserved till, like those used now by other European kings, like our own "Defender of the Faith," they had become at last more grotesque than solemn. The free-thinking Emperor Joseph II, at the end of the eighteenth century, was "Advocate of the Christian Church," "Vicar of Christ," "Imperial head of the faithful," "Leader of the Christian army," "Protector of Palestine, of general councils, of the Catholic faith."*

The title, if it added little to the power, yet certainly seems to have increased the dignity of the Empire, and by consequence the jealousy of other states, of France especially. This did not, however, go so far as to prevent its recognition by the Pope and the French king,† and after the sixteenth century it would have been a breach of diplomatic courtesy to omit it. Nor have imitators been wanting : witness such titles as "Most Christian king." "Catholic king," "Defender of the Faith." ‡

* Moser, *Römische Kayser.*

† Urban IV used the title in 1259; Francis I (of France) calls the Empire " sacrosanctum."

‡ One may compare " Holy Russia." It is almost superfluous to observe that the beginning of the title "Holy" has nothing to do with the beginning of the Empire itself. Essentially and substantially, the Holy Roman Empire was, as has been shown already, the creation of Charles the Great. Looking at it more technically, as the monarchy, not of the whole West, like that of Charles, but of Germany and Italy, with a claim, which was never more than a claim, to universal sovereignty, its beginning is fixed by most of the German writers, whose practice has been followed in the text, at the coronation of Otto the Great. But the title was at least one, and probably two centuries later.

Note.—An interesting illustration of the power of the imperial idea in a country where one would have least looked for it, a country almost wholly cut off, during the earlier middle age, from the ecclesiastical as well as the political influences of the European continent, has been supplied me by the kindness of Sir Henry Maine. In Ireland, before the English Conquest, the custom was for a chieftain or magnate, who seemed to have usually a superfluity of cattle, to give them out among his dependants to be pastured; and thus the expression "to receive stock" from any one comes to denote the owning of a subordinate or vassal position, similar to that of the feudal tenant who receives land as a *beneficium* from his lord. Now the Brehon law, after showing how the inferior princes of the island may receive stock from the King of Erin—the suzerain of the whole island, who, however, even when he existed, had little more than a titular authority—goes on to say, "When the King of Erin is without opposition (i. e. when he holds Dublin, Waterford and Limerick, which were usually in the hands of Norsemen or Danes), he receives stock from the King of the Romans," i. e. the Emperor. And the commentary adds that sometimes it is the successor of Patrick who gives stock to the King of Erin, thereby setting the primate of Ireland in the position beside the Emperor which continental theory assigned to the Pope.

CHAPTER XIII.

FALL OF THE HOHENSTAUFEN.

IN THE three preceding chapters the Holy Empire has been described in what is not only the most brilliant but the most momentous period of its history; the period of its rivalry with the Popedom for the chief place in Christendom. For it was mainly through their relations with the spiritual power, by their friendship and protection at first, no less than by their subsequent hostility, that the Teutonic Emperors influenced the development of European politics. The reform of the Roman Church which went on during the reigns of Otto I and his successors down to Henry III, and which was chiefly due to the efforts of those monarchs, was the true beginning of the grand period of the Middle Ages, the first of that long series of movements, changes and creations in the ecclesiastical system of Europe which was, so to speak, the master current of history, secular as well as religious, during the centuries which followed. The first result of Henry III's purification of the Papacy was seen in Hildebrand's attempt to subject all jurisdiction to that of his own chair, and in the long struggle of the Investitures, which brought out into clear light the opposing pretensions of the temporal and spiritual powers. Although destined in the end to bear far other fruit, the immediate effect of this struggle was to evoke in all classes an intense religious feeling; and, in opening up new fields of ambition to the hierarchy, to stimulate wonderfully their

power of political organization. It was this impulse that
gave birth to the Crusades, and that enabled the Popes,
stepping forth as the rightful leaders of a religious war, to
bend it to serve their own ends : it was thus too that
they struck the alliance — strange as such alliance seems
now — with the rebellious cities of Lombardy, and
proclaimed themselves the protectors of municipal freedom. But the third and crowning triumph of the
Holy See was reserved for the thirteenth century. In
the foundation of the two great orders of ecclesiastical
knighthood, the all-powerful, all-pervading Dominicans
and Franciscans, the religious fervor of the Middle Ages
culminated : in the overthrow of the only power which
could pretend to vie with her in antiquity, in sanctity, in
universality, the Papacy saw herself exalted to rule alone
over the kings of the earth. Of that overthrow, following
with terrible suddenness on the days of strength and glory
which we have just been witnessing, this chapter has now
to speak.

It happened strangely enough that just while their ruin
was preparing, the house of Swabia gained over their ecclesiastical foes what seemed likely to prove an advantage
of the first moment. The son and successor of Barbarossa
was Henry VI, a man who had inherited all his father's
harshness with none of his father's generosity. By his
marriage with Constance, the heiress of the Norman
kings, he had become master of Naples and
Sicily. Emboldened by the possession of what *Henry VI,*
had been hitherto the stronghold of his prede- *1190-*
cessors' bitterest enemies, and able to threaten *1197.*
the Pope from south as well as north, Henry conceived a
scheme which might have wonderfully changed the history
of Germany and Italy. He proposed to the Teutonic
magnates to lighten their burdens by uniting these newly
acquired countries to the Empire, to turn their feudal

lands into allodial, and to make no further demands for
money on the clergy, on condition that they should pronounce the crown hereditary in his family.   Results of the
highest importance would have followed this change,
which Henry advocated by setting forth the perils of interregna, and which he doubtless meant to be but part of
an entirely new system of polity.   Already so strong in
Germany, and with an absolute command of their new
kingdom, the Hohenstaufen might have dispensed with
the renounced feudal services, and built up a firm centralized system, like that which was already beginning to
develop itself in France.   First, however, the Saxon
princes, then some ecclesiastics headed by Conrad of
Mentz, opposed the scheme; the pontiff retracted his consent, and Henry had to content himself with getting his
infant son Frederick II chosen king of the Romans.   On
Henry's untimely death the election was set aside, and the
contest which followed between Otto of Brunswick and

*Philip,
1198–
1208.*

Philip of Hohenstaufen, brother of Henry VI,
gave the Popedom, now guided by the genius
of Innocent III, an opportunity of extending
its sway at the expense of its antagonist.   The
Pope moved heaven and earth on behalf of Otto, whose

*Innocent
III and
Otto IV.*

family had been the constant rivals of the
Hohenstaufen, and who was himself willing to
promise all that Innocent required; but Philip's
personal merits and the vast possessions of his
house gave him while he lived the ascendancy in Germany.
His death by the hand of an assassin, while it seemed to
vindicate the Pope's choice, left the Swabian party without a head, and the Papal nominee was soon recognized
over the whole Empire.   But Otto IV became less submissive as he felt his throne more secure.   If he was
a Guelf by birth, his acts in Italy, whither he had gone
to receive the imperial crown, were those of a Ghibe-

line, anxious to reclaim the rights he had but just forsworn. The Roman Church at last deposed and excommunicated her ungrateful son, and *Otto IV,* Innocent rejoiced in a second successful asser- *1208 (1198)* tion of pontifical supremacy, when Otto was de- *1212.* throned by the youthful Frederick II whom a tragic irony sent into the field of politics as the champion of the Holy See, whose hatred was to embitter his life and extinguish his house.

Upon the events of that terrific strife, for which Emperor and Pope girded themselves up for the last time, the narrative of Frederick II's career, with its romantic adventures, its sad picture of mar- *Frederick* velous powers lost on an age not ripe for *II, 1212-* them, blasted as by a curse in the moment of *1250.* victory, it is not necessary, were it even possible, here to enlarge. That conflict did indeed determine the fortunes of the German kingdom no less than of the republics of Italy, but it was upon Italian ground that it was fought out and it is to Italian history that its details belong. So too of Frederick himself. Out of the long array of the Germanic successors of Charles, he is, with Otto III, the only one who comes before us with a genius and a frame of character that are not those of a Northern or a Teuton.* There dwelt in him, it is true, all the energy and knightly valor of his father Henry and his grandfather Barbarossa. But along with these, and changing their direction, were other gifts, inherited perhaps from his Italian mother and fostered by his education among the orange-groves of

---

* I quote from the Liber Augustalis printed among Petrarch's works the following curious description of Frederick: " Fuit armorum strenus, linguarum peritus, rigorosus, luxuriosus, epicurus, nihil curans vel credens nisi temporale: fuit malleus Romanæ ecclesiæ." As Otto III has been called "mirabilia mundi," so Frederick II is often spoken of in his own time as " stupor mundi Fridericus."

Palermo—a love of luxury and beauty, an intellect refined, subtle, philosophical. Through the mist of calumny and fable it is but dimly that the truth of the man can be discerned, and the outlines that appear serve to quicken rather than appease the curiosity with which we regard one of the most extraordinary personages in history. A sensualist, yet also a warrior and a politician ; a profound lawgiver and an impassioned poet ; in his youth fired by crusading fervor, in later life persecuting heretics while himself accused of blasphemy and unbelief ; of winning manners and ardently beloved by his followers, but with the strain of more than one cruel deed upon his name, he was the marvel of his own generation, and succeeding ages looked back with awe, not unmingled with pity, upon the inscrutable figure of the last Emperor who had braved all the terrors of the Church and died beneath her ban, the last who had ruled from the sands of the ocean to the shores of the Sicilian sea. But while they pitied they condemned. The undying hatred of the Papacy threw round his memory a lurid light; him and him alone of all the imperial line, Dante, the worshiper of the Empire, must perforce deliver to the flames of hell.*

Placed as the Empire was, it was scarcely possible for its head not to be involved in war with the constantly aggressive Popedom—aggressive in her claims of territorial dominion in Italy as well as of ecclesiastical jurisdiction throughout the world. But it was Frederick's peculiar misfortune to have given the Popes a hold over him which they well knew how to use. In a moment of youthful enthusiasm he had taken the cross from the hands of an eloquent monk, and his delay to fulfill the vow was branded as impious neglect. Excommunicated by Gregory IX for

Struggle of Frederick with the Papacy.

---

* "Quà entro è lo secondo Federico." *Inferno*, canto x.

not going to Palestine, he went, and was excommunicated for going : having concluded an advantageous peace, he sailed for Italy, and was a third time excommunicated for returning. To Pope Gregory he was at last after a fashion reconciled, but with the accession of Innocent IV the flame burst out afresh. Upon the special pretexts which kindled the strife it is not worth while to descant: the real causes were always the same, and could only be removed by the submission of one or other combatant. Chief among them was Frederick's possession of Sicily. Now were seen the fruits which Barbarossa had stored up for his house when he gained for Henry his son the hand of the Norman heiress. Naples and Sicily had been for some two hundred years recognized as a fief of the Holy See, and the Pope, who felt himself in danger while encircled by the powers of his rival, was determined to use his advantage to the full and make it the means of extinguishing Imperial authority throughout Italy. But although the struggle was far more of a territorial and political one than that of the previous century had been, it reopened every former source of strife, and passed into a contest between the civil and the spiritual potentate. The old war-cries of Henry and Hildebrand, of Barbarossa and Alexander, roused again the unquenchable hatred of Italian factions; the pontiff asserted the transference of the Empire as a fief, and declared that the power of Peter, symbolized by the two keys, was temporal as well as spiritual : the Emperor appealed to law, to the indelible rights of Cæsar; and denounced his foe as the anti-christ of the New Testament, since it was God's second vicar whom he was resisting. The one scoffed at anathema, upbraided the avarice of the Church, and treated her soldiery, the friars, with a severity not seldom ferocious. The other solemnly deposed a rebellious and heretical prince, offered the imperial crown to Robert of France, to the heir of Denmark, to Hakon

the Norse king ; succeeded at last in raising up rivals in
Henry of Thuringia and William of Holland.   Yet
throughout it is less the Teutonic Emperor who is attacked
than the Sicilian king, the unbeliever and friend of
Mohammedans, the hereditary enemy of the Church, the
assailant of Lombard independence, whose success must
leave the Papacy defenceless.   And as it was from the
Sicilian kingdom that the strife chiefly arose, so was the
possession of the Sicilian kingdom a source rather of weakness than of strength, for it distracted Frederick's forces
and put him in the false position of a liegeman resisting
his lawful suzerain.   Truly, as the Greek proverb says,
the gifts of foes are no gifts, and bring no profit with them.
The Norman kings were more terrible in their death than
in their life: they had sometimes baffled the Teutonic
Emperor; their heritage destroyed him.

With Frederick fell the Empire.   From the ruin that
overwhelmed the greatest of its houses it emerged, living
Conrad IV, indeed, and destined to a long life, but so
1250-1254. shattered, crippled and degraded, that it could
never more be to Europe and to Germany what
it once had been.   In the last act of the tragedy were
joined the enemy who had now blighted its strength and
the rival who was destined to insult its weakness and at
last blot out its name.   The murder of Frederick's grandson Conradin—a hero whose youth and whose chivalry
might have moved the pity of any other foe—was approved,
if not suggested, by Pope Clement; it was done by the minions of Charles, of France.

The Lombard league had successfully resisted Frederick's armies and the more dangerous Ghibeline nobles:
Italy lost to their strong walls and swarming population
the Empire. made defeats in the open field hardly felt; and
now that South Italy too had passed away from
a German line—first to an Angevin, afterward to an Ara-

gonese dynasty—it was plain that the peninsula was irre-
trievably lost to the Emperors. Why, however, should
they not still be strong beyond the Alps? was their position
worse than that of England when Normandy and Aquitaine
no longer obeyed a Plantagenet? The force that had
enabled them to rule so widely would be all the greater in
a narrow sphere.

So indeed it might once have been, but now it was too
late. The German kingdom broke down beneath the
weight of the Roman Empire. To be univer-
sal sovereign Germany had sacrificed her own   *Decline of
political existence. The necessity which their   imperial
projects in Italy and disputes with the Pope   power in
laid the Emperors under of purchasing by con-   Germany.*
cessions the support of their own princes, the ease with
which in their absence the magnates could usurp, the
difficulty which the monarch returning found in resuming
the privileges of his crown, the temptation to revolt and
set up pretenders to the throne which the Holy See held
out, these were the causes whose steady action laid the
foundation of that territorial independence which rose into
a stable fabric at the era of the Great Interregnum.*
Frederick II had by two Pragmatic Sanctions, A.D. 1220
and 1232, granted, or rather confirmed, rights
already customary, such as to give the bishops   *The Great
and nobles legal sovereignty in their own towns   Interreg-
and territories, except when the Emperor   num.*
should be present; and thus his direct jurisdiction became
restricted to his narrowed domain, and to the cities immediately dependent on the crown. With so much less to do,
an Emperor became altogether a less necessary personage;
and hence the seven magnates of the realm, now by law or
custom sole electors, were in no haste to fill up the place
of Conrad IV, whom the supporters of his father Frederick

had acknowledged.   William of Holland was in the field,
Double elec- but rejected by the Swabian party : on his
tion of   death a new election was called for, and at last
Richard of   set on foot.   The archbishop of Cologne ad-
England   vised his brethren to choose some one rich
and Alfonso   enough to support the dignity, not strong
of Castile.   enough to be feared by the electors : both
requisites met in the Plantagenet Richard, earl of Cornwall, brother of the English Henry III.   He received three,
eventually four votes, came to Germany, and was crowned
at Aachen.   But three of the electors, finding that his
bribe to them was lower than to the others, seceded
in disgust, and chose Alfonso X of Castile,† who,
shrewder than his competitor, continued to watch
the stars at Toledo, enjoying the splendors of his
title while troubling himself about it no further than
to issue now and then a proclamation.   Meantime the
condition of Germany was frightful.   The new Didius
                Julianus, the chosen of princes baser than
State of   the prætorians whom they copied, had neither
Germany   the character nor the outward power and re-
during the   sources to make himself respected.   Every
Interreg-   flood-gate of anarchy was opened: prelates and
num.   barons extended their domains by war : robber-
knights infested the highways and the rivers : the misery
of the weak, the tyranny and violence of the strong, were
such as had not been seen for centuries.   Things were even
worse than under the Saxon and Franconian Emperors ;
for the pretty nobles who had then been in some measure
controlled by their dukes, were now, after the extinction

---

* The interregnum is by some reckoned as the two years before
Richard's election; by others, as the whole period from the death of
Frederick II, or that of his son Conrad IV, till Rudolf's accession
in 1273.

† Surnamed, from his scientific tastes, "the Wise."

of the great houses, left without any feudal superior. Only in the cities was shelter or peace to be found. Those of the Rhine had already leagued themselves for mutual defence, and maintained a struggle in the interests of commerce and order against universal brigandage. At last, when Richard had been some time dead, it was felt that such things could not go on forever : with no public law, and no courts of justice, an Emperor, the embodiment of legal government, was the only resource. The Pope himself, having now sufficiently improved the weakness of his enemy, found the disorganization of Germany beginning to tell upon his revenues, and threatened that if the electors did not appoint an Emperor, he would. Thus urged, they chose, in A.D. 1273, Rudolf, count of Hapsburg, founder of the house of Austria.*

Rudolph of Hapsburg, 1272–1292.

From this point there begins a new era. We have seen the Roman Empire revived in A.D. 800, by a prince whose vast dominions gave ground to his claim of universal monarchy: again erected in A.D. 962, on the narrower but firmer basis of the German kingdom. We have seen Otto the Great and his successors during the three following centuries, a line of monarchs of unrivaled vigor and abili-

Change in the position of the Empire.

---

* "Electores imperii ad indictum et mandatum domini papæ apud Franchenfurte super electione convienentes, comitem Rudolfum . . . in regem elegerunt."—Ann. S. Rudb. Salisb. ad ann. (Pertz, *M.G.H.* ix.) Hapsburg is a castle (built about A.D. 1020) in the Aargau on the banks of the Aar, and near the line of railway from Olten to Zürich, from a point on which a glimpse of it may be had. "Within the ancient walls of Vindonissa," says Gibbon, "the castle of Hapsburg, the abbey of Königsfelden, and the town of Brugg have successively arisen. The philosophic traveler may compare the monuments of Roman conquests, of feudal or Austrian tyranny, of monkish superstition, and of industrious freedom. If he be truly a philosopher. he will applaud the merit and happiness of his own time."

ties, strain every nerve to make good the pretensions of
their office against the rebels in Italy and the ecclesiastical power. These efforts had now failed signally and
hopelessly. Each successive Emperor had entered the
strife with resources scantier than his predecessors, each
had been more decisively vanquished by the Pope, the
cities, and the princes. The Roman Empire might, and
so far as its practical utility was concerned, ought now to
have been suffered to expire; nor could it have ended
more gloriously than with the last of the Hohenstaufen.
That it did not so expire, but lived on six hundred years
more, till it became a piece of antiquarianism hardly more
venerable than ridiculous—till, as Voltaire said, all that
could be said about it was that it was neither holy, nor
Roman, nor an empire—was owing partly indeed to the
belief, still unshaken, that it was a necessary part of the
world's order, yet chiefly to its connection, which was by
this time indissoluble, with the German kingdom. The
Germans had confounded the two characters of their sovereign so long, and had grown so fond of the style and pretensions of a dignity whose possession appeared to exalt
them above the other peoples of Europe, that it was now
too late for them to separate the local from the universal
monarch. If a German king was to be maintained at all,
he must be Roman Emperor; and a German king there
must still be. Deeply, nay, mortally wounded as the event
proved his power to have been by the disasters of the
Empire to which it had been linked, the time was by no
means come for its extinction. In the unsettled state of
society, and the conflict of innumerable petty potentates,
no force save feudalism was able to hold society together;
and its efficacy for that purpose depended, as the anarchy
of the recent interregnum showed, upon the presence of
the recognized feudal head.

That head, however, was no longer what he had been.

The relative position of Germany and France was now
exactly the reverse of that which they had
occupied two centuries earlier. Rudolf was as
conspicuously a weaker sovereign than Philip
III of France, as the Franconian Emperor
Henry III had been stronger than the Capetian
Philip I. In every other state of Europe the tendency of events had been to centralize the administration and increase the power of the monarch,
*Decline of
the regal
power in
Germany as
compared
with France
and Eng-
land.*
even in England, not to diminish it: in Germany alone
had political union become weaker, and the independence
of the princes more confirmed. The causes of this change
are not far to seek. They all resolve themselves into this
one, that the German king attempted too much at once.
The rulers of France, where manners were less rude than
in the other Transalpine lands, and where the Third
Estate rose into power more quickly, had reduced one by
one the great feudataries by whom the first Capetians had
been scarcely recognized. The English kings had annexed
Wales, Cumbria and part of Ireland, had obtained a prerogative great if not uncontrolled, and exercised no doubtful sway through every corner of their country. Both had
won their successes by the concentration on that single
object of their whole personal activity, and by the skillful
use of every device whereby their feudal rights, personal,
judicial and legislative, could be applied to fetter the vassal.
Meantime the German monarch, whose utmost efforts it
would have needed to tame his fierce barons and maintain
order through wide territories occupied by races unlike in
dialect and customs, had been struggling with the Lombard cities and the Normans of South Italy, and had been
for full two centuries the object of the unrelenting enmity
of the Roman pontiff. And in this latter contest, by
which more than by any other the fate of the Empire was
decided, he fought under disadvantages far greater than

his brethren in England and France. William the Conqueror had defied Hildebrand, William Rufus had resisted
Anselm; but the Emperors Henry IV and Barbarossa had
to cope with prelates who were Hildebrand and Anselm in
one ; the spiritual heads of Christendom as well as the
primates of their special realm, the Empire. And thus,
while the ecclesiastics of Germany were a body more formidable from their possessions than those of any other
European country, and enjoying far larger privileges, the
Emperor could not, or could with far less effect, win them
over by invoking against the Pope that national feeling
which made the cry of Gallican liberties so welcome even
to the clergy of France.

After repeated defeats, each more crushing than the
last, the imperial power, so far from being able to look
down on the papal, could not even maintain itself on an
equal footing. Against no pontiff since Gregory VII had
the monarch's right to name or confirm a pope, undisputed
in the days of the Ottos and of Henry III,
Relations of been made good. It was the turn of the Em-
the Papacy peror to repel a similar claim of the Holy See
and the to the function of reviewing his own election,
Empire. examining into his merits, and rejecting him if
unsound, that is to say, impatient of priestly tyranny. A
letter of Innocent III, who was the first to make this demand in terms, was inserted by Gregory IX in his digest
of the Canon Law, the inexhaustible armory of the churchman, and continued to be quoted thence by every canonist
till the end of the sixteenth century.* It was not difficult
to find grounds on which to base such a doctrine. Gregory
VII deduced it with characteristic boldness from the

---

* *Corpus Iuris Canonici*, Decr. Greg. i. 6, cap. 34, *Venerabilem:*
"Ius et authoritas examinandi personam electam in regem et pro-
movendem ad imperium, ad nos spectat, qui eum inungimus, consec-
ramus, et coronamus."

power of the keys, and the superiority over all other dignities which must needs appertain to the Pope as arbiter of
eternal weal or woe. Others took their stand on the analogy of clerical ordination, and urged that since the Pope in
consecrating the Emperor gave him a title to the obedience
of all Christian men, he must have himself the right of
approving or rejecting the candidate according to his
merits. Others again, appealing to the Old Testament,
showed how Samuel discarded Saul and anointed David in
his room,* and argued that the Pope now must have
powers at least equal to those of the Hebrew prophets.
But the ascendancy of the doctrine dates from the time of
Pope Innocent III, whose ingenuity discovered for it an
historical basis. It was by the favor of the Pope, he declared, that the Empire was taken away from the Greeks
and given to the Germans in the person of Charles, † and
the authority which Leo then exercised as God's representative must abide thenceforth and forever in his successors,
who can therefore at any time recall the gift, and bestow it
on a person or a nation more worthy than its present hold-
ers. This is the famous theory of the Translation of the
Empire, which plays so large a part in controversy down

---

* Lewis II, not presaging the future, uses this parallel in his letter
(before referred to) to Basil: " Nam Francorum principes primo reges,
deinde vero imperatores, dicti sunt ii dum taxat qui a Romano pontifice ad hoc oleo sancto perfusi sunt. . . . Porro is calumpniaris
Romanum pontificem, quod gesserit, poteris calumpniari et Samuel,
quod spreto Saule, quem ipse unxerat, David in regem ungere non
renuerit."

† " Illis principibus," writes Innocent, " ius et potestatem eligendi
regem [Romanorum] in imperatorem postmodum promovendum re-
cognoscimus, ad quos de iure ac antiqua consuetudine noscitur pertinere, præsertim quum ad eos ius et potestas huiusmodi ab apostolica sede pervenerit, quæ Romanum imperium in persona magnifici
Caroli a Græcis transtulit in Germanos."—Decr. Greg. i. 6, cap. 34,
Venerabilem.

till the seventeenth century,* a theory with plausibility enough to make it generally successful, yet one which to an impartial eye appears far removed from the truth of the facts.† Leo III did not suppose, any more than did Charles himself, that it was by his sole pontifical authority that the crown was given to the Frank; nor do we find such a notion put forward by any of his successors down to the twelfth century. Gregory VII in particular, in a remarkable letter dilating on his prerogative, appeals to the substitution by papal interference of Pipin for the last Merovingian king, and even goes back to cite the case of Theodosius humbling himself before St. Ambrose, but says never a word about this "translatio," excellently as it would have served his purpose.

Sound or unsound, however, these arguments did their work, for they were urged skillfully and boldly, and none denied that it was by the Pope alone that the crown could be lawfully imposed.‡ In some instances the rights claimed were actually made good. Thus Innocent III withstood Philip and overthrew Otto IV; thus another haughty priest commanded the electors to choose the Landgrave of Thuringia (A.D. 1246), and was by some of them obeyed; thus Gregory X compelled the recognition of Rudolf. The further pretensions of the Popes to the vicariate of the Empire during interregna the Germans

---

* Its influence, however, as Döllinger (*Das Kaiserthum Karls des Grossen und seiner Nachfolger*) remarks, first became great when this letter, some forty or fifty years after Innocent wrote it, was inserted in the digest of the canon law.

† Vid. supra, pp. 52–58.

‡ Upon this so-called "Translation of the Empire," many books remain to us: many more have probably perished. A good although far from impartial summary of the controversy may be found in Vagedes, *De Ludibriis Aulæ Romanæ in transferendo Imperio Romano.*

never admitted.* Still their place was now generally felt
to be higher than that of the monarch, and their control
over the three spiritual electors and the whole body of the
clergy was far more effective than his. A spark of national
feeling was at length kindled by the exactions and shameless subservience to France of the papal court at Avignon;†
and the infant democracy of industry and intelligence
represented by the cities and by the English Franciscan
Occam, supported Lewis IV in his conflict with John
XXII, till even the princes who had risen by the help of
the Pope were obliged to oppose him. In their famous
meeting at Rhense in 1338, the electors of the Empire
formally declared that the imperial dignity was derived
from God alone, that it was by their choice that the sovereign obtained his right to the title of King and Emperor,
and that in consequence he did not need to be approved or
confirmed by the Apostolic chair. The Diet held at Frank-

---

* "Vacante imperio Romano, cum in illo ad sæcularem iudicem
nequeat haberi recursus, ad summum pontificem, cui in persona B.
Petri terreni simul et cœlestis imperii iura Deus ipse commisit, imperii prædicti iurisdictio regimen et dispositio devolvitur."—Bull *Si
fratrum* (of John XXII, in A.D. 1316), in *Bullar. Rom.* So again:
"Attendentes quod Imperii Romani regimen cura et administratio
tempore quo illud vacare contingit ad nos pertinet, sicut dignoscitur
pertinere." So Boniface VIII, refusing to recognize Albert I, because
he was ugly and one-eyed ("est homo monoculus et vultu sordido,
non potest esse Imperator"), and had taken a wife from the serpent
brood of Frederick II ("de sanguine viperali Friderici"), declared
himself Vicar of the Empire, and assumed the crown and sword of
Constantine. Pope John VIII, in the ninth century, dated his documents during vacancies of the imperial throne, "imperatore domino
nostro Iesu Christo," a form not uncommon in the Middle Ages.

† Avignon was not yet in the territory of France; it lay within the
bounds of the kingdom of Arles. But the French power was nearer
than that of the Emperor; and pontiffs, many of them French
by extraction, sympathized, as was natural, with princes of their
own race.

fort in the same year confirmed this declaration, and even asserted the lawfulness of his assuming the imperial title before coronation by the Pope. The same sentiment dictated the reforms of Constance, but the imperial power which might have floated onward and higher on the turning tide of popular opinion lacked men equal to the occasion : the Hapsburg Frederick III, timid and superstitious, abased himself before the Romish court, and his house has generally adhered to the alliance then struck.

CHAPTER XIV.

THE GERMANIC CONSTITUTION : THE SEVEN ELECTORS.

THE reign of Frederick II was not less fatal to the domestic power of the German king than to the European supremacy of the Emperor. His two Pragmatic Sanctions had conferred rights that *Territorial* made the feudal aristocracy almost independ- *Sovereignty* ent, and the long anarchy of the Interregnum *Princes.* had enabled them not only to use but to extend and fortify their power. Rudolph of Hapsburg had striven, not wholly in vain, to coerce their insolence, but the contest between his son Albert *Adolf,* and Adolf of Nassau which followed his death, *1292–1298.* the short and troubled reign of Albert himself, the absence of Henry VII in Italy, the civil war of Lewis of Bavaria and Frederick, Duke of Austria, rival claimants of the imperial throne, *Albert I,* the diffculties in which Lewis, the successful *1298–1308.* competitor, found himself involved with the Pope—all these circumstances tended more and more to narrow the influence of the crown and complete the emancipation of the turbulent nobles. *Henry VII.* They now became virtually supreme in their *1308–1314.* own domains, enjoying full jurisdiction, certain appeals excepted, the right of legislation, privileges of coining money, of levying tolls and taxes : some were without even a feudal bond to *Lewis IV,* remind them of their allegiance. The num- *1314–1347.* bers of the immediate nobility—those who held directly of the crown—had increased prodigiously by the

extinction of the dukedoms of Saxony, Franconia and
Swabia : along the Rhine the lord of a single tower was
usually a sovereign prince. The petty tyrants whose boast
it was that they owed fealty only to God and the Emperor
showed themselves in practice equally regardless of both
powers. Pre-eminent were the three great houses of
Austria, Bavaria and Luxemburg, this last having acquired Bohemia, A.D. 1309; next came the electors, already
considered collectively more important than the Emperor,
and forming for themselves the first considerable principalities. Brandenburg and the Rhenish Palatinate are
strong independent states before the end of this period ;
Bohemia and the three archbishoprics almost from its
beginning.

The chief object of the magnates was to keep the monarch in his present state of helplessness. Till the expenses
which the crown entailed were found ruinous to its wearer,
their practice was to confer it on some petty prince, such
as were Rudolf and Adolf of Nassau and Günther of
Schwartzburg, seeking when they could to keep it from
settling in one family. They bound the newly elected to
respect all their present immunities, including those which
they had just extorted as the price of their votes ; they
checked all his attempts to recover lost lands
Policy   or rights: they ventured at last to depose their
of the   anointed head, Wenzel of Bohemia. Thus
Emperors.   fettered, the Emperor sought only to make the
most of his short tenure, using his position to aggrandize
his family and raise money by the sale of crown estates and
privileges. His individual action and personal relation to
the subject was replaced by a merely legal and formal one:
he represented order and legitimate ownership, and so far
was still necessary to the political system. But progresses
through the country were abandoned : unlike his predecessors, who had resigned their patrimony when they as-

sumed the scepter, he lived mostly in his own states, often without the Empire's bounds.

How thoroughly the national character of the office was gone is shown by the repeated attempts to bestow it on foreign potentates, who could not fill the place of a German king of the good old vigorous type. Not to speak of Richard and Alfonso, Charles of Valois was proposed against Henry VII, Edward III of England actually elected against Charles IV (his parliament forbade him to accept), George Podiebrad, king of Bohemia, against Frederick III. Sigismund was virtually a Hungarian king. The Emperor's only hope would have been in the support of the cities. During the thirteenth and fourteenth centuries they had increased wonderfully in population, wealth and boldness: the Hanseatic confederacy was the mightiest power of the North, and cowed the Scandinavian kings : the towns of Swabia and the Rhine formed great commercial leagues, maintained regular wars against the counter-associations of the nobility, and seemed at one time, by an alliance with the Swiss, on the point of turning West Germany into a federation of free municipalities. Feudalism, however, was still too strong; the cavalry of the nobles was irresistible in the field, and the thoughtless Wenzel let slip a golden opportunity of repairing the losses of two centuries. After all, the Empire was perhaps past redemption, for one fatal ailment paralyzed all its efforts. The Empire was poor. The crown lands, which had suffered heavily under Frederick II, were further usurped during the confusion that followed; till at last, through the reckless prodigality of sovereigns who sought only their immediate interest, little was left of the vast and fertile domains along the Rhine from which the Saxon and Franconian Emperors had drawn the chief part of their revenue. Regalian rights, the second fiscal resource, had

Power of the Cities.

Financial distress.

fared no better—tolls, customs, mines, rights of coining, of harboring Jews, and so forth, were· either seized or granted away: even the advowsons of churches had been sold or mortgaged ; and the imperial treasury depended mainly on an inglorious traffic in honors and exemptions. Things were so bad under Rudolph that the electors refused to make his son Albert king of the Romans, declaring that, while Rudolph lived, the public revenue which with difficulty supported one monarch, could much less maintain two at the same time.* Sigismund told his Diet, " Nihil esse imperio spoliatius, nihil egentius, adeo ut qui sibi ex Germaniæ principibus successurus esset, qui præter patrimonium nihil aliud habuerit, apud eum non imperium sed potius servitium sit futurum." † Patritius, the secretary of Frederick III, declared that the revenues of the Empire scarcely covered the expenses of its ambassadors. ‡ Poverty such as these expressions point to, a poverty which became greater after each election, not only involved the failure of the attempts which were sometimes made to recover usurped rights,§ but put every project of reform within or war without at the mercy of a jealous Diet.

---

* Quoted by Moser, *Römische Kayser*, from *Chron. Hirsaug.*: "Regni vires temporum iniuria nimium contritæ vix uni alendo regi sufficerent, tantum abesse ut sumptus in nutriendos duos reges ferre queant."

† At Rupert's death, under whom the mischief had increased greatly, there were, we are told, many bishops better off than the Emperor.

‡ " Proventus Imperii ita minimi sunt ut legationibus vix suppetant."—Quoted by Moser. In 1495 Maximilian told his Diet ' Das Römische Reich sei jetziger Zeit ein grosser Last und falle davon kleiner Beth;" and Granvella, Charles V's minister, said at the Diet of Speyer: " The Emperor has, for the support of his dignity, not a hazelnut's worth of profit from the Empire."

§ Albert I tried in vain to wrest the tolls of the Rhine from the grasp of the Rhenish electors.

The three orders of which that Diet consisted, electors, princes, and cities, were mutually hostile, and by consequence selfish ; their niggardly grants did no more than keep the Empire from dying of inanition.

The changes thus briefly described were in progress when Charles IV, king of Bohemia, son of that blind king John of Bohemia who fell at Cressy, and grandson of the Emperor Henry VII, was chosen to ascend the throne. His skillful and consistent policy aimed at settling what he perhaps despaired of reforming, and the famous instrument which, under the name of the Golden Bull, became the corner-stone of the Germanic constitution, confessed and legalized the independence of the electors and the powerlessness of the crown. *Charles IV (A.D. 1347- 1378), and his electoral constitution.* The most conspicuous defect of the existing system was the uncertainty of the elections, followed as they usually were by a civil war. It was this which Charles set himself to redress.

The kingdoms founded on the ruins of the Roman Empire by the Teutonic invaders presented in their original form a rude combination of the elective with the hereditary principle. One family in each tribe had, as the offspring of the gods, an indefeasible claim to rule, but from among the members of such a family the warriors were *German kingdom not originally elective.* free to choose the bravest or the most popular as king.* That the German crown came to be purely elective, while in France, Castile, Arragon, England, and most other European states, the principle of strict hereditary succession established itself, was due to the failure of male heirs in three successive dynasties ; to the restless ambition of the

* The Æthelings of the line of Cerdic, among the West Saxons, the Swedish Ynglings, the Bavarian Agilolfings, may thus be compared with the Achæmenids of Persia or the heroic houses of early Greece.

nobles, who, since they were not, like the French, strong
enough to disregard the royal power, did their best to
weaken it; to the intrigues of the churchmen, zealous for
a method of appointment prescribed by their own law
and observed in capitular elections; to the wish of the
Popes to gain an opening for their own influence and make
effective the veto which they claimed ; above all, to the
conception of the imperial office as one too holy to be, in
the same manner as the regal, transmissible by blood.
Had the German, like other feudal kingdoms, remained
merely local, feudal and national, it would without doubt
have ended by becoming a hereditary monarchy.   Transformed as it was by the Roman Empire, this could not be.
The headship of the human race being, like the Papacy,
the common inheritance of all mankind, could not be confined to any family, nor pass like a private estate by the
ordinary rules of descent.

The right to choose the war-chief belonged, in the ear
liest ages, to the whole body of freemen.   Their suffrage,
which must have been very irregularly exer-
Electoral   cised, became by degrees vested in their leaders,
body in   but the assent of the multitude, although en-
primitive   sured already, was needed to complete the
times.   ceremony.   It was thus that Henry the Fowler,
and St. Henry, and Conrad the Franconian duke, were
chosen.*   Though even tradition might have commem-

---

* Wippo, describing the election of Conrad the Franconian, says:
" Inter confinia Moguntiæ et Wormatiæ convenerunt cuncti primates
et, ut ita dicam, vires et viscera regni." So Bruno says that Henry IV
was elected by the "*populus.*"   So Amandus, secretary of Frederick
Barbarossa, in describing his election, says, "Multi illustres heroes
ex Lombardia, Tuscia, Ianuensi et aliis Italiæ dominiis, ac maior et
potior pars principum ex Transalpino regno."—Quoted by Mur. *Antiq.*
Diss. iii.   And see many other authorities to the same effect, collected
by Pfeffinger, *Vitriarius illustratus.*

orated what extant records place beyond a doubt, it was commonly believed, till the end of the sixteenth century, that the elective constitution had been established, and the privilege of voting confined to seven persons, by a decree of Gregory V and Otto III, which a famous jurist describes as "lex a pontifice de imperatorum comitiis lata, ne ius eligendi penes populum Romanum in posterum esset."* St. Thomas says, "Election ceased from times of Charles the Great to those of Otto III, when Pope Gregory V established that of the seven princes, which will last as long as the holy Roman Church, who ranks above all other powers, shall have judged expedient for Christ's faithful people."† Since it tended to exalt the papal power, this fiction was accepted, no doubt honestly accepted, and spead abroad by the clergy. And indeed, like so many other fictions, it had a sort of foundation in fact. The death of Otto III, the fourth of a line of monarchs among whom son had regularly succeeded to father, threw back the crown into the gift of the nation, and was no doubt one of the chief causes why it did not in the end become hereditary.‡

Thus, under the Saxon and Franconian sovereigns, the throne was theoretically elective, the assent of the chiefs and their followers being required, though little more

---

* Alciatus, *De Formula Romani Imperii.* He adds that the Gauls and Italians were incensed at the preference shown to Germany. So too Landolfo Colonna

† Quoted by Gewoldus, *De Septemviratu Sacri Imperii Romani,* himself a violent advocate of Gregory's decree, though living as late as the days of Ferdinand II. As late as A.D. 1648 we find Pope Innocent X maintaining that the sacred number *Seven* of the electors was "apostolica auctoritate olim præfinitus."—Bull *Zelo Domus* in *Bullar. Rom.*

‡ Sometimes we hear of a decree made by Pope Sergius IV and his cardinals (of course equally fabulous with Otto's). So John Villani, iv. 2.

likely to be refused than it was to an English or a French
king: practically hereditary, since both of these dynasties
succeeded in occupying it for four generations, the father
procuring the son's election during his own lifetime.
And so it might well have continued, had the right of
choice been retained by the whole body of the aristocracy,

*Encroach-
ments of the
great nobles.*
But at the election of Lothar II, A. D. 1125, we
find a certain small number of magnates exercising the so-called right of prætaxation; that
is to say, choosing alone the future monarch,
and then submitting him to the rest for their approval. A
supreme electoral college, once formed, had both the will
and the power to retain the crown in their own gift, and
still further exclude their inferiors from participation.
So before the end of the Hohenstaufen dynasty, two
great changes had passed upon the ancient constitution.   It had become a fundamental doctrine that
the Germanic throne, unlike the thrones of other
countries, was purely elective :* nor could the influence
and the liberal offers of Henry VI prevail on the
princes to abandon what they rightly judged the keystone of their powers.   And at the same time the right
of prætaxation had ripened into an exclusive privilege of
election, vested in a small body :† the assent of the rest

---

* In 1152 we read, "Id iuris Romani Imperii apex habere dicitur
ut non per sanguinis propaginem sed per principum electionem reges
creentur."—Otto of Freysing.   Gulielmus Brito, writing not much
later, says (quoted by Freher):

> " Est etenim talis dynastia Theutonicorum
> Ut nullus regnet super illos, ni prius illum
> Eligat unanimis cleri populique voluntas."

† Innocent III, during the contest between Philip and Otto IV,
speaks of "principes ad quos principaliter spectat regis Romani
electio."

of the nobility being at first assumed, finally altogether dispensed with. On the double choice of Richard and Alfonso A.D. 1257, the only question was as to the majority of votes in the electoral college; neither then nor afterward was there a word of the rights of the other princes, counts and barons, important as their voices had been two centuries earlier.

The origin of that college is a matter somewhat intricate and obscure. It is mentioned A.D. 1152, and in somewhat clearer terms in 1198, as a distinct body; but without anything to show who composed it. First in A.D. 1263 does a letter of Pope Urban *The Seven Electors.* IV. say that by immemorial custom the right of choosing the Roman king belonged to seven persons, the seven who had just divided their votes on Richard of Cornwall and Alfonso of Castile. · Of these seven, three, the archbishops of Mentz, Treves and Cologne, pastors of the richest Transalpine sees, represented the German church, the other four ought, according to the ancient constitution, to have been the dukes of the four nations, Franks, Swabians, Saxons, Bavarians, to whom had also belonged the four great offices of the imperial household. But of these dukedoms the two first named were now extinct, and their place and power in the state, as well as the household offices they had held, had descended upon two principalities of more recent origin, those, namely, of the Palatinate of the Rhine and the Margraviate of Brandenburg. The Saxon duke, though with greatly narrowed dominions, retained his vote and office of archmarshal, and the claim of his Bavarian compeer would have been equally indisputable had it not so happened that both he and the Palsgrave of the Rhine were members of the great house of Wittelsbach. This house had acquired the dukedom of Bavaria in 1180 and the Palatine, which represented the vote of the extinct dukedom of Lorraine, in 1214; but as

both dignities were united in one person, no difficulty arose
until the death of duke Otto the illustrious in 1253.
When his sons shared his dominions, Lewis becoming
Palsgrave, and Henry duke of Bavaria, nothing was settled as to the vote and other rights of an elector, and
before long both sons claimed these, and both with apparently reasonable grounds. The number seven had now,
however, become recognized as sacred : the king of
Bohemia* would not relinquish the place which he laid
claim to as cup-bearer; and the other electors were unwilling to see two votes enjoyed by one family. Thus a contest, which more than once nearly led to war, arose between
the rival lines of Wittelsbach, and between the Bavarian line
(whose title was thought the weaker of the two) and the king
of Bohemia. Rudolf, who in 1289 pronounced in favor of
Bohemia, and Lewis IV, who directed that the vote should
be exercised by the two lines alternately, in vain attempted
to settle it, nor was it laid to rest until the issuing and
confirming, at the Diet of Nürnberg and Metz in 1356, of
Charles IV's Golden Bull. This instrument,
*Golden
Bull of
Charles IV,
A.D. 1356.* thenceforth regarded as a fundamental law of
the Empire, after finally assigning the disputed
vote and office of cup-bearer to Bohemia (of
which Charles was then king) proceeds to lay
down a variety of rules for the conduct of imperial elections. Frankfort is fixed as the place of election ; the
archbishop of Mentz named convener of the electoral

---

* The claim of the king of Bohemia seems to have been made technically in respect of his office of cup-bearer, practically because he
was the equal in power and rank of any of the other electors. It was
disputed partly on the ground that his kingdom was not properly
German. "Rex Bohemiæ qui pincerna est non eligit quia non est
Teutonicus" (Albert. Stad. A.D. 1240). So the *Sachsenspiegel*, "Die
schenke des rikes die koning von behemen, die ne heuet nenen kore,
umme dat he nicht düdesch nis."

college; to Bohemia is given the first, to the Count Palatine the second place among the secular electors. A
majority of votes was in all cases to be decisive. As to
each electorate there was attached a great office, it was
supposed that this was the title by which the vote was
possessed ; though it was in truth rather an effect than a
cause. The three prelates were archchancellors of Germany,
Gaul and Burgundy, and Italy respectively: Bohemia cup-
bearer, the Palsgrave seneschal, Saxony marshal and
Bradenburg chamberlain.*

These arrangements, under which disputed elections
became far less frequent, remained undisturbed till the
breaking out of the Thirty Years' War, when the Emperor
Ferdinand II by an unwarranted stretch of prerogative de-

---

* The names and offices of the seven are concisely given in these
lines, which appear in the treatise of Marsilius of Padua, *De Imperio Romano :*

"Moguntinensis, Trevirensis, Coloniensis,
Quilibet imperii sit Cancellarius horum ;
Et Palatinus dapifer, Dux portitor ensis,
Marchio præpositus cameræ, pincerna Bohemus,
Hi statuunt dominum cunctis per sæcula summum."

It is worth while to place beside this the first stanza of Schiller's
ballad, *Der Graf von Hapsburg :*

"Zu Aachen in seiner Kaiserpracht
Im alterthümlichen Saale,
Sass König Rudolphs heilige Macht
Beim festlichen Krönungsmahle.
Die Speisen trug der Pfalzgraf des Rheins,
Es schenkt der Böhme des perlenden Weins,
Und alle die Wähler, die sieben,
Wie der Sterne Chor um die Sonne sich stellt,
Umstanden geschäftig den Herrscher der Welt,
Die Würde des Amtes zu üben."

It is a poetical license, however (as Schiller himself admits), to
bring the Bohemian there, for King Ottocar was far away at home,
mortified at his own rejection, and already meditating war.

prived (in 1621) the Palsgrave Frederick (king of Bohemia and husband of Elizabeth, the daughter of James I of England) of his electoral vote, and transferred it (1623) to his own partisan, Maximilian of Bavaria.   At the peace of

Eighth Electorate.

Westphalia the Palsgrave was reinstated as eighth elector, Bavaria retaining her vote and rank, but with a provision that if the Bavarian branch of the house of Wittelsbach should come to an end, the Palsgrave should step into its place, which accordingly happened on the extinction of the Bavarian line in 1777. The sacred number having been once broken through, less scruple was felt in making further changes.   In A.D. 1692,

Ninth Electorate.

the Emperor Leopold I conferred a ninth electorate on the house of Brunswick-Lüneburg which was then in possession of the duchy of Hanover, and succeeded to the throne of Great Britain in 1714; and in A.D. 1708, the assent of the Diet thereto was obtained.   It was in this way that English kings came to vote at the election of a Roman Emperor.

It is not a little curious that the only potenate who continued down to our own days actually to entitle himself Elector* should be one who never joined in electing an Emperor, having been under the arrangements of the old Empire a simple Landgrave.   In A.D. 1803, Napoleon, among other sweeping changes in the Germanic constitution, procured the extinction of the electorates of Cologne

---

* The electoral prince (Kurfürst) of Hessen-Cassel.   His retention of the title had this advantage, that it enabled the Germans readily to distinguish electoral Hesse (Kur-Hes-sen) from the Grand Duchy (Hessen-Darmstadt) and the landgraviate (Hessen-Homburg).   This last relic of the electoral system passed away in 1866, when the elector of Hessen was dethroned, and his territories (to the great satisfaction of the inhabitants, whom he had worried by a long course of petty tyrannies) annexed to the Prussian kingdom, along with Hanover, Nassau, and the free city of Frankfort.

and Treves, annexing their territories to France, and gave the title of Elector, as the highest after that of king, to the Duke of Würtemberg, the Margrave of Baden, the Landgrave of Hessen-Cassel, and the archbishop of Salzburg.* Three years afterward the Empire itself ended, and the title became meaningless.

As the Germanic Empire is the most conspicuous example of a monarchy not hereditary that the world has ever seen, it may not be amiss to consider for a moment what light its history throws upon the character of elective monarchy in general, a contrivance which has always had, and will probably always continue to have, seductions for a certain class of political theorists.

First of all then it deserves to be noticed how difficult, one might almost say impossible, it was found to maintain in practice the elective principle. In point of law, the imperial throne was from the tenth century to the nineteenth absolutely open to any orthodox Christian candidate. But as a matter of fact, the competition was confined to a few very powerful families, and there was always a strong tendency for the crown to become hereditary in some one of these. *Objects of an elective monarchy: how far attained in Germany.* Thus the Franconian Emperors held it from A. D. 1024 till 1125, the Hohenstaufen, themselves the heirs *Choice of the fittest.* of the Franconians, for a century or more ; the house of Luxemberg (kings of Bohemia) enjoyed it through three successive reigns, and when in the fifteenth century it fell into the tenacious grasp of the Hapsburgs, they managed to retain it thenceforth (with but one trifling interruption)

---

* France having annexed the whole left bank of the Rhine, the archiepiscopal chair of Mentz was transferred to Regensburg. It was now the only spiritual electorate, for the archbishopric of Salzburg had been secularized for the archduke Ferdinand of Austria, in order to compensate him for the loss of Tuscany.

till it vanished out of nature altogether. Therefore the
chief benefit which the scheme of elective sovereignty
seems to promise, that of putting the fittest man in the
highest place, was but seldom attained, and attained even
then rather by good fortune than design.

No such objection can be brought against the second
ground on which an elective system has sometimes been
Restraint of the sovereign. advocated, its operation in moderating the
power of the crown, for this was attained in the
fullest and most ruinous measure. We are
reminded of the man in the fable, who opened
a sluice to water his garden, and saw his house swept away
by the furious torrent. The power of the crown was not
moderated but destroyed. Each successful candidate was
forced to purchase his title by the sacrifice of rights which
had belonged to his predecessors, and must repeat the
same shameful policy later in his reign to procure the election of his son. Feeling at the same time that his family
could not make sure of keeping the throne, he treated it
as a life-tenant is apt to treat his estate, seeking only to
make out of it the largest present profit. And the
electors, aware of the strength of their position, presumed
upon it and abused it to assert an independence such as
the nobles of other countries could never have aspired to.

Modern political speculation supposes the method of
appointing a ruler by the votes of his subjects, as opposed
Recognition of the popular will. to the system of hereditary succession to be
an assertion by the people of their own will
as the ultimate fountain of authority, an
acknowledgment by the prince that he is no
more than their minister and deputy. To the theory of
the Holy Empire nothing could be more repugnant. This
will best appear when the aspect of the system of election
at different epochs in its history is compared with the corresponding changes in the composition of the electoral

body which have been described as in progress from the
ninth to the fourteenth century. In very early times, the
tribe chose a war chief, who was, even if he belonged to
the most noble family, no more than the first among his
peers, with a power circumscribed by the will of his subjects. Several ages later, in the tenth and eleventh centuries, the right of choice had passed into the hands of the
magnates, and the people were only asked to assent. In
the same measure had the relation of prince and subject
taken a new aspect. We must not expect to find, in such
rude times, any very clear apprehension of the technical
quality of the process, and the throne had indeed become
for a season so nearly hereditary that the election was often
a mere matter of form. But it seems to have been
regarded, not as a delegation of authority by the nobles
and people, with a power of resumption implied, but
rather as their subjection of themselves to the monarch
who enjoys, as of his own right, a wide and ill defined prerogative. In yet later times, when, as has been shown
above, the assembly of the chieftains and the applauding
shout of the host had been superseded by the secret con-
clave of the seven electoral princes, the strict legal view of
election became fully established, and no one was supposed
to have any title to the crown except what a majority of
votes might confer upon him. Meantime, however, the
conception of the imperial office itself had been thoroughly
penetrated by religious ideas, and the fact that the sovereign did not, like other princes, reign by hereditary right,
but by the choice of certain persons, was supposed to be
an enhancement and consecration of his dignity. The electors, to draw what may seem a *Conception
of the elec-*
subtle, but is nevertheless a very real distinc- *toral func-*
tion, selected, but did not create. They only *tion.*
named the person who was to receive what it
was not theirs to give. God, say the mediæval writers,

not deigning to interfere visibly in the affairs of this world, has willed that these seven princes of Germany should discharge the function which once belonged to the senate and people of Rome, that of choosing his earthly viceroy in matters temporal. But it is immediately from Himself that the authority of this viceroy comes, and men can have no relation toward him except that of obedience. It was in this period, therefore, when the Emperor was in practice the mere nominee of the electors, that the belief in his divine right stood highest, to the complete exclusion of the mutual responsibility of feudalism, and still more of any notion of a devolution of authority from the sovereign people.

Peace and order appeared to be promoted by the institutions of Charles IV, which removed one fruitful cause of civil war. But these seven electoral princes acquired, with their extended privileges, a marked and dangerous predominance in Germany. They had once already in their famous meeting at Rhense * in 1338, acted as an independent body, repudiating in the name of the nation the extravagant claims of the Pope, and declaring that it was by their election alone that the Emperor acquired his rights. The position which they had then assumed in a heartily patriotic spirit, was now legalized and made permanent. They were to enjoy full re-

General results of Charles IV's policy.

---

* Rhense is a hamlet on the left bank of the Rhine, some four or five miles above Coblentz. A little way north of it, and on the very shore, between the stream and the railway, stands, half hidden by walnut-trees, the so-called Königsstuhl, a modern restoration of the building erected by Charles IV in 1376 for the meetings of the electors, who from long time past had been wont to assemble here. It was the point where the territories of the four Rhenish electors touched one another. Here several imperial elections were made: the last, Rupert's, in 1400.

galian rights in their territories;* causes were not to be evoked from their courts, save when justice should have been denied: their consent was necessary to all public acts of consequence. Their persons were held to be sacred, and the seven mystic luminaries of the Holy Empire, typified by the seven lamps of the Apocalypse, soon gained much of the Emperor's hold on popular reverence, as well as that actual power which he lacked. To Charles, who viewed the German Empire much as Rudolf had viewed the Roman, this result came not unforeseen. He saw in his office a means of serving personal ends, and to them, while appearing to exalt by elaborate ceremonies its ideal dignity, he deliberately sacrificed what real strength was left. The object which he sought steadily through life was the prosperity of the Bohemian kingdom, and the advancement of his own house. In the Golden Bull, whose seal bears the legend:

" Roma caput mundi regit orbis frena rotundi,"†

there is not a word of Rome or of Italy. To Germany he was indirectly a benefactor, by the foundation of the University of Prague, the mother of all her schools: otherwise her bane. He legalized anarchy, and called it a constitution. The sums expended in obtaining the ratification of the Golden Bull, in procuring the election of his son Wenzel, in aggrandizing Bohemia at the expense of

---

* Goethe, whose imagination was wonderfully attracted by the splendors of the old Empire, has given in the second part of *Faust* a sort of fancy sketch of the origin of the great offices and the territorial independence of the German princes. Two lines express concisely the fiscal rights granted by the Emperor to the electors:

" Dann Steuer Zins und Beed', Lehn und Geleit und Zoll,
    Berg- Salz- und Münz-regal euch angehören soll."

Maximilian said of Charles IV: "Carolo quarto pestilentior pestis nunquam alias contigit Germaniæ."

† This line is said to be as old as the time of Otto III.

Germany, had been amassed by keeping a market in which honors and exemptions, with what lands the crown retained, were put up openly to be bid for. In Italy the Ghibelines saw, with shame and rage, their chief hasten to Rome with a scanty retinue, and return from it as swiftly, at the mandate of an Avignonese Pope, halting on his route only to traffic away the last rights of his Empire. The Guelf might cease to hate a power he could now despise.

Thus, alike at home and abroad, the German king had become practically powerless by the loss of his feudal privileges, and saw the authority that had once been his parcelled out among a crowd of greedy and tyrannical nobles. Meantime how had it fared with the rights which he claimed by virtue of the Imperial crown?

CHAPTER XV.

THE EMPIRE AS AN INTERNATIONAL POWER.

THAT the Roman Empire survived the seemingly mortal wound it had received at the era of the Great Interregnum, and continued to put forth pretensions which no one was likely to make good where the Hohenstaufen had failed, has been attributed to its identification with the German kingdom, in which some life was still left. But this was far from being the only cause which saved it from extinction. It had not ceased to be upheld in the fourteenth and fifteenth centuries by the same singular theory which had in the ninth and tenth been strong enough to re-establish it in the West. The character of that theory was indeed somewhat changed, for if not positively less religious, it was less exclusively so. In the days of Charles and Otto, the Empire, in so far as it was anything more than a tradition from times gone by, rested solely upon the belief that with the visible Church there must be coextensive a single Christian state under one head and governor. But now that the Emperor's headship had been repudiated by the Pope, and his interference in matters of religion denounced as a repetition of the sin of Uzziah; now that the memory of mutual injuries had kindled an unquenchable hatred between the champions of the ecclesiastical and those of the civil power, it was natural that the latter, while they urged, fervently as ever, the divine sanction given to the imperial office, should

Theory of the Roman Empire in the fourteenth and fifteenth centuries.

at the same time be led to seek some further basis whereon
to establish its claims.   What that basis was, and how they
were guided to it, will best appear when a word or two has
been said on the nature of the change that had passed on
Europe in the course of the three preceding centuries, and
the progress of the human mind during the same period.

Such has been the accumulated wealth of literature,
and so rapid the advances of science among us since the
close of the Middle Ages, that it is not now possible by
any effort fully to enter into the feelings with which the
relics of antiquity were regarded by those who saw in
them their only possession.   It is indeed true that modern
art and literature and philosophy have been produced by
the working of new minds upon old materials : that in
thought, as in nature, we see no new creation.   But with
us the old has been transformed and overlaid by the new
till its origin is forgotten : to them ancient books were
the only standard of taste, the only vehicle of truth, the
only stimulus to reflection.   Hence it was that the most
learned man was in those days esteemed the greatest :
hence the creative energy of an age was exactly pro-
portioned to its knowledge of and its reverence for the
written monuments of those that had gone before.   For
until they can look forward, men must look back : till
they should have reached the level of the old civilization,
the nations of mediæval Europe must continue to live
upon its memories.   Over them, as over us, the common
dream of all mankind had power; but to them, as to the
ancient world, that golden age which seems now to glim-
mer on the horizon of the future was shrouded in the
clouds of the past.   It is to the fifteenth and sixteenth
centuries that we are accustomed to assign that new birth
of the human spirit—if it ought not rather to be called a
renewal of its strength and quickening of its sluggish life
—with which the modern time begins.   And the date is

well chosen, for it was then first that the transcendently
powerful influence of Greek literature began to work upon
the world. But it must not be forgotten that
for a long time previous there had been in *Revival of*
progress a great revival of learning, and still *learning*
more of zeal for learning, which being caused *and litera-*
by and directed toward the literature and in- *ture A. D.*
stitutions of Rome, might fitly be called the *1100-1400.*
Roman Renaissance. The twelfth century saw this
revival begin with that passionate study of the legislation
of Justinian, whose influence on the doctrines of imperial
prerogative has been noticed already. The thirteenth
witnessed the rapid spread of the scholastic philosophy, a
body of systems most alien, both in subject and manner,
to anything that had arisen among the ancients, yet one
to whose development Greek metaphysics and the theology
of the Latin fathers had largely contributed, and the
spirit of whose reasonings was far more free than the presumed orthodoxy of its conclusions suffered to appear. In
the fourteenth century there arose in Italy the first great
masters of painting and song; and the literature of the
new languages, springing into the fullness of life in the
Divina Commedia, adorned not long after by the names
of Petrarch and Chaucer, assumed at once its place as a
great and ever-growing power in the affairs of men.

Now, along with the literary revival, partly caused by,
partly causing it, there had been also a wonderful stirring
and uprising in the mind of Europe. The
yoke of church authority still pressed heavily *Growing*
on the souls of men; yet some had been found *freedom of*
to shake it off, and many more murmured in *spirit.*
secret. The tendency was one which showed itself in
various and sometimes apparently opposite directions.
The revolt of the Albigenses, the spread of the Cathari
and other so-called heretics, the excitement created by the

writings of Wickliffe and Huss, witnessed to the fearlessness wherewith it could assail the dominant theology.   It
was present, however skillfully disguised, among those
scholastic doctors who busied themselves with proving by
natural reason the dogmas of the Church: for the power
which can forge fetters can also break them.   It took a
form more dangerous because of a more direct application
to facts, in the attacks, so often repeated from Arnold of
Brescia downward, upon the wealth and corruptions of
the clergy, and above all of the papal court.   For the agitation was not merely speculative.   There was

*Influence
of thought
upon the
arrange-
ments of
society.*
beginning to be a direct and rational interest
in life, a power of applying thought to practical ends, which had not been seen before.
Man's life among his fellows was no longer a
mere wild beast's struggle; man's soul no more,
as it had been, the victim of ungoverned passion, whether it was awed by supernatural terrors or captivated by examples of surpassing holiness.   Manners were
still rude, and governments unsettled ; but society was
learning to organize itself upon fixed principles; to recognize, however faintly, the value of order, industry, equality; to adapt means to ends, and conceive of the common
good as the proper end of its own existence.   In a word,
Politics had begun to exist, and with them there had
appeared the first of a class of persons whom friends and
enemies may both, though with different meanings, call
ideal politicians; men who, however various have been the
doctrines they have held, however impracticable many of
the plans they have advanced, have been nevertheless alike
in their devotion to the highest interests of humanity, and
have frequently been derided as theorists in their own age
to be honored as the prophets and teachers of the next.

Now it was toward the Roman Empire that the hopes
and sympathies of these political speculators as well as of

the jurists and poets of the fourteenth and fifteenth centuries were constantly directed. The cause may be gathered from the circumstances of the time. The most remarkable event in the history of the last three hundred years had been the formation of nationalities, each distinguished by a peculiar language and character, and by steadily increasing differences of habits and institutions. And as upon this national basis there had been in most cases established strong monarchies, Europe was *Separation of the peoples of Europe into hostile kingdoms: consequent need of an international power.* broken up into disconnected bodies, and the cherished scheme of a united Christian state appeared less likely than ever to be realized. Nor was this all. Sometimes through race-hatred, more often by the jealousy and ambition of their sovereigns, these countries were constantly involved in war with one another, violating on a larger scale and with more destructive results than in time past the peace of the religious community ; while each of them was at the same time torn within by frequent insurrections, and desolated by long and bloody civil wars. The new nationalities were too fully formed to allow the hope that by their extinction a remedy might be applied to these evils. They had grown up in spite of the Empire and the Church, and were not likely to yield in their strength what they had won in their weakness. But it still appeared possible to soften, if not to overcome, their antagonism. What might not be looked for from the erection of a presiding power common to all Europe, a power which, while it should oversee the internal concerns of each country, not dethroning the king, but treating him as an hereditary viceroy, should be more especially charged to prevent strife between kingdoms, and to maintain the public order of Europe by being not only the fountain of international law, but also the judge in its causes and the enforcer of its sentences?

To such a position had the Popes aspired. They were
indeed excellently fitted for it by the respect which the
sacredness of their office commanded ; by their
*The Popes
as inter-
national
Judges.*
control of the tremendous weapons of excommunication and interdict; above all, by their
exemption from those narrowing influences of
place, or blood, or personal interest, which it
would be their chiefest duty to resist in others. And there
had been pontiffs whose fearlessness and justice were
worthy of their exalted office, and whose interference was
gratefully remembered by those who found no other help-
ers. Nevertheless, judging the Papacy by its conduct as a
whole, it had been tried and found wanting. Even when
its throne stood firmest and its purposes were most pure,
one motive had always biased its decisions—a partiality to
the most submissive. During the greater part of the fourteenth century it was at Avignon the willing tool of
France : in the pursuit of a temporal principality it had
mingled in and had been contaminated by the unhallowed
politics of Italy ; its supreme council, the college of
cardinals, was distracted by the intrigues of two bitterly
hostile factions. And while the power of the Popes had
declined steadily, though silently, since the days of Boniface VIII, the insolence of the great prelates and the vices
of the inferior clergy had provoked throughout Western
Christendom a reaction against the pretensions of all
sacerdotal authority. As there is no theory at first sight
more attractive than that which entrusts all government
to a supreme spiritual power, which, knowing what is best
for man, shall lead him to his true good by appealing to
the highest principles of his nature, so there is no disappointment more bitter than that of those who find that the
holiest office may be polluted by the lusts and passions of
its holder; that craft and hypocrisy lead while fanaticism
follows ; that here too, as in so much else, the corruption

of the best is worst. Some such disappointment there was in Europe now, and with it a certain disposition to look with favor on the secular power: a wish to escape from the unhealthy atmosphere of clerical despotism to the rule of positive law, harsher, it might be, yet surely less corrupting. Espousing the cause of the Roman Empire as the chief opponent of priestly claims, this tendency found it, with shrunken territory and diminished resources, fitter in some respects for the office of an international judge and mediator than it had been as a great national power. For though far less widely active, it was losing that local character which was fast gathering round the Papacy. With feudal rights no longer enforcible, and removed, except in his patrimonial lands, from direct contact with the subject, the Emperor was not, as heretofore, conspicuously a German and a feudal king, and occupied an ideal position far less marred by the incongruous accidents of birth and training, of national and dynastic interests.

To that position three cardinal duties were attached. He who held it must typify spiritual unity, must preserve peace, must be a fountain of that by which alone among imperfect men peace is preserved and restored, law and justice. The first of these three objects was sought not only on religious grounds, but also from that longing for a wider brotherhood of humanity toward which, ever since the barrier between Jew and Gentile, Greek and barbarian, was broken down, the aspirations of the higher minds of the world have been constantly directed. Placed in the midst of Europe, the Emperor was to bind its tribes into one body, reminding them of their common faith, their common blood, their common interest in each other's welfare. And he was therefore, above all things, professing indeed to be upon earth the representative of the Prince of Peace, bound to listen to complaints, and to redress

Duties attributed to the Empire.

the injuries inflicted by sovereigns or peoples upon each
other ; to punish offenders against the public order of
Christendom ; to maintain through the world, looking
down as from a serene height upon the schemes and
quarrels of meaner potentates, that supreme good without
which neither arts nor letters, nor the gentler virtues of
life, can rise and flourish.   The mediæval Empire was in
its essence what the modern despotisms that mimic it
profess themselves : the Empire was peace:* the oldest
and noblest title of its head was " Imperator pacificus."†
And that he might be the peacemaker, he must be the
expounder of justice and the author of its concrete embodiment, positive law ; chief legislator and supreme judge of

---

* See esp. Ægidi, *Der Fürstenrath nach dem Luneviller Frieden*,
and the passages by him quoted.

† The archbishop of Mentz addresses Conrad II on his election
thus : " Deus quum a te multa requirat tum hoc potissimum de-
siderat ut facias iudicium et iustitiam et pacem patriæ quæ respicit
ad te, ut sis defensor ecclesiarum et clericorum, tutor viduarum et
orphanorum."—Wipo, Vita Chuonradi, c. 3, *ap.* Pertz. So Pope
Urban IV writes to Richard : " Ut Imperii Romani fastigium et eius
culmen præsidens specialis advocati et defensoris præcipui circa
ecclesiam gerat officium et . . . inimicis consternatis eiusdem in
pacis pulchritudine sedat populus Christianus et requie opulenta
quiescat."—Raynald. Ann. Eccl. ad ann. 1263.   Compare also the
" Edictum de crimine læsæ maiestatis" issued by Henry VII in Italy :
" Ad reprimenda multorum facinora qui ruptis totius debitæ fidelita-
tis habenis adversus Romanum imperium, in cuius tranquillitate
totius orbis regularitas requiescit, hostili animo armati conentur
nedum humana, verum etiam divina præcepta, quibus iubetur quod
omnis anima Romanorum principi sit subiecta, scelestissimis facin-
oribus et rebellionibus demoliri," etc.—Pertz, *M. G. H.*, legg. ii, p.
544. See also a curious passage in the Life of St. Adalbert, describing the beginning of the reign at Rome of the Emperor Otto III, and
his cousin and nominee Pope Gregory V : " Lætantur cum primati-
bus minores civitatis : cum afflicto paupere exultant agmina viduarum, quia novus imperator dat iura populis ; dat iura novus papa."

appeal, like his predecessor, the compiler of the Corpus
Iuris, the one and only source of all legitimate authority.
In this sense, as governor and administrator, not as owner,
is he, in the words of the jurists, Lord of the world; not
that its soil belongs to him in the same sense in which the
soil of France or England belongs to their respective kings:
he is the steward of Him who has received the nations for
his inheritance and the uttermost parts of the earth for
his possession. It is, therefore, by him alone that the
idea of pure right, acquired not by force but by legitimate
devolution from those whom God himself had' set up, is
visibly expressed upon earth. To find an external and
positive basis for that idea is a problem which it has
at all times been more easy to evade than to solve, and
one peculiarly distressing to those who could neither
explain the phenomena of society by reducing it to its
original principles, nor inquire historically how its existing
arrangements had grown up. Hence the at-
tempt to represent human government as an *Divine*
emanation from divine: a view from which all *right of the*
the similar but far less logically consistent *Emperor.*
doctrines of divine right which have prevailed in later
times are borrowed. As has been said already, there is
not a trace of the notion that the Emperor reigns by an
hereditary right of his own or by the will of the people,
for such a theory would have seemed to the men of the
middle ages an absurd and wicked perversion of the true
order. Nor do his powers come to him from those who
choose him, but from God, who uses the electoral princes
as mere instruments of nomination. Having such an
origin, his rights exist irrespective of their actual exercise,
and no voluntary abandonment, not even an express grant,
can impair them. Boniface VIII* reminds the king of

---

* "Vicarius Iesu Christi et successor Petri transtulit potestatem
imperii a Græcis in Germanos ut ipsi Germani . . . possint

France, and imperialist lawyers till the seventeenth century repeated the claim, that he, like other princes, is of right and must ever remain subject to the Roman Emperor. And the sovereigns of Europe long continued to address the Emperor in language, and yield to him a precedence, which admitted the inferiority of their own position.*

There was in this theory nothing that was absurd, though much that was impracticable. The ideas on which it rested are still unapproached in grandeur and simplicity, still as far in advance of the average thought of Europe, and as unlikely to find men or nations fit to apply them, as when they were promulgated five hundred years ago. The practical evil which the establishment of such a universal monarchy was intended to meet, that of wars and hardly less ruinous preparations for war between the states of Europe, remains what it was then. The remedy which mediæval theory proposed has been in some measure ap-

eligere regem Romanorum qui est promovendus in Imperatorem et monarcham omnium regum et principum terrenorum. Nec insurgat superbia Gallicorum quæ dicat quod non recognoscit superiorem : mentiuntur, quia de iure sunt et esse debent sub rege Romanorum et Imperatore."—Speech of Boniface VIII, April 30, 1303—Pfeffinger, Corp. iur. publ. i. 377. It is curious to compare with this the words addressed nearly five centuries earlier by Pope John VIII to Lewis, king of Bavaria: "Si sumpseritis Romanum imperium, omni regna vobis subiecta existent."—Jaffé, Reg. Pont. p. 281.

* So Alfonso, king of Naples, writes to Frederick III : "Nos reges omnes debemus reverentiam Imperatori, tanquam summo regi, qui est Caput ex Dux regum." — Quoted by Pfeffinger, i. 379. And Francis I (of France), speaking of a proposed combined expedition against the Turks, says : "Cæsari nihilominus principem ea in expeditione locum non gravarer ex officio cedere."—Marquard Freher, Script. rer. Germ. iii. 425. For a long time no European sovereign save the Emperor ventured to use the title of "majesty." The imperial chancery conceded it in 1633 to the kings of England and Sweden ; in 1641 to the king of France.—Zedler, *Universal Lexicon,* s. v. Majestät.

plied by the construction and reception of international law; the greater difficulty of erecting a tribunal to arbitrate and decide, with the power of enforcing its decisions, is as far from a solution as ever.

It is easy to see how it was to the Roman Emperor, and to him only, that the duties and privileges above mentioned could be attributed. Being Roman, he was of no nation, and therefore fittest to judge between contending states, and appease the animosities of race. His was the imperial tongue of Rome, not only the vehicle of religion and law, but also, since no other was understood everywhere in Europe, the necessary medium of diplomatic intercourse. *Roman Empire why an international power.* As there was no Church but the Holy Roman Church, and he its temporal head, it was by him that the communion of the saints in its outward form, its secular side, was represented, and to his keeping that the sanctity of peace must be entrusted. As direct heir of those who from Julius to Justinian had shaped the existing law of Europe,* he was, so to speak, legality personified;† the only sovereign on earth who, being possessed of power by an unimpeachable title, could by his grant confer upon others rights equally valid. And as he claimed to perpetuate the greatest political system the world had known, a system which still moves the wonder of those who see before their eyes empires as much wider than the Roman as they are less symmetrical, and whose vast and complex machinery far surpassed anything the fourteenth

---

* For with the progress of society and the growth of commerce the old feudal customs were through the greater part of western Europe, and especially in Germany, either giving way to or being remodeled and supplemented by the civil law.

† "Imperator est animata lex in terris."—Quoted by Von Raumer, v. 81, from a letter of the bishops of Salzburg and Regensburg to Pope Gregory IX.

century possessed or could hope to establish, it was not strange that he and his government (assuming them to be what they were entitled to be) should be taken as the ideal of a perfect monarch and a perfect state.

Of the many applications and illustrations of these doctrines which mediæval documents furnish, it will suffice to

Illustrations.

adduce two or three. No imperial privilege was prized more highly than the power of creating kings, for there was none which raised the Emperor so much above them. In this, as in other inter-

Right of creating Kings.

national concerns, the Pope soon began to claim a jurisdiction, at first concurrent, then separate and independent. But the older and more reasonable view assigned it, as flowing from the possession of supreme secular authority, to the Emperor; and it was from him that the rulers of Burgundy, Bohemia, Hungary, perhaps Poland also, received the regal title.* The prerogative was his in the same manner in which that of conferring titles is still held to belong to the sovereign in every modern kingdom. And so when Charles the Bold, last duke of French Burgundy, proposed to consolidate his wide dominions into a kingdom, it was from Frederick III that he sought permission to do so.

---

* Thus we are told of the Emperor Charles the Bald, that he confirmed the election of Boso, king of Burgundy and Provence, "Dedit Bosoni Provinciam (*sc.* Carolus Calvus), et corona in vertice capitis imposita, eum regem appellari iussit, ut more priscorum imperatorum regibus videretur dominari."—Regin. Chron. ad ann. 877. This statement is incorrect, but it evidences the views of the time. Frederick II made his son Enzio (that famous Enzio whose romantic history every one who has seen Bologna will remember) king of Sardinia, and also erected the duchy of Austria into a kingdom, although for some reason the title seems never to have been used ; and Lewis IV gave to Humbert of Dauphiné the title of king of Vienne, A.D. 1336. Otto III is said to have conferred the title of king on Boleslas of Poland.

The Emperor, however, was greedy and suspicious, the Duke uncompliant; and when Frederick found that terms could not be arranged between them, he stole away suddenly, and left Charles to carry back, with ill-concealed mortification, the crown and scepter which he had brought ready-made to the place of interview.*

In the same manner, as representing what was common to and valid throughout all Europe, nobility, and more particularly knighthood, centered in the Empire. The great Orders of Chivalry were inter- *Chivalry.* national institutions, whose members, having consecrated themselves a military priesthood, had no longer any country of their own, and could therefore be subject to no one save the Emperor and the Pope. For knighthood was constructed on the analogy of priesthood, and knights were conceived as being to the world in its secular aspect exactly what priests, and more especially the monastic orders, were to it in its religious aspect: to the one body was given the sword of the flesh, to the other the sword of the spirit; each was universal, each had its autocratic head.† Singularly, too, were these notions brought into harmony with the feudal polity. Cæsar was lord paramount of the world: its countries great fiefs, whose kings were his tenants in chief, the suitors of his court, owing to him homage, fealty, and military service against the infidel.

One illustration more of the way in which the empire was held to be something of and for all mankind, cannot be omitted. Although from the practical union of the

---

* The Duke of Lithuania is said to have treated with Sigismund for the bestowal on him of the title of King.—Cf. Pfeffinger, Corp. iur. publ. i. 424.

† It is probably for this reason that the *Ordo Romanus* directs the Emperor and Empress to be crowned (in St. Peter's) at the altar of St. Maurice, the patron saint of knighthood.

imperial with the German throne none but Germans were
chosen to fill it,* it remained in point of law absolutely
free from all restrictions of country or birth.   In an age
of the most intense aristocratic exclusiveness
Persons eligible as Emperors. the highest office in the world was the only
secular one open to all Christians. The old
writers, after debating at length the qualifica-
cations that are or may be desirable in an Emperor, and
relating how in Pagan times Gauls and Spaniards, Moors
and Pannonians, were thought worthy of the purple, decide that two things, and no more, are required of the candidate for Empire: he must be free-born, and he must be
orthodox.†

---

* See especially Gerlach Buxtorff, *Dissertatio ad Auream Bullam;*
and Augustinus Stenchus, *De Imperio Romano;* quoted by Marquard
Freher. It was keenly debated, while Charles V and Francis I (of
France) were rival candidates, whether any one but a German was
eligible. By birth Charles was either a Spaniard or a Fleming; but
this difficulty his partisans avoided by holding that he had been, according to the civil law, *in potestate* of Maximilian his grandfather.
However, to say nothing of the Guidos and Berengars of earlier days,
the examples of Richard and Alfonso are conclusive as to the eligi-
bility of others than Germans.   Edward III of England was, as has
been said, actually elected; Henry VIII was a candidate. And attempts were frequently made to elect the kings of France.—Cf.
Pfeffinger, Vitriarius illustratus, 69 sqq.

† The mediæval practice seems to have been that which still prevails, in the Roman Catholic Church—to presume the doctrinal
orthodoxy and eternal conformity of every citizen, whether lay or
clerical, until the contrary be proved. Of course when heresy was
rife it went hard with suspected men, unless they could either clear
themselves or submit to recant. But no one was required to pledge
himself beforehand, as a qualification for any office, to certain doctrines. And thus, important as an Emperor's orthodoxy was, he does
not appear to have been subjected to any test (in the modern sense of
the word), although the Pope pretended to the right of catechizing
him in the faith and rejecting him if unsound.   In the *Ordo Romanus*
we find a long series of questions which the Pontiff was to adminis-

It is not without a certain surprise that we see those who were engaged in the study of ancient letters, or felt indirectly their stimulus, embrace so fervently the cause of the Roman Empire. Still more difficult is it to estimate the respective influence exerted by each of the three revivals which it has been attempted to distinguish. The spirit of the ancient world by which the men who led these *The Empire and the new learning.* movements fancied themselves animated, was in truth a pagan, or at least a strongly secular spirit, in many respects inconsistent with the associations which had now gathered round the imperial office. And this hostility did not fail to show itself when at the beginning of the sixteenth century, in the fullness of the Renaissance, a direct and for the time irresistible sway was exercised by the art and literature of Greece, when the mythology of Euripides and Ovid supplanted that which had fired the imagination of Dante and peopled the visions of St. Francis ; when men forsook the image of the saint in the cathedral for the statue of the nymph in the garden; when the uncouth jargon of scholastic theology was equally distasteful to the scholars who formed their style upon Cicero and the philosophers who drew their inspiration from Plato. That meanwhile the admirers of antiquity did ally themselves with the defenders of the Empire, was due partly indeed to the false notions that were entertained regarding the

---

ter, but it does not appear, and is in the highest degree unlikely, that such a programme was ever carried out. At the German coronation, however (performed in earlier days at Aachen, afterward at Frankfort), the custom was for the Emperor before he was anointed to declare his orthodoxy by an oath taken on the famous copy of the Gospels which was held to have been used by Charles, and on a casket containing earth soaked with the blood of the martyr Stephen. The charge of heresy was one of the weapons used with most effect against Frederick II.

early Cæsars, yet still more to the common hostility of both schools to the Papacy. It was as successor of old Rome, and by virtue of her traditions, that the Holy See had established so wide a dominion ; yet no sooner did Arnold of Brescia and his republicans arise, claiming liberty in the name of the ancient constitution of the Roman city, than they found in the Popes their bitterest foes, and turned for help to the secular monarch against the clergy. With similar aversion did the Romish court view the revived study of the ancient jurisprudence, so soon as it became, in the hands of the school of Bologna, and afterward of the jurists of France, a power able to assert its independence and resist ecclesiastical pretensions. In the ninth century, Pope Nicholas I had himself judged in the famous case of Teutberga, wife of Lothar, according to the civil law: in the thirteenth, his successors * forbade its study, and the canonists strove to expel it from Europe.†
And as the current of educated opinion among the laity was beginning, however imperceptibly at first, to set against sacerdotal tyranny, it followed that the Empire would find sympathy in any effort it could make to regain its lost position. Thus the Emperors became, or might have become had they seen the greatness of the opportunity and been strong enough to improve it, the exponents and guides of the political movement, the pioneers, in part at least, of the Reformation. But the revival came too late to arrest, if not to adorn, the decline of their office. The growth of a national sentiment in the several countries of Europe, which had already gone too far to be arrested, and was urged on by forces far stronger than the theories of

---

* Honorius II in 1229 forbade it to be studied or taught in the University of Paris. Innocent IV published some years later a still more sweeping prohibition.

† See v. Savigny, *History of Roman Law in the Middle Ages,* vol. iii. pp. 81, 341–347.

catholic unity which opposed it, imprinted on the resistance to papal usurpation, and even on the instincts of political freedom, that form of narrowly local patriotism which they long retained and have not yet wholly lost. It can hardly be said that upon any occasion, except the gathering of the council of Constance by Sigismund, did the Emperor appear filling a truly international place. For the most part he exerted in the politics of Europe no influence greater than that of other princes. In actual resources he *The doctrine of the Empire's rights and functions never carried out in fact.* stood below the kings of France and England, far below his vassals the Visconti of Milan.* Yet this helplessness, such was men's faith or their timidity, and such their unwillingness to make prejudice bend to facts, did not prevent his dignity from being extolled in the most sonorous language by writers whose imaginations were enthralled by the halo of traditional glory which surrounded it.

We are thus brought back to ask, What was the connection between imperialism and the literary revival?

To moderns who think of the Roman Empire as the heathen persecuting power, it is strange to find it depicted as the model of a Christian commonwealth. It is stranger still that the study of antiquity should have made men advocates of arbitrary power. Democratic Athens, oligarchic Rome, *Attitude of the men of letters.* suggest to us Pericles and Brutus : the moderns who have striven to catch their spirit have been men like Algernon Sidney, and Vergniaud, and Shelley. The explanation is the same in both cases.† The ancient world was known

---

* Charles the Bold of Burgundy was a potentate incomparably stronger than the Emperor Frederick III from whom he sought the regal title.

† Cf. Sismondi, *Républiques Italiennes,* iv. chap. xxvii.

to the earlier middle ages by tradition, freshest for what
was latest, and by the authors of the Empire. Both presented to them the picture of a mighty despotism and a
civilization brilliant far beyond their own. Writings of
the fourth and fifth centuries, unfamiliar to us, were to
them authorities as high as Tacitus or Livy; yet Virgil and
Horace too had sung the praises of the first and wisest of
the Emperors. To the enthusiasts of poetry and law,
Rome meant universal monarchy ;* to those of religion,
her name called up the undimmed radiance of the Church
under Sylvester and Constantine. Petrarch,

Petrarch. the apostle of the dawning Renaissance, is excited by the last attempt to revive even the shadow of
imperial greatness: as he had hailed Rienzi, he welcomes
Charles IV into Italy, and execrates his departure. The
following passage is taken from his letter to the Roman
people asking them to receive back Rienzi : " When was
there ever such peace, such tranquillity, such justice, such
honor paid to virtue, such rewards distributed to the good
and punishments to the bad, when was ever the state so
wisely guided, as in the time when the world had obtained
one head, and that head Rome; the very time wherein God
deigned to be born of a virgin and dwell upon earth. To
every single body there has been given a head; the whole
world therefore also, which is called by the poet a great
body, ought to be content with one temporal head. For
every two-headed animal is monstrous; how much more
horrible and hideous a portent must be a creature with a
thousand different heads, biting and fighting against one
another ! If, however, it is necessary that there be more
heads than one, it is nevertheless evident that there ought
to be one to restrain all and preside over all, that so the
peace of the whole body may abide unshaken. Assuredly

---

* See Dante, *Paradise,* canto vi.

both in heaven and in earth the sovereignty of one has always been best."

His passion for the heroism of Roman conquest and the ordered peace to which it brought the world is the center of Dante's political hopes: he is no more an exiled Ghibeline, but a patriot whose fervid *Dante.* imagination sees a nation arise regenerate at the touch of its rightful lord. Italy, the spoil of so many Teutonic conquerors, is the garden of the Empire which Henry is to redeem: Rome the mourning widow, whom Albert is denounced for neglecting.* Passing through purgatory, the poet sees Rudolf of Hapsburg seated gloomily apart, mourning his sin in that he left unhealed the wounds of Italy.† In the deepest pit of hell's ninth circle lies Lucifer, huge, three-headed ; in each mouth a sinner whom he crunches between his teeth, in one mouth Iscariot the traitor to Christ, in the others the two traitors to the first Emperor of Rome, Brutus and Cassius.‡ To multiply illustrations from others parts of the poem would be an endless task; for the idea is ever present in Dante's mind, and displays itself in a hundred unexpected forms. Virgil himself is selected to be the guide of the pilgrim through hell and purgatory, not so much as being the great poet of antiquity, as because he " was born under Julius and lived beneath the good Augustus;" because he was divinely charged to sing of the Empire's earliest and brightest glories. Strange, that the shame of one age should be the glory of another. For Virgil's melancholy panegyrics upon the destroyer of the republic are no more like Dante's appeals

---

* " Vieni a veder la tua Roma, che piagne
    Vedova, sola e dì e notte chiama:
  ' Cesare mio, perchè non m' accompagne ?' "
                Purgatorio, canto vi. 112.

† *Purgatorio,* canto vii. 94.
‡ *Inferno,* canto xxxiv. 52.

to the coming saviour of Italy than is Cæsar Octavianus to Henry count of Luxemburg.

The visionary zeal of the man of letters was seconded by the more sober devotion of the lawyer. Conqueror, theologian and jurist, Justinian is a hero greater than either Julius or Constantine, for his enduring work bears him witness. Absolutism was the civilian's creed:* the phrases "legibus solutus," "lex regia," whatever else tended in the same direction, were taken to express the prerogative of him whose official style of Augustus, as well as the vernacular name of "Kaiser," designated the legitimate successor of the compiler of the Corpus Juris. Since it was upon this legitimacy that his claim to be the fountain of law rested, no pains were spared to seek out and observe every custom and precedent by which old Rome seemed to be connected with her representative.

Attitude of the Jurists.

Of the many instances that might be collected, it would be tedious to enumerate more than a few. The offices of the imperial household, instituted by Constantine the Great, were attached to the noblest families of Germany. The Emperor and Empress, before their coronation at Rome, were lodged in the chambers called those of Augustus and Livia;† a bare sword was borne before them by the prætorian prefect; their processions were adorned by the standards, eagles, wolves and dragons, which had figured in the train of

Imitations of old Rome.

---

* Not that the doctors of the civil law were necessarily political partisans of the Emperors. Savigny says that there were on the contrary more Guelfs than Ghibelines among the jurists of Bologna.— *Roman Law in the Middle Ages,* vol. iii. p. 80.

† Cf. Palgrave, *Normandy and England,* vol. ii. (of Otto and Adelheid). The *Ordo Romanus* talks of a "Camera Iuliæ" in the Lateran palace, reserved for the Empress.

Hadrian or Theodosius.* The constant title of the
Emperor himself, according to the style introduced by
Probus, was "semper Augustus," or "perpetuus Augustus," which erring etymology translated "at all times
increaser of the Empire."† Edicts issued by a Franconian
or Swabian sovereign were inserted as Novels‡ in the Corpus Juris, in the latest editions of which custom still
allows them a place. The *pontificatus maxims* of his pagan
predecessors was supposed to be preserved by the admission
of each Emperor as a canon of St. Peter's at Rome and St.
Mary's at Aachen.§ Sometimes we even find him talking
of his consulship.‖ Annalists invariably number the place
of each sovereign from Augustus downward.¶ The notion
of an uninterrupted succession, which moves the stranger's
wondering smile as he sees ranged round the magnificent
Golden Hall of Augsburg the portraits of the Cæsars,
laurelled, helmeted and periwigged, from Julius the conqueror of Gaul to Joseph the partitioner of Poland, was to
those generations not an article of faith only because its
denial was inconceivable.

---

* See notes to *Chron. Casin.* in Muratori, *S. R. I.* iv. 515.

† Zu aller Zeiten Mehrer des Reichs.

‡ *Novellæ Constitutiones.*

§ Marquard Freher, Scr. rer. Germ. iii. The question whether the
seven electors vote as *singuli* or as a *collegium*, is solved by showing
that they have stepped into the place of the senate and people of
Rome, whose duty it was to choose the Emperor, though (it is
naïvely added) the soldiers sometimes usurped it.—Peter de Andlo,
De Imperio Romano.

‖ Thus Charles, in a capitulary added to a revised edition of the
Lombard law issued in A.D. 801, says, "Anno consulatus nostri
primo." So Otto III calls himself "Consul Senatus populique
Romani."

¶ Francis II, the last Emperor, was one hundred and twentieth
from Augustus. Some chroniclers call Otto the Great Otto II, counting in Salvius Otho, the successor of Galba.

And all this historical antiquarianism, as one might call
it, which gathers round the Empire, is but one instance,
though the most striking, of that eager wish
Reverence for ancient forms and phrases in the Middle Ages. to cling to the old forms, use the old phrases,
and preserve the old institutions to which the
annals of mediæval Europe bear witness. It
appears even in trivial expressions, as when a
monkish chronicler says of evil bishops deposed,
Tribu moti sunt, or talks of the " senate and people of
the Franks," when he means a council of chiefs surrounded
by a crowd of half-naked warriors. So throughout Europe
charters and edicts were drawn upon Roman precedents;
the trade guilds, though often traceable to a different
source, represented the old *collegia ;* villenage was the
offspring of the system of *coloni* under the later Empire.
Even in remote Britain, the Teutonic invaders used Roman
ensigns, and stamped their coins with Roman devices;
called themselves " Basileis " and " Augusti."* Especially
did the cities perpetuate Rome through her most lasting
boon to the conquered, municipal self-government ; those
of later origin emulating in their adherence to antique
style others who, like Nismes and Cologne, Zürich and
Augsburg, could trace back their institutions to the *coloniæ*
and *municipia* of the first centuries. On the walls and
gates of hoary Nürnburg† the traveler still sees emblaz-
oned the imperial eagle, with the words " Senatus populusque Norimbergensis," and is borne in thought from the
quiet provincial town of to-day to the stirring republic of
the middle ages: thence to the Forum and the Capitol of
her greater prototype. For, in truth, through all that

---

* See p. 43 and note to p. 140.

† Nürnberg herself was not of Roman foundation. But this makes
the imitation all the more curious. The fashion even passed from
the cities to rural communities like some of the Swiss cantons. Thus
we find " Senatus populusque Uronensis."

period which we call the Dark and Middle Ages, men's minds were possessed by the belief that all things continued as they were from the beginning, that no chasm never to be recrossed lay between them and that ancient world to which they had not ceased to look back. We who are centuries removed can see that there had passed a great and wonderful change upon thought, and art, and literature, and politics, and society itself : a change whose best illustration is to be found in the process whereby there arose out of the primitive basilica the Romanesque cathedral, and from it in turn the endless varieties of Gothic. But so gradual was the change that each generation felt it passing over them no more than *Absence of* a man feels that perpetual transformation by *the idea of* which his body is renewed from year to year ; *change or* while the few who had learning enough to *progress.* study antiquity through its contemporary records, were prevented by the utter want of criticism, and of that which we call historical feeling, from seeing how prodigious was the contrast between themselves and those whom they admired. There is nothing more modern than the critical spirit which dwells upon the difference between the minds of men in one age and in another; which endeavors to make each age its own interpreter, and judge what it did or produced by a relative standard. Such a spirit was, before the last century or two, wholly foreign to art as well as to metaphysics. The converse and the parallel of the fashion of calling mediæval offices by Roman names, and supposing them therefore the same, is to be found in those old German pictures of the siege of Carthage or the battle between Porus and Alexander, where in the foreground two armies of knights, mailed and mounted, are charging each other like Crusaders, lance in rest, while behind, through the smoke of cannon, loom out the Gothic spires and towers of the be-

leagured city. And thus, when we remember that the
notion of progress and development, and of change as
the necessary condition thereof, was unwelcome or unknown in mediæval times, we may better understand,
though we do not cease to wonder, how men, never doubt-
ing that the political system of antiquity had descended to
them, modified indeed, yet in substance the same, should
have believed that the Frank, the Saxon, and the Swabian
ruled all Europe by a right which seems to us not less fantastic than that fabled charter whereby Alexander the
Great bequeathed his empire to the Slavic race for the love
of Roxolana.

It is a part of that perpetual contradiction of which the
history of the Middle Ages is full, that this belief had
hardly any influence on practical politics. The more ab-
jectly helpless the Emperor becomes, so much the more
sonorous is the language in which the dignity of his crown
is described. His power, we are told, is eternal, the provinces having resumed their allegiance after the barbarian
irruptions; * it is incapable of diminution or injury: exemptions and grants by him, so far as they tend to limit his
own prerogative, are invalid: † all Christendom is still of
right subject to him, though it may contumaciously refuse
obedience. ‡ The sovereigns of Europe are solemnly

---

* Æneas Sylvius, _De Ortu et Authoritate Imperii Romani._

† Thus some civilians held Constantine's Donation null ; but the
canonists, we are told, were clear as to its legality.

‡ "Et idem dico de istis aliis regibus et principibus, qui negant se
esse subditos regi Romanorum, ut rex Franciæ, Angliæ, et similes.
Si enim fatentur ipsum esse Dominum universalem, licet ab illo universali domino se subtrahant ex privilegio vel ex præscriptione vel
consimili, non ergo desunt esse cives Romani, per ea quæ
dicta sunt. Et per hoc omnes gentes quæ obediunt S. matri
ecclesiæ sunt de populo Romano. Et forte si quis diceret
dominum Imperatorem non esse dominum et monarcham totius orbis,

warned that they are resisting the power ordained of God.* No laws can bind the Emperor, though he may choose to live according to them : no court can judge him, though he may condescend to be sued in his own : none may presume to arraign the conduct or question the motives of him who is answerable only to God.† So writes Æneas Sylvius, while Frederick III, chased from his capital by the Hungarians, is wandering from convent to convent, an imperial beggar; while the princes, whom his subserviency to the Pope has driven into rebellion, are offering the imperial crown to Podiebrad, the Bohemian king.

But the career of Henry VII in Italy is the most remarkable illustration of the Emperor's position: and imperialist doctrines are set forth most strikingly in the treatise which the greatest spirit of the age wrote to herald or commemorate the advent of that hero, the *De Monarchia* of Dante.‡

Henry VII
A. D. 1308-
1313.

---

esset hæreticus, quia diceret contra determinationem ecclesiæ et textum S. evangelii, dum dicit, ' Exivit edictum a Cæsare Augusto ut describeretur universus orbis.' Ita et recognovit Christus Imperatorem ut dominum."—Bartolus, *Commentary on the Pandects*, xlviii. i. 24, *De Captivis et postliminio reversis*.

* Peter de Andlo, *multis locis* (see esp. cap. viii), and other writings of the time. Cf. Dante's letter to Henry VII : " Romanorum potestas nec metis Italiæ nec tricornis Siciliæ margine coarctatur. Nam etsi vim passa in angustum gubernacula sua contraxit undique, tamen de inviolabili iure fluctus Amphitritis attingens vix ab inutili unda Oceani se circumcingi dignatur. Scriptum est enim

    ' Nascetur pulchra Troianus origine Cæsar,
    Imperium Oceano, famam qui terminet astris.' "

So Fr. Zoannetus, in the sixteenth century, declares it to be a mortal sin to resist the Empire, as the power ordained of God.

† Æneas Sylvius Piccolomini (afterward Pope Pius II), *De Ortu et Authoritate Imperii Romani*. Cf. Gerlach Buxtorff, *Dissertatio ad Auream Bullam*.

‡ It has hitherto been the common opinion that the *De Monarchia*

Rudolf, Adolf of Nassau, Albert of Hapsburg, none of them crossed the Alps or attempted to aid the Italian Ghibelines who battled away in the name of their throne. Concerned only to restore order and aggrandize his house, and thinking apparently that nothing more was to be made of the imperial crown, Rudolf was content never to receive it, and purchased the Pope's good will by surrendering his jurisdiction in the capital, and his claims over the bequest of the Countess Matilda. Henry the Luxemburger ventured on a bolder course ; urged perhaps only by his lofty and chivalrous spirit, perhaps in despair at effecting anything with his slender resources against the princes of Germany. Crossing from his Burgundian dominions with a scanty following of knights, and descending from the Cenis upon Turin, he found his prerogative higher in men's belief after sixty years of neglect than it had stood under the last Hohenstaufen. The cities of Lombardy opened their gates ; Milan decreed a vast subsidy ; Guelf and Ghibeline exiles alike were restored, and imperial vicars appointed everywhere : supported by the Avignonese pontiff, who dreaded the restless ambition of his French neighbor, King Philip IV, Henry had the interdict of the Church as well as the ban of the Empire at his command. But the illusion of success vanished as soon as men, recovering from their first impression, began to be again governed by their ordinary passions and interests, and not by an imaginative reverence for the glories of the past. Tumults and revolts broke out in Lombardy; at Rome the king of Naples held St. Peter's, and the coronation must take place in St. John Lateran, on the southern bank of the Tiber. The hostility of the Guelfic league, headed by the Florentines, Guelfs even

was written in the view of Henry's expedition. But latterly weighty reasons have been advanced for believing that its date must be placed some years later.

against the Pope, obliged Henry to depart from his impartial and republican policy, and to purchase the aid of the
Ghibeline chiefs by granting them the government of
cities. With few troops, and encompassed
by enemies, the heroic Emperor sustained
an unequal struggle for a year longer,
till, in A. D. 1313, he sank beneath the fevers of
the deadly Tuscan summer. His German followers
believed, nor has history wholly rejected the tale, that
poison was given him by a Dominican monk in sacramental
wine.

*Death of
Henry VII.*

Others after him descended from the Alps, but they
came, like Lewis IV, Rupert, Sigismund, at the behest of
a faction, which found them useful tools for a
time, then flung them away in scorn ; or like
Charles IV and Frederick III, as the humble
minions of a French or Italian priest. With
Henry VII ends the history of the Empire in Italy, and
Dante's book is an epitaph instead of a prophecy. A
sketch of its argument will convey a notion of the feelings
with which the noblest Ghibelines fought, as well as of the
spirit in which the Middle Age was.accustomed to handle
such subjects.

*Later Em-
perors in
Italy.*

Weary of the endless strife of princes and cities, of the
factions within every city against each other, seeing municipal freedom, the only mitigation of turbu-
lence, vanish with the rise of domestic tyrants,
Dante raises a passionate cry for some power
to still the tempest, not to quench liberty or
supersede local self-government, but to correct and moderate them, to restore unity and peace to hapless Italy. His
reasoning is throughout closely syllogistic: he is alternately
the jurist, the theologian, the scholastic metaphysician :
the poet of the Divina Commedia is betrayed only by the
compressed energy of diction, by his clear vision of the unseen, rarely by a glowing metaphor.

*Dante's
feelings and
theories.*

Monarchy is first proved to be the true and rightful form of government.* Men's objects are best attained during universal peace: this is possible only under a monarch. And as he is the image of the Divine unity, so man is through him made one, and brought most near to God. There must, in every system of forces, be a "primum mobile;" to be perfect,ᐧ every organization must have a center, into which all is gathered, by which all is controlled.† Justice is best secured by a supreme arbiter of disputes, himself unsolicited by ambition, since his dominion is already bounded only by ocean. Man is best and happiest when he is most free; to be free is to exist for one's own sake. To this grandest end does the monarch and he alone guide us; other forms of government are perverted,‡ and exist for the benefit of some class ; he seeks the good of all alike, being to that very end appointed.§

The De Monarchia.

Abstract arguments are then confirmed from history. Since the world began there has been but one period of perfect peace, and but one of perfect monarchy, that, namely, which existed at our Lord's birth, under the scepter of Augustus; since then the heathen have raged, and the kings of the earth have stood up; they have set themselves against their Lord, and his anointed the Roman

---

* More than half a century earlier the envoys of the Norwegian king, in urging the chiefs of the republic of Iceland assembled at their Althing to accept Hakon as their suzerain, had argued that monarchy was the only rightful form of government, and had appealed to the fact that in all continental Europe there was no such thing as an absolutely independent republic.

† Suggesting the celestial hierarchies of Dionysius the Areopagite.

‡ Quoting Aristotle's *Politics.*

§ " Non enim cives propter consules nec gens propter regem, sed e converso consules propter cives, rex propter gentem."

prince.* The universal dominion, the need for which has been thus established, is then proved to belong to the Romans. Justice is the will of God, a will to exalt Rome shown through her whole history.† Her virtues deserves honor: Virgil is quoted to prove those of Æneas, who by descent and marriage was the heir of three continents: of Asia through Assaracus and Creusa; of Africa by Electra (mother of Dardanus and daughter of Atlas) and Dido; of Europe by Dardanus and Lavinia. God's favor was approved in the fall of the shields to Numa, in the miraculous deliverance of the capital from the Gauls, in the hailstorm after Cannæ. Justice is also the advantage of the state: that advantage was the constant object of the virtuous Cincinnatus, and the other heroes of the republic. They conquered the world for its own good, and therefore justly, as Cicero attests;‡ so that their sway was not so much " imperium " as " patrocinium orbis terrarum." Nature herself, the fountain *The De Monarchia.* of all right, had, by their geographical position and by the gift of a genius so vigorous, marked them out for universal dominion:

> " Excudent alii spirantia mollius æra,
> Credo equidem: vivos ducent de marmore vultus;
> Orabunt causas melius, cœlique meatus
> Describent radio, et surgentia sidera dicent:
> Tu regere imperio populos, Romane, memento;
> Hæ tibi erunt artes; pacisque imponere morem,
> Parcere subiectis, et debellare superbos."

Finally, the right of war asserted, Christ's birth, and

---

* " Reges et principes in hoc unico concordantes, ut adversentur Domino suo et uncto suo Romano Principi," having quoted " Quare fremuerunt gentes."

† Especially in the opportune death of Alexander the Great.

‡ Cic. *De Off.*, ii. " Ita ut illud patrocinium orbis terrarum potius quam imperium poterat nominari."

death under Pilate, ratified their government. For Christian doctrine requires that the procurator should have been a lawful judge,* which he was not unless Tiberius was a lawful Emperor.

The relations of the imperial and papal power are then examined, and the passages of Scripture (tradition being rejected), to which the advocates of the Papacy appeal, are elaborately explained away. The argument from the sun and moon† does not hold, since both lights existed before man's creation, and at a time when, as still sinless, he needed no controlling powers. Else *accidentia* would have preceded *propria* in creation. The moon, too, does not receive her being nor all her light from the sun, but so much only as makes her more effective. So there is no reason why the temporal should not be aided in a corresponding measure by the spiritual authority. This difficult text disposed of, others fall more easily; Levi and Judah, Samuel and Saul, the incense and gold offered by the Magi;‡ the two swords, the power of binding and loosing given to Peter. Constantine's donation was illegal: no single Emperor nor Pope can disturb the everlasting foun-

---

* " Si Pilati imperium non de iure fuit, peccatum in Christo non fuit adeo punitum."

† There is a curious seal of the Emperor Otto IV (figured in J. M. Heineccius, *De veteribus Germanorum atque aliarum nationum sigillis*), on which the sun and moon are represented over the head of the Emperor. Heineccius says he cannot explain it, but there seems to be no reason why we should not take the device as typifying the accord of the spiritual and temporal powers which was brought about at the accession of Otto, the Guelfic leader, and the favored candidate of Pope Innocent III. The analogy between the lights of heaven and the potentates of earth is one which the mediæval writers are very fond of. It seems to have originated with Gregory VII.

‡ Typifying the spiritual and temporal powers, Dante meets this by distinguishing the homage paid to Christ from that which his Vicar can rightfully demand.

dations of their respective thrones : the one had no right to bestow, nor the other to receive, such a gift. Leo III gave the Empire to Charles wrongfully: *" usurpatio iuris nom facit ius."* It is alleged that all things of one kind are reducible to one individual, and so all men to the Pope. But Emperor and Pope differ in kind, and so far as they are men, are reducible only to God, on whom the Empire immediately depends; for it existed before Peter's see, and was recognized by Paul when he appealed to Cæsar. The temporal power of the Papacy can have been given neither by natural law, nor divine ordinance, nor universal consent: nay, it is against its own Form and Essence, the life of Christ, who said, "My kingdom is not of this world."

Man's nature is twofold, corruptible and incorruptible; he has therefore two ends, active virtue on earth, and the enjoyment of the sight of God hereafter ; the one to be attained by practice conformed to the precepts of philosophy, the other by the theological virtues. Hence two guides are needed, the Pontiff and the Emperor, the latter of whom, in order that he may direct mankind in accordance with the teachings of philosophy to temporal blessedness, must preserve universal peace in the world. Thus are the two powers equally ordained of God, and the Emperor, though supreme in all *The De* that pertains to the secular world, is in some *Monarchia conclusion.* things dependent on the Pontiff, since earthly happiness is subordinate to eternal. " Let Cæsar, therefore, show toward Peter the reverence wherewith a first-born son honors his father, that, being illumined by the light of his paternal favor, he may the more excellently shine forth upon the whole world, to the rule of which he has been appointed by Him alone who is of all things, both spiritual and temporal, the King and Governor." So ends the treatise.

Dante's arguments are not stranger than his omissions.

No suspicion is breathed against Constantine's donation; no proof is adduced, for no doubt is felt, that the Empire of Henry VII is the legitimate continuation of that which had been swayed by Augustus and Justinian. Yet Henry was a German, sprung from Rome's barbarian foes, the elected of those who had neither part nor share in Italy and her capital.

CHAPTER XVI.

THE CITY OF ROME IN THE MIDDLE AGES.

" It is related," says Sozomen, in the ninth book of his Ecclesiastical History, " that when Alaric was hastening against Rome, a holy monk of Italy admonished him to spare the city, and not to make himself the cause of such fearful ills. But Alaric answered, ' It is not of my own will that I do this ; there is One who forces me on, and will not let me rest, bidding me spoil Rome.' "*

Toward the close of the tenth century the Bohemian Woitech, famous in after legend as St. Adalbert, forsook his bishopric of Prague to journey into Italy, and settled himself in the Roman monastery of Sant' Alessio. After some few years passed there in religious solitude, he was summoned back to resume the duties of his see, and labored for a while among his half-savage countrymen. Soon, however, the old longing came over him : he re-sought his cell upon the brow of the Aventine, and there, wandering among the ancient shrines, and taking on himself the menial offices of the convent, he abode happily for a space. At length the reproaches of his metropolitan, the archbishop of Mentz, and the express commands of Pope Gregory V, drove him back over the Alps, and he set off in the train of Otto III, lamenting, says his biographer, that he should no more enjoy his beloved quiet

---

* Hist. Eccl. 1. ix. c. 6: τὸν δὲ φάναι, ὡς οὐχ ἑκὼν τάδε ἐπιχειρεῖ, ἀλλά τις συνεχῶς ἐνοχλῶν αὐτὸν βιάζεται, καὶ ἐπιτάττει τὴν Ῥώμην πορθεῖν.

in the mother of martyrs, the home of the Apostles, golden Rome. A few months later he died a martyr among the pagan Lithuanians of the Baltic.*

Nearly four hundred years later, and nine hundred after the time of Alaric, Francis Petrarch writes thus to his friend John Colonna:

"Thinkest thou not that I long to see that city to which there has never been any like nor ever shall be; which even an enemy called a city of kings; of whose people it hath been written, 'Great is the valor of the Roman people, great and terrible their name;' concerning whose unexampled glory and incomparable empire, which was, and is, and is to be, divine prophets have sung; where are the tombs of the apostles and martyrs and the bodies of so many thousands of the saints of Christ."†

It was the same irresistible impulse that drew the warrior, the monk, and the scholar toward the mystical city which was to mediæval Europe more than Delphi had been to the Greek or Mecca to the Islamite, the Jerusalem of Christianity, the city which once ruled the earth, and now ruled the world of disembodied spirits.‡ For there was

---

* See the two Lives of St. Adalbert in Pertz, *M. G. H.*, iv, evidently compiled soon after his death.

† Another letter of Petrarch's to John Colonna, written immediately after his arrival in the city, deserves to be quoted, it is so like what a stranger would now write off after his first day in Rome: "In præsens nihil est quod inchoare ausim, miraculo rerum tantarum et stuporis mole obrutus . . . præsentia vero, mirum dictu, nihil imminuit sed auxit omnia: vere maior fuit Roma maioresque sunt reliquiæ quam rebar: iam non orbem ab hac urbe domitum sed tam sero domitum miror. Vale."

‡ The idea of the continuance of the sway of Rome under a new character is one which mediæval writers delight to illustrate. In Appendix, Note D, there is quoted as a specimen a poem upon Rome, by Hildebert (bishop of Le Mans, and afterward archbishop of Tours), written in the beginning of the twelfth century.

then, as there is now, something in Rome to attract men of every class. The devout pilgrim came to pray at the shrine of the Prince of the Apostles, too happy if he could carry back to his monastery in the forests of Saxony or by the bleak Atlantic shore the bone of some holy martyr ; the lover of learning and poetry dreamed of Virgil and Cicero among the shattered columns of the Forum ; the Germanic kings, in spite of pestilence, treachery and seditions, came with their hosts to seek in the ancient capital of the world the fountain of temporal dominion. Nor has the spell yet wholly lost its power. To half the Christian nations Rome is the metropolis of religion, to all the metropolis of art. In her streets, and hers alone among the cities of the world, may every form of human speech be heard: she is more glorious in her decay and desolation than the stateliest seats of modern power.

But while men thought thus of Rome, what was Rome herself.

The modern traveler, after his first few days in Rome, when he has looked out upon the Campagna from the summit of St. Peter's, paced the chilly corridors of the Vatican, and mused under the echoing dome of the Pantheon, when he has passed in review the monuments of regal and republican and papal Rome, begins to seek for some relics of the twelve hundred years that lie between Constantine and Pope Julius II, "Where," he asks, "is the Rome of the Middle Ages, the Rome of Alberic and Hildebrand and Rienzi ; the Rome which dug the graves of so many Teutonic hosts ; whither the pilgrims flocked ; whence came the commands at which kings bowed? Where are the memorials of the brightest age of Christian architecture, the age which reared Cologne and Rheims and Westminster, which gave to Italy the cathedrals of Tuscany and the wave-washed palaces of Venice?" To this question there is no answer. Rome, the mother of the arts, has scarcely a building to commemorate those times, for to her they were times of turmoil and misery, times in which the shame of the present was embittered by recollections of a brighter past. Nevertheless a minute scrutiny may still discover, hidden in dark corners or disguised under an unbecoming modern dress, much that carries us back to the mediæval town, and helps us to realize its social and political condition. Therefore, a brief notice of the state of Rome during the Middle Ages, with especial reference to those monumen's which the visitor may still examine for himself, may not be without its use, and is at any rate no unfitting pendant to an account of the institution which drew from the city its name and its magnificent pretensions. Moreover, as will appear more fully in the sequel, the history of the Roman people is an instructive illustration of the influence of those ideas upon which the Empire itself rested, as well in their weakness as in their strength.*

It is not from her capture by Alaric, nor even from the more destructive ravages of the Vandal Genseric, that the material and social ruin of Rome must be dated, but rather from the repeated sieges which she sustained

Causes of the rapid decay of the city.

in the war of Belisarius with the Ostrogoths. This struggle, however, long and exhausting as it was, would not have proved so fatal had the previous condition of the city been sound and healthy. Her wealth and population in the middle of the fifth century were probably little inferior to what they had been in the most prosperous days of the imperial government. But this wealth was entirely gathered

---

* In writing this chapter I have derived much assistance from the interesting work of Ferdinand Gregorovius, *Geschichte der Stadt Rom in Mittelalter.* Unfortunately no English translation of it exists; but I am informed by the author that one is likely ere long to appear.

into the hands of a small and effeminate aristocracy. The crowd that filled her streets was composed partly of poor and idle freemen, unaccustomed to arms and debarred from political rights; partly of a far more numerous herd of slaves, gathered from all parts of the world, and morally even lower than their masters. There was no middle class, and no system of municipal institutions, for although the senate and consuls with many of the lesser magistracies continued to exist, they had for centuries enjoyed no effective power, and were nowise fitted to lead and rule the people. Hence it was that when the Gothic war and the subsequent inroads of the Lombards had reduced the great families to beggary, the framework of society dissolved and could not be replaced. In a state rotten to the core there was no vital force left for reconstruction. The old forms of political activity had been too long dead to be recalled to life : the people wanted the moral force to produce new ones, and all the authority that could be said to exist in the midst of anarchy tended to center itself in the chief of the new religious society.

So far Rome's condition was like that of the other great towns of Italy and Gaul. But in two points her case differed from theirs, and to these the difference of her after fortunes may be traced. Her bishop had no temporal potentate to overshadow his dignity or check his ambition, for the vicar of the Eastern court lived far away at Ravenna, and seldom interfered *Peculiari-* except to ratify a papal election or punish a more *ties in the* than commonly outrageous sedition. Her pop- *of Rome.* ulation received an all but imperceptible infusion of that Teutonic blood and those Teutonic customs by whose stern discipline the inhabitants of northern Italy were in the end renovated. Everywhere the old institutions had perished of decay : in Rome alone there was nothing except the ecclesiastical system out of which new ones could arise. Her condition was therefore the most pitiable in which a community can find itself, one of struggle without purpose or progress. The citizens were divided into three orders: the military class, including what was left of the ancient aristocracy; the clergy, a host of priests, monks and nuns, attached to the countless churches and convents; and the people or *plebs*, as they are called, a poverty-stricken rabble without trade, without industry, with little municipal organization to bind them together. Of these two latter classes the Pope was the natural leader, the first was divided into factions headed by some three or four of the great families, whose quarrels kept the town in incessant bloodshed. The internal history of Rome from the sixth to the twelfth century is an obscure and tedious record of the contests of these factions with each other, and of the aristocracy as a whole with the slowly growing power of the Chuch.

The revolt of the Romans from the Iconoclastic Emperors of the East, followed as it was by the reception of the Franks as patricians and emperors, is an event of the highest importance in the history of Italy and of the popedom. In the domestic constitution of Rome it made little change. With the instinct of a profound genius, Charles the Great saw that Rome, though it might be ostensibly the capital, could not be the real center of his dominions. He continued to reside in Germany, and did not even build a palace at Rome. For a time the awe of his power, the presence of his *missus* or lieutenant, and the occasional visits of his successors Lothar and Lewis II to the city, repressed her internal disorders. But after the death of the prince last named, and still more after the dissolution of the Carolingian Empire itself, Rome relapsed into a state of profligacy and barbarism to which, even in that age, Europe supplied no parallel, a barbarism which

Her condition in the ninth and tenth centuries.

had inherited all the vices of civilization without any of its virtues. The papal office in particular seems to have lost its religious character, as it had certainly lost all claim to moral purity. For more than a century the chief priest of Christendom was no more than a tool of some ferocious faction among the nobles. Criminal means had raised him to the throne ; violence, sometimes going the length of mutilation or murder, deprived him of it. The marvel is, a marvel in which papal historians have not unnaturally discovered a miracle, that after sinking so low, the Papacy should ever have risen again. Its rescue and exaltation to the pinnacle of glory was accomplished not by the Romans but by the efforts of the Transalpine Church, aiding and prompting the Saxon and Franconian Emperors. Yet even the religious reform did not abate intestine turmoil, and it was not till the twelfth century that a new spirit began to work in politics, which ennobled if it could not heal the sufferings of the Roman people.

Ever since the days of Alberic their pride had revolted against the haughty behavior of the Teutonic emperors. From still earlier times they had been jealous of sacerdotal authority, and now watched with alarm the rapid extension of its influence. The events of the twelfth century gave these feelings a definite direction. It was the time of the struggle of the Investitures, in which Hildebrand and his disciples had been striving to draw all the things of this world as well as of the next into *Growth of a republican feeling: hostility to the Popes.* their grasp. It was the era of the revived study of Roman law, by which alone the extravagant pretensions of the decretalists could be resisted. The Lombard and Tuscan towns had become flourishing municipalities, independent of their bishops, and at open war with their Emperor. While all these things were stirring the minds of the Romans, Arnold of Brescia came preaching reform,

denouncing the corrupt life of the clergy, not perhaps,
like some others of the so called schismatics of
Arnold of Brescia. his time, denying the need of a sacerdotal order,
but at any rate urging its restriction to purely
spiritual duties. On the minds of the Romans such teaching fell like the spark upon dry grass; they threw off the
yoke of the Pope,* drove out the imperial prefect, reconstituted the senate and the equestrian order, appointed
consuls, struck their own coins, and professed to treat the
German Emperors as their nominees and dependants. To
have successfully imitated the republican constitution of
the cities of northern Italy would have been much, but
with this they were not content. Knowing in a vague,
ignorant way that there had been a Roman republic before
there was a Roman empire, they fed their vanity with
visions of a renewal of all their ancient forms, and saw in
fancy their senate and people sitting again upon the Seven
Hills and ruling over the kings of the earth. Stepping, as
it were, into the arena where Pope and Emperor were contending for the headship of the world, they rejected the
one as a priest, and declaring the other to be only their
creature, they claimed as theirs the true and lawful inheritance of the world-dominion which their ancestors had won.
Antiquity was in one sense on their side, and to us now it
seems less strange that the Roman people should aspire to
rule the earth than that a German barbarian should rule it
in their name. But practically the scheme was absurd,
and could not maintain itself against any serious opposition. As a modern historian aptly expresses it, " they
were setting up ruins:" they might as well have raised the

---

* Republican forms of some sort had existed before Arnold's arrival, but we hear the name of no other leader mentioned ; and
doubtless it was by him chiefly that the spirit of hostility to the
clerical power was infused into the minds of the Romans.

broken columns that strewed their Forum and hoped to
rear out of them a strong and stately temple. The reverence which the men of the Middle Ages felt for Rome was
given altogether to the name and to the place, nowise to
the people. As for power, they had none : so far from
holding Italy in subjection, they could scarcely maintain
themselves against the hostility of Tusculum. But it
would have been well worth the while of the
Teutonic Emperors to have made the Romans *Short-*
their allies, and bridled by their help the tem- *sighted*
poral ambition of the Popes. The offer was *policy of the*
actually made·to them, first to Conrad III, who *Emperors.*
seems to have taken no notice of it; and afterward, as has
been already stated, to Frederick I, who repelled in the
most contumelious fashion the envoys of the senate.
Hating and fearing the Pope, he always respected him :
toward the Romans he felt all the contempt of a feudal
king for burghers, and of a German warrior for Italians.
At the demand of Pope Hadrian, whose foresight thought
no heresy so dangerous as one which threatened the
authority of the clergy, Arnold of Brescia was seized by
the imperial prefect, put to death, and his ashes cast into
the Tiber, lest the people should treasure them up as
relics. But the martyrdom of their leader did not quench
the hopes of his followers. The republican constitution
continued to exist, and rose from time to time, during the
weakness or the absence of the Popes, into a brief and
fitful activity.* Once awakened, the idea, seductive at once

---

* The series of papal coins is interrupted (with one or two slight
exceptions) from A.D. 984 (not long after the time of Alberic) to A.D.
1304. In their place we meet with various coins struck by the municipal authorities, some of which bear on the obverse the head of the
Apostle Peter, with the legend Roman. Pricipe: on the reverse the
head of the Apostle Paul, legend, Senat. Popul. Q. R. Gregorovius
ut supra.

to the imagination of the scholar and the vanity of the
Roman citizen, could not wholly disappear, and two centuries after Arnold's time it found a more brilliant if less
disinterested exponent in the tribune Nicholas Rienzi.

The career of this singular personage is misunderstood
by those who suppose him to have been possessed of profound political insight, a republican on modern
*Character
and career
of the
tribune
Rienzi.*
principles. He was indeed, despite his overween-
ing conceit, and what seems to us his charla-
tanry, both a patriot and a man of genius, in tem-
perament a poet, filled with soaring ideas. But
those ideas, although dressed out in gaudier
colors by his lively fancy, were after all only the old ones,
memories of the long-faded glories of the heathen republic, and a series of scornful contrasts levelled at her
present oppressors, both of them showing no vista of
future peace except through the revival of those ancient
names to which there were no things to correspond. It
was by declaiming on old texts and displaying old monuments that the tribune enlisted the support of the Roman
populace, not by any appeal to democratic principles;
and the whole of his acts and plans, though they astonished men by their boldness, do not seem to have been
regarded as novel or impracticable.*   In the breasts of

---

* Rienzi called himself Augustus as well as tribune; "tribuno Augusto de Roma." (He pretended, or his friends pretended for him—
it was at any rate believed — that he was an illegitimate son
of the Emperor Henry VII). He cited, on becoming Tribune of
Rome, the cardinals to appear before the people of Rome and give
an account of their conduct; and after them the Emperor. "Ancora
citao lo Bavaro (Lewis IV). Puoi citao li elettori de lo imperio in
Alemagna, e disse 'Voglio vedere che rascione haco nella elettione,'
che trovasse scritto che passato alcuno tempo la elettione recadeva a
li Romani."— *Vita di Cola di Rienzi*, c. xxvi (written by a contemporary). I give the spelling as it stands in Muratori's edition.

men like Petrarch, who loved Rome even more than they hated her people, the enthusiasm of Rienzi found a sympathetic echo : others scorned and denounced him as an upstart, a demagogue and a rebel. Both friends and enemies seemed to have comprehended and regarded as natural his feelings and designs, which were altogether those of his age. Being, however, a mere matter of imagination, not of reason, having no anchor, so to speak, in realities, no true relation to the world as it then stood, these schemes of republican revival were as transient and unstable as they were quick of growth and gay of color. As the authority of the Popes became consolidated, and free municipalities disappeared elsewhere throughout Italy, the dream of a renovated Rome at length withered up and fell and died. Its last struggle was made in the conspiracy of Stephen Porcaro, in the time of Pope Nicholas V; and from that time onward there was no question of the supremacy of the bishop within his holy city.

It is never without a certain regret that we watch the disappearance of a belief, however illusive, around which the love and reverence for mankind once clung. But this illusion need be the less regretted that it had only the feeblest influence for good on the state of mediæval Rome. During the three centuries that lie between Arnold of Brescia and Porcaro, the disorders *Causes of* of Rome were hardly less violent than they had *the failure* been in the Dark Ages, and to all appearance *of the* worse than those of any other European city. *struggle for* There was a want not only of fixed authority, *independ-* but of those elements of social stability which *ence.* the other cities of Italy possessed. In the greater republics of Lombardy and Tuscany the bulk of the population were artisans, hard-working orderly people ; while above them stood a prosperous middle class, engaged mostly in commerce, and having in their system of trade-guilds an

organization both firm and flexible. It was by foreign
trade that Genoa, Venice and Pisa became great, as it was
the wealth acquired by manufacturing industry that enabled Milan and Florence to overcome and incorporate the
territorial aristocracies which surrounded them.

Rome possessed neither source of riches. She was ill-
placed for trade; having no market she produced no goods
to be disposed of, and the unhealthiness which long
neglect had brought upon her Campagna made its fertility
unavailable. Already she stood as she stands now, lonely
and isolated, a desert at her very gates. As
Internal there was no industry, so there was nothing
condition of that deserved to be called a citizen class. The
the city.
The people. people were a mere rabble, prompt to follow the
demagogue who flattered their vanity, prompter
still to desert him in the hour of danger. Superstition
was with them a matter of national pride, but they lived
too near sacred things to feel much reverence for them :
they ill-treated the Pope and fleeced the pilgrims who
crowded to their shrines : they were probably the only
community in Europe who sent no recruit to the armies of
the Cross. Priests, monks, and all the nondescript hang-
ers-on of an ecclesiastical court, formed a large part of the
population; while of the rest many were supported in a
state of half mendicancy by the countless religious foundations, themselves enriched by the gifts or the
The nobility. plunder of Latin Christendom. The noble
families were numerous, powerful, ferocious ; they were
surrounded by bands of unruly retainers, and waged a constant war against each other from their castles in the adjoining country or in the streets of the city itself. Had
things been left to take their natural course, one of these
families, the Colonna, for instance, or the Orsini, would
probably have ended by overcoming its rivals, and have
established, as was the case in the republics of Romagna

and Tuscany, a " signoria" or local tyranny, like those
which had once prevailed in the cities of
Greece. But the presence of the sacerdotal *The bishop.*
power, as it had hindered the growth of feudalism, so also it
stood in the way of such a development as this, and in so
far aggravated the confusion of the city. Although the
Pope was not as yet recognized as legitimate sovereign, he
was not only the most considerable person in Rome, but
the only one whose authority had anything of an official
character. But the reign of each pontiff was short; he had
no military force, he was frequently absent from his see.
He was, moreover, very often a member of one of the
great families, and, as such, no better than a faction
leader at home, while venerated by the rest of Europe as
the universal priest.

It remains only to speak of the person who should have
been to Rome what the national king was to the cities of
France, or England, or Germany, that is to
say, of the Emperor. As has been said *The Emperor.*
already, his power was a mere chimera, chiefly
important as furnishing a pretext to the Colonna and
other Ghibeline chieftains for their opposition to the papal
party. Even his abstract rights were matter of controversy. The Popes, whose predecessors had been content
to govern as the lieutenants of Charles and Otto, now
maintained that Rome as a spiritual city could not be subject to any temporal jurisdiction, and that she was therefore no part of the Roman Empire, though at the same
time its capital. Not only, it was urged, had Constantine
yielded up Rome to Sylvester and his successors, Lothar
the Saxon had at his coronation formally renounced his
sovereignty by doing homage to the pontiff and receiving
the crown as his vassal. The Popes felt then as they feel
now, that their dignity and influence would suffer if they
should even appear to admit in their place of residence the

jurisdiction of a civil potentate, and although they could
not secure their own authority, they were at least able to
exclude any other.   Hence it was that they were so uneasy
whenever an Emperor came to them to be crowned, that
they raised up difficulties in his path, and endeavored to
be rid of him as soon as possible.   And here
Visits of the
Emperors
to Rome.
something must be said of the programme, as
one may call it, of these imperial visits to
Rome, and of the marks of their presence which
the Germans left behind them, remembering always that
after the time of Frederick II it was rather the exception
than the rule for an Emperor to be crowned in his capital
at all.

The traveler who enters Rome now, if he comes, as he
most commonly does, by way of Civita Vecchia, slips in
by the railway before he is aware, is huddled into a
vehicle at the terminus, and set down at his hotel in the
middle of the modern town before he has seen anything at
all.   If he comes overland from Tuscany along the bleak
road that passes near Veii and crosses the Milvian bridge,
he has indeed from the slopes of the Ciminian range a
splendid prospect of the sea-like Campagna, girdled in by
glittering hills, but of the city he sees no sign save the
pinnacle of St. Peter's, until he is within the walls.   Far
Their
approach.
otherwise was it in the Middle Ages.   Then
travelers of every grade, from the humble pilgrim to the new-made archbishop who came in
the pomp of a lengthy train to receive from the Pope the
pallium of his office, approached from the north or north-
east side; following a track along the hilly ground on the
Tuscan side of the Tiber until they halted on the brow of
Monte Mario*—the Mount of Joy—and saw the city of

---

* The Germans called this hill, which is the highest in or near
Rome, conspicuous from a beautiful group of stone-pines upon its
brow, Mons Gaudii; the origin of the Italian name, Monte Mario, is

their solemnities lie spread before them, from the great pile of the Lateran far away upon the Cœlian hill, to the basilica of St. Peter's at their feet. They saw it not, as now, a sea of billowy cupolas, but a mass of low red-roofed houses, varied by tall brick towers, and at rarer intervals by masses of ancient ruin, then larger far than now ; while over all rose those two monuments of the best of the heathen Emperors, monuments that still look down, serenely changeless, on the armies of new nations and the festivals of a new religion—the columns of Marcus Aurelius and Trajan.

From Monte Mario the Teutonic host descended, when they had paid their orisons, into the Neronian field, the piece of flat land that lies outside the gate of St. Angelo. Here it was the custom for the elders of the Romans to meet the elected Emperor, present their charters for confirmation, and receive his oath to preserve their good customs.* Then a procession *Their entrance.* was formed : the priests and monks, who had come out with hymns to greet the Emperor, led the way ; the knights and soldiers of Rome, such as they were, came next ; then the monarch, followed by a long array of Transalpine chivalry. Passing into the city they advanced to St. Peter's, where the Pope, surrounded by his clergy, stood on the great staircase of the basilica to welcome and bless the Roman king. On the next day came the coronation, with ceremonies too elaborate for description,† ceremonies which, we may well believe, were seldom

not known, unless it be, as some think, a corruption of Mons Malus. It was on this hill that Otto III hanged Crescentius and his followers.

* I quote this from the *Ordo Romanus* as it stands in Muratori's third Dissertation in the *Antiquitates Italiæ medii ævi.*

† Great stress was laid on one part of the procedure—the holding by the Emperor of the Pope's stirrup for him to mount, and the

duly completed. Far more usual were other rites, of
which the book of ritual makes no mention, unless they
are to be counted among the " good customs of the
Romans;" the clang of war bells, the battle cry of German
and Italian combatants. The Pope, when he
Hostility of could not keep the Emperor from entering
Pope and Rome, required him to leave the bulk of his
people to the host without the walls, and if foiled in this,
Germans. sought his safety in raising up plots and seditions against his too powerful friend. The Roman people,
on the other hand, violent as they often were against the
Pope, had nevertheless a sort of national pride in him. Very
different were their feelings toward the Teutonic chieftain, who came from a far land to receive in their city, yet
without thanking them for it, the ensign of a power which
the prowess of their forefathers had won. Despoiled of
their ancient right to choose the universal bishop, they
clung all the more desperately to the belief that it was they
who chose the universal prince, and were mortified afresh
when each successive sovereign contemptuously scouted
their claims, and paraded before their eyes his rude barbarian cavalry. Thus it was that a Roman sedition was the all
but invariable accompaniment of a Roman coronation.
The three revolts against Otto the Great have been already
described. His grandson Otto III, in spite of his passionate fondness for the city, was met by the same faithless-
ness and hatred, and departed at last in despair at the fail-

---

leading of his palfrey for some distance. Frederick Barbarossa's
omission of this mark of respect when Pope Hadrian IV met him on
his way to Rome, had nearly caused a breach between the two poten
tates, Hadrian absolutely refusing the kiss of peace until Frederick
should have gone through the form, which he was at last forced to
do in a somewhat ignominious way.

ure of his attempts at conciliation.* A century afterward Henry V's coronation produced violent tumults, occasioned by his seizing the Pope and cardinals in St. Peter's, and keeping them prisoners till they submitted to his terms. Remembering this, Pope Hadrian IV would fain have forced the troops of Frederick Barbarossa to remain without the walls, but the rapidity of their movements disconcerted his plans and anticipated the resistance of the Roman populace. Having established himself in the Leonine city,† Frederick barricaded the bridge over the Tiber, and was duly crowned in St. Peter's. But the rite was scarcely finished when the Romans, who had assembled in arms on the Capitol, dashed over the bridge, fell upon the Germans, and were with difficulty repulsed by the personal efforts of Frederick. Into the city he did not venture to pursue them, nor was he at any period of his reign able to make himself master of the whole of it. Finding themselves similarly baffled, his successors at last accepted their position, and were content to take the crown on the Pope's conditions and depart without further question.

Coming so seldom and remaining for so short a time, it is not wonderful that the Teutonic Emperors should, in

---

* A remarkable speech of expostulation made by Otto III to the Roman people (after one of their revolts) from the tower of his house on the Aventine has been preserved to us. It begins thus: " Vosne estis mei Romani? Propter vos quidem meam patriam, propinquos quoque reliqui; amore vestro Saxones et cunctos Theotiscos, sanguinem meum, proieci; vos in remotas partes imperii nostri adduxi, quo patres vestri cum orbem ditione premerent numquam pedem posuerunt; scilicet ut nomen vestrum et gloriam ad fines usque dilatarem; vos filios adoptavi : vos cunctis praetuli."— *Vita S. Bernwardi;* in Pertz, *M. G. H.*, t. iv. (It is from this form " Theotiscus " that the Italian " Tedesco " seems to have been derived).

† The Leonine city, so called from Pope Leo IV, lay between the Vatican and St. Peter's and the river.

the seven centuries from Charles the Great to Charles the
Fifth, have left fewer marks of their presence
Memorials of the Germanic Emperors in Rome. in Rome than Titus or Hadrian alone have
done ; fewer and less considerable even than
those which tradition attributes to those whom
it calls Servius Tullius and the elder Tarquin.
Those monuments which do exist are just sufficient to make the absence of all others more conspicuous.
The most important dates from the time of Otto III, the
only Emperor who attempted to make Rome his permanent
residence. Of the palace, probably nothing
Of Otto III. more than a tower, which he built on the
Aventine, no trace has been discovered ; but the church,
founded by him to receive the ashes of his friend the
martyred St. Adalbert, may still be seen upon the island
in the Tiber. Having received from Benevento relics
supposed to be those of Bartholomew the Apostle,*
it became dedicated to that saint, and is at present the
church of San Bartolommeo in Isola, whose quaintly
picturesque bell-tower of red brick, now gray with extreme
age, looks out from among the orange-trees of a convent
garden over the swift-edying yellow waters of the Tiber.

Otto II, son of Otto the Great, died at Rome, and lies
buried in the crypt of St. Peter's, the only Emperor who
has found a resting-place among the graves of
Of Otto II. the Popes.† His tomb is not far from that of

---

* It would seem that Otto was deceived, and that in reality they
are the bones of St. Paulinus of Nola.

† The only other of the Teutonic Emperors buried in Italy were, so
far as I know, Lewis II (whose tomb, with an inscription commemo-
rating his exploits, is built into the wall of the north aisle of the
famous church of S. Ambrose at Milan), Henry VI and Frederick II,
at Palermo, Conrad IV, at Messina, and Henry VII, whose sarcophagus may be seen in the Campo Santo of Pisa, a city always
conspicuous for her zeal on the imperial side. Eight emperors or

his nephew Pope Gregory V: it is a plain one of roughly chiseled marble. The lid of the superb porphyry sarcophagus in which he lay for a time now serves as the great font of St. Peter's, and may be seen in the baptismal chapel, on the left of the entrance of the church, not far from the tombs of the Stuarts. Last of all must be mentioned a curious relic of the Emperor Frederick II, the ' prince whom of all others one would least expect to see honored in the city of his foes. It is an inscription in the palace of the Conservators upon the Capitoline hill, built into the wall of the great staircase, and relates the victory of Frederick's army over the Milanese, and the capture of the carroccio* of the rebel city, which he sends as a trophy to his faithful Romans. These are all or nearly all the traces of her Teutonic lords that Rome has preserved till now. Pictures indeed there are in abundance, from the mosaic of the Scala Santa at the Lateran† and the curious frescoes in the church of Santi Quattro Incoronati,‡ down to the paint-

Of Frederick II.

kings (Conrad II, Henry III, Henry IV, Henry V, Philip, Rudolf I, Adolf and Albert I) lie in the cathedral of Speyer; five (Charles IV, Wenzel, Ferdinand I, Maximilian II and Rudolf II) at Prague; two (Charles I and Otto III) at Aachen; two (Henry II and Conrad III) at Bamberg; two (Lewis IV and Charles VII) at Munich; two (Arnulf and Lewis the Child) at Regensburg ; Lewis the Pious at Metz, Lothar I at Prüm near Treves, Henry I at Quedlinburg, Otto I at Magdeburg, Otto IV at Brunswick, Rupert at Heidelberg, Sigismund at Nagy Várad, Albert II at Stuhlweissenburg, Charles V in the Escurial, and most of the later ones at Vienna. Of all the tombs the noblest is that of Maximilian I at Innsbruck.

* See note, p. 173.
† See p. 117.
‡ These highly curious frescoes are in the chapel of St. Sylvester attached to the very ancient church of Quattro Santi on the Cœlian hill, and are supposed to have been executed in the time of Pope Innocent III. They represent scenes in the life of the Saint, more particularly the making of the famous donation to him by Constantine, who submissively holds the bridle of his palfrey.

ings of the Sistine antechapel and the Stanze of Raphael in the Vatican, where the triumphs of the Popedom over all its foes are set forth with matchless art and equally matchless unveracity. But these are mostly long subsequent to the events they describe, and these all the world knows.

Associations of the highest interest would have attached to the churches in which the imperial coronation was performed—a ceremony which, whether we regard the dignity of the performers or the splendor of the adjuncts, was probably the most imposing that modern Europe has known. But old St. Peter's disappeared in the end of the fifteenth century, not long after the last Roman coronation, that of Frederick III, while the basilica of St. John Lateran, in which Lothar the Saxon and Henry VII were crowned, has been so wofully modernized that we can hardly figure it to ourselves as the same building.*

Bearing in mind what was the social condition of Rome during the middle ages, it becomes easier to understand

Causes of the want of mediæval monuments in Rome.

the architectural barrenness which at first excites the visitor's surprise. Rome had no temporal sovereign, and there were therefore only two classes who could build at all, the nobles and the clergy. Of these, the former had seldom the wealth, and never the taste, which would have enabled them to construct palaces graceful as the Venetian or massively grand as the Florentine and Genoese. Moreover, the constant practice of domestic war made defense the first object of a house, beauty and convenience the

Barbarism of the aristocracy.

---

* The last imperial coronation, that of Charles V, took place in the church of St. Petronius at Bologna, Pope Clement VII being unwilling to receive Charles in Rome. It is a grand church, but the choir, where the ceremony took place, seems to have been "restored," that is to say modernized, since Charles' time.

second. The nobility, therefore, either adapted ancient edifices to their purpose or built out of their materials those huge square towers of brick, a few of which still frown over the narrow streets in the older parts of Rome. We may judge of their number from the statement that the senator Brancaleone destroyed one hundred and forty of them. With perhaps no more than one exception, that of the so-called House of Rienzi, these towers are the only domestic buildings in the city older than the middle of the fifteenth century. The vast palaces to which strangers now flock for the sake of the picture galleries they contain, have been most of them erected in the sixteenth or seventeenth centuries, some even later. Among the earliest is that of Palazzo Cenci,* whose gloomy low-browed arch so powerfully affected the imagination of Shelley.

It was no want of wealth that hampered the architectural efforts of the clergy, for vast revenues flowed in upon them from every corner of Christendom. A good deal was actually spent upon the erection or repairs of churches and convents, although with a less *Ambition,* liberal hand than that of such great Trans- *weakness,* alpine prelates as Hugh of Lincoln or Conrad *and cor-* of Cologne. But the Popes always needed *ruption of* money for their projects of ambition, and in *the clergy.* times when disorder and corruption were at their height the work of building stopped altogether. Thus it was that after the time of the Carolingians scarcely a church was erected until the beginning of the twelfth century, when the reforms of Hildebrand had breathed new zeal into the priesthood. The Babylonish captivity of Avignon, as it was called, with the great schism of the West that followed

---

* The name of Cenci is a very old one at Rome: it is supposed to be an abbreviation of Crescentius. We hear in the eleventh century of a certain Cencius, who on one occasion made Gregory VII prisoner.

upon it, was the cause of a second similar intermission, which lasted nearly a century and a half.

At every time, however, even when his work went on most briskly, the labors of the Roman architect took the direction of restoring and readorning old churches rather than of erecting new ones. While the Trans-
Tendency of alpine countries, except in a few favored spots,
the Roman such as Provence and part of the Rhineland,
builders to remained during several ages with few and
adhere to rudely built stone churches, Rome possessed,
the ancient as the inheritance of the earlier Christian cen-
manner. turies, a profusion of houses of worship, some
of them still unsurpassed in splendor, and far more than adequate to the needs of her diminished population. In repairing these from time to time, their original form and style of work were usually as far as possible preserved, while in constructing new ones, the abundance of models, beautiful in themselves and hallowed as well by antiquity as by religious feeling, enthralled the invention of the workman, bound him down to be at best a faithful imitator, and forbade him to deviate at pleasure from the old established manner. Thus it befell that while his brethren throughout the rest of Europe were passing by successive steps from the old Roman and Byzantine styles to Romanesque, and from Romanesque to Pointed, the Roman architect scarcely departed from the plan and arrangements of
Absence of the primitive basilica. This is one chief reason
Gothic in why there is so little Gothic work in Rome, so
Rome. little even of Romanesque like that of Pisa.
What there is appears chiefly in the pointed window, more rarely in the arch, seldom or never in spire or tower or column. Only one of the existing churches of Rome is Gothic throughout, and that, the Dominican church of S. Maria sopra Minerva, was built by foreign monks. In some of the other churches, and especially in the

cloisters of the convents, instances may be observed of the same style: in others slight traces, by accident or design almost obliterated.*

The mention of obliteration suggests a third cause of the comparative want of mediæval buildings in the city—the constant depredations and changes of which she has been the subject. Ever since the time of Constantine Rome has been a city of destruction, and Christians have vied with pagans, citizens with enemies, in urging on the fatal work. Her siege and capture by Robert Guiscard,† the ally of Hildebrand against Henry IV, was far more ruinous than the attacks of the Goths or Vandals: and itself yields in atrocity to the sack of Rome in A.D. 1527 by the soldiers of the Catho-

Destruction and alteration of the old buildings:

By invaders.

---

* Thus in the church of San Lorenzo without the walls there are several pointed windows, now bricked up; and similar ones may be seen in the church of Ara Cœli on the summit of the Capitol. So in the apse of St. John Lateran there are three or four windows of Gothic form: and in its cloister, as well as in that of St. Paul without the walls, a great deal of beautiful Lombard work. The elegant porch of the church of Sant' Antonio Abate is Lombard. In the apse of the church of San Giovanni e Paolo on the Cœlian hill there is an external arcade exactly like those of the Duomo at Pisa. Nor are these the only instances. The ruined chapel attached to the fortress of the Caetani family—the family to which Boniface VIII belonged, and which still holds its place among the Roman nobility—is a pretty little building, more like northern Gothic than anything within the walls of Rome. It stands upon the Appian Way, opposite the tomb of Cæcilia Metella, which the Caetani used as a stronghold.

† A good deal of the mischief done by Robert Guiscard, from which the parts of the city lying beyond the Coliseum toward the river and St. John Lateran never recovered, is attributed to the Saracenic troops in his service. Saracen pirates are said to have once before sacked Rome. Genseric was not a heathen, but he was a furious Arian, which, as far as respect to the churches of the orthodox went, was nearly the same thing. The seven-branched candlestick and

lic king and most pious Emperor Charles V.*   Since the
days of the first barbarian invasions the Ro-
By the Ro- mans have gone on building with materials
mans of the
Middle Ages. taken from the ancient temples, theaters, law-
courts, baths and villas, stripping them of their
gorgeous casings of marble, pulling down their walls for
the sake of the blocks of travertine, setting up their own
hovels on the top or in the midst of these majestic piles.
Thus it has been with the memorials of paganism: a somewhat different cause has contributed to the
By modern disappearance of the mediæval churches.
restorers
of churches. What pillage, or fanaticism, or the wanton
lust of destruction did in the one case, the
ostentatious zeal of modern times has done in the other.
The era of the final establishment of the Popes as temporal
sovereigns of the city, is also that of the supremacy of the
Renaissance style in architecture.   After the time of
Nicholas V, the pontiff against whom, it will be remembered, the spirit of municipal freedom made its last
struggle in the conspiracy of Porcaro, nothing was built
in Gothic, and the prevailing enthusiasm for the antique
produced a corresponding dislike to everything mediæval, a
dislike conspicuous in men like Julius the Second and Leo
X, from whom the grandeur of modern Rome may be said
to begin.   Not long after their time the great religious
movement of the sixteenth century, while triumphing in
the north of Europe, was in the south met and overcome
by a counter-reformation in the bosom of the old church
herself, and the construction or restoration of ecclesias-

---

other vessels of the Temple, which Titus had brought from Jerusalem to Rome, are said to have been carried off by him and lost on
the voyage to Africa.

* We are told that one cause of the ferocity of the German part of
the army of Charles was their anger at the ruinous condition of the
imperial palace.

tical buildings became again the passion of the devout.* No employment, whether it be called an amusement or a duty, could have been better suited to the court and aristocracy of Rome. They were indolent; wealthy, and fond of displaying their wealth; full of good taste, and anxious, especially when advancing years had chased away youth's pleasures, to be full of good works also. Popes and cardinals and the heads of the great families vied with one another in building new churches and restoring or enlarging those they found till little of the old was left; raising over them huge cupolas, substituting massive pilasters for the single-shafted columns, adorning the interior with a profusion of rare marbles, of carving and gilding, of frescoes and altar-pieces, by the best masters of the sixteenth and seventeenth centuries. None but a bigoted mediævalist can refuse to acknowledge the warmth of tone, the repose, the stateliness, of the churches of modern Rome; but even in the midst of admiration the sated eye turns away from the wealth of ponderous ornament, and we long for the clear pure color, the simple yet grand proportions that give a charm to the buildings of an earlier age.

Few of the ancient churches have escaped untouched ; many have been altogether rebuilt. There are also some, however, in which the modernizers of the sixteenth and subsequent centuries have spared *Existing* two features of the old structure, its round *relics of the* apse or tribune and its bell-tower. The apse *Dark and* has its interior usually covered with mosaics, *Middle* exceedingly interesting, both from the ideas *Ages.* they express and as the only monuments of pictorial art

* Under the influence, partly of this anti-pagan spirit, partly of his own restless vanity, partly of a passion to be doing something, Pope Sixtus V did a great deal of mischief in the way of destroying or spoiling the monuments of antiquity.

that remain to us from the Dark Ages.* To speak of
them, however, as they deserve to be spoken
The Mosaics. of, would involve a digression for which there
is no space here. The campanile or bell-
tower is a quaint little square brick tower, of no great
height, usually standing detached from the church, and
having in its topmost, sometimes also in its
The Bell-towers. other upper stories, several arcade windows,
divided by tiny marble pillars.† What with
these campaniles, then far more numerous than they are
now, and with the huge brick fortresses of the nobles,
towers must have held in the landscape of the mediæval
city very much the part which domes do now. Although

---

* The finest of the similar Ravenna mosaics are rather older than
these Roman ones: but some there, as well as few others elsewhere
in Italy (e. g. the superb ones at Torcello), date from the seventh,
eighth and ninth centuries.

† These campaniles are generally supposed to date from the ninth
and tenth centuries. I am informed, however, by Mr. J. H. Parker,
of Oxford, whose antiquarian skill is well known, that he is led to
believe by an examination of their moldings that few or none,
unless it be that of Santa Prassede, are older than the twelfth century. This of course applies only to the existing buildings. The
type of tower may be, and indeed no doubt is, older. Somewhat
similar towers may be observed in many parts of the Italian Alps,
especially in the wonderful mountain land north of Venice, where
such towers are of all dates from the eleventh or twelfth down to
the nineteenth century, the ancient type having in these remote
valleys been adhered to because the builder had no other models
before him. In the valley of Cimolais (not very far from Longarone
in Val d'Ampezzo) I have seen such a campanile in course of erection,
precisely similar to others in the neighboring villages some eight
centuries old. The very curious round towers of Ravenna, some
four or five of which are still standing, seem to have originally had
similar windows, though these have been all, or nearly all, stopped
up. The Roman towers are all square.

less imposing, they were probably more picturesque, the latter as in the earlier part of the Middle Ages the houses and churches, which are now mostly crowded together on the flat of the Campus Martius, were scattered over the heights and slopes of the Cœlian, Aventine and Esquiline hills.* Modern Rome lies chiefly on the opposite or north-eastern side of the Capitol, and the change from the old to the new site of the city, which can hardly be said to have distinctly begun before the destruction of the south-western part of the town by Robert Guiscard, was not completed until the sixteenth century. In A.D. 1536, in anticipation of the entry of Charles V, the rebuilding of the Capitol (afterward carried on by Michael Angelo) was begun upon foundations that had been laid by the first Tarquin; and the palace of the Senator, the greatest municipal edifice of Rome, which had hitherto looked toward the Forum and the Coliseum, was made to front in the direction of St. Peter's and the modern town.

The Rome of to-day is no more like the city of Rienzi than she is to the city of Trajan; just as the Roman church of the nineteenth century differs profoundly, however she may strive to disguise it, from the *Changed aspect of the city of Rome.* church of Hildebrand. But among all their changes, both church and city have kept themselves wonderfully free from the intrusion of foreign, at least of Teutonic, elements, and have faithfully preserved at all times something of an old Roman charac-

---

* The Palatine hill seems to have been then, as it is for the most part now, a waste of stupendous ruins. In the great imperial palace upon its northern and eastern sides was the residence of an official of the Eastern court in the beginning of the eighth century. In the time of Charles, some seventy years later, this palace was no longer habitable.

ter. Latin Christianity inherited from the imperial
system of old that firmly knit yet flexible
Analogy between her architecture and her civil and ecclesiastical constitution. organization, which was one of the grand
secrets of its power ; the great men whom
mediæval Rome gave to or trained up for the
Papacy were, like their progenitors, adminis-
trators, legislators, statesmen; seldom enthusiasts themselves, but perfectly understanding
how to use and guide the enthusiasm of others
—of the French and German crusaders, of men like Francis
of Assissi and Dominic and Ignatius. Between Catholicism in Italy and Catholicism in Germany or England there
was always, as there is still, a very perceptible difference.
So also, if the analogy be not too fanciful, was it with
Rome the city. Socially she seemed always drifting toward
feudalism ; yet she never fell into its grasp.
Preservation of an antique character in both. Materially, her architecture was at one time
considerably influenced by Pointed forms, yet
Gothic never became, as in the rest of Europe,
the dominant style. It approached Rome late,
and departed from her early, so that we scarcely
notice its presence, and seem to pass almost without a
break from the old Romanesque * to the Græco-Roman of
the Renaissance. Thus regarded, the history of the city,
both in her political state and in her buildings, is seen to
be intimately connected with that of the Holy Empire
itself. The Empire in its title and its pretensions expressed the idea of the permanence of the institutions of
the ancient world ; Rome the city had, in externals at
least, carefully preserved their traditions : the names of
her magistracies, the character of her buildings, all spoke
of antiquity, and gave it a strange and shadowy life in the
midst of new races and new forms of faith.

---

* Such as we see it in the later and lesser churches of basilica form.

In its essence the Empire rested on the feeling of the unity of mankind ; it was the perpetuation of the Roman dominion by which the old nationalities had been destroyed, with the addition of the Chris- *Relation of* tian element which had created a new nation- *the City* ality that was also universal. By the extension *and the* of her citizenship to all her subjects heathen *Empire.* Rome had become the common home, and, figuratively, even the local dwelling-place of the civilized races of man. By the theology of the time Christian Rome had been made the mystical type of humanity, the one flock of the faithful scattered over the whole earth, the holy city whither, as to the temple on Moriah, all the Israel of God should come to worship. She was not merely an image of the mighty world, she was the mighty world itself in miniature. The pastor of her local church is also the universal bishop; the seven suffragans who consecrate him are the overseers of petty sees in Ostia, Antium, and the like, towns lying close round Rome : the cardinal priests and deacons who join these seven in electing him derive their title to be princes of the Church, the supreme spiritual council of the Christian world, from the incumbency of a parochial cure within the precincts of the city. Similarly, her ruler, the Emperor, is ruler of mankind; he is chosen by the acclamations of her people : * he can be lawfully

---

* It was thus that most of the earlier Teutonic Emperors, and notably Charles and Otto, professed to have obtained the crown ; although practically it was partly a matter of conquest and partly of private arrangement with the Pope. In later times, the seven Germanic princes were recognized as the legally qualified electoral body, but their appearance on the stage was a result of the confusion of the German kingdom with the Roman Empire, and in strictness they had nothing to do with the Roman crown at all. The right to bestow it could only—on principle—belong to some Roman authority, and those who felt the difficulty were driven to support a formal cession of their privilege by the Roman people to the seven electors. See p.

crowned nowhere but in one of her basilicas. She is, like
Jerusalem of old, the mother of us all.

There is yet another way in which the record of the
domestic contests of Rome throws light upon the history
of the Empire. From the eleventh century to the fifteenth
her citizens ceased not to demand in the name of the old
republic their freedom from the tyranny of the nobles and
the Pope, and their right to rule over the world at large.
These efforts—selfish and fantastic we may call them, yet
men like Petrarch did not disdain to them their sympathy
—issued from the same theories and were directed to the
same ends as those which inspired Otto III and Frederick
Barbarossa and Dante himself. They witness to the same
incapacity to form any ideal for the future except a revival
of the past; the same belief that one universal state is both
desirable and possible, but possible only through the means
of Rome; the same refusal to admit that a right which has
once existed can ever be extinguished. In the days of the
Renaissance these notions were passing silently away: the
succeeding century brought with it misfortunes that broke
the spirit of the nation. Italy was the battle-field of
.Europe: her wealth became the prey of a rapacious sol-
dierly: Florence, the noblest of her republics, was enslaved
by an unfeeling Emperor, and handed over as the pledge
of amity to a selfish Medicean Pope. When the
*Extinction
of the
Florentine
republic,
A.D. 1530.* hope of independence had been lost, the people
turned away from politics to live for art and
literature, and found, before many generations
had passed, how little such exclusive devotion
could compensate for the departure of freedom,
and a national spirit, and the activity of civic life. A
century after the golden days of Ariosto and Raphael,

227 *supra;* and cf Matthew Villani (iv. 77), "Il popolo Romano, non
da se, ma la chiesa per lui, concedette la elezione degli Imperadori a
sette principi della Magna."

Italian literature had become frigid and affected, while Italian art was dying of mannerism.

At length, after long ages of sloth, the stagnant waters were troubled. The Romans, who had lived in listless contentment under the paternal sway of the Popes, received new ideas from the advent of the revolutionary armies of France, and have found the Papal system, since its re-establishment fifty years ago as a modern bureaucratic despotism, far less tolerable than it was of yore. Our own days have seen the name of Rome become again *Feelings of* a rallying-cry for the patriots of Italy, but in a *the modern* sense most unlike the old one. The contem- *toward* poraries of Arnold and Rienzi desired freedom *Rome.* only as a step to universal domination: their descendants, more wisely, yet not more from patriotism than from a pardonable civic pride, seek only to be the capital of the Italian kingdom. Dante prayed for a monarchy of the world, a reign of peace and Christian brotherhood: those who invoke his name as the earliest prophet of their creed strive after an idea that never crossed his mind—the national union of Italy.*

Plain common-sense politicians in other countries do not understand this passion for Rome as a capital, and think it their duty to lecture the Italians on their flightiness. The latter do not themselves pretend that the shores of the Tiber are a suitable site for a capital: Rome is lonely, unhealthy, and in a bad strategical position ; she has no particular facilities for trade : her people, with some fine qualities, are less orderly and industrious than the Tuscans or the Piedmontese. Nevertheless, all Italy cries with one voice for Rome, firmly believing that

* That which Dante, Arnold of Brescia, and the rest really have in common with the modern Italian "party of movement" is their hostility to the temporal power of the Popes. (This chapter was written in 1865.)

national life can never thrill with a strong and steady pulsation till the ancient capital has become the nation's heart.   They feel that it is owing to Rome—Rome pagan as well as Christian—that they once played so grand a part in the drama of European history, and that they have now been able to attain that fervid sentiment of unity which has brought them at last together under one government.   Whether they are right, whether if right they are likely to be successful, need not be inquired here. But it deserves to be noted that this enthusiasm for a famous name—for it is nothing more—is substantially the same feeling as that which created and hallowed the Holy Empire of the Middle Ages.   The events of the last few years on both sides of the Atlantic have proved that men are not now, any more than they ever were, chiefly governed by calculations of material profit and loss.   Sentiments, fancies, theories, have not lost their power ; the spirit of poetry has not wholly passed away from politics. Strange, therefore, as seems to us the worship paid to the name of mediæval Rome by those who saw the sins and the misery of her people, it can hardly have been an intenser feeling than is the imaginative reverence wherewith the Italians of to-day look on the city whence, as from a fountain, all the streams of their national life have sprung, and in which, as in an ocean, they are all again to mingle.

CHAPTER XVII.

THE RENAISSANCE: CHANGE IN THE CHARACTER OF THE EMPIRE.

IN Frederick III's reign the Empire sank to its lowest point. It had shot forth a fitful gleam under Sigismund, who in convoking and presiding over the council of Constance had revived one of the highest functions of his predecessors. The precedents of the first great œcumenical councils, and especially of the council of Nicæa, had established the principle that it belonged to the Emperor, even more properly than to the Pope, to convoke ecclesiastical assemblies from the whole Christian world. The tenet commended itself to the reforming party in the church, headed by Gerson, the chancellor of Paris, whose aim it was, while making no changes in matters of faith, to correct the abuses which had grown up in discipline and government, and limit the power of the Popes by exalting the authority of general councils, to whom there was now attributed an immunity from error superior to that, whatever it might be, which resided in the successor of Peter. And although it was only the sacerdotal body, not the whole Christian people, who were thus made the exponents of the universal religious consciousness, the doctrine was nevertheless a foreshadowing of that fuller freedom which was soon to follow. The existence of the Holy Empire and the existence of general councils were, as has been

Wenzel,
1378–
1400.
Rupert,
1400–
1410.
Sigismund,
1410–
1438.
Council of
Constance.

already remarked, necessary parts of one and the same theory,* and it was therefore more than a coincidence that the last occasion on which the whole of Latin Christendom met to deliberate and act as a single commonwealth,† was also the last on which that commonwealth's lawful temporal head appeared in the exercise of his international functions. Never afterward was he, in the eyes of Europe, anything more than a German monarch.

It might seem doubtful whether he would long remain a monarch at all. When in A.D. 1493 the calamitous reign of Frederick III ended, it was impossible for the princes to see with unconcern the condition into which their selfishness and turbulence had brought the Empire. The time was indeed critical. Hitherto the Germans had been protected rather by the weakness of their enemies than by their own strength. From France there had been little to fear while the English menaced her on one side and the Burgundian dukes on the other: from England still less while she was torn by the strife of York and Lancaster. But now throughout Western Europe the power of the feudal oligarchies was broken ; and its chief countries were being, by the establishment of fixed rules of succession and the absorption of the smaller into the larger principalities, rapidly built up into compact and aggressive military monarchies. Thus Spain became a

Weakness of Germany as compared with the other states of Europe. Albrecht II, 1438-1440. Frederick III, 1440-1493.

---

* It is not without interest to observe that the council of Basel showed signs of reciprocating imperial care by claiming those very rights over the Empire to which the Popes were accustomed to pretend.

† The councils of Basel and Florence were not recognized from first to last by all Europe, as was the council of Constance. When the assembly of Trent met, the great religious schism had already made a general council, in the true sense of the word, impossible.

great state by the union of Castile and Arragon, and the conquest of the Moors of Granada. Thus in England there arose the popular despotism of the Tudors. Thus France, enlarged and consolidated under Lewis XI and his successors, began to acquire that predominant influence on the politics of Europe which her commanding geographical position, the martial spirit of her people, and, it must be added, the unscrupulous ambition of her rulers, have secured to her in every succeeding century. Meantime there had appeared in the far East a foe still more terrible. The capture of Constantinople gave the Turks a firm hold on Europe, and inspired them with the hope of effecting in the fifteenth century what Abderrahman and his Saracens had so nearly effected in the eighth—of establishing the faith of Islam through all the provinces that obeyed the Western as well as the Eastern Cæsars. The navies of the Ottoman Sultans swept the Mediterranean; their well-appointed armies pierced Hungary and threatened Vienna.

Nor was it only that formidable enemies had arisen without: the frontiers of Germany herself were exposed by the loss of those adjoining territories which had formerly owned allegiance to the Emperors. Poland, once tributary, had shaken off the yoke at the interregnum, and had *Loss of imperial territories.* recently wrested West Prussia from the Teutonic knights, and compelled their Grand Master to swear allegiance for East Prussia, which they still retained. Bohemia, where German culture had struck deeper roots, remained a member of the Empire; but the privileges she had obtained from Charles IV, and the subsequent acquisition of Silesia and Moravia, made her virtually independent. The restless Hungarians avenged their former vassalage to Germany by frequent inroads on her eastern border.

Imperial power in Italy ended with the life of Henry

VII. Rupert did indeed cross the Alps, but it was
as the hireling of Florence ; Frederick III re-
Italy. ceived the Lombard crown, but it no longer
conveyed the slightest power. In the beginning of the
fourteenth century Dante still hopes for the renovation of his
country from the action of the Teutonic Emperors. Some
fifty years later Matthew Villani sees clearly that they do
not and cannot reign to any purpose south of the Alps.*
Nevertheless the phantom of imperial authority lingers on
for a time. It is put forward by the Ghibeline tyrants of
the cities to justify their attacks on their Guelfic neighbors: even resolute republicans like the Florentines do not
yet venture altogether to reject it, however unwilling to
permit its exercise. Before the middle of the fifteenth
century, the names of Guelf and Ghibeline had ceased to
have any sense or meaning ; the Pope was no longer the
protector nor the Emperor the assailant of municipal freedom
for municipal freedom itself had well-nigh disappeared. But
the old war-cries of the Church and the Empire were still repeated as they had been three centuries before, and the rival
principles that had once enlisted the noblest spirits of Italy
on one or other side had now sunk into a pretext for wars of
aggrandizement or of mere unmeaning hate. That which
had been remarked long before in Greece was seen to be
true here; the spirit of faction outlived the cause of fac-

---

* "E pero venendo gl' imperadori della Magna col supremo titolo,
e volendo col senno e colla forza della Magna reggiere gli Italiani,
non lo fanno e non lo possono fare."—M. Villani, iv. 77. Matthew
Villani's etymology of the two great faction names of Italy is worth
quoting, as a fair sample of the skill of mediævals in such matters:
"La Italia tutta e divisa mistatemente in due parti, l' una che
seguita ne' fatti del mondo la santa chiesa—e questi son dinominati
Guelfi; cioè, guardatori di fè. E l' altra parte seguitano lo 'mperio o
fedele o enfedele che sia delle cose del mondo a santa chiesa. E chia-
mansi Ghibellini, quasi guida belil; cioè, guidatori di battaglie."

tion, and became itself the new and prolific source of a useless, endless strife.

After Frederick III no Emperor was crowned in Rome, and almost the only trace of that connection between Germany and Italy, to maintain which so much had been risked and lost, was to be found in the obstinate belief of the Hapsburg Emperors, that their own claims, though often purely dynastic and personal, could be enforced by an appeal to the imperial rights of their predecessors. Because Barbarossa had overrun Lombardy with a Transalpine host they fancied themselves entitled to demand duchies for themselves and their relatives, and to entangle the Empire in wars wherein no interest but their own was involved.

The kingdom of Arles, if it had never added much strength to the Empire, had been useful as an outwork against France. And thus its loss—Dauphiné passing over, partly in A. D. 1350, finally in *Burgundy.* 1457, Provence in 1486—proved a serious calamity, for it brought the French nearer to Switzerland, and opened to them a tempting passage into Italy. The Emperors did not for a time expressly renounce their feudal suzerainty over these lands, but if it was hard to enforce a feudal claim over a rebellious landgrave in Germany, how much harder to control a vassal who was also the mightiest king in Europe.

On the north-west frontier, the fall in A. D. 1477 of the great principality which the dukes of French Burgundy were building up, was seen with pleasure by the Rhinelanders whom Charles the last duke had incessantly alarmed. But the only effect of its fall was to leave France and Germany directly confronting each other, and it was soon seen that the balance of strength lay on the side of the less numerous but better organized and more active nation.

Switzerland, too, could no longer be considered a part of
the Germanic realm. The revolt of the Forest Cantons,

Switzerland. in A. D. 1313, was against the oppressions
practiced in the name of Albert count of Hapsburg, rather than against the legitimate authority of
Albert the Emperor. But although several subsequent
sovereigns, and among them conspicuously Henry VII
and Sigismund, favored the Swiss liberties, yet while the
antipathy between the Confederates and the territorial
nobility gave a peculiar direction to their policy, the
accession of new cantons to their body, and their brilliant
success against Charles the Bold in A.D. 1477, made them
proud of a separate national existence, and not unwilling
to cast themselves loose from the stranded hulk of the
Empire. Maximilian tried to conquer them, but after a
furious struggle, in which the valleys of Western Tyrol
were repeatedly laid waste by the peasants of the Engadin,
he was forced to give way, and in A.D. 1500 recognized
them by treaty as practically independent. Not, however,
till the peace of Westphalia, in A.D. 1648, was the Swiss
Confederation in the eye of public law a sovereign state,
and even after that date some of the towns continued to
stamp their coins with the double eagle of the Empire.

If those losses of territory were serious, far more serious
was the plight in which Germany herself lay. The country

*Internal
weakness.* had now become not so much an empire as an
aggregate of very many small states, governed
by sovereigns who would neither remain at
peace with each other nor combine against a foreign
enemy, under the nominal presidency of an Emperor who
had little lawful authority, and could not exert what he
had. *

---

* " Nam quamvis Imperatorem et regem et dominum vestrum esse
fateamini, precario tamen ille imperare videtur: nulla ei potentia est;
tantum ei paretis quantum vultis, vultis autem minimum."—Æneas
Sylvius to the princes of Germany, quoted by Hippolytus a Lapide.

There was another cause, besides those palpable and obvious ones already enumerated, to which this state of things must be ascribed. That cause is to be found in the theory which regarded the Empire as an international power, supreme among Christian states. From the day when Otto the Great was crowned at Rome, the characters of German king and Roman Emperor were united in one person, and it has been shown how that union tended more and more to become a fusion. If the two offices, in their nature and origin so dissimilar, had been held by different persons, the Roman Empire would most probably have soon disappeared, while the German kingdom grew into a robust national monarchy. Their connection gave a *Influence of the theory of the Empire as an international power upon the Germanic constitution.* longer life to the one and a feebler life to the other, while at the same time it transformed both. So long as Germany was only one of the many countries that bowed beneath their scepter it was possible for the Emperors, though we need not suppose they troubled themselves with speculations on the matter, to distinguish their imperial authority, as international and more than half religious, from their royal, which was, or was meant to be, exclusively local and feudal. But when within the narrowed bounds of Germany these international functions had ceased to have any meaning, when the rulers of England, Spain, France, Denmark, Hungary, Poland, Italy, Burgundy, had in succession repudiated their control, and the Lord of the World found himself obeyed by none but his own people, he would not sink from being lord of the world into a simple Teutonic king, but continued to play in the more contracted theater the part which had belonged to him in the wider. Thus did Germany instead of Europe become the sphere of his international jurisdiction; and her electors and princes, originally mere vassals, no greater

than a Count of Champagne in France, or an Earl of
Chester in England, stepped into the place which it had
been meant that the several monarchs of Christendom
should fill. If the power of their head had been what it
was in the eleventh century, the additional dignity so
assigned to them might have signified very little. But
coming in to confirm and justify the liberties already won,
this theory of their relation to the sovereign had a great,
though at the time scarcely perceptible, influence in
changing the German Empire, as we may now begin
to call it, from a state into a sort of confederation or
body of states, united indeed for some of the purposes of government, but separate and independent
for others more important. Thus, and that in its
ecclesiastical as well as its civil organization, Germany
became a miniature of Christendom.* The Pope, though
he retained the wider sway which his rival had lost,
was in an especial manner the head of the German clergy,
as the Emperor was of the laity: the three Rhenish prelates
sat in the supreme college beside the four temporal electors:
the nobility of prince-bishops and abbots was as essential a
part of the constitution and as influential in the deliberations of the Diet as were the dukes, counts and margraves
of the Empire. The world-embracing Christian state was
to have been governed by a hierarchy of spiritual pastors,
whose graduated ranks of authority should exactly correspond with those of the temporal magistracy, who were
to be like them endowed with worldly wealth and power,
and to enjoy a jurisdiction co-ordinate although distinct.
This system, which it was in vain attempted to establish
in Europe during the eleventh and twelfth centuries, was

---

* See Ægidi, *Der Fürstenrath nach dem Luneviller Frieden ;* a
book which throws more light than any other with which I am
acquainted on the inner nature of the Empire.

in its main features that which prevailed in the Germanic Empire from the fourteenth century onward. And conformably to the analogy which may be traced between the position of the archdukes of Austria in Germany and the place which the four Saxon and the two first Franconian Emperors had held in Europe, both being recognized as leaders and presidents in all that concerned the common interest, in the one case of the Christian, in the other of the whole German people, while neither of them had any power of direct government in the territories of local kings and lords ; so the plan by which those who chose Maximilian emperor sought to strengthen their national monarchy was in substance that which the Popes had followed when they conferred the crown of the world on Charles and Otto. The pontiffs then, like the electors now, finding that they could not give with the title the power which its functions demanded, were driven to the expedient of selecting for the office persons whose private resources enabled them to sustain it with dignity. The first Frankish and the first Saxon Emperors were chosen because they were already the mightiest potentates in Europe ; Maximilian because he was the strongest of the German princes. The parallel may be carried one step further. Just as under Otto and his successors the Roman Empire was Teutonized, so now under the Hapsburg dynasty, from whose hands the scepter departed only once thenceforth, the Teutonic Empire tends more and more to lose itself in an Austrian monarchy.

Position of the Emperor in Germany, compared with that of his predecessors in Europe.

Of that monarchy and of the power of the house of Hapsburg, Maximilian was, even more than Rudolf his ancestor, the founder.* Uniting in his person those wide

---

* The two immediately preceding Emperors, Albert II (1438–1439) and Frederick III, father of Maximilian (1439–1493), had been Hapsburgs. It is nevertheless from Maximilian that the ascendancy of that family must be dated.

domains through Germany which had been dispersed
among the collateral branches of his house,
Beginning of the Hapsburg influence in Germany. and claiming by his marriage with Mary of
Burgundy most of the territories of Charles
the Bold, he was a prince greater than any who
had sat on the Teutonic throne since the death
of Frederick II. But it was as archduke of
Austria, count of Tyrol, duke of Styria and Carinthia,
feudal superior of lands in Swabia, Alsace and Switzerland,
that he was great, not as Roman Emperor. For just as
from him the Austrian monarchy begins, so with him the
Holy Empire in its old meaning ends. That strange
system of doctrines, half religious, half political, which
had supported it for so many ages, was growing obsolete,
and the theory which had wrought such changes on Germany
and Europe, passed ere long so completely from
remembrance that we can now do no more than call up a
faint and wavering image of what it must once have been.

For it is not only in imperial history that the accession
of Maximilian is a landmark. That time — a time of
change and movement in every part of human
Character of the epoch of Maximilian. life, a time when printing had become common,
and books were no longer confined to the
clergy, when drilled troops were replacing the
feudal militia, when the use of gunpowder was
changing the face of war—was especially marked by one
event, to which the history of the world offers no parallel
before or since, the discovery of America.
The discovery of America. The cloud which from the beginning of things
had hung thick and dark round the borders of
civilization was suddenly lifted : the feeling of
mysterious awe with which men had regarded the firm
plain of earth and her encircling ocean ever since the
days of Homer, vanished when astronomers and geographers
taught them that she was an insignificant globe, which,

so far from being the center of the universe, was itself swept round in the motion of one of the least of its countless systems. The notions that had hitherto prevailed regarding the life of man and his relations to nature and the supernatural, were rudely shaken by the knowledge that was soon gained of tribes in every stage of culture, and living under every variety of condition, who had developed apart from all the influences of the Eastern hemisphere. In A.D. 1453 the capture of Constantinople and extinction of the Eastern Empire had dealt a fatal blow to the prestige of tradition and an immemorial name: in A.D.1492 there was disclosed a world whither the eagles of the all-conquering Rome had never winged their flight. No one could now have repeated the arguments of the *De Monarchia.*

Another movement, too, widely different, but even more momentous, was beginning to spread from Italy beyond the Alps. Since the barbarian tribes settled in the Roman provinces, no change had come to pass in Europe at all comparable to that which *The Renaissance.* followed the diffusion of the new learning in the latter half of the fifteenth century. Enchanted by the beauty of the ancient models of art and poetry, more particularly those of the Greeks, men came to regard with aversion and contempt all that had been done or produced from the days of Trajan to those of Pope Nicholas V. The Latin style of the writers who lived after Tacitus was debased : the architecture of the Middle Ages was barbarous : the scholastic philosophy was an odious and unmeaning jargon: Aristotle himself, Greek though he was, Aristotle who had been for three centuries more than a prophet or an apostle, was hurled from his throne, because his name was associated with the dismal quarrels of Scotists and Thomists. That spirit, whether we call it analytical, or sceptical, or earthly, or simply secular, for it is more or less all of these

—the spirit which was the exact antithesis of mediæval mysticism, had swept in and carried men away, with all the force of a pent-up torrent. People were content to gratify thei.· tastes and their senses, caring little for worship, and still less for doctrine: their hopes and ideas were no longer such as had made their forefathers crusaders or ascetics : their imagination was possessed by associations far different from those which had inspired Dante : they did not revolt against the church, but they had no enthusiasm for her, and they had enthusiasm for whatever was fresh and graceful and intelligible. From all that was old and solemn, or that seemed to savor of feudalism or monkery, they turned away, too indifferent to be hostile. And so, in the midst of the Renaissance, so, under the consciousness that former things were passing from the earth, and a new order opening, so, with the other beliefs and memories of the Middle Age, the shadowy rights of the Roman Empire melted away in the fuller modern light. Here and there a jurist muttered that no neglect could destroy its universal supremacy, or a priest declaimed to listless hearers on its duty to protect the Holy See; but to Germany it had become an ancient device for holding together the discordant members of her body, to its possessors an engine for extending the power of the house of Hapsburg.

Henceforth, therefore, we must look upon the Holy Roman Empire as lost in the German; and after a few faint

Empire henceforth German. attempts to resuscitate old-fashioned claims, nothing remains to indicate its origin save a sounding title and a precedence among the states of Europe. It was not that the Renaissance exerted any direct political influence either against the Empire or for it; men were too busy upon statues and coins and manuscripts to care what befell Popes or Emperors. It acted rather by silently withdrawing the whole system of doctrines upon which the Empire had rested, and thus leaving it, since it had previously no support but that of opinion, without any support at all.

During Maximilian's eventful reign several efforts were made to construct a new constitution, but it is to German rather than to imperial history that they properly belong. Here, indeed, the history of the Holy Empire might close, did not the title unchanged beckon us on, and were it not that the events of these later centuries may in their causes be traced back to times when the name of Roman was not wholly a mockery. *Attempts to reform the Germanic Constitution.* It may be enough to remark that while the preservation of peace and the better administration of justice were in some measure attained by the Public Peace and Imperial Chamber, established in A.D. 1495, schemes still more important failed through the bad constitution of the Diet, and the unconquerable jealousy of the Emperor and the Estates. Maximilian refused to have his prerogative, indefinite though weak, restricted by the appointment of an administrative council,* and when the Estates extorted it from him, did his best to ensure its failure. In the Diet, which consisted of three colleges, electors, princes and cities, the lower nobility and knights of the Empire were unrepresented, and resented every decree that affected their position, refusing to pay taxes in voting which they had no voice. The interests of the princes and the cities were often irreconcilable, while the strength of the crown would not have been sufficient to make its adhesion to the latter of any effect. The policy of conciliating the commons, which Sigismund had tried, succeeding Emperors seldom cared to repeat, content to gain their point by raising factions among the territorial magnates, and so to stave off the un-

---

* Reichsregiment.

welcome demand for reform. After many earnest attempts
to establish a representative system, such as might resist
the tendency to local independence and cure the evils of
separate administration, the hope so often baffled died
away. Forces were too nearly balanced : the
sovereign could not extend his personal control,
nor could the reforming party limit him by a
strong council of government, for such a measure would have equally trenched on the independence of the states. So ended the first
great effort for German unity, interesting from its bearing
on the events and aspirations of our own day: interesting,
too, as giving the most convincing proof of the decline of
the imperial office. For the projects of reform did not
propose to effect their objects by restoring to Maximilian
the authority his predecessors had once enjoyed, but by
setting up a body which would resemble far more nearly
the senate of a federal state than the administrative council which surrounds a monarch. The existing system developed itself further: relieved from external pressure, the
princes became more despotic in their own territories: distinct codes were framed, and new systems of administration introduced : the insurgent peasantry were crushed
down with more confident harshness. Already had leagues
of princes and cities been formed * (that of Swabia was
one of the strongest forces in Germany, and often the
monarch's firmest support); now alliances begin to be contracted with foreign powers, and receive a direction of formidable import from the rivalry which the pretensions on
Naples and Milan of Charles VIII and Lewis XII of
France kindled between their house and the Austrian. It
was no slight gain to have friends in the heart of the

Causes of the failure of the projects of reform.

---

* Wenzel had encouraged the leagues of the cities, and incurred
thereby the hatred of the nobles.

enemy's country, such as French intrigue found in the Elector Palatine and the count of Würtemberg.

Nevertheless this was also the era of the first conscious feeling of German nationality, as distinct from imperial. Driven in on all hands, with Italy and the Slavic lands and Burgundy hopelessly lost, Teutschland learned to separate itself from Welschland.* The Empire became the representative of a narrower but more practicable national union. It is not a mere coincidence that at this date there appear several notable changes of style. "Nationis Teutonicæ" (Teutscher Nation) is added to the simple "sacrum imperium Romanum." The title of "Imperator electus," which Maximilian obtains leave from Pope Julius II to assume,† when the Venetians prevent him from reaching his capital, marks the severance of Germany from Rome. No subsequent Emperor received his crown from the ancient capital (Charles V was indeed crowned by the Pope's hands, but the ceremony took place at Bologna, and was therefore of at least questionable validity); each assumed after his German coronation§ the title of Emperor Elect,‡ and employed

Germanic nationality.

Change of Titles.

---

* The Germans, like our own ancestors, called foreign, *i. e.* non-Teutonic nations, Welsh ; yet apparently not all such nations, but only those which they in some way associated with the Roman Empire, the Cymry of Roman Britain, the Romanized Kelts of Gaul, the Italians, the Roumans or Wallachs of Transylvania and the Principalities. It does not appear that either the Magyars or any Sclavonic people were called by any form of the name. In the Icelandic writings of the thirteenth century France (Francia occidentalis) is called "Valland."

† Julius was well pleased to give it, as he had no desire to see Maximilian in Italy.

‡ Erwählter Kaiser. See Appendix, Note C.

§ The German crown was received at Aachen, the ancient Frankish capital, where may still be seen, in the gallery of the basilica, the

this in all documents issued in his name. But the word

The title "Imperator Electus." "elect" being omitted when he was addressed by others, partly from motives of courtesy, partly because the old rules regarding the Roman coronation were forgotten or remembered only by antiquaries, he was never called, even when formality was required, anything but Emperor. The substantial import of another title now first introduced is the same. Before Otto I, the Teutonic king had called himself either "rex" alone, or "Francorum orientalium rex," or "Francorum atque Saxonum rex": after A.D. 962, all lesser dignities had been merged in the "Romanorum Imperator."[*] To this Maximilian appended "Germaniæ rex," or, adding Frederick II's bequest,[†] "Konig in Germanien und Jerusalem." It has been thought that from a mixture of the title King of Germany, and that of Emperor, has been formed the phrase "German Emperor," or less correctly, "Emperor of Germany."[‡] But more probably the terms

marble throne on which the Emperors from the days of Charles to those of Ferdinand I were crowned. It was upon this chair that Otto III had found the body of Charles seated, when he opened his tomb in A.D. 1001. After Ferdinand I, the coronation as well as the election took place at Frankfort. An account of the ceremony may be found in Goethe's *Wahrheit und Dichtung.* Aachen, though it remained and indeed is still a German town, lay in too remote a corner of the country to be a convenient capital, and was moreover in dangerous proximity to the West Franks, as stubborn old Germans continue to call them. As early as A.D. 1353 we find Bishop Leopold of Bamberg complaining that the French had arrogated to themselves the honors of the Frankish name, and called themselves "reges Franciæ" instead of "reges Franciæ occidentalis."—Lupoldus Bebenburgensis, apud Schardium, *Sylloge Tractatuum.*

[*] Romanorum rex (after Henry II) till the coronation at Rome.

[†] But the Emperor was only one of many claimants to this kingdom; they multiplied as the prospect of regaining it died away.

[‡] This latter does not occur, even in English books, till comparatively recent times. English writers of the seventeenth century

"German Emperor" and "Emperor of Germany" are nothing but convenient corruptions of the technical description of the Germanic sovereign.*

That the Empire was thus sinking into a merely German power cannot be doubted. But it was only natural that those who lived at the time should not discern the tendency of events. Again and again did the restless and sanguine Maximilian propose the recovery of Burgundy and Italy—his last scheme was to adjust the relations of Papacy and Empire by becoming Pope himself; nor were successive Diets less zealous to check private war, still the scandal of Germany, to set right the gear of the imperial chamber, to make the imperial officials permanent, and their administration uniform throughout the country. But while they talked the heavens darkened, and the flood came and destroyed them all.

---

always call him "The Emperor," pure and simple, just as they invariably say "the French king." But the phrase "Empereur d'Almayne" may be found in very early French writers.

* See Moser, *Römische Kayser;* Goldast's and other collections of imperial edicts and proclamations.

CHAPTER XVIII.

THE REFORMATION AND ITS EFFECTS UPON THE EMPIRE.

THE Reformation falls to be mentioned here, of course, not as a religious movement, but as the cause of political changes, which still further rent the Empire, and struck at the root of the theory by which it had been created and upheld. Luther completed the work of Hildebrand. Hitherto it had seemed not impossible to strengthen the German state into a monarchy, compact if not despotic ; the very Diet of Worms, where the monk of Wittenberg proclaimed to an astonished church and Emperor that the day of spiritual tyranny was past, had framed and presented a fresh scheme for the construction of a central council of government. The great religious schism put an end to all such hopes, for it became a source of political disunion far more serious and permanent than any that had existed before, and it taught the two factions, into which Germany was henceforth divided, to regard each other with feelings more bitter than those of hostile nations.

The breach came at the most unfortunate time possible. After an election, more memorable than any preceding,

Accession of Charles V (1519-1558). an election in which Francis I of France and Henry VIII of England had been his competitors, a prince had just ascended the imperial throne who united dominions vaster than any Europe had seen since the days of his great namesake. Spain and Naples, Flanders, and other parts of the Burgundian lands, as well as large regions in eastern Germany, obeyed Charles: he drew inexhaustible revenues from a new empire beyond the Atlantic. Such a power, directed by a mind more resolute and profound than that of Maximilian his grandfather, might have well been able, despite the stringency of his coronation engagements * and the watchfulness of the electors,†. to override their usurped privileges, and make himself practically as well as officially the head of the nation. Charles V, though from the coldness of his manner ‡ and his Flemish speech never a favorite among the Germans, was in point a fact far stronger than Maximilian or any other Emperor who had reigned for three centuries. In Italy, he succeeded, after long struggles with the Pope and the French, in rendering himself supreme : England he knew how to lead, by flattering Henry and cajoling Wolsey : from no state but France had he serious opposition to fear. To this'strength his imperial dignity was indeed a mere accident: its sources were the infantry of Spain, the looms of Flanders, the sierras of Peru. But the conquest once achieved, might could lose itself in right ; and as an earlier Charles had veiled the terror of the Frankish sword under the mask of Roman election, so might his successor sway a hundred provinces with the sole name of Roman Emperor, and transmit to his race a dominion as wide and more enduring. .

One is tempted to speculate as to what might have hap-

---

* The so-called "Wahlcapitulation."

† The electors long refused to elect Charles, dreading his great hereditary power, and were at last induced to do so only by their overmastering fear of the Turks.

‡ Nearly all the Hapsburgs seem to have wanted that sort of genial heartiness which, apt as it is to be stifled by education in the purple, has nevertheless been possessed by several other royal lines, greatly contributing to their vitality ; as, for instance, by more than one prince of the houses of Brunswick and Hohenzollern.

pened had Charles espoused the reforming cause. His
reverence for the Pope's person is sufficiently seen in the
sack of Rome and the captivity of Clement; the traditions
of his office might have led him to tread in the
Attitude of steps of the Henrys and the Fredericks, into
Charles
toward the which even the timid Lewis IV and the unsta-
religious ble Sigismund had sometimes ventured ; the
movement. awakening zeal of the German people, exasper-
ated by the exactions of the Romish court,
would have strengthened his hands, and enabled him,
while moderating the excesses of change, to fix his throne
on the deep foundations of national love. It may well be
doubted—Englishmen at least have reason for the doubt—
whether the Reformation would not have lost as much as it
could have gained by being entangled in the meshes of
royal patronage. But, setting aside Charles' personal
leaning to the old faith, and forgetting that he was king of
the most bigoted race of Europe, his position as Emperor
made him almost perforce the Pope's ally. The Empire
had been called into being by Rome, had vaunted the protection of the Apostolic See as its highest earthly privilege, had latterly been wont, especially in Hapsburg hands,
to lean on the Papacy for support. Itself founded entirely
on prescription and the traditions of immemorial reverence, how could it abandon the cause which the longest
prescription and the most solemn authority had combined
to consecrate? With the German clergy, despite occasional
quarrels, it had been on better terms than with the lay
aristocracy; their heads had been the chief ministers of
the crown; the advocacies of their abbeys were the last
source of imperial revenue to disappear. To turn against
them now, when furiously assailed by heretics; to abrogate
claims hallowed by antiquity and a hundred laws, would be
to pronounce its own sentence, and the fall of the eternal
city's spiritual dominion must involve the fall of what still

professed to be her temporal. Charles would have been glad to see some abuses corrected; but a broad line of policy was called for, and he cast in his lot with the Catholics.*

Of many momentous results only a few need be noticed here. The reconstruction of the old imperial system, upon the basis of Hapsburg power, proved in the end impossible. Yet for some years it had seemed actually accomplished. When the Smal- kaldic league had been dissolved and its leaders captured, the whole country lay pros- trate before Charles. He overawed the Diet at *Ultimate failure of the repres- sive policy of Charles.* Augsburg by his Spanish soldiery: he forced formularies of doctrine upon the vanquished Protestants : he set up and pulled down whom he would throughout Germany, amid the muttered discontent of his own partisans. Then, as in the beginning of the year 1552, he lay at Innsbruck, fondly dreaming that his work was done, waiting the spring weather to cross to Trent, where the Catholic fathers had again met to settle the world's faith for it, news was sud-

---

* See this brought out with great force in the very interesting work of Padre Tosti, *Prolegomeni alla Storia Universale della Chiesa*, from which I quote one passage, which bears directly on the matter in hand: " Il grido della riforma clericale aveva un eco terribile in tutta la compagnia civile dei popoli: essa percuoteva le cime del laicale potere, e rimbalzava per tutta la gerarchia sociale. Se l' imperatore Sigismondo nel consilio di Costanza non avesse fiutate queste conse- quenze nella eresia di Hus e di Girolamo di Praga, forse non avrebbe con tantò zelo mandati alle fiamme que' novatori. Rotto da Lutero il vincolo di suggezione al Papa ed ai preti in fatti di religione, avvenne che anche quello che sommetteva il vassallo al barone, il barone al imperadore si allentasse. Il popolo con la Bibbia in mano era prete, vescovo, e papa; e se prima contristato della prepotenza di chi gli soprastava, ricorreva al successore di San Pietro, ora ricorreva a se stesso, avendogli commesse Fra Martino le chiavi del regno dei Cieli."—vol. ii. pp. 398–9.

denly brought that North Germany was in arms, and that
the revolted Maurice of Saxony had seized Donauwerth,
and was hurrying through the Bavarian Alps to surprise
his sovereign.* Charles rose and fled south over the snows
of the Brenner, then eastward, under the blood-red cliffs
of dolomite that wall in the Pusterthal, far away into the
silent valleys of Carinthia: the council of Trent broke up in
consternation: Europe saw and the Emperor acknowledged
that in his fancied triumph over the spirit of revolution he
had done no more than block up for the moment an irresistible torrent. When this last effort to produce religious uniformity by violence had failed as hopelessly as the
previous devices of holding discussions of doctrine and
calling a general council, a sort of armistice was agreed to
in 1555, which lasted in mutual fear and suspicion for
more than sixty years. Four years after this disappointment
of the hopes and projects which had occupied his busy life,
Charles, weighed down by cares and with the shadow of
coming death already upon him, resigned the sovereignty
of Spain and the Indies, of Flanders and Naples, into the
hands of his son Philip II ; while the imperial scepter
passed to his brother Ferdinand, who had been
Ferdi- some time before (1531) chosen King of the
nand I,
1558-1564. Romans. Fedinand was content to leave things
much as he found them, and the amiable
Maximilian II, who succeeded him, though person-
ally well inclined to the Protestants, found
Maximilian himself fettered by his position and his allies,
II,
1564-1576. and could do little or nothing to quench the
flame of religious and political hatred. Germany remained divided into two omnipresent factions,
and so further than ever from harmonious action, or a

---

* Maurice is reported to have been just as well pleased at Charles'
escape. "I have no cage big enough," said he, "for such a bird."

tightening of the long-loosened bond of feudal allegiance. The states of either creed being gathered into *Destruction* a league, there could no longer be a recognized *of the Ger-* center of authority for judicial or administra- *manic state-* tive purposes. Least of all could a center be *system.* sought in the Emperor, the leader of the papal party, the suspected foe of every Protestant. Too closely watched to do anything of his own authority, too much committed to one party to be accepted as a mediator by the other, he was driven to attain his own objects by falling in with the schemes and furthering the selfish ends of his adherents, by becoming the accomplice or the tool of the Jesuits. The Lutheran princes addressed themselves to reduce a power of which they had still an oversensitive dread, and found, when they exacted from each successive sovereign engagements more stringent than his predecessor's, that in this, and this alone, their Catholic brethren were not unwilling to join them. Thus obliged to strip himself one by one of the ancient privileges of his crown, the Emperor came to have little influence on the government except that which his intrigues might exercise. Nay, it became almost impossible to maintain a government at all. For when the Reformers found themselves outvoted at the Diet, they declared that in matters of religion a majority ought not to bind a minority. As the measures were few which did not admit of being reduced to this category, for whatever benefited the Emperor or any other Catholic prince injured the Protestants, nothing could be done save by the assent of two bitterly hostile factions. Thus scarce anything was done; and even the courts of justice were stopped by the disputes that attended the appointment of every judge or assessor.

In the foreign politics of Germany another result followed. Inferior in military force and organization, the Protestant princes at first provided for their safety by

forming leagues among themselves. The device was an old
one, and had been employed by the monarch
Alliance of himself before now, in despair at the effete and
the Protest- cumbrous forms of the imperial system. Soon
ants with
France. they began to look beyond the Vosges, and found
that France, burning heretics at home, was only
too happy to smile on free opinions elsewhere. The alliance
was easily struck; Henry II assumed in 1552 the title of
" Protector of the Germanic liberties," and a pretext for
interference was never wanting in future.

These were some of the visible political consequences of
the great religious schism of the sixteenth century. But
beyond and above them there was a change far
The Ref- more momentous than any of its immediate
ormation results. There is perhaps no event in history
spirit, and
its influence which has been represented in so great a variety
upon the of lights as the Reformation. It has been
Empire. called a revolt of the laity against the clergy,
or of the Teutonic races against the Italians, or
of the kingdoms of Europe against the universal monarchy of the Popes. Some have seen in it only a burst of
long-repressed anger at the luxury of the prelates and the
manifold abuses of the ecclesiastical system ; others a
renewal of the youth of the church by a return to primitive forms of doctrine. All these, indeed, to some extent
it was ; but it was also something more profound, and
fraught with mightier consequences than any of them. It
was in its essence the assertion of the principle of individuality—that is to say, of true spiritual freedom. Hitherto the personal consciousness had been a faint and
broken reflection of the universal ; obedience had been
held the first of religious duties; truth had been conceived
as a something external and positive, which the priesthood
who were its stewards were to communicate to the passive
layman, and whose saving virtue lay not in its being felt

and known by him to be truth, but in a purely formal
and unreasoning acceptance. The great principles which
mediæval Christianity still cherished were obscured by the
limited, rigid, almost sensuous forms which had been
forced on them in times of ignorance and barbarism.
That which was in its nature abstract, had been able to
survive only by taking a concrete expression. The universal consciousness became the Visible Church : the
Visible Church hardened into a government and degene-
rated into a hierarchy. Holiness of heart and life was
sought by outward works, by penances and pilgrimages,
by gifts to the poor and to the clergy, wherein there
dwelt often little enough of a charitable mind. The presence of divine truth among men was symbolized under
one aspect by the existence on earth of an infallible Vicar
of God, the Pope ; under another, by the reception of
the present Deity in the sacrifice of the mass; in a third,
by the doctrine that the priest's power to remit sins and
administer the sacraments depended upon a transmission
of miraculous gifts which can hardly be called other than
physical. All this system of doctrine, which might, but
for the position of the church as a worldly, and therefore
obstructive, power, have expanded, renewed and purified
itself during the four centuries that had elapsed since its
completion,* and thus remained in harmony with the
growing intelligence of mankind, was suddenly rent in
pieces by the convulsion of the Reformation, and flung
away by the more religious and more progressive peoples
of Europe. That which was external and concrete, was
in all things to be superseded by that which was inward
and spiritual. It was proclaimed that the individual
spirit, while it continued to mirror itself in the world-
spirit, had nevertheless an independent existence as a

---

* It was not till the end of the eleventh century that transubstan-
tiation was definitely established as a dogma.

center of self-issuing force, and was to be in all things active rather than passive. Truth was no longer to be truth to the soul until it should have been by the soul recognized, and in some measure even created; but when so recognized and felt, it is able under the form of faith to transcend outward works and to transform the dogmas of the understanding; it becomes the living principle within each man's breast, infinite itself, and expressing itself infinitely through his thoughts and acts. He who as a spiritual being was delivered from the priest, and brought into , direct relation with the Divinity, needed not, as heretofore, to be enrolled a member of a visible congregation of his fellows, that he might live a pure and useful life among them. Thus by the Reformation the Visible Church, as well as the priesthood, lost that paramount importance which had hitherto belonged to it, and sank from being the depositary of all religious tradition, the source and center of religious life, the arbiter of eternal happiness or misery, into a mere association of Christian men, for the expression of mutual

Effect of the Reformation on the doctrines regarding the Visible Church.

sympathy and the better attainment of certain common ends. Like those other doctrines which were now assailed by the Reformation, this mediæval view of the nature of the Visible Church had been naturally, and so, it may be said, necessarily developed between the third and the twelfth century, and must therefore have represented the thoughts and satisfied the wants of those times. By the Visible Church the flickering lamp of knowledge and literary culture, as well as of religion, had been fed and tended through the long night of Dark Ages. But, like the whole theological fabric of which it formed a part, it was now hard and unfruitful, identified with its own worst abuses, capable apparently of no further development, and unable to satisfy minds which in growing stronger had grown more conscious of their strength. Before the awakened zeal of the northern nations it stood a cold and lifeless system, whose organization as a hierarchy checked the free activity of thought, whose bestowal of worldly power and wealth on spiritual pastors drew them away from their proper duties, and which by maintaining alongside of the civil magistracy a co-ordinate and rival government, maintained also that separation of the spiritual element in man from the secular, which had been so complete and so pernicious during the Middle Ages, which debases life, and severs religion from morality.

The Reformation, it may be said, was a religious movement: and it is the Empire, not the Church, that we have here to consider. The distinction in only apparent. The Holy Empire is but another *Consequent* name for the Visible Church. It has been *effect upon* *the Empire.* shown already how mediæval theory constructed the State on the model of the Church ; how the Roman Empire was the shadow of the Popedom—designed to rule men's bodies as the pontiff ruled their souls. Both alike claimed obedience on the ground that Truth is One, and that where there is one faith there must be One government.* And, therefore, since it was this very principle of Formal Unity that the Reformation overthrew, it became a revolt against despotism of every kind ; it erected the standard of civil as well as of religious liberty, since both of them are needed, though needed in a different measure, for the worthy development of the individual spirit. The Empire had never been conspicuously the antagonist of popular freedom, and was, even under Charles V, far less formidable to the commonalty than were the petty princes of Germany. But submission, and submission on the ground of indefeasible transmitted right,

---

* See the passages quoted in note, p. 95 ; and note§, p. 107.

upon the ground of Catholic traditions and the duty of the Christian magistrate to suffer heresy and schism as little as the parallel sins of treason and rebellion, had been its constant claim and watchword. Since the days of Julius Cæsar it had passed through many phases, but in none of them had it ever been a constitutional monarchy, pledged to the recognition of popular rights. And hence the indirect tendency of the Reformation to narrow the province of government and exalt the privileges of the subject was as plainly adverse to the Empire as the Protestant claim of the right of private judgment was to the pretensions of the Papacy and the priesthood.

The remark must not be omitted in passing, how much less than might have been expected the religious movement did at first actually effect in the way of *Immediate influence of the Refor- mation on political and relig- ious liberty.* promoting either political progress or freedom of conscience. The habits of centuries were not to be unlearned in a few years, and it was natural that ideas struggling into exis t nce and activity should work erringly and imperfectly for a time. By a few inflammable minds liberty was carried into antinomianism, and produced the wildest excesses of life and doctrine. Several fantastic sects arose, refusing to conform to the ordinary rules without which human society could not subsist. But these commotions neither spread widely nor lasted long. Far more pervading and more remarkable was the other error, if that can be called an error which was the almost unavoidable result of the circumstances of the time. The prin- *Conduct of the Protest- ant States.* ciples which had led the Protestants to sever themselves from the Roman Church, should have taught them to bear with the opinions of others, and warned them from the attempt to connect agreement in doctrine or manner of worship with the necessary forms of civil government.

Still less ought they to have enforced that agreement by civil penalties; for faith, upon their own showing, had no value save when it was freely given. A church which does not claim to be infallible is bound to allow that some part of the truth may possibly be with its adversaries: a church which permits or encourages human reason to apply itself to revelation has no right first to argue with people and then to punish them if they are not convinced. But whether it was that men only half saw what they had done, or that finding it hard enough to unrivet priestly fetters, they welcomed all the aid a temporal prince could give, the result was that religion, or rather religious creeds, began to be involved with politics more closely than had ever been the case before. Through the greater part of Christendom wars of religion raged for a century or more, and down to our own days feelings of theological antipathy continue to affect the relations of the powers of Europe. In almost every country the form of doctrine which triumphed associated itself with the state, and maintained the despotic system of the Middle Ages, while it forsook the grounds on which that system had been based. It was thus that there arose National Churches, which were to be to the several Protestant countries of Europe that which the Church Catholic had been to the world at large; churches, that is to say, each of which was to be co-extensive with its respective state, was to enjoy landed wealth and exclusive political privilege, and was to be armed with coercive powers against recusants. It was not altogether easy to find a set of theoretical principles on which such churches might be made to rest, for they could not, like the old church, point to the historical transmission of their doctrines; they could not claim to have in any one man or body of men an infallible organ of divine truth; they could not even fall back upon general councils, or the argument, whatever it may be worth, *" Securus iudicat orbis terra-*

rum." But in practice these difficulties were soon got over, for the dominant party in each state, if it was not infallible, was at any rate quite sure that it was right, and could attribute the resistance of other sects to nothing but moral obliquity. The will of the sovereign, as in England, or the will of the majority, as in Holland, Scandinavia and Scotland, imposed upon each country a peculiar form of worship, and kept up the practices of mediæval intolerance without their justification. Persecution, which might be at least excused in an infallible Catholic and Apostolic Church, was peculiarly odious when practiced by those who were not catholic, who were no more apostolic than their neighbors, and who had just revolted from the most ancient and venerable authority in the name of rights which they now denied to others. If union with the visible church by participation in a material sacrament be necessary to eternal life, persecution may be held a duty, a kindness to perishing souls. But if the kingdom of heaven be in every sense a kingdom of the spirit, if saving faith be possible out of one visible body and under a diversity of external forms, persecution becomes at once a crime and a folly. Therefore the intolerance of Protestants, if the forms it took were less cruel than those practiced by the Roman Catholics, was also far less defensible; for it had seldom anything better to allege on its behalf than motives of political expediency, or, more often, the mere headstrong passion of a ruler or a faction to silence the expressions of any opinions but their own. To enlarge upon this theme, did space permit it, would not be to digress from the proper subject of this narrative. For the Empire, as has been said more than once already, was far less an institution than a theory or doctrine. And hence it is not too much to say, that the ideas which have but recently ceased to prevail regarding the duty of the magistrate to compel uniformity in doctrine and worship by the civil

arm, may all be traced to the relation which that theory
established between the Roman Church and the Roman
Empire; to the conception, in fact, of an Empire Church
itself.

Two of the ways in which the Reformation affected the
Empire have been now described: its immediate political
results, and its far more profound doctrinal importance, as
implanting new ideas regarding the nature of
freedom and the province of government. A
third, though apparently almost superficial,
cannot be omitted. Its name and its traditions, little as they retained of their former
magic power, were still such as to excite the
antipathy of the German reformers. The
*Influence
of the Ref-
ormation
on the name
and asso-
ciations of
the Empire.*
form which the doctrine of the supreme importance of one faith and one body of the faithful
had taken was the dominion of the ancient capital
of the world through her spiritual head, the Roman
bishop, and her temporal head, the Emperor. As
the names of Roman and Christian had been once convertible, so long afterward were those of Roman and Catholic.
The Reformation, separating into its parts what had hitherto been one conception, attacked Romanism but not
Catholicity, and formed religious communities which,
while continuing to call themselves Christian, repudiated
the form with which Christianity had been so long identified in the West. As the Empire was founded upon the
assumption that the limits of Church and State are exactly co-extensive, a change which withdrew half of its subjects from the one body while they remained members of
the other, transformed it utterly, destroyed the meaning
and value of its old arrangements, and forced the Emperor
into a strange and incongruous position. To his Protestant subjects he was merely the head of the administration,
to the Catholics he was also the Defender and Advocate of
their church. Thus from being chief of the whole state

he became the chief of a party within it, the Corpus Catholicorum, as opposed to the Corpus Evangelicorum; he lost what had been hitherto his most holy claim to the obedience of the subject; the awakened feeling of German nationality was driven into hostility to an institution whose title and history bound it to the center of foreign tyranny. After exulting for seven centuries in the heritage of Roman rule, the Teutonic nations cherished again the feeling with which their ancestors had resisted Julius Cæsar and Germanicus. Two mutually repugnant systems could not exist side by side without striving to destroy one an-another. The instincts of theological sympathy overcame the duties of political allegiance, and men who were subjects both of the Emperor and of their local prince, gave all their loyalty to him who espoused their doctrines and protected their worship. For in North Germany princes as well as people were mostly Lutheran: in the southern and especially the south-eastern lands, where the magnates held to the old faith, Protestants were scarcely to be found except in the free cities. The same causes which injured the Emperor's position in Germany swept away the last semblance of his authority through other countries. In the great struggle which followed, the Protestants of England and France, of Holland and Sweden, thought of him only as the ally of Spain, of the Vatican, of the Jesuits; and he of whom it had been believed a century before that by nothing but his existence was the coming of Antichrist on earth delayed, was in the eye of the northern divines either Antichrist himself or Antichrist's foremost champion. The earthquake that opened a chasm in Germany was felt through Europe; its states and peoples marshaled themselves under two hostile banners, and with the Empire's expiring power vanished that united Christendom it had been created to lead.*

* Henry VIII of England when he rebelled against the Pope called

Some of the effects thus sketched began to show themselves as early as that famous Diet of Worms, from Luther's
appearance at which, in A.D. 1521, we may date
the beginning of the Reformation. But just *Troubles of*
as the end of the religious conflict in England *Germany.*
can hardly be placed earlier than the Revolution in 1688,
nor in France than the Revocation of the Edict of Nantes in
1685, so it was not till after more than a century of doubtful strife that the new order of things was fully
and finally established in Germany. The *Rudolf II,*
arrangements of Augsburg, like most treaties *1576-1612.*
on the basis of *uti possidetis*, were no better than a hollow
truce, satisfying no one, and consciously made to be
broken. The church lands which Protestants had seized,
and Jesuit confessors urged the Catholic
princes to reclaim, furnished an unceasing *Matthias,*
ground of quarrel; neither party yet knew the *1612-1619.*
strength of its antagonists sufficiently to abstain from insulting or persecuting their modes of worship, and the
smouldering hate of half a century was kindled by the
troubles of Bohemia into the Thirty Years' War.

The imperial scepter had now passed from the indolent
and vacillating Rudolf II (1576-1612), the corrupt and reckless policy of whose ministers had done much to
exasperate the already suspicious minds of the *Thirty*
Protestants into the firmer grasp of Ferdinand *Years'*
II.* Jealous, bigoted, implacable, skillful in *War,*
forming and concealing his plans, resolute to *1618-1648.*

himself King of Ireland (his predecessors had used only the title
" Dominus Hiberniæ ") without asking the Emperor's permission, in
order to show that he repudiated the temporal as well as the spiritual
dominion of Rome. So the Statute of Appeals is careful to deny and
reject the authority of " other foreign potentates," meaning, no doubt,
the Emperor as well as the Pope.

* Matthias, brother of Rudolf II, reigned from 1612 till 1619.

obstinacy in carrying them out in action, the house of
Hapsburg could have had no abler and no more unpopular
leader in their second attempt to turn the
German Empire into an Austrian military
monarchy. They seemed for a time as near
to the accomplishment of the project as Charles
V had been. Leagued with Spain, backed by the Catholics of Germany, served by such a leader as Wallenstein,
Ferdinand proposed nothing less than the extension of the Empire to its old limits, and the
recovery of his crown's full prerogative over all
its vassals. Denmark and Holland were to be
attacked by sea and land: Italy to be reconquered with the
help of Spain: Maximilian of Bavaria and Wallenstein to
be rewarded with principalities in Pomerania and Mecklenburg. The latter general was all but master of Northern
Germany when the successful resistance of Stralsund
turned the wavering balance of the war. Soon after (A.D.
1630), Gustavus Adolphus crossed the Baltic, and saved
Europe from an impending reign of the Jesuits. Ferdinand's high-handed proceedings had already alarmed even
the Catholic princes. Of his own authority he had put
the Elector Palatine and other magnates to the ban of the
Empire : he had transferred an electoral vote to Bavaria ;
had treated the districts overrun by his generals as spoils of
war to be portioned out at his pleasure ; had unsettled all
possession by requiring the restitution of church property
occupied since A.D. 1555. The Protestants
were helpless; the Catholics, though they complained of the flagrant illegality of such conduct, did not dare to oppose it : the rescue of Germany
was the work of the Swedish king. In four campaigns he
destroyed the armies and the prestige of the Emperor ;
devastated his lands, emptied his treasury, and left him at
last so enfeebled that no subsequent successes could make

Ferdinand II, A.D. 1619-1637.

Plans of Ferdinand II.

Gustavus Adolphus.

him again formidable. Such, nevertheless, was the self-ishness and apathy of the Protestant princes, divided by the mutual jealousy of the Lutheran and the Calvinist party—some, like the Saxon elector, most in-glorious, of his inglorious house, bribed by the *Ferdinand* cunning Austrian; others afraid to stir lest a *III,* 1637-1658. reverse should expose them unprotected to his vengeance—that the issue of the long protracted contest would have gone against them but for the interference of France. It was the leading principle of Richelieu's policy to depress the house of Hapsburg and keep Germany disunited : hence he fostered Protestantism abroad while trampling it down at home. The triumph he *The peace of* did not live to see was sealed in A.D. 1648, on *Westphalia.* the utter exhaustion of all the combatants, and the treaties of Münster and Osnabrück were thenceforward the basis of the Germanic constitution.

CHAPTER XIX.

THE PEACE OF WESTPHALIA : LAST STAGE IN THE DECLINE
OF THE EMPIRE.

THE Peace of Westphalia is the first, and, with the exception perhaps of the Treaties of Vienna in 1815, the most important of those attempts to reconstruct by diplomacy the European states-system which have played so large a part in modern history. It is important, however, not as marking the introduction of new principles, but as winding up the struggle which had convulsed Germany since the revolt of Luther, sealing its results, and closing definitely the period of the Reformation. Although the causes of disunion which the religious movement called into being had now been at work for more than a hundred years, their effects were not fully seen till it became necessary to establish a system which should represent the altered relations of the German states. It may thus be said of this famous peace, as of the other so-called "fundamental law of the Empire," the Golden Bull, that it did no more than legalize a condition of things already in existence, but which by being legalized acquired new importance. To all parties alike the result of the Thirty Years' War was thoroughly unsatisfactory : to the Protestants, who had lost Bohemia, and still were obliged to hold an inferior place in the electoral college and in the Diet: to the Catholics, who were forced to permit the exercise of heretical worship, and leave the church land in the grasp of sacrilegious spoilers : to the princes, who could not throw off the burden of imperial supremacy : to the emperor, who could turn that supremacy to no practical account.

No other conclusion was possible to a contest in which every one had been vanquished and no one victorious : which had ceased because while the reason for war continued the means of war had failed. Nevertheless, the substantial advantage remained with the German princes, for they gained the formal recognition of that territorial independence whose origin may be placed as far back as the days of Frederick II, and the maturity of which had been hastened by the events of the last preceding century. It was, indeed, not only recognized but justified as rightful and necessary. For while the political situation, to use a current phrase, had changed within the last two hundred years, the eyes with which men regarded it had changed still more. Never by their fiercest enemies in earlier times, not once by the Popes or Lombard republicans in the heat of their strife with the Franconian and Swabian Cæsars, had the Emperors been reproached as mere German kings, or their claim to be the lawful heirs of Rome denied. The Protestant jurists of the sixteenth or rather of the seventeenth century were the first persons who ventured to scoff at the pretended lordship of the world, and declare their Empire to be nothing more than a German monarchy, in dealing with which no superstitious reverence need prevent its subjects from making the best terms they could for themselves, and controlling a sovereign whose religious predilections made him the friend of their enemies.

It is very instructive to turn suddenly from Dante or Peter de Andlo to a book published shortly before A.D. 1648, under the name of Hippolytus a Lapide,* and notice the matter-of-fact way, the almost contemptuous spirit in which, disregarding the traditional glories of the Empire, he comments on its actual condition and prospects. Hippoly-

The treatise of Hippolytus a Lapide.

---

* *De Ratione Status in Imperio nostro Romano-Germanico.*

tus, the pseudonym which the jurist Chemnitz assumed, urges with violence almost superfluous that the Germanic constitution must be treated entirely as a native growth: that the so-called "lex regia" and the whole system of Justinianean absolutism which the Emperors had used so dexterously, were in their applications to Germany not merely incongruous but positively absurd. With eminent learning, Chemnitz examines the early history of the Empire, draws from the unceasing contests of the monarch with the nobility the unexpected moral that the power of the former has been always dangerous, and is now more dangerous than ever, and then launches out into a long invective against the policy of the Hapsburgs, an invective which the ambition and harshness of the late Emperor made only too plausible. The one real remedy for the evils that menace Germany he states concisely—" domus Austriacæ extirpatio:" but, failing this, he would have the Emperor's prerogative restricted in every way, and provide means for resisting or dethroning him. It was by these views, which seem to have made a profound impression in Germany, that the states, or rather France and Sweden acting on their behalf, were guided in the negotiations of Osnabrück and Münster. By extorting a full recognition of the sovereignty of all the princes, Catholics and Protestants alike, in their respective territories, they bound the Emperor from any direct interference with the administration, either in particular districts or throughout the Empire. All affairs of public importance, including the rights of *Rights of* making war or peace, of levying contributions, *the Em-* raising troops, building fortresses, passing or *peror and* interpreting laws, were henceforth to be left *the Diet, as* entirely in the hands of the Diet. The Aulic *settled in* Council, which had been sometimes the engine *A.D. 1648.* of imperial oppression, and always of imperial intrigue, was so restricted as to be harmless for the future.

The "reservata" of the Emperor were confined to the rights of granting titles and confirming tolls. In matters of religion, an exact though not perfectly reciprocal equality was established between the two chief ecclesiastical bodies, and the right of "Itio in partes," that is to say, of deciding questions in which religion was involved by amicable negotiations between the Protestant and Catholic states, instead of by a majority of votes in the Diet, was definitely conceded. Both Lutherans and Calvinists were declared free from all jurisdiction of the Pope or any Catholic prelate. Thus the last link which bound Germany to Rome was snapped, the last of the principles by virtue of which the Empire had existed was abandoned. For the Empire now contained and recognized as its members persons who formed a visible body at open war with the Holy Roman Church; and its constitution admitted schismatics to a full share in all those civil rights which, according to the doctrines of the early Middle Age, could be enjoyed by no one who was out of the communion of the Catholic Church. The Peace of Westphalia was therefore an abrogation of the sovereignty of Rome, and of the theory of Church and State with which the name of Rome was associated. And in this light was it regarded by Pope Innocent X, who commanded his legate to protest against it, and subsequently declared it void by the bull "Zelo domus Dei." *

---

* Even the Roman pontiffs had lapsed into that scolding, anile tone (so unlike the fiery brevity of Hildebrand, or the stern precision of Innocent III) which is now seldom absent from their public utterances. Pope Innocent X pronounces the provisions of the treaty, "Ipso iure nulla, irrita, invalida, iniqua, iniusta, damnata, reprobata, inania, viribusque et effectu vacua, omnino fuisse, esse, et perpetuo fore."—In spite of which they were observed. This bull may be found in vol. xvii. of the *Bullarium*. It bears date Nov. 20th, A.D. 1648.

The transference of power within the Empire, from its
head to its members, was a small matter compared with
the losses which the Empire suffered as a whole. The
real gainers by the treaties of Westphalia were those who
had borne the brunt of the battle against Ferdinand II and his son. To France were ceded
Brisac, the Austrian part of Alsace, and the lands
of the three bishoprics in Lorraine—Metz,
Toul and Verdun, which her armies had seized in A. D.
1552: to Sweden, northern Pomerania, Bremen and Verden.
There was, however, this difference between the position
of the two, that whereas Sweden became a member of the
German Diet for what she received (as the king of Holland was, until 1866, a member for Dutch Luxemburg, and
as the kings of Denmark, up till the accession of the present sovereign in 1863, were for Holstein), the acquisitions
of France were delivered over to her in full sovereignty, and
forever (as it seemed) severed from the Germanic body.
And as it was by their aid that the liberties of the Protestants
had been won, these two states obtained at the same time
what was more valuable than territorial accessions—the
right of interfering at. imperial elections, and generally
whenever the provisions of the treaties of Osnabrück and
Münster, which they had guaranteed, might be supposed
to be endangered. The bounds of the Empire were
further narrowed by the final separation of two countries,
once integral parts of Germany, and up to this time
legally members of her body. Holland and Switzerland
were, in A. D. 1648, declared independent.

The Peace of Westphalia is an era in imperial history
not less clearly marked than the coronation of Otto the
Great, or the death of Frederick II. As from the days of
Maximilian it had borne a mixed or transitional character,
well expressed by the name Romano-Germanic, so henceforth it is in everything but title purely and solely a

*Loss of
imperial
territories.*

German Empire. Properly, indeed, it was no longer an Empire at all, but a Confederation, and that of the loosest sort. For it had no common treasury, no efficient common tribunals,* no means of coercing a refractory member;† its states were of different religions, were governed according to different forms, were administered judicially and financially without any regard to each other. The traveler in Central Germany used, up till 1866, to be amused to find, every hour or two, by the change in the soldiers' uniforms, and in the color of the stripes on the railway fences, that he had passed out of one and into another of its miniature kingdoms. Much more surprised and embarrassed would he have been a century ago, when, instead of the present twenty-nine there were three hundred petty principalities between the Alps and the Baltic, each with its own laws, its own court (in which the ceremonious pomp of Versailles was faintly reproduced), its little army, its separate coinage, its tolls and custom-houses on the frontier, its crowd of meddlesome and pedantic officials, presided over by a prime minister who was generally the unworthy favorite of his prince and the pensioner of some foreign court. This vicious system, which para-

Germany after the Peace.

Number of petty independent states: effects of such a system on Germany.

---

* The Imperial Chamber (Kammergericht) continued, with frequent and long interruptions, to sit while the Empire lasted. But its slowness and formality passed that of any other legal body the world has yet seen, and it had no power to enforce its sentences. Till 1689 it sat at Speyer, whence the saying "Spirae lites spirant et non exspirant;" in that year the French laid Speyer in ashes, and the chamber was in 1693 established at Wetzlar. The Aulic council was little more efficient, and was generally disliked as the tool of imperial intrigue.

† The "matricula" specifying the quota of each state to the imperial army could not be any longer employed.

lyzed the trade, the literature, and the political thought of Germany, had been forming itself for some time, but did not become fully established until the Peace of Westphalia, by emancipating the princes from imperial control, had made them despots in their own territories. The impoverishment of the inferior nobility and the decline of the commercial cities caused by a war that had lasted a whole generation, removed every counterpoise to the power of the electors and princes, and made absolutism supreme just where absolutism wants all its justification, its states too small to have any public opinion, states in which everything depends on the monarch, and the monarch depends on his favorites. After A.D. 1648 the provincial estates or parliaments became obsolete in most of these principalities and powerless in the rest. Germany was forced to drink to its very dregs the cup of feudalism, feudalism from which all the feelings that once ennobled it had departed.

It is instructive to compare the results of the system of feudality in the three chief countries of modern Europe.

Feudalism in France, England, Germany. In France, the feudal head absorbed all the powers of the state, and left to the aristocracy only a few privileges, odious indeed, but politically worthless. In England, the mediæval system expanded into a constitutional monarchy, where the oligarchy was still strong, but the commons had won the full recognition of equal civil rights. In Germany, everything was taken from the sovereign, and nothing given to the people; the representatives of those who had been fief-holders of the first and second rank before the Great Interregnum were now independent potentates; and what had been once a monarchy was now an aristocratic federation. The Diet, originally an assembly of magnates meeting from time to time like our early English Parliaments, became in A.D. 1654 a permanent body, at which the electors, princes and cities were represented by their envoys. In other words, it was now not a national council, but an international congress of diplomatists.

Where the sacrifice of imperial, or rather federal, rights to state rights was so complete, we may wonder that the farce of an Empire should have been retained at all. A mere German Empire would *Causes of* probably have perished ; but the Teutonic *the contin-* people could not bring itself to abandon the *uance of* venerable heritage of Rome. Moreover, the *the Empire.* Germans were of all European peoples the most slow-moving and long-suffering; and as, if the Empire had fallen, something must have been erected in its place, they preferred to work on with the clumsy machine so long as it would work at all. Properly speaking, it has no history after this; and the history of the particular states of Germany which takes its place is one of the dreariest chapters in the annals of mankind. It would be hard to find, from the Peace of Westphalia to the French Revolution, a single grand character or a single noble enterprise ; a single sacrifice made to great public interests, a single instance in which the welfare of nations was preferred to the selfish passions of their princes.* The military history of those times will always be read with interest; but free and progressive countries have a history of peace not less rich and varied than that of war ; and when we ask for an account of the political life of Germany in the eighteenth century, we hear nothing but the scandals of buzzing courts, and the wrangling of diplomatists at never-ending congresses.

---

* There was indeed one ruler of consummate powers; but his policy was self-regarding throughout, and though he did much for his state and people, he did nothing by them, and gave no opportunity for the development of political life among them.

Useless and helpless as the Empire had become, it was not without its importance to the neighboring countries, with whose fortunes it had been linked by the Peace of Westphalia. It was the pivot on which the political system of Europe was to revolve : the scales, so to speak, which marked the equipoise of power that had become the grand object of the policy of all states. This modern caricature of the plan by which the theorists of the fourteenth century had proposed to keep the world at peace, used means less noble and attained its end no better than theirs had done. No one will deny that it was and is desirable to prevent a universal monarchy in Europe. But it may be asked whether a system can be considered successful which allowed Frederick of Prussia to seize Silesia, which did not check the aggressions of Russia and France upon their neighbors, which was forever bartering and exchanging lands in every part of Europe without thought of the inhabitants, which permitted and has never been able to redress that greatest of public misfortunes, the partitionment of Poland. And if it be said that bad as things have been under this system, they would have been worse without it, it is hard to refrain from asking whether any evils could have been greater than those which the people of Europe have suffered through constant wars with each other, and through the withdrawal, even in time of peace, of so large a part of their population from useful labor to be wasted in maintaining a standing army.

The Empire and the balance of power.

The result of the extended relations in which Germany now found herself to Europe, with two foreign kings never wanting an occasion, one of them never the wish, to interfere, was that a spark from her set the Continent ablaze, while flames kindled elsewhere was sure to spread hither. Matters grew worse as her princes inherited or created so many

Position of the Empire in Europe.

thrones abroad. The Duke of Holstein acquired Denmark, the Count Palatine Sweden, the Elector of Saxony Poland, the Elector of Hanover England, the Archduke of Austria Hungary and Bohemia, while the Elector (originally Margrave) of Brandenburg assumed, on the strength of non-imperial territories to the north-eastward, which had come into his hands, the style and title of King of Prussia. Thus the Empire seemed again about to embrace Europe; but in a sense far different from that which those words would have expressed under Charles and Otto. Its history for a century and a half is a dismal list of losses and disgraces. The chief external danger was from French influence, for a time supreme, always menacing. For though Lewis XIV, on whom, in A.D. 1658, half the electoral college wished to confer the imperial crown, was before the end of his life an object of intense hatred, officially entitled " Hereditary enemy of the Holy Empire,"* France had nevertheless a strong party among the princes always at her beck. The Rhenish and Bavarians electors were her favorite tools. The "*réunions*" begun in A.D. 1680, a pleasant euphemism for robbery in time of peace, added Strasburg and other places in Alsace, Lorraine, and Franche Comté to the monarchy of Lewis, and brought him nearer the heart of the Empire; his ambition and cruelty were witnessed to by repeated wars, and by the devastation of the Rhine countries; the ultimate though short-lived triumph of his policy was attained when Marshal Belleisle dictated the election of Charles VII in A.D. 1742. In the Turkish wars, when the princes left Vienna to be saved by the Polish Sobieski, the Empire's weakness appeared in a still more pitiable light. There was, indeed, a complete loss of hope and interest in the old system.

---

* *Erbfeind des heiligen Reichs.*

The princes had been so long accustomed to consider
themselves the natural foes of a central govern-

Weakness and stagnation of Germany.

ment, that a request made by it was sure to be
disregarded ; they aped in their petty courts
the pomp and etiquette of Vienna or Paris, grum
bling that they should be required to garrison
the great frontier fortresses which alone protected them
from an encroaching neighbor.   The Free Cities had never
recovered the famines and sieges of the Thirty Years' War.
Hanseatic greatness had waned, and the southern towns
had sunk into languid oligarchies.   All the vigor of the
people in a somewhat stagnant age either found its sphere
in rising states like the Prussia of Frederick the Great, or
turned away from politics altogether into other channels.
The Diet had become contemptible from the slowness with
which it moved, and its tedious squabbles on matters the
most frivolous.   Many sittings were consumed in the discussion of a question regarding the time of keeping Easter,
more ridiculous than that which had distracted the Western churches in the seventh century, the Protestants refusing to reckon by the reformed calendar because it was the
work of a Pope.   Collective action through the old organs
was confessed impossible, when the common object of
defense against France was sought by forming a league
under the Emperor's presidency, and when at European
congresses the Empire was not represented at all.*   No
change could come from the Emperor, whom the capitulation of A.D. 1658 deposed *ipso facto* if he violated its
provisions.   As Dohm† said, to keep him from doing
harm, he was kept from doing anything.

Yet little was lost by his inactivity, for what could have

---

* Only the envoys of the several states were present at Utrecht
in 1713.

† Quoted by Ludwig Haüsser, *Deutsche Geschichte.*

been hoped from his action? From the election of
Albert II, A.D. 1437, to the death of Charles VI,
A.D. 1740, the scepter had remained in the
hands of one family. So far from being fit
subjects for undistinguishing invective, the
Hapsburg Emperors may be contrasted favor-
ably with the contemporary dynasties of France,
Spain or England. Their policy, viewed as a whole, from
the days of Rudolf downward, had been neither conspicuously tyrannical, nor faltering, nor dishonest.
But it had been always selfish. Entrusted with
an office which might, if there be any power in
those memories of the past to which the champions of hereditary monarchy so constantly
appeal, have stirred their sluggish souls with some enthusiasm for the heroes on whose throne they sat, some wish
to advance the glory and the happiness of Germany, they had
cared for nothing, sought nothing, used the Empire as an
instrument for nothing but the attainment of their own
personal or dynastic ends. Placed on the eastern verge of
Germany, the Hapsburgs had added to their ancient lands
in Austria proper, Styria and Tyrol, non-German territories far more extensive, and had thus become the chiefs
of a separate and independent state. They endeavored to
reconcile its interests with the interests of the Empire, so
long as it seemed possible to recover part of the old imperial prerogative. But when such hopes were dashed by
the defeats of the Thirty Years' War, they hesitated no
longer between an elective crown and the rule of their
hereditary states, and comported themselves thenceforth in
European politics not as the representatives of Germany,
but as heads of the great Austrian monarchy. There would
have been nothing culpable in this had they not at the same
time continued to entangle Germany in wars with which she
had no concern: to waste her strength in tedious com-

*Leopold I,
1658-1705.
Joseph I,
1705-1711.
Charles VI,
1711-1740.*

*The Haps-
burg Em-
perors and
their policy.*

bats with the Turks, or plunge her into a new struggle
with France, not to defend her frontiers or recover the
lands she had lost, but that some scion of the house of
Hapsburg might reign in Spain or Italy. Watching the
whole course of their foreign policy, marking how in A.D.
1736 they had bartered away Lorraine for Tuscany, a German for a non-German territory, and seeing how at home
they opposed every scheme of reform which could in the
least degree trench upon their own prerogative, how they
strove to obstruct the imperial chamber lest it should interfere with their own Aulic council, men were driven to
separate the body of the Empire from the imperial office
and its possessors,* and when plans for reinvigorating the
one failed, to leave the others to their fate.

Causes of the long retention of the throne by Austria. Still the old line clung to the crown with that
Hapsburg grip which has almost passed into a
proverb. Odious as Austria was, no one could
despise her, or fancy it easy to shake her commanding position in Europe. Her alliances
were fortunate: her designs were steadily pursued: her dis-
membered territories always returned to her. Though
the throne continued strictly elective, it was impossible
not to be influenced by long prescription. Projects were
repeatedly formed to set the Hapsburgs aside by electing
a prince of some other line,† or by passing a law that
there should never be more than two, or four, successive

---

* The distinction is well expressed by the German "Reich" and
"Kaiserthum," to which we have unfortunately no terms to correspond.

† So the Elector of Saxony proposed in 1532 that, Albert II, Frederick III and Maximilian having been all of one house, Charles V's
successor should be chosen from some other.—Moser, *Römische
Kayser.* See the various attempts of France in Moser. The coronation engagements (Wahlcapitulation) of every Emperor bound him
not to attempt to make the throne hereditary in his family.

Emperors of the same house. France* ever and anon renewed her warnings to the electors, that their freedom was passing from them, and the scepter becoming hereditary in one haughty family. But it was felt that a change would be difficult and disagreeable, and that the heavy expense and scanty revenues of the Empire required to be supported by larger patrimonial domains than most German princes possessed. The heads of states like Prussia and Hanover, states whose size and wealth would have made them suitable candidates, were Protestants, and so excluded both by the connection of the imperial office with the Church, and by the majority of Roman Catholics in the electoral college,† who, however jealous they might be of Austria, were led both by habit and sympathy to rally round her in moments of peril. The one occasion on which these considerations were disregarded showed their force. On the extinction of the male line of Hapsburg in the person of Charles VI, the intrigues of the French envoy, Marshal Belleisle, procured the election of Charles Albert of Bavaria, who stood first among the Catholic princes. His *Charles VII, 1742–1745.* reign was a succession of misfortunes and ignominies. Driven from Munich by the Austrians, the head of the Holy Empire lived in Frankfort on the

---

* In 1658 France offered to subsidize the Elector of Bavaria if he would become Emperor.

† Whether an Evangelical was eligible for the office of Emperor was a question often debated, but never actually raised by the candidature of any but a Roman Catholic prince. The "exacta æqualitas" conceded by the Peace of Westphalia might appear to include so important a privilege. But when we consider that the peculiar relation in which the Emperor stood to the Holy Roman Church was one which no heretic could hold, and that the coronation oaths could not have been taken by, nor the coronation ceremonies (among which was a sort of ordination) performed upon a Protestant, the conclusion must be unfavorable to the claims of any but a Catholic.

bounty of France, cursed by the country on which his
own ambition had brought the miseries of a
Francis I,   protracted war.* The choice in 1745 of Duke
1745-
1765.   Francis of Lorraine, husband of the archduchess
of Austria and queen of Hungary, Maria Theresa, was meant to restore the crown to the only power
capable of wearing it with dignity: in Joseph II, her
son, it again rested on the brow of a Hapsburg.† In
the war of the Austrian succession, which followed on the
death of Charles VI, the Empire as a body took no part ;
in the Seven Years' War its whole might broke in vain
against one resolute member.   Under Frederick
Seven
Years' War.   the Great Prussia approved herself at least a
match for France and Austria leagued against
her, and the semblance of unity which the predominance

---

* " The bold Bavarian, in a luckless hour,
    Tries the dread summits of Cæsarean power;
    With unexpected legions bursts away,
    And sees defenceless realms receive his sway. . .
    The baffled prince in honor's flattering bloom
    Of hasty greatness finds the fatal doom;
    His foes' derision and his subjects' blame,
    And steals to death from anguish and from shame."
              JOHNSON, *Vanity of Human Wishes.*

† The following nine reasons for the long continuance of the Empire in the House of Hapsburg are given by Pfeffinger (*Vitriarius
Illustratus*), writing early in the eighteenth century:

1. The great power of Austria.
2. Her wealth, now that the Empire was so poor.
3. The majority of Catholics among the electors.
4. Her fortunate matrimonial alliances.
5. Her moderation.
6. The memory of benefits conferred by her.
7. The example of evils that had followed a departure from the
   blood of former Cæsars.
8. The fear of the confusion that would ensue if she were deprived
   of the crown.
9. Her own eagerness to have it.

of a single power had hitherto given to the Empire was replaced by the avowed rivalry of two military monarchies. The Emperor Joseph II, a sort of philosopher-king, than whom few have more narrowly missed greatness, made a desperate effort to set *Joseph II, 1765-1790.* things right, striving to restore the disordered finances, to purge and vivify the Imperial Chamber. Nay, he renounced the intolerant policy of his ancestors, quarreled with the Pope,* and presumed to visit Rome, whose streets heard once more the shout that had been silent for three centuries, "Evviva il nostro imperatore! Siete a casa vostra: siete il padrone."† But his indiscreet haste was met by a sullen resistance, and he died disappointed in plans for which the time was not yet ripe, leaving no result save the league of princes which Frederick the Great had formed to oppose his designs on Bavaria. His successor, Leopold II, abandoned the projected reforms, and a calm, the calm before the hurricane, settled down again upon Germany. The existence of the *Leopold II, 1790-1792.* Empire was almost forgotten by its subjects: there was nothing to remind them of it but a feudal invest-iture now and then at Vienna (real feudal rights were obsolete);‡ a concourse of solemn old lawyers *Last phase of the Em-pire.* at Wetzlar puzzling over interminable suits ;§ and some thirty diplomatists at Regensburg,‖

---

* The Pope undertook a journey to Vienna to mollify Joseph, and met with a sufficiently cold reception. When he saw the famous minister Kaunitz and gave him his hand to kiss, Kaunitz took it and shook it.

† "You are in your own house: be the master." Joseph was the first Emperor since Charles the Bald who had kept his Christmas at Rome.

‡ Joseph II was foiled in his attempt to assert them.

§ Goethe spent some time in studying law at Wetzlar among those who practiced in the Kammergericht.

‖ Cf. Pütter, *Historical Development of the Political Constitution of the German Empire*, vol. iii.

the relics of that Imperial Diet where once a hero-
king, a Frederick or a Henry, enthroned amid mitered
prelates and steel - clad barons, had issued laws for
every tribe from the Mediterranean to the
The Diet.   Baltic.* The solemn triflings of this so-called
" Diet of Deputation" have probably never been equaled
elsewhere.† Questions of precedence and title, questions
whether the envoys of princes should have chairs of red
cloth like those of the electors, or only of the less honorable green, whether they should be served on gold or on
silver, how many hawthorn boughs should be hung up
before the door of each on May-day ; these, and such as
these, it was their chief employment not to settle but to
discuss. The pedantic formalism of old Germany passed
that of Spaniards or Turks ; it had now crushed under a
mountain of rubbish whatever meaning or force its old
institutions had contained. It is the penalty of greatness
that its form should outlive its substance: that gilding and
trappings should remain when that which they were meant
to deck and clothe has departed. So our sloth or our timidity, not seeing that whatever is false must be also bad, maintains in being what once was good long after it has become
helpless and hopeless: so now at the close of the eighteenth
century, strings of sounding titles were all that was left
of the Empire which Charles had founded, and Frederick
adorned, and Dante sung.

The German mind, just beginning to put forth the blossoms of its wondrous literature, turned away in disgust
Feelings of   from the spectacle of ceremonious imbecility
the German   more than Byzantine. National feeling seemed
people.   gone from princes and people alike. Of Fred-

---

* Frederick the Great said of the Diet, " Es ist ein Schattenbild,
eine Versammlung aus Publizisten die mehr mit Formalien als mit
Sachen sich beschäftigen, und, wie Hofhunde, den Mond anbellen."

† Cf. Häusser, *Deutsche Geschichte;* Introduction.

erick the Great, of Joseph II, there is no need
to speak, but even Lessing, who did more than any one
else to create the German literary spirit, says, "Of the love
of country I have no conception: it appears to me at best
a heroic weakness which I am right glad to be without." *
There were nevertheless persons who saw how fatal such a
system was, lying like a nightmare on the people's soul.
Speaking of the union of princes formed by Frederick of
Prussia to preserve the existing condition of things,
Johannes von Müller writes: † "If the German Union
serves for nothing better than to maintain the *status quo*,
it is against the eternal order of God, by which neither the
physical nor the moral world remains for a moment in the
status quo, but all is life and motion and progress. To
exist without law or justice, without security from arbitrary imposts, doubtful whether we can preserve from day
to day our children, our honor, our liberties, our rights,
our lives, helpless before superior force, without a beneficial connection between our states, without a national
spirit at all, this is the *status quo* of our nation. And it
was this that the Union was meant to confirm. If it be
this and nothing more, then bethink you how when Israel
saw that Rehoboam would not hearken, the people gave
answer to the king and spake, 'What portion have we in
David, or what inheritance in the son of Jesse? to your
tents, O Israel: David, see to thine own house.' See
then to your own houses, ye princes."

Nevertheless, though the Empire stood like a corpse
brought forth from some Egyptian sepulchre, ready to
crumble at a touch, there seemed no reason why it should
not stand so for centuries more. Fate was kind, and slew
it in the light.

---

* Quoted by Häusser.

† *Deutschelands Erwartungen vom Fürstenbunde,* quoted in the
Staats Lexikon.

CHAPTER XX.

FALL OF THE EMPIRE.

GOETHE has described the uneasiness with which, in the days of his childhood, the burghers of his native Frankfort saw the walls of the Roman Hall covered with the portraits of Emperor after Emperor, till space was left for few, at last for one.* In A.D. 1792 Francis II mounted the throne of Augustus, and the last place was filled. Three years before there had arisen on the western horizon a little cloud, no bigger than a man's hand, and now the heaven was black with storms of ruin. There was a prophecy,† dating from the first days of the Empire's decline, that when all things were falling to pieces, and wickedness rife in the world, a second Frankish Charles should rise as Emperor to purge and heal, to bring back peace and purify religion. If this was not exactly the mission of the new ruler of the West Franks, he was at least anxious to tread in the steps and revive the glories of the hero whose throne he professed to have again erected. It were a task superfluously easy to show how delusive is that minute historical parallel of which every Parisian was full in A.D. 1804, the parallel

Francis II, 1792-1806.

---

* *Wahrheit und Dichtung*, bk. i. The Römer Saal is still one of the sights of Frankfort. The portraits, however, which one now sees in it, seem to be all or nearly all of them modern; and few have any merit as works of art.

† *Jordanis Chronica*, ap. Schardium, *Sylloge Tractatuum.*

between the heir of a long line of fierce Teutonic chieftains, whose vigorous genius had seized what it could of
the monkish learning of the eighth century, and the son
of the Corsican lawyer, with all the brilliance of a French-
man and all the resolute profundity of an
Italian, reared in, yet only half believing, the   *Napoleon,*
Emperor of
ideas of the Encyclopædists, swept up into the   *the West.*
seat of absolute power by the whirlwind of a
revolution. Alcuin and Talleyrand are not more unlike
than are their masters. But though in the characters and
temper of the men there is little resemblance, though
their Empires agree in this only, and hardly even in this,
that both were founded on conquest, there is nevertheless
a sort of grand historical similarity between their positions. Both were the leaders of fiery and warlike nations,
the one still untamed as the creatures of their native
woods, the other drunk with revolutionary fury. Both
aspired to found, and seemed for a time to have succeeded in founding, universal monarchies. Both were
gifted with a strong and susceptible imagination, which if
it sometimes overbore their judgment, was yet one of the
truest and highest elements of their greatness. As the one
looked back to the kings under the Jewish theocracy and
the Emperors of Christian Rome, so the other thought to
model himself after Cæsar and Charlemagne. For, useful
as was the fancied precedent of the title and career of the
great Carolingian to a chief determined to be king, yet
unable to be king after the fashion of the Bourbons, and
seductive as was such a connection to the imaginative
vanity of the French people, it was no studied purpose or
stimulating art that led Napoleon to remind his subjects so
frequently of the hero he claimed to represent. No one
who reads the records of his life can doubt that he believed, as fully as he believed anything, that the same
destiny which had made France the center of the modern

world had also appointed him to sit on the throne and
carry out the projects of Charles the Frank,
Belief of to rule all Europe from Paris, as the Cæsars
Napoleon had ruled it from Rome.* It was in this belief
that he was that he went to the ancient capital of the
the succes-
sor of Char- Frankish Emperors to receive there the Austrian
lemagne. recognition of his imperial title: that hetalked of
"revendicating" Catalonia and Arragon, be-
cause they had formed a part of the Carolingian realm,
though they had never obeyed any descendant of Hugh
Capet : that he undertook a journey to Nimeguen, where
he had ordered the ancient palace to be restored, and inscribed on its walls his name below that of Charles: that
he summoned the Pope to attend his coronation as
Stephen had come ten centuries before to install Pipin in
the throne of the last Merovingian.† The same desire

---

* In an address by Napoleon to the Senate in 1804, bearing date
10th Frimaire (1st Dec.), are the words, "Mes descendans conserve-
ront longtemps ce trône, le premier de l'univers." Answering a
deputation from the department of the Lippe, Aug. 8th, 1811, "La
Providence, qui a voulu que je rétablisse le trône de Charlemagne,
vous a fait naturellement rentrer, avec la Hollande et les villes
anséatiques, dans le sein de l'Empire."—*Œuvres de Napoleon*, tom.
v. p. 521. "Pour le Pape, je suis Charlemagne, parce que, comme
Charlemagne, je réunis la couronne de France à celle des Lombards,
et que mon Empire confine avec l'Orient." (Quoted by Lanfrey, *Vie
de Napoleon*, iii. 417). "Votre Sainteté est souveraine de Rome,
mais j'en suis l'Empereur." (Letter of Napoleon to Pope Pius, Feb.
13th, 1806. Lanfrey). "Dites bien," says Napoleon to Cardinal
Fesch, "que je suis Charlemagne, leur Empereur [of the Papal
Court] que je dois être traité de même. Je fais connaitre au Pape
mes intentions en peu de mots, s'il n'y acquiesce pas, je le réduirai à
la même condition qu'il était avant Charlemagne." (Lanfrey, *Vie de
Napoleon*, iii. 420).

† Napoleon said on one occasion, "Je n'ai pas succédé a Louis
Quatorze, mais a Charlemagne."—Bourrienne, *Vie de Napoleon*, vi.
256, who adds that in 1804, shortly before he was crowned, he had
the imperial insignia of Charles brought from the old Frankish

to be regarded as lawful Emperor of the West showed
itself in his assumption of the Lombard crown at Milan;
in the words of the decree by which he annexed Rome to
the Empire, revoking " the donations which my predecessors, the French Emperors, have made;"* in the title
" King of Rome," which he bestowed on his ill-fated son,
in imitation of the German " King of the Romans."† We
are even told that it was at one time his intention to eject
the Hapsburgs, and be chosen Roman Emperor in their
stead. Had this been done, the analogy would have been
complete between the position which the French ruler held
to Austria now, and that in which Charles and Otto had
stood to the feeble Cæsars of Byzantium. It
was curious to see the head of the Roman   *Attitude of*
church turning away from his ancient ally to   *the Papacy*
the reviving power of France—France, where   *toward*
                                               Napoleon.
the Goddess of Reason had been worshiped
eight years before—just as he had sought the help of the
first Carolingians against his Lombard enemies.‡ The

---

capital, and exhibited them in a jeweler's shop in Paris, along with
those which had just been made for his own coronation. But if
there was not in this a trick of Napoleon's, there must be a mistake
of Bourrienne's, for these insignia had been removed from Aachen by
Austria in 1798. (Cf. Bock, *Die Kleinodien des h. Römischen
Reiches*, p. 4). Somewhat in the same spirit in which he displayed
the Bayeux embroidery, in order to incite his subjects to the conquest
of England.

* " Je n'ai pu concilier ces grands interêts (of political order and
the spiritual authority of the Pope) qu'en annulant les donations des
Empereurs Français, mes prédécesseurs, et en réunissant les états
Romains à la France."—Proclamation issued in 1809; *Œuvres*, iv.

† See Appendix, Note C.

‡ Pope Pius VII wrote to the First Consul, "Carissime in Christo
Fili noster . . . tam perspecta sunt nobis tuæ voluntatis studia
erga nos, ut *quotiescunque* ope aliqua in rebus nostris indigemus, eam
a te fidenter petere non dubitare debeamus."—Quoted by Ægidi.

difference was indeed great between the feelings wherewith
Pius VII addressed his " very dear son in Christ," and
those that had pervaded the intercourse of Pope Hadrian
I with the son of Pipin; just as the contrast is strange
between the principles that shaped Napoleon's policy and
the vision of a theocracy that had floated before the mind
of Charles. Neither comparison is much to the advantage
of the modern; but Pius might be pardoned for catching
at any help in his distress, and Napoleon found that the
protectorship of the church strengthened his position in
France, and gave him dignity in the eyes of Christendom.*

A swift succession of triumphs had left only one thing
still preventing the full recognition of the Corsican warrior
as sovereign of Western Europe, and that one was the existence of the old Romano-Germanic Empire.
The French Empire. Napoleon had not long assumed his new title
when he began to mark a distinction between
" la France " and " l'Empire Français." France had, since
A.D. 1792, advanced to the Rhine, and, by the annexation
of Piedmont, had overstepped the Alps; the French Empire included, besides the kingdom of Italy, a mass of dependent states, Naples, Holland, Switzerland and many
German principalities, the allies of France in the same
sense in which the " socii populi Romani " were allies of

---

* Let us place side by side the letters of Hadrian to Charles in the
Codex Carolinus, and the following preamble to the Concordat of A.D.
1801, between the First Consul and the Pope (which I quote from the
Bullarium Romanum), and mark the changes of a thousand years.
" Gubernium reipublicæ [Gallicæ] recognoscit religionem Catholicam
Apostolicam Romanam eam esse religionem quam longe maxima pars
civium Gallicæ reipublicæ profitetur. Summus pontifex pari modo
recognoscit eandem religionem maximam utilitatem maximumque
decus percepisse et hoc quoque tempore præstolari ex catholico cultu
in Gallia constituto, necnon ex peculiari eius professione quam
faciunt reipublicæ consules."

Rome.* When the last of Pitt's coalitions had been destroyed at Austerlitz, and Austria had made her submission by the peace of Presburg, the conqueror felt that his hour was come. He had now overcome two Emperors, those of Austria and Russia, claiming to represent the old and the new Rome respectively, and had in eighteen months created more kings than the occupants of the Germanic throne in as many centuries. It was time, he thought, to sweep away obsolete pretensions, and claim the sole inheritance of that Western Empire, of which the titles and ceremonies of his court presented a grotesque imitation.† The task was an easy one after what had been already accomplished. Previous wars and treaties had so redistributed the territories and changed the constitution of the Germanic Empire that it could hardly be said to exist in anything but name. *Napoleon in Germany.* In French history Napoleon appears as the restorer of peace, the rebuilder of the shattered edifice of social order, the author of a code and an administrative system which the Bourbons who dethroned him were glad to preserve. Abroad he was the true child of the Revolution, and conquered only to destroy. It was his mission —a mission more beneficent in its results than in its means‡—to break up in Germany and Italy the abominable system of petty states, to reawaken the spirit of the people,

---

* Cf. Heeren, *Political System*, vol. iii. p. 273.

† He had arch-chancellors, arch-treasurers, and so forth. The Legion of Honor, which was thought important enough to be mentioned in the coronation oath, was meant to be something like the mediæval orders of knighthood, whose connection with the Empire has already been mentioned.

‡ Napoleon's feelings toward Germany may be gathered from the phrase he once used, " Il faut depayser l'Allemagne." Again, in a letter to his brother Lonis, he says, " You must know that the annihilation of German nationality is a necessary leading principle of my policy."

to sweep away the relics of an effete feudalism, and leave the ground clear for the growth of newer and better forms of political life. Since A.D. 1797, when Austria at Campo Formio perfidiously exchanged the Netherlands for Venetia, the work of destruction had gone on apace. All the German sovereigns west of the Rhine had been dispossessed, and their territories incorporated with France, while the rest of the country had been revolutionized by the arrangements of the peace of Luneville and the "Indemnities," dictated by the French to the Diet in February, 1803. New kingdoms were erected, electorates created and extinguished, the lesser princes mediatized, the free cities occupied by troops and bestowed on some neighboring potentate. More than any other change, the secularization of the dominions of the prince-bishops and abbots proclaimed the fall of the old constitution, whose principles had required the existence of a spiritual alongside of the temporal aristocracy. The Emperor Francis, partly foreboding the events that were at hand, partly in order to meet Napoleon's assumption of the imperial name by depriving that name of its peculiar meaning, began in A.D. 1805 to style himself "Hereditary Emperor of Austria," while retaining at the same time his former title.* The next act of the drama was one in which we may more readily pardon the ambition of a foreign conqueror than the traitorous selfishness of the German princes, who broke every tie of ancient friendship and duty to grovel at his throne. By the Act of the Confederation†

The Confederation of the Rhine. of the Rhine, signed at Paris, July 17, 1806, Bavaria, Würtemberg, Baden, and several other states, sixteen in all, withdrew from the

---

* Thus in documents issued by the Emperor during these two years he is styled "Roman Emperor Elect, Hereditary Emperor of Austria," (erwählter Römischer Kaiser, Erbkaiser von Oesterreich)

† This Act of Confederation of the Rhine (Rheinbund) is printed in

body and repudiated the laws of the Empire, while on
August 1st the French envoy at Regensburg announced to
the Diet that his master, who had consented to become
Protector of the Confederate princes, no longer recognized
the existence of the Empire. Francis II resolved at once
to anticipate this new Odoacer, and by a declaration, dated August 6, 1806, resigned the im-   *Abdication*
perial dignity. His deed states that finding it   *of the*
impossible, in the altered state of things, to   *Emperor*
fulfill the obligations imposed by his capitula-   *Francis II.*
tion, he considers as dissolved the bonds which attached
him tò the Germanic body, releases from their allegiance
the states who formed it, and retires to the government
of his hereditary dominions under the title of " Emperor
of Austria."* Throughout, the term " German Empire "
(*Deutsches Reich*) is employed. But it was the crown of
Augustus, of Constantine, of Charles, of Maximilian, that

Koch's *Traités* (continued by Schöll), vol. viii., and Meyer's *Corpus
Iuris Confœderationis Germanicæ*, vol. i. It has every appearance of
being a translation from the French, and was no doubt originally
drawn up in that language. Napoleon is called in one place " Der
nämliche Monarch, dessen Absichten sich stets mit den wahren In-
teressen Deutschlands übereinstimmend gezeigt haben." The phrase
" Roman Empire " does not occur : we hear only of the " German
Empire," " body of German states " (Staatskörper), and so forth.
This Confederation of the Rhine was eventually joined by every German State except Austria, Prussia, Electoral Hessen and Brunswick.

* *Histoire des Traités*, vol. viii. The original may be found in
Meyer's *Corpus Iuris Confœderationis Germanicæ*, vol. i. p. 70. It is
a document in no way remarkable, except from the ludicrous resemblance which its language suggests to the circular in which a trades-
man, announcing the dissolution of an old partnership, solicits, and
hopes by close attention to merit, a continuance of his customers'
patronage to his business, which will henceforth be carried on under
the name of, etc., etc.

Francis of Hapsburg laid down, and a new era in the world's
history was marked by the fall of its most ven-
End of the
erable institution.   One thousand and six
Empire.
years after Leo the Pope had crowned the
Frankish king, eighteen hundred and fifty-eight years
after Cæsar had conquered at Pharsalia, the Holy Roman
Empire came to its end.

There was a time when this event would have been
thought a sign that the last days of the world were at
hand. But in the whirl of change that had bewildered
men since A.D. 1789, it passed almost unnoticed. No one
could yet fancy how things would end, or what sort of a
new order would at last shape itself out of chaos. When
Napoleon's universal monarchy had dissolved, and old
landmarks showed themselves again above the receding
waters, it was commonly supposed that the Empire would
be re-established on its former footing.* Such was indeed
the wish of many states, and among them of Hanover,
representing Great Britain.† Though a simple revival of
the old Romano-Germanic Empire was plainly out of the
question, it still appeared to them that Germany would be
best off under the presidency of a single head, entrusted
with the ancient office of maintaining peace among the
members of the confederation.   But the new kingdoms,
Bavaria especially, were unwilling to admit a superior;
Prussia, elated at the glory she had won in the war of
independence, would have disputed the crown with Aus-

---

* Koch (Schöll), *Histoire des Traités*, vol. xi. p. 257, sqq.; Häusser,
Deutsche Geschichte, vol. iv.

† Great Britain had refused in 1806 to recognize the dissolution of
the Empire. And it may indeed be maintained that in point of law
the Empire was never extinguished at all, but lives on as a disembodied spirit to this day. For it is clear that, technically speaking,
the abdication of a sovereign can destroy only his own rights, and
does not dissolve the state over which he presides.

tria; Austria herself cared little to resume an office shorn of much of its dignity, with duties to perform and no resources to enable her to discharge them. Use was therefore made of an expression in the Peace of Paris which spoke of uniting Germany by a federative bond,* and the Congress of Vienna was decided by the wishes of Austria and the difficulty of bringing the various states to agree to anything else, to establish a federal league. Thus was brought into existence the Germanic Confederation, an institution confessed almost from its birth to be a temporary expedient — an unsatisfactory compromise between the reality of local sovereignty and the semblance of national union, which, after an ignoble and often-threatened life of half a century, fell unregretted upon the fields of Königgrätz and Langensalza.

Congress of Vienna.

The Germanic Confederation. Its end in A.D. 1866.

* " Les états d'Allemagne seront independans et unis par un lien federatif."—*Histoire des Traités,* vol. xi. p. 257.

CHAPTER XXI.

CONCLUSION.

AFTER the attempts already made to examine separately
each of the phases of the Empire, little need be said, in
General summary. conclusion, upon its nature and results in general. A general character can hardly help
being either vague or false. For the aspects
which the Empire took are as many and as various as the
ages and conditions of society during which it continued
to exist. Among the exhausted peoples around the Mediterranean, whose national feeling had died out, whose faith
was extinct or turned to superstition, whose thought and
art was a faint imitation of the Greek, there arises a huge
despotism, first of a city, then of an administrative system,
which presses with equal weight on all its subjects, and
becomes to them a religion as well as a government. Just
when the mass is at length dissolving, the tribes of the
North come down, too rude to maintain the institutions
they found subsisting, too few to introduce their own, and
a weltering confusion follows, till the strong hand of the
first Frankish Emperor raises the fallen image and bids the
nations bow down to it once more. Under him it is for
some brief space a theocracy; under his German successors
the first of feudal kingdoms, the center of European chivalry. As feudalism wanes, it is again transformed, and
after promising for a time to become an hereditary Haps-

burg monarchy, sinks at last into the presidency, not more dignified than powerless, of an international league. To us moderns a perpetuation under conditions so diverse of the same name and the same pretensions appear at first sight absurd,

Perpetuation of the name of Rome.

a phantom too vain to impress the most superstitious mind. Closer examination will correct such a notion. No power was ever based on foundations so pure and deep as those which Rome laid during three centuries of conquest and four of undisturbed dominion. If her empire had been an hereditary or local kingdom, it might have fallen with the extinction of the royal line, the conquest of the tribe, the destruction of the city to which it was attached. But it was not so limited. It was imperishable because it was universal ; and when its power had ceased, it was remembered with awe and love by the races whose separate existence it had destroyed, because it had spared the weak while it smote down the strong; because it had granted equal rights to all, and closed against none of its subjects the path of honorable ambition. When the military power of the conquering city had departed, her sway over the world of thought began: by her the theories of the Greeks had been reduced to practice; by her the new religion had been embraced and organized; her language, her theology, her laws, her architecture, made their way where the eagles of war had never flown, and with the spread of civilization have found new homes on the Ganges and the Mississippi.

Nor is such a claim of government prolonged under changed conditions by any means a singular phenomenon. Titles sum up the political history of nations and are as often causes as effects : if not insignificant now, how much less so in ages of ignorance and unreason. It would be an instructive, if it were not a tedious task,

Parallel instances.

to examine the many pretensions that are still being put forward to represent the Empire of Rome,

Claims to represent the Roman Empire. all of them baseless, none of them effectless. Austria clings to a name which seems to give her a sort of precedence in Europe, and was wont, while she held Lombardy, to justify her position there by invoking the feudal rights of the Hohenstaufen. With no more legal right

Austria. than a prince of Reuss or a landgrave of Homburg might pretend to, she has assumed the arms and devices of the old Empire, and being almost the youngest of European monarchies, is respected as the oldest and most conservative. Bonapartean France, as the self-

France. appointed heir of the Carolingians, grasped for a time the scepter of the West, and under her lately fallen ruler aspired to hold the balance of European politics, and be recognized as the leader and patron of the so-called Latin races on both sides of the Atlantic.* Professing the creed of Byzantium, Russia claims the crown

Russia. of the Byzantine Cæsars, and trusts that the capital which prophecy has promised for a thousand years will not be long withheld. The doctrine of Panslavism, under an imperial head of the whole Eastern church, has become a formidable engine of aggression in the hands of a crafty and warlike despotism. Another

Greece. testimony to the enduring influence of old political combinations is supplied by the eagerness with which modern Hellas has embraced the notion of gathering all the Greek races into a revived Empire of the

The Turks. East, with its capital on the Bosphorus. Nay, the intruding Ottoman himself, different in faith as well as in blood, has more than once declared

---

* See Louis Napoleon's letter to General Forey, explaining the object of the expedition to Mexico.

himself the representative of the Eastern Cæsars, whose dominion he extinguished. Solyman the Magnificent assumed the name of Emperor, and refused it to Charles V: his successors were long preceded through the streets of Constantinople by twelve officers, bearing straws aloft, a faint semblance of the consular fasces that had escorted a Quinctius or a Fabius through the Roman forum. Yet in no one of these cases has there been that apparent legality of title which the shouts of the people and the benediction of the pontiff conveyed to Charles and Otto.*

These examples, however, are minor parallels: the complement and illustration of the history of the Empire is to be found in that of the Holy See. The Papacy, *Parallel of* whose spiritual power was itself the offspring *the Papacy.* of Rome's temporal dominion, evoked the phantom of her parent, used it, obeyed it, rebelled and overthrew it, in its old age once more embraced it, till in its downfall she has heard the knell of her own approaching doom.†

Both Papacy and Empire rose in an age when the human spirit was utterly prostrated before authority and tradition, when the exercise of private judgment was impossible to most and sinful to all. Those who believed the miracles recorded in the *Acta Sanctorum*, and did not question the Isidorian decretals, might well recognize as ordained of God the twofold authority of Rome, founded, as it seemed to be, on so many texts of Scripture, and confirmed by five centuries of undisputed possession.

---

* One may also compare the retention of the office of consul at Rome till the time of Justinian: indeed it even survived his formal abolition. The relinquishment of the title "King of Great Britain, France and Ireland," seriously distressed many excellent persons.

† I speak, of course, of the Papacy as an autocratic power claiming a more than spiritual authority.

Both sanctioned and satisfied the passion of the Middle Ages for unity. Ferocity, violence, disorder, were the conspicuous evils of that time : hence all the aspirations of the good were for something which, breaking the force of passion and increasing the force of sympathy, should teach the stubborn wills to sacrifice themselves in the view of a common purpose. To those men, moreover, unable to rise above the sensuous, not seeing the true connection or the true difference of the spiritual and the secular, the idea of the Visible Church was full of awful meaning. Solitary thought was helpless, and strove to lose itself in the aggregate, since it could not create for itself that which was universal. The schism that severed a man from the congregation of the faithful on earth was hardly less dreadful than the heresy which excluded him from the company of the blessed in heaven. He who kept not his appointed place in the ranks of the church militant had no right to swell the rejoicing anthems of the church triumphant. Here, as in so many other cases, the continued use of traditional language seems to have prevented us from seeing how great is the difference between our own times and those in which the phrases we repeat were first used, and used in full sincerity. Whether the world is better or worse for the change which has passed upon its feelings in these matters is another question: all that is necessary to note here is that the change is a profound and pervading one. Obedience, almost the first of mediæval virtues, is now often spoken of as if it were fit only for slaves or fools. Instead of praising, men are wont to condemn the submission of the individual will, the surrender of the individual belief, to the] will or the belief of the community. Some persons declare variety of opinion to be a positive good. The great mass have certainly no longing for an abstract unity of faith. They have no horror of schism. They do not, cannot, understand the intense fascination which the idea of one all-pervading church exercised upon their mediæval forefathers. A life in the church, for the church, through the church; a life which she blessed in mass at morning and sent to peaceful rest by the vesper hymn; a life which she supported by the constantly recurring stimulus of the sacraments, relieving it by confession, purifying it by penance, admonishing it by the presentation of visible objects for contemplation and worship—this was the life which they of the Middle Ages conceived of as the rightful life of man; it was the actual life of many, the ideal of all. The unseen world was so unceasingly pointed to, and its dependence on the seen so intensely felt, that the barrier between the two seemed to disappear. The church was not merely the portal to heaven; it was heaven anticipated; it was already self-gathered and complete. In one sentence from a famous mediæval document may be found a key to much which seems strangest to us in the feelings of the Middle Ages : " The church is dearer to God than heaven. For the church does not exist for the sake of heaven, but conversely, heaven for the sake of the church."*

Again, both Empire and Papacy rested on opinion rather than on physical force, and when the struggle of the eleventh century came, the Empire fell, because its rival's hold over the souls of men was firmer, more direct, enforced by penalties more terrible than the death of the body. The ecclesiastical body under Alexander and Innocent was animated by a loftier spirit and more wholly devoted to a single aim than the knights and nobles who followed the banner of the Swabian Cæsars. Its allegi-

---

* "Ipsa enim ecclesia charior Deo est quam cœlum. Non enim propter cœlum ecclesia, sed e converso propter ecclesiam cœlum." From the tract entitled "A Letter of the four Universities to Wenzel and Urban VI," quoted in an earlier chapter.

ance was undivided ; it comprehended the principles for which it fought: they trembled at even while they resisted the spiritual power.

Both sprang from what might be called the accident of name.   The power of the great Latin patriarchate was a Form: the ghost, it has been said, of the older

Papacy and Empire compared as perpetuations of a name.

Empire, favored in its growth by circumstances, but really vital because capable of wonderful adaptation to the character and wants of the time.   So, too, though far less perfectly, was the Empire.   Its Form was the tradition of the universal rule of Rome; it met the needs of successive centuries by civilizing barbarous people, by maintaining unity in confusion and disorganization, by controlling brute violence through the sanctions of a higher power, by being made the keystone of a gigantic feudal arch, by assuming in its old age the presidency of a European confederation.   And the history of both, as it shows the power of ancient names and forms, shows also within what limits such perpetuation is possible, and how it sometimes deceives men, by preserving the shadow while it loses the substance.   This perpetuation itself, what is it but the expression of the belief of mankind, a belief incessantly corrected yet never weakened, that their old institutions do and may continue to subsist unchanged, that what has served their fathers will do well enough for them, that it is possible to make a system perfect and abide in it forever?   Of all political instincts this is perhaps the strongest; often useful, often grossly abused, but never so natural and so fitting as when it leads men, who feel themselves inferior to their predecessors, to save what they can from the wreck of a civilization higher than their own.   It was thus that both Papacy and Empire were maintained by the generations who had no type of greatness and wisdom save that which they associated with the name of Rome. And therefore it is that no examples show so convincingly how hopeless are all such attempts to preserve in life a system which arose out of ideas and under conditions that have passed away. Though it never could have existed save as a prolongation, though it was and remained through the Middle Ages an anachronism, the Empire of the tenth century had little in common with the Empire of the second. Much more was the Papacy, though it too hankered after the forms and titles of antiquity, in reality a new creation. And in the same proportion as it was new, and represented the spirit not of a past age but of its own, was it a power stronger and more enduring than the Empire. More enduring, because younger, and so in fuller harmony with the feelings of its contemporaries: stronger, because at the head of the great ecclesiastical body, in and through which, rather than through secular life, all the intelligence and political activity of the Middle Ages sought its expression. The famous simile of Gregory VII is that which best describes the Empire and the Popedom. They were indeed the " two lights in the firmament of the militant church," the lights which illumined and ruled the world all through the Middle Ages. And as moonlight is to sunlight, so was the Empire to the Papacy. The rays of the one were borrowed, feeble, often interrupted : the other shone with an unquenchable brilliance that was all her own.

The Empire, it has just been said, was never truly mediæval. Was it then Roman in anything but name ? and was that name anything better than a piece of fantastic antiquarianism? It is easy *In what* to draw a comparison between the Antonines *sense was* and the Ottos which should show nothing but *the Empire* unlikeness. What the Empire was in the *Roman ?* second century every one knows. In the tenth it was a feudal monarchy, resting on a strong territorial oli-

garchy. Its chiefs were barbarians, the sons of those who
had destroyed Varus and baffled Germanicus, sometimes
unable even to use the tongue of Rome. Its powers were
limited. It could scarcely be said to have a regular organization at all, whether judicial or administrative. It was
consecrated to the defence, nay, it existed by virtue of the
religion which Trajan and Marcus had persecuted.
Nevertheless, when the contrast has been stated in the
strongest terms, there will remain points of resemblance.
The thoroughly Roman idea of universal denationalization
survived, and drew with it that of a certain equality among
all free subjects. It has been remarked already, that the
world's highest dignity was for many centuries the only
civil office to which any free-born Christian was legally
eligible. And there was also, during the earlier ages,
that indomitable vigor which might have made Trajan or
Severus seek their true successors among the woods of Germany rather than in the palaces of Byzantium, where
every office and name and custom had floated down from
the court of Constantine in a stream of unbroken legitimacy. The ceremonies of Henry VII's coronation would
have been strange indeed to Caius Julius Cæsar Octavianus
Augustus; but how much nobler, how much more Roman
in force and truth than the childish and unmeaning forms
with which a Palæologus was installed ! It was not in
purple buskins that the dignity of the Luxemburger lay.*
To such a boast the Germanic Empire had long ere its
death lost right : it had lived on, when honor and nature
bade it die: it had become what the empire of the Moguls
was, and that of the Ottomans is now, a curious relic of
antiquity, over which the imaginative might muse, but
which the mass of men would push aside with impatient
contempt. But institutions, like men, should be judged
by their prime.

---

*Von Raumer, *Geschichte der Hohenstaufen*, v.

The comparison of the old Roman Empire with its Germanic representative raises a question which has been a good deal canvassed of late years. That wonderful system which Julius Cæsar and his subtle nephew erected upon the ruins of the republican constitution of Rome has been made the type of a certain form of government and of a certain set of social as well as political *" Imperialism: " Roman, French and mediæval.* arrangements, to which, or rather to the theory whereof they are a part, there has been given the name of Imperialism. The sacrifice of the individual to the mass, the concentration of all legislative and judicial powers in the person of the sovereign, the centralization of the administrative system, the maintenance of order by a large military force, the substitution of the influence of public opinion for the control of representative assemblies, are commonly taken, whether rightly or wrongly, to characterize that theory. Its enemies cannot deny that it has before now given and may again give to nations a sudden and violent access of aggressive energy; that it has often achieved the glory (whatever that may be) of war and conquest : that it has a better title to respect in the ease with which it may be made, as it was by the Flavian and Antonine Cæsars of old, and at the beginning of this century by Napoleon in France, the instrument of comprehensive reforms in law and government. The parallel between the Roman world under the Cæsars and the French people in the days of the last-named monarch is indeed less perfect than those who dilate upon it fancy. That equalizing despotism which was a good to a medley of tribes, the force of whose national life had spent itself and left them languid, yet restless, with all the evils of isolation and none of its advantages, was not necessarily a good to a country then the strongest and most united in Europe—a country where the administration is only too perfect, and the pressure of social uniformity only too strong. But whether it be a good or an evil, no one can doubt that there is a sense in which France represents, and has always represented, the imperialist spirit of Rome more truly than those whom the Middle Ages recognized as the legitimate heirs of her name and dominion. Like her, the French people have a deep-rooted belief that to them it naturally belongs to lead the world and control the policy of neighboring states: like her, they regard war not as a sometimes necessary evil, but as a thing to be enjoyed for its own sake—a noble, perhaps the noblest employment of human force and genius. And in their political character, whether it be the result of the five centuries of Roman rule in Gaul, or rather due to the original instincts of the Gallic race, there may be found a claim, better founded than any which Napoleon put forward, to be the Romans* of the modern world. The tendency of the *Political character of the Teutonic and Gallic races.* Teuton was and is to the independence of the individual life, to the mutual repulsion, if the phrase may be permitted, of the social atoms, as contrasted with Keltic and so-called Romanic peoples, among which the unit is more completely absorbed in the mass, who live possessed by a common idea which they are driven to realize in the concrete. Teutonic states have been little more successful than their neighbors in the establishment of free constitutions. Their assemblies meet, and vote, and are dissolved, and nothing comes of it : their citizens endure, without greatly resenting, outrages that would raise the more excitable French or Italians in revolt. But, whatever may have been the form of government, the body of the people have in Germany always enjoyed a freedom of thought which has made them comparatively

* Meaning thereby not the citizens of Rome in her republican days, but the Italo-Hellenic subjects of the Roman Empire.

careless of politics; and the absolutism of the Elbe is at this day* no more like that of the Seine than a revolution at Dresden is to a revolution at Paris. The rule of the Hohenstaufen had nothing either of the good or the evil of the imperialism which Tacitus painted, or of that which the panegyrists of the lately fallen system in France were wont to paint in colors somewhat different from his.

There was, nevertheless, such a thing as mediæval imperialism, a theory of the nature of the state and the best form of government, which has been described once already, and need not be described again. *Essential principles of the mediæval Empire.* It is enough to say, that from three leading principles all its properties may be derived. The first and the least essential was the existence of the state as a monarchy. The second was the exact coincidence of the state's limits, and the perfect harmony of its workings with the limits and the workings of the church. The third was its universality. These three were vital. Forms of political organization, the presence or absence of constitutional checks, the degree of liberty enjoyed by the subject, the rights conceded to local authorities, all these were matters of secondary importance. But although there brooded over all the shadow of a despotism, it was a despotism not of the sword but of law; a despotism not chilling and blighting, but one which, in Germany at least, looked with favor on municipal freedom, and everywhere did its best for learning, for religion, for intelligence; a despotism not hereditary, but one which constantly maintained in theory the principle that he should rule who was found the fittest. To praise or to decry the Empire as a despotic power is to misunderstand it altogether. We need not, because an unbounded prerogative was useful in ages of turbulence,

---

* Written in 1865.

advocate it now; nor need we, with Sismondi, blame the
Frankish conqueror because he granted no "constitutional
charter" to all the nations that obeyed him. Like the
Papacy, the Empire expressed the political ideas of a time,
and not of all time : like the Papacy, it decayed when
those ideas changed ; when men became more capable of
rational liberty ; when thought grew stronger, and the
spiritual nature shook itself more free from the bonds of
sense.

The influence of the Empire upon Germany is a subject
too wide to be more than glanced at. There is much to
make it appear altogether unfortunate. For
Influence
of the Holy
Empire on
Germany.
many generations the flower of Teutonic chivalry crossed the Alps to perish by the sword of
the Lombards, or the deadlier fevers of Rome.
Italy terribly avenged the wrongs she suffered.
Those who destroyed the national existence of another
people forfeited their own: the German kingdom, crushed
beneath the weight of the Roman Empire, could never recover strength enough to form a compact and united monarchy, such as arose elsewhere in Europe; the race whom
their neighbors had feared and obeyed till the fourteenth century saw themselves, down even to our own day,
the prey of intestine feuds, and their country the battlefield
of Europe. Spoiled and insulted by a neighbor restlessly
aggressive and superior in all the arts of success, they came
to regard France as the persecuted Slav regards them.
The want of national union and political liberty from Germany has suffered, and to some extent suffers still, need
not be attributed to the differences of her races; for, conspicuous as that difference was in the days of Otto the
Great, it was no greater than in France, where intruding
Franks, Goths, Burgundians and Northmen were mingled
with primitive Kelts and Basques; not so great as in Spain,
or Italy, or Britain. Rather is it due to the decline of

the central government, which was induced by its strife with the Popedom, its endless Italian wars, and the passion for universal dominion, which made it the assailant of all the neighboring countries. The absence or the weakness of the monarch enabled his feudal vassals to establish petty despotisms, debarring the nation from united political action, and greatly retarding the emancipation of the commons. Thus, while the princes became shamelessly selfish, justifying their resistance to the throne as the defense of their own liberty—liberty to oppress the subject—and ready on the least occasion to throw themselves into the arms of France, the body of the people were deprived of all political training, and have found the lack of such experience impede their efforts to this day.

For these misfortunes, however; there has not been wanting some compensation. The inheritance of the Roman Empire made the Germans the ruling race of Europe, and the brilliance of that glorious dawn has never faded and can never fade entirely from their name. A peaceful people now, peaceful in sentiment even now when they have become a great military power, acquiescent in paternal government, and given to the quiet enjoyments of art, music and meditation, they delight themselves with memories of the time when their conquering chivalry was the terror of the Gaul and the Slav, the Lombard and the Saracen. The national life received a keen stimulus from the sense of exaltation which victory brought, and from the intercourse with countries where the old civilization had not wholly perished. It was this connection with Italy that raised the German lands out of barbarism, and did for them the work which Roman conquest had performed in Gaul, Spain and Britain. From the Empire flowed all the richness of their mediæval life and literature: it first awoke in them a consciousness of national existence; its history has inspired and served as material to their poetry; to many ardent politicians the splendors of the past have become the beacon of the future.* There was a bright side even to that long political disunion, which can hardly be said to have yet disappeared. When they complained that they were not a nation, and sighed for the harmony of feeling and singleness of aim which their great rival seemed to display, the example of the Greeks might have brought them some comfort. To the variety which so many small governments have produced may be partly attributed the breadth of development in German thought and literature, by virtue of which it transcends the French hardly less than the Greek surpassed the Roman. Paris, no doubt, is great, but a country may lose as well as gain by the predominance of a single city; and Germany need not mourn that she alone among modern states has not and never has had a capital.

The merits of the old Empire were not long since the subject of a brisk controversy among several German professors of history. The spokesmen of the *Austria as heir of the Holy Empire.* Austrian or Roman Catholic party, a party which, ten years ago, was not less powerful in some of the minor South German States than in Vienna, claimed for the Hapsburg monarchy the honor of being the legitimate representative of the mediæval Empire, and declared that only by again accepting Hapsburg leadership could Germany win back the glory and the strength that once were hers. The North German liberals ironically applauded the comparison. " Yes," they replied, " your Austrian Empire, as it calls itself, is the true daughter of the old despotism: not less tyrannical, not less aggressive, not less retrograde; like its

---

* See especially Von Sybel, *Die Deutsche Nation und das Kaiserreich;* and the answers of Ficker and Von Wydenbrugk; also Höfler, *Kaiserthum und Papstthum,* and Waitz, *Deutsche Kaiser von Karl dem Grossen bis Maximilian.*

progenitor, the friend of priests, the enemy of free thought, the trampler upon the national feeling of the peoples that obey it. It is you whose selfish and anti-national policy blasts the hope of German unity now, as Otto and Frederick blasted it long ago by their schemes of foreign conquest. The dream of Empire has been our bane from first to last." It is possible, one may hope, to escape the alternative of admiring the Austrian Empire or denouncing the Holy Roman. Austria has indeed, in some things, but too faithfully reproduced the policy of the Saxon and Swabian Cæsars.* Like her, they oppressed and insulted the Italian people: but it was in the defense of rights which the Italians themselves admitted. Like her, they lusted after a dominion over the races on their borders, but that dominion was to them a means of spreading civilization and religion in savage countries, not of pampering upon their revenue a hated court and aristocracy. Like her, they strove to maintain a strong government at home, but they did it when a strong government was the first of political blessings. Like her, they gathered and maintained vast armies ; but those armies were composed of knights and barons who lived for war alone, not of peasants torn away from useful labor and condemned to the cruel task of perpetuating their own bondage by crushing the aspirations of another nationality. They sinned grievously, no doubt, but they sinned in the dim twilight of a half-barbarous age, not in the noon-day blaze of modern civilization. The enthusiasm for mediæval faith and simplicity which was so fervid some years ago has run its course, and is not likely soon to revive. He who reads the history of the Middle Ages will not deny that its heroes, even the grandest of them, were in some respects little better than savages. But when he

---

* Written in 1865; Austria, taught by adversity, has turned over a new leaf since then.

approaches more recent times, and sees how, during the last three hundred years, kings have dealt with their subjects and with each other, he will forget the ferocity of the Middle Ages, in horror at the heartlessness, the treachery, the injustice all the more odious because it sometimes wears the mask of legality, which disgraces the annals of the military monarchies of Europe. With regard, however, to the pretensions of modern Austria, the truth is that this dispute about the worth of the old system has no bearing upon them at all. The day of imperial greatness was already past when Rudolf the first Hapsburg reached the throne ; while during what may be called the Austrian period, from Maximilian to Francis II, the Holy Empire was to Germany a mere clog and incumbrance, which the unhappy nation bore because she knew not how to rid herself of it. The Germans are welcome to appeal to the old Empire to prove that they were once a united people. Nor is there any harm in their comparing the politics of the twelfth century with those of the nineteenth, although to argue from the one to the other seems to betray a want of historical judgment. But the one thing which is wholly absurd is to make Francis Joseph of Austria the successor of Frederick of Hohenstaufen, and justify the most sordid and ungenial of modern despotisms by the example of the mirror of mediæval chivalry, the noblest creation of mediæval thought.

We are not yet far enough from the Empire to comprehend or state rightly its bearing on European progress. *Bearing of the Empire upon the progress of European civilization.* The mountain lies behind us, but miles must be traversed before we can take in at a glance its peaks and slopes and buttresses, picture its form, and conjecture its height. Of the perpetuation among the peoples of the West of the arts and literature of Rome it was both an effect and a cause—a cause only less powerful than the church. It would be endless to show in how many ways it affected the political institutions of the Middle Ages, and through them the whole civilized world. Most of the attributes of modern royalty, to take the most obvious instance, belonged originally and properly to the Emperor, and were borrowed from him by other monarchs. The once famous doctrine of divine right had the same origin. To the existence of the Empire is chiefly to be ascribed the prevalence of Roman law through Europe, and its practical importance in our own days. For while in Southern France and Central Italy, where the subject population greatly outnumbered their conquerors, the old system would have in any case survived, it cannot be doubted that in Germany, as in England, a body of customary Teutonic law would have grown up, had

Influence upon modern jurisprudence.

it not been for the notion that since the German monarch was the legitimate successor of Justinian, the Corpus Juris must be binding on all his subjects. This strange idea was received with a faith so unhesitating that even the aristocracy, who naturally disliked a system which the Emperors and the cities favored, could not but admit its validity, and before the end of the Middle Ages Roman law prevailed through all Germany.* When it is considered how great are the services which German writers have rendered and continue to render to the study of scientific jurisprudence throughout Europe generally, this result will appear far from insignificant. But another of still wider import followed. When by the Peace of Westphalia a crowd of petty principalities were recognized as practically independent states, the need of a code to regulate their intercourse became pressing. Such a code Grotius and his successors formed out of what was then the private law of

---

* Modified of course by the canon law, and not superseding the feudal law of the land.

Germany, which thus became the foundation whereon the system of international jurisprudence has been built up during the last two centuries. That system is, indeed, entirely a German creation,* and could have arisen in no country where the law of Rome had not been the fountain of legal ideas and the groundwork of positive codes. In Germany, too, was it first carried out in practice, and that with a success which is the best, some might say the only, title of the later Empire to the grateful remembrance of mankind. Under its protecting shade small princedoms and free cities lived unmolested beside states like Saxony and Bavaria—each member of the Germanic body feeling that the rights of the weakest of his brethren were also his own.

The most important chapter in the history of the Empire is that which describes its relation to the Church and *Influence of the Empire upon the history of the Church.* the Papacy. Of the ecclesiastical power it was alternately the champion and the enemy. In the ninth and tenth centuries the Emperors extended the dominion of Peter's chair : in the tenth and eleventh they rescued it from an abyss of guilt and shame to be the instrument of their own downfall. The struggle which Gregory VII began, although it was political rather than religious, awoke in the Teutonic nations a hostility to the pretensions of the Romish court. That struggle ended, with the death of the last Hohenstaufen, in the victory of the priesthood— a victory whose abuse by the insolent and greedy pontiffs of the fourteenth and fifteenth centuries made it more ruinous than a defeat. The anger which had long smouldered in the breasts of the northern nations of Europe burst out in the sixteenth with a violence which alarmed those whom it had hitherto defended, and made the

---

* Holland was then practically German.

Emperors once more the allies of the Popedom, and the partners of its declining fortunes. But the nature of that alliance and of the hostility which had preceded it must not be misunderstood. It is a *Nature of* natural, but not the less a serious error to suppose, as modern writers often seem to do, that *between the* the pretensions of the Empire and the Popedom were mutually exclusive; that each claimed *and the* all the rights, spiritual and secular, of a universal monarch. So far was this from being the case, that we find mediæval writers and statesmen, even Emperors and Popes themselves, expressly recognizing a divinely appointed duality of government—two potentates, each supreme in the sphere of his own activity, Peter in things eternal, Cæsar in things temporal. The relative position of the two does indeed in course of time undergo a signal alteration. In the days of Charles, the barbarous age of modern Europe, when men were and could not but be governed chiefly by physical force, the Emperor was practically, if not theoretically, the grander figure. Four centuries later, in the era of Pope Innocent III, when the power of ideas had grown stronger in the world, and was able to resist or to bend to its service the arms and the wealth of men, we see the balance inclined the other way. Spiritual authority is conceived of as being of a nature so high and holy that it must inspire and guide the civil administration. But it is not proposed to supplant that administration nor to degrade its head : the great struggle of the eleventh and two following centuries does not aim at the annihilation of one or other power, but turns solely upon the character of their connection. Hildebrand, the typical representative of the Popedom, requires the obedience of the Emperor on the ground of his own personal responsibility for the souls of their common subjects: he demands, not that the functions of

temporal government shall be directly committed to himself, but that they shall be exercised in conformity with
the will of God, whereof he is the exponent.   The imperialist party had no means of meeting this argument, for
they could not deny the spiritual supremacy of the Pope,
nor the transcendant importance of eternal salvation.
They could therefore only protest that the Emperor, being
also divinely appointed, was directly answerable to God,
and remind the Pope that his kingdom was not of this
world.   There was in truth no way out of the difficulty, for
it was caused by the attempt to sever things that admit of
no severance, life in the soul and life in the world, life for
the future and life in the present.   What it is most pertinent to remark is that neither combatant pushed his
theory to extremities, since he felt that his adversary's
title rested on the same foundations as his own.   The
strife was keenest at the time when the whole world believed fervently in both powers ; the alliance came when
faith had forsaken the one and grown cold toward the
other; from the Reformation onward Empire and Popedom fought no longer for supremacy, but for existence.
One is fallen already, the other shakes with every blast.

Nor was that which may be called the inner life of the
Empire less momentous in its influence upon the minds of
men than were its outward dealings with the
Roman Church upon her greatness and decline.
In the Middle Ages, men conceived of the communion of the saints as the formal unity of an
organized body of worshipers, and found the
concrete realization of that conception in their
universal religious state, which was in one
aspect the Church, in another the Empire.   Into the
meaning and worth of the conception, into the nature of
the connection which subsists or ought to subsist between
the Church and the State, this is not the place to inquire.

Ennobling influence of the conception of the World-Empire.

That the form which it took in the Middle Ages was always imperfect, and became eventually rigid and unprogressive, was sufficiently proved by the event. But by it the European peoples were saved from the isolation, and narrowness, and jealous exclusiveness which had checked the growth of the earlier civilizations of the world, and which we see now lying like a weight upon the kingdoms of the East : by it they were brought into that mutual knowledge and co-operation which is the condition if it be not the source of all true culture and progress. For as by the Roman Empire of old the nations were first forced to own a common sway, so by the Empire of the Middle Ages was preserved the feeling of a brotherhood of mankind, a commonwealth of the whole world, whose sublime unity transcended every minor distinction.

As despotic monarchs claiming the world for their realm, the Teutonic Emperors strove from the first against three principles, over all of which their forerunners of the elder Rome had triumphed—those of Nationality, Aristocracy and Popular Freedom. Their *Principles adverse to the Empire.* early struggles were against the first of these, and ended with its victory in the emancipation, one after another, of England, France, Poland, Hungary, Denmark, Burgundy and Italy. The second, in the form of feudalism, menaced even when seeming to embrace and obey them, and succeeded, after the Great Interregnum, in destroying their effective strength in Germany. Aggression and inheritance turned the numerous independent principalities thus formed out of the greater fiefs, into a few military monarchies, resting neither on a rude loyalty, like feudal kingdoms, nor on religious duty and tradition, like the Empire, but on physical force, more or less disguised by legal forms. That the hostility to the Empire of the third was accidental rather than necessary is seen by this, that the very same monarchs who strove to crush

the Lombard and Tuscan cities favored the growth of the
free towns of Germany. Asserting the rights of the
individual in the sphere of religion, the Reformation
weakened the Empire by denying the necessity of external
unity in matters spiritual: the extension of the same principle to the secular world, whose fullness is still withheld
from the Germans, would have struck at the doctrine of
imperial absolutism had it not found a nearer and deadlier
foe in the actual tyranny of the princes. It is more than
a coincidence, that as the proclamation of the liberty of
thought had shaken it, so that of the liberty of action
made by the revolutionary movement, whose beginning
the world saw and understood not in 1789, whose end we
see not yet, should have indirectly become the cause which
overthrew the Holy Empire.

Its fall in the midst of the great convulsion that changed
the face of Europe marks an era in history, an era whose
character the events of every year are further
Change marked by its fall. unfolding : an era of the destruction of old
forms and systems and the building up of new.
The last instance is the most memorable.
Under our eyes, the work which Theodoric and Lewis II,
Guido and Ardoin and the second Frederick essayed in vain,
has been achieved by the steadfast will of the Italian people.
The fairest province of the Empire, for which Franconian
and Swabian battled so long, is now a single monarchy under
the Burgundian count, whom Sigismund created imperial
vicar in Italy, and who, now that he holds the ancient capital, might call himself " King of the Romans " more truly
than Greek or Frank or Austrian has done since Constantine forsook the Tiber for the Bosphorus. No longer the
prey of the stranger, Italy may forget the past, and sympathize, as she has now indeed, since the fortunate alliance
of 1866, begun to sympathize, with the efforts after national
unity of her ancient enemy—efforts confronted by so many

obstacles that a few years ago they seemed all but hopeless, but now crowned with a success which, if it be not yet complete, has in it all the promise of completeness in the future. For if the name of German Empire does not denote a united monarchy, it does nevertheless denote not only a nation but also a state—a state whose strength lies in the community of interests and feelings among its members, and in which this unity of sentiment, based upon the glorious memories of the Middle Ages, built up by the literature of more recent times, cemented by the last great struggle against France, promises to grow in each succeeding generation more hearty and more trustful. On the new shapes that may emerge in this general reconstruction it would be idle to speculate. Yet one prediction may be ventured. No universal monarchy is likely to arise. More frequent intercourse, and the progress of thought, have done much to change the character of national distinctions, substituting for ignorant prejudice and hatred a genial sympathy and the sense of a common interest. They have not lessened their force. No one who reads the history of the last three hundred years, no one, above all, who studies attentively the career of Napoleon, can believe it possible for *Relations* any state, however great her energy and ma- *of the Em-* terial resources, to repeat in modern Europe *pire to the* the part of ancient Rome: to gather into one *ties of* vast political body races whose national indi- *Europe.* dividuality has grown more and more marked in each successive age. Nevertheless, it is in great measure due to Rome and to the Roman Empire of the Middle Ages that the bonds of national union are on the whole both stronger and nobler than they were ever before. The latest historian of Rome, after summing up the results to the world of his hero's career, closes his treatise with these words : " There was in the world as Cæsar

found it the rich and noble heritage of past centuries, and
an endless abundance of splendor and glory, but little
soul, still less taste, and, least of all, joy in and through
life. Truly it was an old world, and even Cæsar's genial
patriotism could not make it young again. The blush of
dawn returns not until the night has fully descended.
Yet with him there came to the much-tormented races of
the Mediterranean a tranquil evening after a sultry day;
and when, after long historical night, the new day broke
once more upon the peoples, and fresh nations in free self-
guided movement began their course toward new and higher
aims, many were found among them in whom the seed of
Cæsar had sprung up, many who owed him, and who owe him
still, their national individuality."* If this be the glory of
Julius, the first great founder of the Empire, so is it also
the glory of Charles, the second founder, and of more
than one among his Teutonic successors. The work of
the mediæval Empire was self-destructive; and it fostered,
while seeming to oppose, the nationalities that were destined to replace it. It tamed the barbarous races of the
North, and forced them within the pale of civilization.
It preserved the arts and literature of antiquity. In times
of violence and oppression, it set before its subjects the
duty of rational obedience to an authority whose watch-
words were peace and religion. It kept alive, when
national hatreds were most bitter, the notion of a great
European Commonwealth. And by doing all this, it was
in effect abolishing the need for a centralizing and despotic
power like itself : it was making men capable of using
national independence aright : it was teaching them to
rise to that conception of spontaneous activity, and a freedom which is above law but not against it, to which
national independence itself, if it is to be a blessing at all,

---

* Mommsen, *Römische Geschichte*, iii. *sub fin.*

must be only a means. Those who mark what has been the tendency of events since A.D. 1789, and who remember how many of the crimes and calamities of the past are still but half redressed, need not be surprised to see the so-called principle of nationalities advocated with honest devotion as the final and perfect form of political development. But such undistinguishing advocacy is after all only the old error in a new shape. If all other history did not bid us beware the habit of taking the problems and the conditions of our own age for those of all time, the warning which the Empire gives might alone be warning enough. From the days of Augustus down to those of Charles V the whole civilized world believed in its existence as a part of the eternal fitness of things, and Christian theologians were not behind heathen poets in declaring that when it perished the world would perish with it. Yet the Empire is gone, and the world remains, and hardly notes the change.

This is but a small part of what might be said upon an almost inexhaustible theme : inexhaustible not from its extent but from its profundity : not because there is so much to say, but because, pursue we it never so far, more will remain unexpressed, since incapable of expression. For that which it is at once most necessary and least easy to do, is to look at the Empire as a whole: a single institution, in which centers the history of eighteen centuries—whose outer form is the same, while its essence and spirit are constantly changing. It is when we come to consider it in this light that the difficulties of so vast a subject are felt in all their force. Try to explain in words the theory and inner meaning of the Holy Empire, as it appeared to the saints and poets of the Middle Ages, and that which we cannot but conceive as noble and fertile in its life, sinks into a heap of barren and scarcely intelligible

Difficulties arising from the nature of the subject.

formulas.   Who has been able to describe the Papacy in
the power it once wielded over the hearts and imaginations of men?   Those persons, if such there still be, who
see in it nothing but a gigantic upas-tree of fraud and
superstition, planted and reared by the enemy of mankind,
are hardly further from entering into the mystery of its
being than the complacent political philosopher, who explains in neat phrases the process of its growth, analyzes
it as a clever piece of mechanism, enumerates and measures
the interests it appealed to, and gives, in conclusion, a sort
of tabular view of its results for good and for evil.   So,
too, is the Holy Empire above all description or explanation; not that it is impossible to discover the beliefs which
created and sustained it, but that the power of those
beliefs cannot be adequately apprehended by men whose
minds have been differently trained, and whose imaginations are fired by different ideals.   Something, yet still
how little, we should know of it if we knew what were the
thoughts of Julius Cæsar when he laid the foundations on
which Augustus built: of Charles, when he reared anew
the stately pile : of Barbarossa and his grandson, when
they strove to avert the surely coming ruin.   Something
more succeeding generations will know, who will judge the
Middle Ages more fairly than we, still living in the midst
of a reaction against all that is mediæval, can hope to do,
and to whom it will be given to see and understand new
forms of political life, whose nature we cannot so much as
conjecture.   Seeing more than we do, they will also see
some things less distinctly.   The Empire which to us still
looms largely on the horizon of the past, will to them sink
lower and lower as they journey onward into the future.
But its importance in universal history it can never lose.
For into it all the life of the ancient world was gathered:
out of it all the life of the modern world arose.

SUPPLEMENTARY CHAPTER.

THE NEW GERMAN EMPIRE.

IN 1806 the Holy Empire died and was buried, and to all appearance soon forgotten. No out-worn shape of the past could have seemed less likely to be ever recalled to life, for the forces which had so long assailed and at last destroyed it were stronger than ever, and threatened with extinction even that feeble shadow which, under the name of the Germanic Confederation, affected in some sort to represent the unity of the German nation. Fifty years passed away ; new questions arose ; Europe ranged itself into new parties; men's minds began to be swayed by new feelings ; time drove fast onward, and the Holy Roman Empire seemed left so far behind among the mists of the past that it was hard to believe that living men had seen it and borne part in its government. Then suddenly there arises from these cold ashes a new, vigorous, self-confident German Empire, a State which, although most different, as well in its inner character as in its form and legal aspect, from its venerable predecessor, is nevertheless in a very real sense that predecessor's representative. An account of this new creation of our own days, perhaps the most striking and fertile epoch in European annals, is therefore a fitting, if not a necessary, pendant to the history of the elder Empire; it is, in fact, the latest act of a long drama, which gives a new and happier meaning to all that has gone before. For not only does the new Empire hold that central and commanding place among Continental States which the old Empire once filled: it is, in a moral and intellectual sense, the offspring of the old Empire, and, but for the pre-existence of the other, could never have itself come into being.

It has been shown in the earlier chapters of this treatise, how from the days of the Emperor Henry III, when the Holy Empire reached the maximum of its power, every succeeding change tended to weaken it morally and politically, to loosen its cohesion, diminish its material resources, destroy its hold on the love and faith of its subjects. The first crisis was marked by the death of Frederick II, when Italy was lost beyond hope of recovery; the second by the Reformation, and particularly by the Treaty of 1555 ; the third by the Peace of Westphalia, when Germany was legally reconstituted as a sort of federation of mutually suspicious and unfriendly states; the fourth, one may perhaps say, by the Seven Years' War, when one vigorous member successfully resisted the whole force of Austria and the other German powers, backed by the armies of France and Russia. It is easy for us now to see, that as after the first of these crises the Empire had no longer any chance of making good its claim to be a world-monarchy, co-extensive with Christianity, so after the second its prospects as a national State, claiming to unite all Germany under a single effective administration, were practically hopeless. The Germans, however, as was natural, did not see this until in 1648 the admission of the substantial independence of the princes had turned the imperial dignity into a mask under which the harsh features of the Hapsburg sovereigns tried in vain to conceal themselves. Over the sentiment of the people its name still retained some power, for it was associated with all the glories of their earlier history, with heroic memories enshrined in song, with claims of world-supremacy which they could not bring themselves to forget. But it was no longer a rallying-point for national feeling, a center to which the country looked for inspiration and guidance. There was indeed but little national feeling in the Germany of that age, little political hope or ardor, little interest in the welfare of the State as a whole, for there was nothing to stir men's feelings as Germans or citizens, no struggles for great common objects against foreign powers, no free political life at home, no assemblies, no press, no local self-government. But, even if a national feeling had been awake, it would hardly have attached itself to the old Empire, which was not only cumbrous and antiquated, but seemed strange and un-German, just because it was more than German ; and which found the support of Rome now almost as injurious as her enmity had been in times gone by, since the friendship of Rome meant the hatred and jealousy of the Protestants. It can hardly be said that the Empire was so utterly dead but that it might have been vivified by a really great man, just as such an one might perhaps make the English monarchy a power even now. But had this come to pass, it would have been because the genius gave life to the office, not, as of old, because the office inspired its holder. And it was not so to be. The imperial throne found no man of the first order to fill it; and continued to stand rather because nobody appeared to overthrow it, than because any good reason remained for it in the new order of things.

The denationalization of Germany had indeed gone beyond politics. As after the establishment of foreign rule in Italy, Italian art and letters had become frigid and affected, so with that extinction of any free or united state life in Germany which followed the Thirty Years' War, the blossoms of literature which had put themselves forth in the age of the Reformation were nipped and withered away. In Lewis XIV's time, French influence became dominant in Germany, no less in poetry and criticism, than in matters of dress, furniture and etiquette; and the ambition of German men of letters was to put off what they were hardly ashamed to call their native barbarism, and imitate the sparkling elegance of their Western neighbors and enemies. French was the fashionable language; French ideas and modes of thought were no less supreme than Greek ideas had been at Rome in the last century of the Republic; French men of letters and science were imported, as apostles of enlightenment, by the best of the German princes, just as Germans have in later times been drawn into Russia by the Czars.

Just when this reign of foreign taste was most undisputed, just when the political life and national sentiment of Germany seemed bound in a frozen sleep, a change began ; and it began, like so many other great changes, in an unpromising quarter and an unconscious way.

From the time of the Swabian emperors, the Margrave of Brandenburg was one of the most considerable princes *The Mar-* of the Empire, and by the reign of Rudolf I he *graviate of* had become definitely recognized as an Elector *Branden-* with the office of Archchamberlain.* His *burg and* dominions consisted of the Mark proper, or old *the house* Mark, to which were added the New and the *of Hohen-* Middle Mark, a flat, sandy territory of heaths *zollern.* and woods lying along the Elbe and the Havel, which had been conquered from the Wends in the days of Henry the Fowler, and gradually filled by a Teutonic population, together with a more or less vague authority, or claims of authority, over the Slavic tribes to the north and east. In A.D. 1411 this territory was delivered over to Frederick, sixth Burggrave of Nürnberg, by the Emperor

---

* A sketch of the earlier history of Prussia and the house of Hohenzollern may be found in the first volume of Mr. Carlyle's " History of Friedrich II."

Sigismund, whom he had served faithfully, and to whom
he had advanced moneys, which the latter in this way
repaid, giving Brandenburg as a sort of pledge which was
not likely to be redeemed: and in 1415 Sigismund formally
conferred the Mark and the electoral dignity upon Frederick and his heirs, still, however, reserving (but on the
occasion of the formal investiture of 1417 omitting this
reservation) the right of redeeming his grant by the payment of 400,000 Hungarian gold gulden, and retaining to
himself and his male heirs the reversion in the Electorate,
expectant on the extinction of Frederick's line, an event
which has not yet happened. This Burggrave Frederick
was the lineal descendant of a certain Conrad of Hohenzollern (first Burggrave in the days of Frederick Barbarossa), scion of an old Swabian family whose ancestral
castle stands in the high limestone plateau of the Rauhe
Alp, not very far from Hohenstaufen and from Altorf,
the original seat of the Welfs; and this Conrad is the
twenty-third lineal ancestor of the present Emperor
William. From the time of Elector Frederick the house of
Hohenzollern held Brandenburg, adding to it by slow
degrees various other scattered territories and claims to
territories which for a time could not be made good, and
in particular acquiring, in 1605 and 1618, the district
known as East Prussia, lying along the Baltic beyond the
Vistula, as the heirs of Albert the last Grandmaster of the
Teutonic knights.* The Hohenzollerns embraced Protestantism, and after having played (in the person of the

---

* The Duchy of East Prussia was established by the treaty of
Cracow in 1525, under Polish suzerainty. The Electors of Brandenburg, from the time of Joachim II onward, obtained from Poland the
co-investiture of it, but did not get the actual government into their
hands till 1605, nor the full legal dominion till 1618; and the supremacy of Poland remained until released at the peace of Wehlau in
1657.

Elector George William) a rather contemptible part in the Thirty Years' War, produced a really distinguished prince in Frederick the (so-called) Great Elector, who reigned in the latter half of the seventeenth century. He freed East Prussia from the supremacy of Poland, consolidated his straggling dominions into a well-ordered State, and gave to his subjects, by the luster of his military successes, a sort of incipient consciousness of national existence.

In 1700 his son Frederick, having secured or purchased the approval of the Emperor Leopold, but not without a furious protest from Pope Clement XI, whose prophetic spirit dreaded and denounced in Hilde-brandine fashion the admission of a heretic to the most sacred of secular offices, called himself King of Prussia, taking his title from the above-named Duchy of East Prussia, and crowning himself at Königsberg, its ancient capital, on January 18, 1701. This region formed no part of the Holy Empire, and its original inhabitants, the old Prussians,* were of course not Germans at all, but a Lithuanian people, who had remained pagans and barbarians till they were half conquered, half exterminated by the Teutonic knights in the thirteenth and fourteenth centuries, and their country Germanized by a constant immigration from the West. It is a curious freak of history, not unlike that which has given the British name to the Teutonic and Gaelic inhabitants of these islands, that has transferred the name of this vanishing race to the greatest of modern German states.

Erection of the kingdom of Prussia.

This assumption of royalty, the work of a prince who contributed nothing else to the greatness of his house, was a matter of far greater consequence than might have at first appeared. At that time no other member of the Empire (except the Elector of Saxony, who had in 1697

---

* So called from their dwelling next to Russia—po Russia.

been chosen king of Poland) wore a crown, and the new dignity was soon felt to have raised its owner into a different European position ; it made him the fellow of the sovereigns of France, England, Denmark, Sweden, and brought him into what soon became a rivalry with his titular superior the Emperor. Had Austria been wise, she would have rejected a bribe far larger than that by which her compliance was purchased, would even have dispensed with the good-will of Brandenburg in the struggle of the Spanish Succession, rather than have yielded to this young antagonist a moral advantage of such moment. For the time, however, little change seemed to have been made. Frederick I, was feeble and peaceful : the eccentric Frederick William I, who followed him, had a dutiful reverence for his Emperor, and prized his regiment of giants too highly to care to risk them in war. He was, moreover, thrifty to the verge of parsimony ; and his energy, which was considerable, found scope for its exercise in a careful oversight of the revenue and civil service of the country which largely contributed to the successes of his son.

The greatness of the Prussian monarchy begins with Frederick II, certainly the most considerable man who has succeeded to a throne since Charles V. The extraordinary military talents by which *Frederick* Europe knows him best, are a less worthy title *the Great,* to the admiration of posterity, than the ardor *1740-1786.* he showed for good administration, for the prosperity and happiness of his people. Along with the instinctive desire of a powerful and active mind to have every thing done in the best way, he had a complete superiority to prejudice and tradition, and a genuine sympathy, not indeed for political liberty, but for cultivation and enlightenment. It was at bottom this, fully as much as the glories of his campaigns, that made him, in spite of his cold heart and

scornful manners, a favorite with his own people and an
object of interest, even of pride, throughout Germany.
Upon that country the moral effect of his reign was great.
It stirred the national spirit to see a German prince defend
his naturally weak kingdom against the allied might of
Austria, France and Russia, and come out of the terrible
struggle with undaunted confidence and undiminished
territories. While the other states of the Empire were
languishing under a wasteful and old-fashioned misgovernment, Prussia gave the example of an administration
which, while rigidly economical, strove to develop the
resources of the country, of a highly disciplined army, a
codified law, a reformed system of procedure, a capital to
which literary and scientific celebrities were gathered from
all quarters. While Roman Catholicism and feudalism
reigned on the Danube, Frederick made Berlin the center
of light for North Germany; and in this way effected as
much for his kingdom as he had done by the seizure of
wealthy Silesia, giving it a representative position, a claim
on German interest and sympathy which there had been
nothing in its earlier history, or in that of his own house,
to awaken. But in all this it would be a mistake to
attribute to the great king a conception of what it is now
the fashion to call " Prussia's German Mission," the conscious foresight of a German patriot anxious to pave the
way for the unity of the nation. There is little in his
words or acts to show such a feeling ; what he planned
and cared for was the strength and well-being of his own
Prussian State.* And when at the end of his life he took

* The idea was started during the Seven Years' War of uniting
Germany under Prussian supremacy, deposing Francis I, and getting
Frederick himself chosen Emperor; and his favorite minister Winter-
feldt was, in 1757, sanguine enough to believe this could be effected.
(See Schmidt, *Preussens Deutsche Politik*, p. 22). Frederick is said
to have, while Crown Prince, formed the plan of marrying Maria
Theresa, whose hatred he afterward so justly incurred.

a lead in the politics of the Empire, by forming the League of Princes to oppose the ambitious designs of Joseph II, his purpose was simply to maintain the *status quo*—that *status quo* whose impotence was so terribly displayed by the events of the next twenty years.* That League is memorable, not as being in any sense a project of reform, but as the first instance in which Prussia appears heading a party among the German States in hostility to Austria : it is the beginning of that Dualism, as the Germans call it, which at last reached a point where nothing but a struggle for life and death could decide between the rival powers.

What glory Prussia had gained under Frederick II she seemed determined to lose under his two unworthy successors. Nothing, except indeed the behavior of the minor German princes, could have been weaker, meaner, more unpatriotic than her conduct in the struggle with France which began in 1792.† In 1791 she had leagued herself with Austria, but their relations, as might have been expected, soon ceased to be cordial. Frederick *Prussian policy in the wars of the French Revolution.* William II began to negotiate with the French Republic, in the hope of getting something for himself out of the confusion, and in 1795 concluded with France the separate peace of Basel, by which a line of demarcation was drawn between North and South Germany, the former being declared neutral. When in 1806 the Confederation of the Rhine had been formed under Napoleon's protectorate and

---

* This League, which Frederick modeled to some extent upon the Smalkaldic of the sixteenth century, answered its purpose by checking Joseph, and preventing any change in the constitution of the Empire. See upon it Von Ranke's *Die Deutschen Mächte und der Fürstenbund.*

† See for the whole history of this period Von Sybel's *Geschichte der Revolutionszeit.*

the Holy Empire extinguished, Prussia, which by a convention (February 15, 1806) had obtained possession of
Hanover, part, it need hardly be said, of the dominions of
her late ally, the English King George III, endeavored to
unite the Northern States in a league, at whose head
should stand her king, with the title and prerogative of
Emperor, the Direktorium being composed of him and the
sovereigns of Saxony and Hessen-Cassel. Talleyrand,
however, found it easy to baffle this scheme, on which he
had at first pretended to smile (it is memorable as the first
appearance of the conception of a North German Confederation) ; and soon afterward the defeats of Jena and
Auerstadt, followed by that of Friedland, left Prussia at
Napoleon's mercy, if mercy he had any. By the Peace of
Tilsit she submitted, losing her lands west of the Elbe,
and in all more than half of her territories, recognizing
the Confederation of the Rhine, and abandoning all claim
to interfere in German politics. Meanwhile Saxony, the
newly created kingdom of Westphalia, and all the other
purely German members of the old Empire joined the
Rhenish Confederation, that is to say, enrolled themselves
the vassals of the Parisian crown. French domination was
offensive everywhere, but nowhere so offensive as in
Prussia, the feebleness of whose Court seems to have
emboldened Napoleon to treat her with an insolent scorn
he never thought of showing to the more consistent,
though no more patriotic Hapsburgs. Hence, too, when

*The War of
Liberation.*

uprising came, and the swelling wave of popular enthusiasm tossed back the French beyond
the Elbe, the Weser, the Rhine itself, it was
the much-suffering Prussian people that was foremost in
the fight; it was northern heroes of the sword and pen
that drew the admiration and gratitude of a liberated
Fatherland; while the French, who had been wont to treat
the North Germans with a strangely misplaced contempt,

felt for them, after the campaigns of Leipzig and Waterloo, a hatred scarcely less bitter than that they bore to
England herself.

This great deliverance was far more the work of the
people than of King or Court : but as was natural, it induced a burst of loyalty which strengthened and glorified
the Prussian monarchy in the eyes of Germany, and gave
it a great opportunity of placing itself at the head of the
nation. For the national feeling which had smouldered for
two centuries or more, had now risen into a strong and
brilliant flame ; and it was on Prussia, far more than on
any other state, that its light was shed. Austria's merits
as well as her vices do not permit her to be popular ;
Bavaria and Würtemberg had been aggrandized by Napoleon ; Saxony had adhered to him throughout ; Prussia
had endured most and triumphed most signally. Now
would have been the time for her to answer to the great
cry that went up for freedom and unity, to secure by firm
action the rights of the people in a consolidated German
state.

But, as often happens, the hour came without the man.
Frederick William III was well intentioned indeed, but
feeble and narrow-minded ; and his Court had not yet recovered from its horrors at the principles of 1789 and the
acts of 1793. As the want of representative institutions
and the habit of combination for political purposes gave
the desire for unity no means of expressing itself practically, it remained an aspiration, a sentiment—nothing more.
Thus, when the Congress of Vienna met to
reconstitute Europe and Germany, the princes *The Con-*
were masters of the situation ; and they used *gress of*
their advantage with characteristic selfishness. *Vienna.*
The proclamation of Kalisch, issued by the sovereigns of
Prussia and Russia, when they leagued themselves against
Napoleon (March 25, 1813), announced the object of

the two powers to be "to aid the German peoples in recovering freedom and independence, and to afford to them
effective protection and defense in re-establishing a venerable Empire." The reconstitution of the country, it was
added, was to be effected solely by the united action of the
princes and peoples, and was to proceed "from the ancient
and native spirit of the German nation; that Germany, the
more perfectly this work was executed in its principles and
compass, might so much the more appear again among the
peoples of Europe in renovated youth, strength and unity."
But at the Congress nothing was heard, and indeed nothing would have been listened to, of the kind.* When it
opened, Hardenberg, the Prussian minister, presented
a scheme which, although it recognized in the princes an
independence in some respects considerable, and already
conceded to them by the treaties securing their
adhesion against France, proposed to treat Germany
as being for many purposes a united state, under
institutions whose tendency would have been to
make her less and less of a mere league. Austria,
however, under the chilling influence of Metternich,
himself perhaps prompted by the darker spirit
of Frederick von Gentz, received these proposals with
dull disfavor; the minor potentates, headed by Bavaria and
Würtemburg, entered energetic protests against anything
which could infringe on their sovereignty; protests so sweeping that even Austria was obliged to remind them that
under the old Empire certain rights were assured to
German subjects, while the envoy of Hanover exclaimed
againt the "Sultanism" of these members of the late Confederation of the Rhine. At last, after a long period of

---

* For the Congress of Vienna students may refer to L. Häusser's
Deutsche Geschichte; for the subsequent history of the Confederation
to H. Schulze, *Einleitung in das deutsche Straatsrecht,* and K.
Klüpfel, *Die deutschen Einheitsbestrebungen seit,* 1815.

confusion and uncertainty, in which projects for the restoration of the "ancient venerable Empire" were frequently put forward, and supported among others by Stein, a counter-scheme, propounded by Metternich, was molded into the Act of Foundation of the Germanic Confederation. The work was hastily done, under the pressure of alarm at Napoleon's return from Elba, and professed to be only an outline, to be subsequently improved and filled in. The diplomatists were exhausted by a long course of bickerings and intrigues upon this and other questions; many were dissatisfied, but every one saw that his opponent's power of hindering was greater than his own power of forcing a proposition through: and as it was clear something must be done, people brought themselves to a sort of acquiescence, which, though it professed to be only temporary, could not easily be recalled, and of course made it harder to reopen the discussion. So this proposed completion, as was natural in the matter of so much delicacy and difficulty, never took place; and the revised draft of the Act of Confederation, adopted on June 10, 1815, a week before Waterloo, was in all its main features the constitution which lasted down till 1866. Prussia yielded with unaccountable readiness—unaccountable except on the hypothesis that her minister, Hardenberg and William von Humboldt, despaired at such a time and among such people of effecting anything satisfactory—the points on which she had at first insisted; and made little further objection to the carrying out of Metternich's views. Her king was a faithful member of the Holy Alliance: her government adhered to the principles associated with that compact, and was content in internal questions to follow humbly in the wake of Austria. While the reaction was triumphing in the rest of Europe, Particularism* triumphed

Establishment of the Germanic Confederation.

* *Particularismus* is the convenient name which the Germans have given to the policy, feeling or system which maintains the inde-

at Vienna, and the interests of the German people were forgotten or ignored.

The Federal Constitution, while recognizing fully the sovereignty of the princes in their own territories, had made only the feeblest provisions for the concession of popular rights and the establishment of representative institutions in the several states. Almost the only expression which it allowed to be given to the idea of national unity was in the creation of a central federal body, the Diet, wherein only the princes and not their subjects were represented, which was empowered to act in foreign affairs, and might be made by the great princes the means of repressing any liberal movements on the part of an individual member. But this did not satisfy Metternich. The excitement produced by the War of Liberation did not at once subside : the ideas of freedom, national unity, national greatness, which it had called forth, had obtained a dominion over the minds of the German youth ; and were eloquently preached by some of the noblest spirits among its teachers. These ideas, however, innocent as they would now appear, and well founded as was the jealousy of Russian influence which prompted their expression, were marked with fear and suspicion by the narrow minds of the Prussian king and the minister of Francis of Austria. In 1819, therefore, Metternich brought together, as if by accident, the ministers of ten leading German courts at Karlsbad in Bohemia, and procured their assent to a series of measures extinguishing the freedom of the press, restraining university teaching, forbidding societies and political meetings, and erecting a sort of inquisition at Mentz for the discovery and punishment of democratic agitators. These measures were soon after adopted by the Federal Diet at

pendence of the several local potentates, who were or are members of the Germanic body.

Frankfort, and followed by conferences of ministers at Vienna. These produced the instrument known as the Vienna Final Act (Schlussakt) of 1820, whereby the constitution of the Confederation was further modified in a reactionary and anti-national spirit. Such securities as existed for the rights of the subject in the several states were diminished, while the Diet saw its powers enlarged whenever they could be employed for the suppression of free institutions, and received a frightfully wide police jurisdiction through the territories of the minor princes.

This Karlsbad Conference struck the key-note of the policy of the Federal Diet during the three-and-thirty dreary years that lie between 1815 and the brief though bright awakening of 1848.* If the selfishness of rulers were not the commonest moral of history, there would be something extraordinary as well as offensive in the horror of change and reform which was now exhibited *Condition of Germany under the Confederation.* by these very princes who had, with Napoleon's help or connivance, carried out by the mediatization of the weaker neighbors a revolution far more sweeping, and in point of law less defensible, than any which the patriotic reformers now proposed. These potentates, especially those of Northern Germany, were for the most part possessed by the same reactionary feelings as their two great neighbors; their rule was harsh and repressive, conceding little or nothing to the demands of their subjects, and prepared, especially after their alarms had been renewed by the revolution of 1830 in France, to check the most harmless expressions of the aspirations for national unity. Such unity now appeared further off than ever. While the old Empire lasted, princes and peoples owned one common head in the Emperor, and lived under a constitution which had descended, however modified, from the days when the nation formed a single powerful state. Now, by the medi-

* See L. K. Aegidi, *Aus dem Jahre*, 1819.

atization of the lesser principalities, the extinction of the Reichsritterschaft (knights of the Empire), the absorption of all the free cities save four, the class which had formed a link between the princes and the mass of the nation had been removed; the sovereigns had, in becoming fewer, become more isolated and more independent; they were members rather of the European than of the German commonwealth. Those moral effects of the War of Liberation, from which so much had at first been hoped, now seemed to have been lost utterly and forever.

Meanwhile the German liberals labored under the immense difficulty of having no legitimate and constitutional mode of agitation, no lever, so to speak, by *The party of progress in Germany.* which they could move the mass of their countrymen. They were mere speakers and writers, because there was nothing else for them to do; dreamers and theorists, as unthinking people in more fortunate countries called them, because the field of practical politics was closed to them. In only a few of *Its difficulties.* the states did representative assemblies exist; and these were too small and too limited in their powers to be able to stimulate the political interests of their constituents. Prussia herself had no parliament of the whole monarchy until 1847 : up to that year there had been only local " Landes Stände;" estates or diets for the several provinces.

The liberal party had two objects to struggle for—the establishment or extension of free institutions in the several states, and the attainment of national *Its aims: establishment of constitutional government.* unity. As respects the first of these, it may be remarked that the mere passion for freedom in the abstract has never produced a great popular movement. Englishmen, Swiss, and Americans may, through long habit, think it essential to national happiness ; but it is generally desired rather as a means than as an end : and there must always exist in order to rouse a people to disaffection or insurrection, either such a withdrawal of liberties previously enjoyed as wounds its pride and conservative feeling, or else the infliction by the governing power of positive evils which affect the subject in his daily life, his religion, his social and domestic relations. Now in Germany, and particularly in the Prussian State, such liberties had not been known since primitive times; and there were few serious practical grievances to be complained of. From the time of Frederick the Great the country had been well and honestly administered ; conscience was free, trade and industry were growing, taxation was not heavy, the press censorship did not annoy the ordinary citizen, and the other restraints upon personal freedom were only those to which the subjects of all the Continental monarchies had been accustomed. The habit of submission was strong ; and there existed in most places a good deal of loyalty, irrational perhaps, but not therefore the less powerful, toward the long-descended reigning houses. In several of the petty states there was indeed serious misgovernment, and an arbitrary behavior on the sovereign's part which might well have provoked revolt. Hessen-Cassel, for instance, was ruled by the unworthy minions of a singularly contemptible prince ; and in Hanover King Ernest Augustus on his accession in 1837 abolished by a stroke of the pen the constitution which had been granted by his predecessor William. But these states were too small for a vigorous political life ; the nobility depended on the Court and were disposed to side with it ; the power of the Confederation hung like a thunder-cloud on the horizon, ready to burst wherever Austria chose to guide it. It was therefore hard for the liberals to excite their countrymen to any energetic and concerted action ; and when the governments thought fit to repress their attempts at agitation, this could be harshly done with little fear of the consequences.

In laboring for the creation of one united German state out of the multitude of petty principalities, the party of progress found themselves in a still greater dis-

Attainment of national unity. advantage. There was indeed a sentimental wish for it, but only a sentiment ; an idea which worked powerfully upon imaginative minds, but had little hold on the world of fact and reality, little charm for the steady-going burgher and the peasant whose vision was bounded by his own valley. Some considerable practical benefits might no doubt have been expected from its realization, such as the establishment of a common code of laws, the better execution of great public works, the protection of the nation from the aggressions of France and Russia; but these were objects whose importance it was hard to bring home to the average citizen in peaceful times. And where was the movement toward unity to begin ? Not in the Federal Diet, of all places, for it consisted of the envoys of princes who would have been the first to suffer. Not in the local legislatures, for they had no power to deal practically with such questions, and would speedily have been silenced had they attempted by discussing them to influence the policy of their masters. It was therefore only through the carefully guarded press, and occasionally in social or literary gatherings, that appeals to the nation could be made, or the semblance of an agitation kept up. There was no point to start from: it was all aspiration and nothing more; and so this movement, to which so many of the noblest hearts and intellects of Germany devoted themselves (though the two greatest stood aloof), made during many years little apparent progress. The Zollverein was indeed created, and thereby a bond of union established whose advantages were soon felt, but this was done by the

individual action of Prussia and the several States which
one after another entered into her views, not by the Diet
as a national work. Meanwhile the strictness of the
repressive system was still maintained : Prussia, though
now ruled by the more liberal Frederick William IV, was
still silent: the influence of Metternich was still supreme.
Then came the revolution of 1848. The monarchy of
Louis Philippe fell with a crash that sounded over Europe,
and every German and Italian throne rocked to
its foundation. In Vienna, Berlin, Dresden   *The Revo-*
and Munich, not to speak of smaller capitals, *lution of*
there came, sooner or later, risings more or   *1848.*
less formidable; constitutions were promised or granted by
the terrified princes: the Federal Diet, after a hasty declaration in favor of the liberties it had so long withheld,
abdicated to make way for a national Parliament, which
was duly summoned, and met at Frankfort on the 18th of
May, 1848. This assembly appointed as Administrator of
the Empire (Reichsverweser) the Archduke John of Austria, and began to frame a constitution for United Germany. According to the draught, completed early in
1849, Germany was to be a federal state, under a hereditary
emperor, irresponsible, but advised by responsible ministers; and with a parliament of two houses, one representing the states, members of the Empire : the other the
people. On the 28th of March the assembly offered the
imperial dignity to the King of Prussia.* He hesitated

---

* In 1847, when things seemed quiet enough, Frederick William IV
had opened negotiations with Austria with a view to improving the
constitution of the Confederation, and making better provision for
common defense and for internal communication. In the Berlin
revolution of March, 1848, he had behaved with irresolution, no
doubt, but had shown some real sympathy for the people. And
this he had: he heartily desired both the well-being, and, to a certain
extent, the freedom of his own people and the greatness of Germany;
but he was unhappily entangled with notions of divine right and
various other mediæval whimsies and sentiments,

to accept it without the consent of the other sovereigns ;
and exactly a month afterward definitely refused it, fearing
the jealousy of some of the princes, although twenty-nine
of them had already expressed their approval of the
scheme ; disliking several parts of the new constitution,
and feeling himself too weak and irresolute to take the
helm of the German state at a moment of such difficulty
and confusion. His refusal was a great, and as it proved,
a fatal discouragement to the liberals, for it disunited
them, and it destroyed their hopes of a powerful material
support. Nevertheless the Frankfort assembly sat for
some months longer, till, having migrated to Stuttgart, it
dwindled down at last into a sort of rump parliament, and
was suppressed by force, while Prussia, at first in conjunc-
tion with Hanover and Saxony, started other and narrower
plans for national organization, schemes modeled after
those of 1785 and 1806, but of which nothing ever came.*

The Reaction : re-estab-lishment of the Confed-eration. Meantime the governments had recovered
from their first alarm. Austria had recon-
quered North Italy, and had by Russia's help
overpowered the Magyars; France had restored
the Pope; everywhere over Europe the tide of
reaction was rising fast. In 1850 Austria and
Prussia took from the Archduke John such
shadow of power as still remained to him as Reichsverweser, and at the conferences of Olmütz Prussia resumed
her attitude of submissive adherence to Austria's policy.
By the middle of 1851 the Confederation was re-established
on its old footing, with its old powerlessness for good, its
old capacities for mischief, and, it may be added, its old ·
willingness to use those capacities for the suppression of
free institutions in the more progressive states.

The effects, however, of the great uprising of 1848 were

---

* They were debated at great length by an assembly convoked at
Gotha.

not lost in Germany any more than in Italy and Hungary. It has made things seem possible—seem even for a moment accomplished—which had been *Effects of* till then mere visions; it had awakened a keen *the move-* political interest in the people, stirred their *ment of* whole life, and given them a sense of national *1848-49.* unity such as they had not had since 1814. By showing the governments how insecure were the foundations of their arbitrary power, it had made them less unwilling to accept change; it had taught peoples how little was to be expected from the enforced good-will of princes. From this time, therefore, after the first reaction had spent itself, one may observe a real though slow progress toward free constitutional life. In some of the smaller states, and particularly in Baden, it soon came to be the policy of the government to encourage the action of the local parliament; and the Prussian assembly became in its long and spirited struggle with the crown a political school of incomparable value to the rest of Germany as well as to its own great kingdom.

One other thing more the events of 1848-1850 did most effectively for the Germans, if indeed that wanted doing: they made clear to the nation the hopelessness of expecting anything from the Confederation. During the last sixteen years of its existence, nothing, if we except the promulgation under its sanction of a general code of commercial law, was done by the Federal Diet for national objects: its deliberations had for many years been carried on in secret; it spoke with no authority to foreign princes, and behaved with sluggish irresolution in the question which was again beginning to agitate Germany, of the succession of Schleswig and Holstein, and the relation of these duchies to the Danish Crown.

The restoration of the Federal constitution in 1850-51 was at the time regarded as merely provisional, accepted

only because Austria and Prussia could not be got to
agree upon any new scheme ; and the successive projects
of reform which thereafter emanated, sometimes from
governments, sometimes from voluntary associations, kept
the question of the organization of Germany and the
attainment of some sort of national unity, constantly before
the people. Thus, although nothing was done, and the
weary discussions which went on moved the laughter of
other nations, the way was secretly but surely paved for
revolution.   In 1859 the liberals organized themselves in

Parties in Germany. what was called the National Union (National-
Verein), a body containing numerous members
in nearly all the German States, and among
them many distinguished publicists and men of letters. It
held general meetings from time to time; and, when occasion arose, its permanent committee issued pamphlets and
manifestoes, explaining the views and recommending the
policy of the party. This policy was not a very definite
one, so far as practical measures were concerned, yet tolerably clear in its ultimate object—viz., the union of all Germany in one Federal state (whether republican or mon-
archical), and if necessary, the absolute exclusion of Austria therefrom. This last feature procured for it from her
adherents and from the German conservatives generally,
the name of the Little German (Kleindeutsch) party; and
they, assuming the title of Great Germans (Grossdeutschen
i. e., the advocates of a Germany which should include
Austria), founded in 1862 a rival association, which called
itself the Reform Union, and in like manner held meetings
and issued manifestoes. It found strong support in Hanover, Bavaria and Würtemburg, but comparatively little
in the middle states, and of course still less in Prussia.
Its policy was mainly defensive; while the National Union,
whose tendencies would naturally have been philo-Prussian
and aggressive, found itself embarrassed by what seemed

the resolutely reactionary attitude taken up by the Prussian king and ministers in the affairs of their own kingdom. A contest respecting the organization and payment of the army had broken out between the Government and the Chamber—a contest embittered first by the accession to the throne of the feudally-minded King William I (hitherto Regent), whose assertion of the principle of the divine right at his coronation at Königsberg had surprised and displeased thinking people, and afterward by the admission to the chief place in the ministry of a statesman who was then supposed to be the champion of tyranny and feudalism, even of the Austrian alliance. During the struggle which raged in the years 1862–64, and which at some moments seemed to threaten revolution, it was impossible for Germany to hope for anything from a power which refused to work constitutional government at home, and treated the representatives of the people with a roughness under which no one could tell that there lay concealed a substantial community of purpose.

The liberals of the South and West were therefore in 1863 disposed fairly to abjure Prussia as given over to a reprobate mind; and Austria thought she saw her opportunity. Encouraged by the partial success which had attended his efforts to unite and pacify the different provinces of the monarchy by the creation of a Reichsrath, Count Schmerling conceived the hope of recovering by an appeal to the nation the ancient primacy of the Hapsburgs, and thrusting the now unpopular Prussia into the background. Accordingly in August, 1863, the Emperor Francis Joseph invited the reigning princes and representatives of the free cities *The Fursten Congress at Frankfort.* to meet him at Frankfort, to discuss a scheme of federal reform which he there propounded, and which, while it increased the power of Austria, appeared to strengthen the cohesion of the Confederation, and to introduce, though

insufficiently, a popular element into its constitution.   All
save one attended ; but that one was the king of Prussia.
He had in the preceding year taken for his prime minister
Otto Edward Leopold, Freiherr of Bismarck-Schönhausen
in the Old Mark of Brandenburg, a man who, having been
Prussian representative in the Federal Diet from 1851 to
1859, had learned by experience the weakness of that body
and its subservience to Austria, and was now becoming impatient to try some speedier, and if necessary more forcible,
method than diplomatic discussion of putting an end to
the existing dead-lock.   At his suggestion, the Prussian
Court refused to have anything to do with the Austrian
scheme, which fell therewith to the ground, and the Diet
was troubled by no change for the rest of its unhonored
life.

Austria, however, would probably have tried to carry
through her project had not another question suddenly
arisen, which turned all thoughts in a different
direction, threw the German powers into new
relations to one another, and became at last the
cause of the dissolution of the Confederation
itself.   In November, 1863, Frederick VII,
king of Denmark, died; and the contest so long foreseen
and delayed between the Danes and the Germans, respecting their rights over Schleswig and Holstein, broke out
with unexpected vehemence.

The Schleswig-Holstein Question.

The Danish constitution of 1855 had incorporated these
two Duchies with Denmark for all purposes, although
Holstein had always been a part of Germany, while Schleswig was by law indissolubly united to Holstein, and
although the inhabitants even of Schleswig were in great
majority of German speech.   The Federal Diet had protested long ago against this constitution as an infraction
of its rights, but it was not till October, 1863, that it
decreed federal execution against Denmark.   When, a few
weeks later, Christian IX succeeded to the throne in virtue

of· the arrangements which Frederick VII had been
empowered to make by the Treaty of London in 1852, no
steps had as yet been taken to give effect to the decree.
But the eyes of Europe were at once turned upon the new
sovereign, whose title was disputed, and when, under the
pressure of the heated populace of Copenhagen, he acceded
to the constitution incorporating the duchies with Denmark, he found himself and his kingdom at once committed
to the struggle. Prince Frederick of Augustenburg*
claimed Schleswig and Holstein, and was supported not
only by a considerable party in both duchies, but by the
general sentiment of the Germans, who saw in his candidature the only chance of saving them from the Danes.
The agitation in Germany soon grew vehement, and that
the faster because the question was one upon which all
parties and sects could unite. The National Union and
Reform Union met, fraternized, and appointed a joint
permanent committee, which issued addresses to the
nation, established Schleswig-Holstein Unions throughout
the country, and promoted the enlistment of bands of vol-
unteers, who hurried to the border. Even the Federal
Diet, though the opposition of Prussia and Austria prevented it from recognizing Frederick as Duke, carried out
(against the will of those powers) the resolution for federal
execution by sending in December, 1863, a body of Saxons
and Hanoverians to occupy Holstein.

Prussia had a difficult game to play, and she played it
with consummate skill. Her ministers were unwilling to
aid the Prince of Augustenburg, both because *Policy of*
she was bound to Denmark as one of the *Prussia.*
signataries of the Treaty of London,†

---

* Prince Frederick had never assented to Frederick VII's arrangements, and contended that he was not barred by his father's renunciation of the rights of the family.

† The Confederation was not bound by the Treaty of London, as it
had never been laid before the Diet. Prussia and Austria were.

and because their views of the future included other contingencies which it would then have been premature to mention. But if hope and the voice of the nation called on them to act, prudence forbade them to act alone. It was essential to carry Austria along with them, not only because the Austrian alliance would be needed if England, France and Russia threatened war, but because she could in this way be made to share the unpopularity which backwardness in the national cause was bringing upon Prussia, and because she was thus alienated from Bavaria, Hanover, and the other states of the second rank, with which her relations had been, especially since the Frankfort Congress, so close and cordial. When the co-operation of Austria had been secured—partly by adroitly playing on her fears of the democratic and almost revolutionary character which the Schleswig-Holstein movement was taking in Germany, partly by her own reluctance to let Prussia gain any advantage by acting alone against Denmark—the Prussian government resolved to take the control of the quarrel out of the hands of the Diet, so as to decide the fate of the two Duchies in the way most favorable to their own plans for the reconstruction of North Germany. Accordingly Prussia and Austria appealed, as they were undoubtedly entitled to do, to certain provisions of the Treaty of London, recognizing the special rights of Schleswig ; and summoned Denmark to withdraw at once the law of November 18, 1863, whereby Schleswig was finally incorporated with the Danish monarchy. When the Danes refused, a strong Prussian and Austrian force *War with* was poured into the Duchies, not without con-*Denmark.* siderable indignation on the part as well of the rest of Germany as of the Prussian liberals, who believed that the object of this invasion was to check the national movement, expel Prince Frederick, and hand over Schleswig to Christian IX. They were soon better informed. Early in 1864 the united army passed the Danewerk, stormed Düppel, overran Jutland, and had the Danish king and people entirely at their mercy. A Conference was summoned in London; but it broke up without effecting anything; and when the Germans resumed hostilities, and it was clear that the expected help from England, Russia or France* would not be forthcoming, Denmark submitted, and by the Treaty of Vienna (October, 1864) ceded Schleswig, Holstein and Lauenburg to the allied powers absolutely. *Cession of Schleswig and Holstein.* Prussia then pushed the Saxons and Hanoverians out of Holstein, and began to strengthen herself and make arrangements for the administration of the territory she occupied ; while Austria, seeing this, began to hesitate, and suspect, and doubt whether her course had been altogether wise. She was soon to be still more cruelly undeceived.

Now that the Danes were forever dispossessed, the question arose—what was to become of the Duchies. Everybody expected the recognition of Prince Frederick of Augustenberg: the Diet was clearly in his favor, and Austria seemed quite willing. *Questions as to their disposal.* Prussia, however, refused to consent. Her

---

* It had been commonly believed that Russia would not aid the Danes on account of her obligations to Prussia during the Polish insurrection; and that Louis Napoleon refused to stir because he was disgusted at the cold reception given to his proposal for a general European Congress not very long before. The inaction of England was attributed on the Continent partly to the personal influence of the Sovereign, partly to the supposed prevalence of " peace at any price " doctrines. But it really was in a large measure due to the fact. that English statesmen and public writers found, when they looked into the matter, that the Danes were substantially in the wrong, though no doubt the hesitation of France, without whose aid it would have been folly to stir, had something to do with the matter.

crown lawyers, to whom the whole matter had been referred,
while not attempting to advocate certain ancient hereditary claims that had been put forward on behalf of the
house of Hohenzollern, pronounced in an elaborate
opinion that the title of Christian IX, was legally prefer-
able to that of Prince Frederick, and that, as his title had
passed by the cession to the two allied powers, the latter
were now entirely free to deal with the ceded territories
as they pleased.   Nevertheless, she professed herself ready
to recognize Frederick as duke upon certain conditions,
which were declared to be essential to the safety of
Prussia on her north-west frontier, as well as to the
protection of Schleswig-Holstein itself against the hostility of Denmark.   These conditions included not only a
strict defensive and offensive alliance of the new principality with Prussia, but an incorporation of its army and fleet
with hers, an absorption of its postal and telegraphic
system, the cession of its fortresses, and, in fact a pretty
complete subjection to her authority in military matters
and in external politics.   These proposals were, as was
expected, rejected by Prince Frederick, trusting to the
support of Austria, and buoyed up by the general
sympathy which his pretensions found not only in the rest
of Germany, but even in the Prussian Chamber, which
still maintained unshaken its opposition to the ˏforeign
policy and schemes of military organization of Herr von
Bismarck's government.   Meanwhile voices began to be
raised in the Duchies foɪ annexation to Prussia ; Austria
grew more and more suspicious ; the relations of the
officials of the two powers established in the conquered
territory became daily less friendly.   Things seemed fast
ripening toward a war, when, on the mediation of
Bavaria and Saxony, the Convention of Gastein was
signed between the rival sovereigns in the autumn of
1865.   By this treaty Schleswig was in the meantime

to be held by Prussia, Holstein by Austria, the question of the ultimate disposal of both duchies being reserved ; while Austria sold her rights over Lauenburg to Prussia for 2,500,000 rix-dollars. This was felt to be a hollow truce, and its hollowness, despite the efforts of the Diet to arrange matters, was soon manifest. The Austrian authorities, knowing that they could not permanently retain Holstein, allowed an agitation to be kept up there on behalf of Prince Frederick. Prussia vehemently protested against this, and required Austria to maintain the *status quo.* Notes of complaint and recrimination were constantly passing between the two powers ;* notes whose tone became always more menacing. Then each accused the other of arming, Austria summoning the Diet to prepare to restrain Prussia, Prussia beginning to shadow forth plans for a reform in the federal constitution. Meanwhile both states were arming fast, and it became clear that the only question was which could first strike a blow, and upon what allies each could rely.† Prussia had secured Italy : Austria managed to carry with her the majority of the great German princes. In the memorable last sittings of the Diet of June 11th and 14th, 1866, Austria's

---

* Austria at one time proposed to let Prussia have Holstein in exchange for part of Silesia: at another she offered to leave the disposal of the Duchies to be determined by the Diet. Prussia refused both propositions, well knowing, as regards the latter, that the decision of the Diet was foregone.

† The immediate cause of the war was the convocation by Austria of the states of Holstein, in order to pronounce on the rights of Prince Frederick. This Prussia declared to be an infraction of the Convention of Gastein; and her troops accordingly crossed the Eider, in order to re-occupy Holstein in virtue of her condominate rights under the treaty of Vienna. Austria withdrew to avoid a collision; and made her final motion in the Diet which brought on the declaration of war.

motion to mobolize the federal contingents, with a view
to execution against Prussia, was supported by Bavaria,
Saxony, Hanover, Würtemberg, Hessen-Cassel, Hessen-
Darmstadt, and several of the minor states, thus giving
her a large majority ; while, for Prussia's counter-propo-
sition for a reform in the constitution of the Confederation, there voted only Luxemburg and four of the
"curiæ," consisting of northern and middle states of the
third rank, seventeen in all out of the thirty-three.   The
partisans of both sides having thus committed themselves,
there was no use in further resisting Austria in the Diet;
so Prussia, having entered her protest against its proceedings, withdrew from the Confederation, declared war upon
Hanover and Saxony on June 16th, upon Austria on June
18th and pushed her armies forward with a speed which
seemed almost to paralyze her opponents.

The great military events of 1866 and 1870 are too
fresh in our memories to make it necessary to recount
them here ; nor is it worth while to inquire who was
technically in the right in the dispute which had arisen
between Austria and Prussia relative to the administration
of the duchies and the interpretation of the Convention
of Gastein.   Ever since Frederick the Great's time, it had
been plain that the rivalry of the two great monarchies
was an insuperable obstacle to the unity of the nation.
It was no less plain to the resolute and clear-sighted minister who ruled at Berlin that this rivalry could be put an
end to by the sword alone; and the question that remains,
whether the importance of the object to be attained justified an appeal to force, with all its attendant miseries, is
one which men will answer according to their estimate of
the moral and political value of that object.   Fortunately
the military superiority of Prussia, and her alliance with
Italy, made the struggle far shorter than onlookers in the
rest of Europe had expected; and the victors had the good

sense to be content with something short of the complete fulfillment of their designs. For the Pre- *The Peace* liminaries of Nikolsburg and Peace of Prague, *of Prague.* though they followed one of the most decisive victories of modern times, had nevertheless only half solved the problem that lay before Germany, and established a system which to patriotic eyes might well seem unsatisfactory. It is true that Austria was thereby excluded from the Germanic body, and the ground left free for Prussia to form a new Confederation, in which she should be dominant, and which the court of Vienna undertook to recognize. But with Austria went her German population of seven millions, filling the vast territories of Upper and Lower Austria, Tyrol, Styria and part of Bohemia—districts which had during many centuries formed a part of the old Empire. The new league, moreover, at whose head Prussia placed herself, included only the states north of the river Main, and thus, if it drew closer than before the bonds between those states, drew also a more marked distinction than heretofore between the two halves of the country, leaving the great principalities of Bavaria, Würtemburg and Baden in a much more complete isolation. Germany, in fact, might appear to have purchased the completer unity of her northern peoples by the sacrifice of her unity as a whole. It had been stipulated in the Treaty of Prague that the South German States should be at liberty to enter into a separate league of their own ; and the French government doubtless hoped that now, when the scheme of a North German federation, broached in 1806, had been at length carried out, Napoleon's Confederation of the Rhine, under the protectorate of France, would reappear in the South as a counterpoise to Prussia's power. Very different was the turn which events took. Within a few months after the war of 1866, Bavaria, Würtemburg and Baden—induced, it was supposed, by

their desire to be admitted to the new Zollverein which
Prussia was forming—entered into military treaties with
the North German Confederation, whereby they bound
themselves to unite their armies to its army, in the event
of any attack on Germany by a foreign power.

The North German Confederation. Meanwhile the constitution of the North German Confederation, although it left a nominal
independence to the minor princes, permitting
them to send and receive diplomatic agents to
and from other courts, levy local taxes, and summon their
local legislative bodies as heretofore, effected a fusion of
their military forces, which were placed under the command of the king of Prussia; vested in him, as president,
the conduct of the foreign policy of the Confederation,
and the right of making war and peace (this last with the
consent of the federal parliament), and transferred to the
control of the federal parliament, over which the king
presided through his nominee, the federal chancellor, all
legislation upon a variety of important topics, including
the taxation for federal objects, and the control of the
currency and the postal and telegraphic system. Prussia
at the same time not only increased but consolidated her
dominions by annexing the extensive territories of Schleswig-Holstein, Hanover, Hessen-Cassel, Nassau and the
free city of Frankfort. There was thus formed what was
substantially, if not nominally, a single or united rather
than a federal state. And although much that was anomalous and incomplete might be remarked in its constitution, as could hardly fail to be the case where one member
had twenty-four millions of population and the remaining
twenty-one only five millions among them all, it had the
advantage of trying the experiment of union where it was
easiest, among the comparatively homogenous North German States. It formed a cohesive nucleus, all the more
cohesive that it was comparatively small ; and by accus-

toming the citizens of different principalities to act together in a common assembly, the North German Parliament, it gave them a feeling of common citizenship, which mitigated such discontent as might have been produced by the loss of local independence.

Temporary, however, as the organization of the North German Confederation evidently was, no one predicted for it a life of four years only, nor would most people have expected its development into a grander and more comprehensive union to be the work of its bitterest enemy. The alarm of France at the revelation and the increase of Prussia's military power by the *Attitude of the French* campaigns of 1866, was heightened by the *Empire.* publication of the secret treaties with the South German States. Peace was with difficulty preserved when the question of the cession of Luxemburg arose; and from that time, at least, both countries felt that there existed only a truce full of suspicion between them. France seems to have been hurried into speedier action by the belief that the military treaties had been extorted from the South German powers, and that there was serious disaffection among the inhabitants of the newly annexed districts, which ought to be taken advantage of as soon as possible. But men were astonished, and our astonishment is hardly lessened by what we have since learned, that her ruler and his counsellors should have fired the train so suddenly, and should with a sort of judicial blindness, have chosen the most frivolous of pretexts, and done their best to make the war they declared against Prussia with so light a heart, a national war, in which all Germany felt its interests and feelings involved. This it at once became. *The War* Seldom had such a national rising been seen— *with France,* so swift, so universal, so enthusiastic, sweep- *1870-71,* ing away in a moment the heart-burnings of liberals and feudals in Prussia, the jealousies of North and

South Germans, of Protestants and Catholics.   Every citizen, every soldier, felt that this struggle was a struggle for the greatness and freedom of the nation; and the unbroken career of victory which carried the German arms over the east and center of France, and placed them at last triumphant in the capital of their foes, proved, in the truest sense, what strength there is in a righteous cause.   For it was, even more than the admirable organization of their armies, the skill of their generals, the corruption and weakness of the Bonapartist court—it was the passionate ardor of the whole German péopie, who felt that at last a crisis had come when every motive called on them to put forth their utmost efforts, when the cause of patriotism and the cause of justice were absolutely the same, that gave them that courage and devotion, that self-control even in the moment of victory, to which European history scarcely supplies a parallel.

Never before for centuries, nor even in the War of Liberation of 1814, had the whole people felt and acted so completely as one.   All saw that the time had now come to give this practically realized unity its formal political expression ; nor was there a doubt as to what that form should be.   The imperial name under which Germany had won her first glories in the great days of the middle ages, was that to which the sentiment of the nation turned; and it had the advantage of sparing the susceptibilities of the sovereigns whose loyal adherence to the national cause had given them a better claim on the regard of their subjects, than most of them had before possessed.   By a strange caprice of fate, it was in a hall of the palace at Versailles, which the archenemy of Germany had reared, that the first of the German potentates offered to the king of Prussia, in the name of princes and peoples, that imperial crown which his brother had refused in 1849.   On the 31st of December, 1870, sixty-four years after the dissolution of the old Empire, Germany became again a single state in the eyes of Europe.

The constitution of the new Empire is in its main features that of the North German Confederation, modified by the treaties whereby Baden, Würtemberg and Bavaria, respectively, entered the pre-existing body. Each of these states obtained its due representation in the federal council and federal assembly, and each reserved for itself certain powers or immunities beyond those enjoyed by the North German States ; Bavaria, in particular, retaining a control over her army, her postal, railway and telegraphic system, and her general legislation, which leaves her in a position of great comparative independence. It would, therefore, be a serious error to regard the work of unification as complete, or the Germanic Empire as a centralized state.* It is rather to be considered a very peculiar federation, which, as respects the North German members, is a strict one, conceding to them few and unimportant state rights ; but, as regards the two greatest, Bavaria and Würtemberg, is extremely loose, amounting to little more than a close defensive and offensive military alliance, with a joint foreign policy, a common commercial system, and a common legislation on a few topics. How far such a constitution can be smoothly worked, is a problem on which experience alone can throw light. For it cannot be supposed that the same unity of sentiment which displayed itself at a moment of excitement in the presence of a powerful enemy, will necessarily continue to exist in more peaceful times, or under the rule of less able

Constitution of the new German Empire.

---

* The character of the Empire as a State, and not a mere federation, is perhaps most clearly seen in the position assigned to Alsace and the ceded parts of Lorraine as " Reichsländer," territories forming a part of the Empire but not of any one of the States which compose it, and governed immediately by the central imperial administration.

and patriotic ministers. Not only the existence of separate Courts, where a long-descended prince is surrounded
by a dignified nobility, but also the differences of character, habits, historical associations, and religion among the
various German races, place difficulties in the way of a
complete national union, which long years will be needed
to remove. It is hard to estimate the power of these cen-
trifugal forces, as compared with those opposite ones
which the habit of joint political action will create; but it
is at any rate clear that the process of fusion must be a
slow one. Outside, moreover, of this new organization,
there still remain the seven millions of German-speaking
subjects of Austria, of whose reunion to the German state
there is no immediate prospect, and whose admission at
present would make the problem of welding the nation
completely together even more difficult than it now is.

Observers in other countries are hardly less liable to fall
into the opposite error of misunderstanding the nature of
the great political change of the last eight
Causes of   years, of supposing it to be more sudden and
the progress more accidental, so to speak, than it really is,
of Germany
toward   and to be mainly due to the forcible means em-
unity.   ployed by the present Chancellor of the Empire. The truth rather is, that here, as in
many similar instances which might be quoted, there had
been, as years rolled on, a constant ripening toward change
and a growing feeling for unity, although the strength of
this feeling was not revealed till the moment came which
gave it a field for vigorous action. First evoked by the great
struggle of the War of Liberation, it has been slowly developed and directed by a variety of concurrent forces ;
partly by that desire for political freedom and equal civil
rights which found its nearest enemy in the tyranny of
many of the petty princes ; partly by the decline, so evident through all Europe, of the ancient sentiment of per-

sonal loyalty, and the substitution therefor of a rational conception of the nature of government and the power of the popular will; partly by the better knowledge of their brethren which increased facilities of communication gave to every division of the German race ; but most of all by what we call the feeling or passion of nationality, the desire of a people already conscious of a moral and social unity, to see such unity expressed and realized under a single government, which shall give it a place and name among civilized states. The most powerful factors in the creation of this national spirit, were the brilliant literary activity of Germany since the days of Lessing, and the awakened interest and pride of the people in their earlier history, which was one of the first fruits of that literary revival. Causes not dissimilar were at work in Italy, though there the actual oppression of foreign rulers made the sentiment more passionate. And it need not be doubted that the example of the efforts which Italy, Hungary, and Poland, not to speak of smaller peoples, were making to attain or reconquer national political life, had its influence upon the Germans, however little sympathy those efforts may have found among them.

Time, and the long labors of many noble hearts addressing their countrymen through the press and in the Universities, were needed to mature this feeling of moral, to strengthen this passion for political unity, to make it familiar and dear to the mass of the people, to give it a hold upon their imagination. It was not wonderful that in looking on the apathy of their fellow-citizens and the selfishness of their princes, these great men should sometimes have despaired of success. And even when the feeling had been created and the occasion came which displayed its strength, it might have failed to fulfill its work, had not the power to use and guide it been lodged in the hands of a forceful and keen-sighted practical statesman.

It was with Germany even as with Italy, where the work of Gioberti, Manin, Mazzini and their brethren, might have remained unfinished but for Cavour. And, as in Italy, the work was not carried through in the way or by the means which the first laborers had for the most part intended or desired. The creation of a state

Nature of the process in Germany and Italy.

de novo on ground cleared of all the existing principalities, a state which, even if in form a monarchy (though most would have preferred a republic) should be based on the recognition of popular rights, was what the ideal politicians of both countries had looked forward to. But in both it was by the advance of an existing state, which extended itself to include wider and wider territories, and gave to them its organization, that the unity of the nation was brought about. And this was done with little or no change in the internal constitution of the growing kingdom, little or no movement toward a resettlement of society on democratic foundations. In the constitution of the North German Confederation and the new German Empire, there is no mention and little indirect recognition of those "Fundamental Rights of the German people," on which the Frankfort Parliament of 1848–49 spent so much precious time and toil.

Too much has perhaps been said of late years about Prussia's mission. Neither in the words or acts of her great Frederick (nor indeed in those of his

"Prussia's mission:" real character of her policy.

predecessors) is there a trace of what may be called Pan-Teutonic patriotism, of any enthusiasm for the greatness and happiness of Germany as a whole. His purpose is to build up a strong and well-administered Prussian kingdom: for his German neighbors he has no more regard than for Frenchmen or Swedes; for the German language and literature little but contempt. The policy of his three successors was distinctly Prussian rather than German; and the romantic Frederick William IV disappointed the hopes of the nation almost as grievously in 1849 as Frederick William III had done thirty-five years before. No European court has been more consistently practical than that of Berlin; nor any apparently less conscious of a magnificent national vocation. Her rulers have eshewed sentimental considerations themselves, and have seldom tried to awaken them in the minds of the people, or to turn them to account where they existed. When their interests coincided with those of Germany at large, it was well: but they were not accustomed to proclaim themselves her champions, or the apostles of her national regeneration. Nevertheless it had for a long time been evident that if a political regeneration was to be brought about by force, it was from Prussia alone of the existing principalities that anything could be hoped, since she alone united the character, the traditions, and the material power that were needed to lead the country. Ever since the Reformation the Hapsburg princes and their policy has been regarded with aversion by the more intelligent and progressive part of the nation ; while Prussia, recognized from the days of the Great Elector as the leading Protestant power, naturally became the representative of intellectual liberality and enlightenment. In recent times she had, by the *Causes of her success.* foundation and wise encouragement of the two great universities of Berlin and Bonn, conferred eminent benefits on German learning and science, and gained a corresponding hold upon the respect of the educated classes. If her people were in some respects less richly gifted than those of the middle and southern states, she yet possessed a practical energy and decision in which they were sometimes deficient; she acted while they speculated and waited. She had given the

first example in Germany of a well-governed modern
state, compact, effective, full of life ; and in creating it
she was really rendering the greatest possible service to
the German people. For this state being a strong
reality, which had stood the test of adversity and been
matured by experience, whose well knit administrative
organization commanded the respect, if not always the
affection, of its subjects, was found able to expand
itself, so as to embrace the other populations and territories which from time to time were added to it. And
it expanded, not only, as Austria had done in earlier
centuries, toward the east, among peoples alien in blood
and speech, who remained unfriendly to the original
German nucleus, but also and chiefly westward, or at
least over districts whose inhabitants, being themselves
Germans, were rapidly fused and became not less
patriotically-minded than those of the Mark of Brandenburg itself. After the fall of Napoleon it acquired and
soon assimilated the superb Rhenish and Westphalian
provinces : in 1866 it was enlarged by other territories
hardly less important, while at the same time its military,
and to a great extent its financial system, were applied to
Saxony, Mecklenburg, and the minor North German
principalities. Thus the enormous difficulty of creating
a state *de novo* was avoided by the extension of the
existing state ; and if Germany, as the more idealistic
school of politicians complain, has been in this way
turned into a larger Prussia, the practical school may ask
whether this result (if the matter be more than a question
of names) is not one that may be acquiesced in when
the object of national aspiration has been substantially
attained. Moreover, if Germany is Prussianized, so will
Prussia be in the same process Germanized by the infusion
or addition of the South German races.

Looking therefore to the form which the political reconstruction of Germany has taken, this reconstruction may fairly be said to be Prussia's work. But that work could never have been accomplished without the efforts of those very "sentimental" or "romantic" politicians who found themselves first persecuted as agitators, and then pushed aside when the moment for action came. For it was they who prepared the feelings of the nation for this revolution, and who raised to the height of a great national movement, justified by the popular will, what would otherwise have been a career of violent, self-aggrandizement. It was with Germany as with Italy, where the work of Cavour could never have been accomplished without the previous labors of the greater and loftier Mazzini.

The question which has often been asked of late, How far this new Empire is the lawful successor or representative of the Empire which expired in 1806, need not, after what has been said in earlier *Relation of the new German Empire to the Holy Roman Empire.* chapters, receive here more than a passing mention. For it will be remembered that the Holy Roman Empire of the German nation, the creation of Otto the Great, was formed by the union (which eventually became a fusion) in one person of two quite distinct political entities, the German kingdom, which was then passing from primitive tribe-chieftainship into a feudal monarchy, and the Roman Empire with its claims of universal autocratic sway, expressing on its historical side in traditional reverence for the name of Rome, and on its theological the idea of the unity of all Christians in a visible state and church. In the new Empire there is no such union: it represents one only of those two elements, the German kingdom which Otto received from his father before his fatal journey to Rome. It has put away, let us hope forever, the dream of dominion over peoples of a different blood and speech, for it is based upon, has indeed been created in virtue of, that very principle of nationality to which the theory of the Holy Empire was most conspicuously opposed.

The imperial name has indeed been revived, both on account of its venerable associations and because it best seems to express the titular superiority of the head of the state over the kings and grand dukes whose dominions compose its body. But the idea of an Emperor of a district, be it great or small, was wholly repugnant to mediæval doctrine, which could imagine one Emperor only, lord of all Christians, just as it could recognize only one Pope. And it is, perhaps, some lingering respect for this feeling that has caused the official style of the present sovereign to be " German Emperor," that is, " Emperor in Germany," instead of " Emperor of Germany."

It is therefore in strictness not to Otto the Great and his long line of successors down to Francis II that the Emperor William succeeds, but to the German kings Conrad I and Henry the Fowler, that Henry the Fowler who in one of his expeditions against the Wendish heathen stormed their · fort of Brannibor, and founded there, to guard the northeastern frontier, that Mark of Brandenburg which has grown into the Prussian monarchy. The power of the modern sovereign is indeed of a very different nature from that of those remote predecessors, far more effective in his patrimonial lands than Henry's was in Saxony; far more limited over Bavaria than was that of the Frankish and Saxon princes, even in the days of Duke Arnulf the Wicked. This loose and anomalous federal constitution is the heritage of the old Empire, which in endeavoring to win for the Emperor a commanding European international position, allowed kings and princes to spring up beside him in Germany, and wrest from him nearly all the domestic power which had once been his. But if in this the influence of that great shadow of the past be thought pernicious, it ought not the less to be remembered, that to it is in great measure due this last renewal of national life. It is the tradition of a glorious unity, in the days when Germany led the world, that has made Germany again the central power of continental Europe, and the arbiter of its destinies.

The parallelism between the course of events in Germany and in Italy which has several times already been referred to, appears most strikingly in the events of 1870. As it was by the war of 1866, which, in putting an end to the long dualism of Austria and Prussia, made a united Germany possible, that Italy recovered her Venetian provinces, so it was the war of 1870 that, even while it re-established the Germanic Empire, completed the unity of Italy by making Rome again her possession and her capital. The Popedom which, in the twelfth and thirteenth centuries inflicted a fatal wound upon the Holy Empire, had in modern times allied itself with Austria and the petty despotisms of the peninsula, had done its utmost to check as well the union as the freedom of the Italian people, and had raised those pretensions to a temporal sway which had been one chief cause of its hostility to the mediæval Emperors almost to the rank of an article of faith. It now found itself involved in the fall of its ancient ally France, and saw that temporal dominion perish with the triumph of its ancient Teutonic enemies. The first German victories compelled the recall of the French troops from Rome, and allowed the Italians to establish themselves there ; a few months later the swelling current of success brought about the union of North and South Germany in a single state. The same great struggle which restored political unity to the one nation completed it in the other; and at the very moment when the imperial name was revived in the Transalpine countries, the ancient imperial seat upon the Tiber

National unity in Italy and Germany.

became the capital of an Italian monarchy. The two great races whose national life had been sacrificed to the mediæval Empire regain it together, and regain it by the defeat of that Empire's old antagonists, the ecclesiastical power and the French monarchy. The triumph of the principle of nationality is complete; the old wrongs are redressed; the old problems solved: we seem to have closed one great page in the world's history, and pause to wonder and conjecture what the next may have to unfold. No one who has looked below the surface of the events that have passed in Europe during the last thirty years can have failed to be struck by the rapidity and completeness of the changes those years have witnessed, and by the new aspect which political thought, as well as practical politics, has taken. Through western and central Europe the small states have disappeared, and the great states have reached their natural boundaries of race and language. Free and even comparatively democratic constitutions have been established in many; and where this has not been the case, the rights of the subject have yet been in theory substantially admitted. It is now the passions and interests of peoples rather than of princes that are the potent factors in politics. The divine right of kings and aristocracies, the authority of the state to control the individual conscience or enforce religious conformity, find scarcely a defender : the principles of the Holy Alliance seem to lie centuries behind. Meanwhile other questions, other difficulties, begin to thicken upon us, as on a stormy day a new mass of clouds rises from the darkening west before the last one has been scattered into the blue or swept beneath the opposite horizon. One of these problems, an old one indeed in a new form—that which respects the attitude of an infallible church under an infallible head to the temporal government — the German state has already been called on to confront: others of an economical rather a purely political character threaten the stability of society there as they have long done in France. The foundation of kingdoms on a national basis does not seem to have made the contagion of social disturbances less dangerous ; nor need Germany think that with the restoration of the Empire there has begun for her, any more than for the rest of Europe, an era of peace, ease and happiness. Yet there is reason to trust that that spirit of patriotism and self-control which lately shown forth on so great a theater and with such splendid results, will enable the German people to succeed, not only in perfecting the internal unity of their state and developing the popular element in its constitution, but also in overcoming the more serious perils which threaten it, like the other great industrial communities of the world, from the mutual jealousies and conflicting interests of different classes in society. To have created a great military state is much, yet it is only a small part of the task which lies before the civilized nations of the present.

APPENDIX.

NOTE A.

ON THE BURGUNDIES.

IT would be hard to mention any geographical name which, by its application at different times to different districts, has caused, and continues to cause, more confusion than this name Burgundy. There may, therefore, be some use in a brief statement of the more important of those applications. Without going into the minutiæ of the subject, the following may be given as the ten senses in which the name is most frequently to be met with:

I. The kingdom of the Burgundian (*regnum Burgundionum*) founded A.D. 406, occupying the whole valley of the Saone and lower Rhone, from Dijon to the Mediterranean, and including also the western half of Switzerland. It was destroyed by the sons of Clovis in A.D. 534.

II. The kingdom of Burgundy (*regnum Burgundiæ*), mentioned occasionally under the Merovingian kings as a separate principality, confined within boundaries apparently somewhat narrower than those of the older kingdom last named.

III. The kingdom of Provence or Burgundy (*regnum Provinciæ seu Burgundiæ*)—also, though less accurately, called the kingdom of Cis-Jurane Burgundy—was founded by Boso in A.D. 879, and included Province, Dauphiné, the southern part of Savoy, and the country between the Saone and the Jura.

IV. The kingdom of Trans-Jurane Burgundy (*regnum Iureuse, Burgundia Transiurensis*), founded by Rudolf in A.D. 888, recognized in the same year by the Emperor Arnulf, included the northern part of Savoy, and all Switzerland between the Reuss and the Jura.

V. The kingdom of Burgundy or Arles (*regnum Burgundiæ, regnum Arelatense*), formed by the union, under Conrad the Pacific, in A.D. 937, of the kingdoms described above as III and IV. On the death, in 1032, of the last independent king, Rudolf III, it came partly by bequest, partly by conquest, into the hands of the Emperor Conrad II (the Salic), and thenceforward formed a part of the Empire. In the thirteenth century, France began to absorb it, bit by bit, and has now (since the annexation of Savoy in 1861) acquired all except the Swiss portion.

VI. The Lesser Duchy (*Burgundia Minor*), (Klein Burgund), corresponded very nearly with what is now Switzerland west of the Reuss, including the Valais. It was Trans-Jurane Burgundy (IV) *minus* the parts of Savoy which had belonged to that kingdom. It disappears from history after the extinction of the house of Zahringen in the thirteenth century. Legally it was part of the Empire till A.D. 1648, though practically independent long before that date.

VII. The Free County or Palatinate of Burgundy (Franche-Comté), (Freigrafschaft), (called also Upper Burgundy), to which the name of Cis-Jurane Burgundy originally and properly belonged, lay between the Saone and the Jura. It formed a part of III and V, and was therefore a fief of the Empire. The French dukes of Burgundy were invested with it in A.D. 1384. Its capital, the imperial city of Besancon, was given to Spain in 1651, and by the treaties of Nimwegen, 1678-9, it was ceded to the crown of France.

VIII. The Landgraviate of Burgundy (Landgrafschaft) lay in what is now Western Switzerland, on both sides of the Aar, between Thun and Solothurn. It was a part of the Lesser Duchy (VI), and, like it, is hardly mentioned after the thirteenth century.

IX. The circle of Burgundy (Kreis Burgund), an administrative division of the Empire, was established by Charles V in 1548; and included the Free County of Burgundy (VII) and the seventeen provinces of the Netherlands, which Charles inherited from his grandmother Mary, daughter of Charles the Bold.

X. The Duchy of Burgundy (Lower Burgundy) (Bourgogne), the most northerly part of the old kingdom of the Burgundians, was always a fief of the crown of France, and a province of France till the Revolution. It was of this Burgundy that Philip the Good and Charles the Bold were Dukes. They were also Counts of the Free County (VII).

There was very nearly being an eleventh Burgundy. In 1784 Joseph II proposed to the Elector of Bavaria to give him the Austrian Netherlands, except the citadels of Luxemburg and Limburg, with the title of King of Burgundy, in exchange for his Bavarian dominions, which Joseph was anxious to get hold of. The Elector consented, France (bribed by the offer of Luxemburg and Limburg) and Russia approved, and the project was only baffled by the promptitude of Frederick the Great in forming the League of Princes to preserve the integrity of German territories.

The most copious and accurate information regarding the obscure history of the Burgundian kingdoms (III, IV and V) is to be found in the contributions of Baron Frederic de Gingins la Saraz, a Vaudois historian, to the *Archiv für Schweizer Geschichte*. See also an Essay entitled *The Franks and the Gauls* in Mr. E. A. Freeman's *Historical Essays*.

NOTE B.

ON THE RELATIONS TO THE EMPIRE OF THE KINGDOM
OF DENMARK, AND THE DUCHIES OF SCHLESWIG AND
HOLSTEIN.

THE history of the relations of Denmark and the
Duchies to the Romano-Germanic Empire is a very small
part of the great Schleswig-Holstein controversy. But
having been unnecessarily mixed up with two questions
properly quite distinct—the first, as to the relation of
Schleswig to Holstein, and of both jointly to the Danish
crown; the second, as to the diplomatic engagements which
the Danish kings have in recent times contracted with the
German powers—it has borne its part in making the whole
question the most intricate and interminable that has
vexed Europe for two centuries and a half. Setting aside
irrelevant matter, the facts as to the Empire are as follows:

I. The Danish kings began to own the supremacy of
the Frankish Emperors early in the ninth century. Having
recovered their independence in the confusion that followed
the fall of the Carolingian dynasty, they were again subdued by Henry the Fowler and Otto the Great, and continued tolerably submissive till the death of Frederick II
and the period of anarchy which followed. Since that
time Denmark has always been independent, although her
king was, until the treaty of A.D. 1865, a member of the
German Confederation as duke of Holstein and Lauenburg.

II. Schleswig was in Carolingian times Danish; the
Eyder being, as Eginhard tells us, the boundary between
Saxonia Transalbiana (Holstein), and the Terra Nortman
norum (wherein lay the town of Sliesthorp), inhabited
by the Scandinavian heathen. Otto the Great conquered
all Schleswig, and, it is said, Jutland also, and added the

southern part of Schleswig to the immediate territory of
the Empire, erecting it into a .margraviate. So it remained till the days of Conrad II, who made the Eyder
again the boundary, retaining of course his suzerainty over
the kingdom of Denmark as a whole. But by this time
the colonization of Schleswig by the Germans had begun :
and ever since the numbers of the Danish population
seem to have steadily declined, and the mass of the people
to have grown more and more disposed to sympathize with
their southern rather than their northern neighbors.

III. Holstein always was an integral part of the Empire,
as it was afterward of the Germanic Confederation and is
now of the new German Empire.

NOTE C.

ON CERTAIN IMPERIAL TITLES AND CEREMONIES.

THIS subject is a great deal too wide and too intricate to
be more than touched upon here. But a few brief state-
ments may have their use; for the practice of the Germanic
Emperors varied so greatly from time to time, that the
reader becomes hopelessly perplexed without some clue.
And if there were space to explain the causes of each
change of title, it would be seen that the subject, dry as it
may appear, is very far from being a barren or a dull one.

I. TITLES OF EMPERORS.

Charles the Great styled himself " Carolus serenissimus
Augustus, a Deo coronatus, magnus et pacificus imperator, Romanum (*or* Romanorum) gubernans imperium, qui
et per misericordiam Dei rex Francorum et Langobardorum."

Subsequent Carolingian Emperors were usually entitled

simply "Imperator Augustus." Sometimes "rex Francorum et Langobardorum" was added.*

Conrad I and Henry I (the Fowler) were only German
kings.

A Saxon Emperor was, before his coronation at Rome,
"rex," or "rex Francorium Orientalium," or "Francorum
atque Saxonum rex;" after it, simply "Imperator Augustus." Otto III is usually said to have introduced the form
"Romanorum Imperator Augustus," but some authorities
state that it occurs in documents of the time of Lewis I.

Henry II and his successors, not daring to take the title
of Emperor till crowned at Rome (in conformity with the
superstitious notion which had begun with Charles the
Bald), but anxious to claim the sovereignty of Rome, as
indissolubly attached to the German crown, began to call
themselves "reges Romanorum." The title did not, however, become common or regular till the time of Henry IV,
in whose proclamations (issued before his Roman coronation) it occurs constantly.

From the eleventh century till the sixteenth, the invariable practice was for the monarch to be called "Romanorum rex semper Augustus," till his coronation at Rome
by the Pope; after it, "Romanorum Imperator semper
Augustus."

In A.D. 1508, Maximilian I, being refused a passage to
Rome by the Venetians, obtained a bull from Pope Julius
II permitting him to call himself "Imperator electus"
(erwählter Kaiser). This title Ferdinand I (brother of
Charles V) and all succeeding Emperors took immediately
upon their German coronation, and it was till A.D. 1806
their strict legal designation, † and was always employed

---

* Waitz (*Deutsche Verfassungsgeschichte*) says that the phrase
"semper Augustus" may be found in the times of the Carolingians,
but in no official documents.

† There is some reason to think that toward the end of the Empire

by them in proclamations or other official documents. The term " elect " was however omitted even in formal documents when the sovereign was addressed or spoken of in the third person; and in ordinary practice he was simply " Roman Emperor."

Maximilian added the title " Germaniæ rex," which had never been known before, although the phrase " rex Ger- manorum " may be found employed once or twice in early times. " Rex Teutonicorum," " regnum Teutonicum,"* occur often in the tenth and eleven centuries. A great many titles of less consequence were added from time to time. Charles V had seventy-five, not, of course, as Emperor, but in virtue of his vast hereditary possessions.†

---

people had begun to fancy that " erwählter" did not mean " elect," but "elective." Cf. note, p. 358.

* These expressions seem to have been intended to distinguish the kingdom of the Eastern or Germanic Franks from that of the Western or Gallicized Franks (Francigenæ), which having been for some time " regnum Francorum Occidentalium," grew at last to be simply " regnum Franciæ," the East Frankish kingdom being swallowed up in the Empire. It is not very easy to say precisely when the name " Francia " came to denote, to Europe generally, what we now call France. Leopold of Bamberg, in the fourteenth century, complains of it, as then a fixed use. In the thirteenth century Snorri Sturlason speaks of Otto the Great as collecting an army from " Saxonland, Frakland, Friesland and Vendland," apparently denoting by Frak- land the old Frankish country (*F. orientalis*) *Heimskringla, Olafs Saga Tryggvasonar*). In England the name had no doubt changed its meaning sometime earlier.

† It is right to remark that what is stated here can be taken as only generally and probably true : so great are the discrepancies among even the most careful writers on the subject, and so numerous the forgeries of a later age, which are to be found among the genuine documents of the early Empire. Goldast's *Collections*, for instance, are full of forgeries and anachronisms. Detailed information may be found in Pfeffinger, Moser and Pütter, and in the host of writers to whom they refer.

It is perhaps worth remarking that the word "Emperor" has not at all the same meaning now that it had even so lately as two centuries ago. It is now a commonplace, not to say vulgar, title, somewhat more pompous than that of King, and supposed to belong especially to despots. It is given to all sorts of barbarous princes, like those of China and Abyssinia, in default of a better name. It is peculiarly affected by new dynasties; and has indeed grown so fashionable, that what with Emperors of Brazil, of Hayti and of Mexico, the good old title of King seems in a fair way to become obsolete.* But in former times there was, and could be but one Emperor; he was always mentioned with a certain reverence: his name summoned up a host of thoughts and associations, which we cannot comprehend or sympathize with. His office, unlike that of modern Emperors, was by his very nature elective and not hereditary; and, so far from resting on conquest or the will of the people, rested on and represented pure legality. War could give him nothing which law had not given him already: the people could delegate no power to him who was their lord and the viceroy of God.

II. The Crowns.

Of the four crowns something has been said in the text. They were those of Germany, taken at Aachen in earlier times, latterly at Frankfort, once or twice at Regensburg ; of Burgundy, at Arles ; of Italy, sometimes at Pavia, more usually at Milan or Monza ; of the world, at Rome.

The German crown was taken by every Emperor after the time of Otto the Great ; that of Italy by every one,

---

* We in England may be thought to have made some slight movement in the same direction, by calling the united great council of the Three Kingdoms the Imperial Parliament.

or almost every one, who took the Roman down to
Frederick III, but by none after him ; that of Burgundy,
it would appear, by four Emperors only, Conrad II, Henry
III, Frederick I, and Charles IV. The imperial crown
was received at Rome by most Emperors till Frederick
III ; after him by none save Charles V, who obtained
both it and the Italian at Bologna in a somewhat informal
manner. From Ferdinand I onward the Emperor bound
himself by his capitulation, " sich zum besten befleissigen
zu wollen die kayserliche Cron auch in ziemlich gelegener
Zeit zum schiersten zu erlangen." At the Diet of Ratisbon
in 1653 (when Ferdinand archduke of Austria was chosen
king of the Romans) the Protestants protested against
this article ; but the Emperor, appealing to the Golden
Bull, insisted on its retention. In the capitulation of
Leopold I, however, and his successors down to Francis
II, the article was modified so as to bind the new sovereign
" die Römische-Königliche Cron forderlichst zu empfan-
gen, und alles dasjenige dabey zu thun so sich derenthal,
ben gebühret."

It should be remembered that none of these inferior
crowns were necessarily connected with that of the Roman
Empire, which might have been held by a simple knight
without a foot of land in the world. For as there had
been Emperors (Lothar I, Lewis II, Lewis of Provence,
son of Boso, Guy, Lambert, and Berengar) who were
not kings of Germany, so there were several (all those
who preceded Conrad II) who were not kings of Burgundy, and others (Arnulf for example), who were not
kings of Italy. And it is also worth remarking, that
although no crown save the German was assumed by
the successors of Charles V, their wider rights remained
in full force, and were never subsequently relinquished.
There was nothing, except the practical difficulty and

absurdity of such a project, to prevent Francis II from having himself crowned at Arles,* Milan, and Rome.

III. The King of the Romans (Römischer König).

It has been shown above how and why, about the time of Henry II, the German monarch began to entitle himself "Romanorum rex." Now it was not uncommon in the Middle Ages for the heir-apparent to a throne to be crowned during his father's lifetime, that at the death of the latter he might step at once into his place. (Coronation, it must be remembered, which is now merely a spectacle, was in those days not only a sort of a sacrament, but a matter of great political importance.) This plan was specially useful in an elective monarchy, such as Germany was after the twelfth century, for it avoided the delays and dangers of an election while the throne was vacant. But it seemed against the order of nature to have two Emperors at once,† and as the sovereign's authority in Germany depended not on the Roman but on the German coronation, the practice came to be that each Emperor during his own life procured, if he could, the election of his successor, who was crowned at Aachen, in later times at Frankfort, and took the title of "King of the Romans." During the presence of the Emperor in Germany he exercised no more authority than a Prince of

---

* Although to be sure the Burgundian dominions had all passed from the Emperor to France, the kingdom of Sardinia, and the Swiss Confederation.

† Nevertheless, Otto II was crowned Emperor, and reigned for some time along with his father, under the title of "Co-Imperator." So Lothar I was associated in the Empire with Lewis the Pious, as Lewis himself had been crowned in the lifetime of Charles. Many analogies to the practice of the Romano-Germanic Empire in this respect might be abduced from the history of the old Roman, as well as of the Byzantine Empire.

Wales does in England, but on the Emperor's death he succeeded at once, without any second election or coronation, and assumed (after the time of Ferdinand I) the title of " Emperor Elect,"* Before Ferdinand's time, he would have been expected to go to Rome to be crowned there. While the Hapsburgs held the scepter, each monarch generally contrived in this way to have his son or some other near relative chosen to succeed him. But many were foiled in their attempts to do so ; and, in such cases, an election was held after the Emperor's death, according to the rules laid down in the Golden Bull.

The first person who thus became king of the Romans in the lifetime of an Emperor seems to have been Henry VI, son of Frederick I.

It was in imitation of this title that Napoleon called his son king of Rome.

A few weeks ago (May, 1876) the Royal Titles Bill gave rise to much discussion in England respecting the meaning of the name of Emperor, particularly whether or no it implies a superiority to kings. Although the subject has been referred to in the text, it may be worth while to repeat here that beyond all doubt the title of Emperor was, during the Dark and Middle Ages, not only superior to that of King, but involved the conception of a sovereignty over kings, and a power of creating them (see p. 246 and note). For there was then, and could be (according to the received theory), only one Emperor, God's temporal vice-regent, of whom kings were no more than local deputies or officers. These notions vanished in the sixteenth century, but the idea of the Emperor's primacy survived till 1806, although latterly various devices were resorted to to avoid the admission of it at diplo-

---

* Maximilian had obtained this title, " Emperor Elect," from the Pope. Ferdinand took it as of right, and his successors followed the example.

matic gatherings.   It was doubtless because they thought
it more imposing that the Czar of Muscovy, and afterward
Napoleon, wishing to assert their equality with the legitimate successor of Augustus and Otto the Great, assumed the
imperial title; and it was because he hoped to retain the
old splendor of his crown in a new form that Francis II,
presaging the extinction of the Holy Empire, adopted the
style, which would have seemed absurd three centuries
earlier, of Hereditary Emperor of Austria.   Some similar
belief in the dignity of the title must have prompted its
assumption by the sovereigns of Brazil and Hayti (this
last intending to imitate Napoleon), by the unfortunate
Maximilian in Mexico, and by Louis Napoleon, who of
course had to claim his uncle's inheritance.   The old sentiment of reverence has, however, been so much used up,
not to say outraged, by these modern attempts to take
advantage of it, that it can scarcely be said to survive in
our days.   Except in the case of the German Emperor,
the associations of the imperial name are no longer
specially dignified: Emperor is only a pretentious synonym
for king.

It is otherwise with the German Emperor, because he
has a substantial, if not a formal and technical claim, to
represent the mediæval empire, with its line of magnificent
sovereigns from Henry the Fowler to Frederick II.   Moreover a title different from and apparently higher than that
of king was wanted for the head of the new Germanic state,
because the kingdoms of Saxony, Bavaria and Würtemburg
are members of it.

There was a certain resemblance between the position in
Hindostan of the Mogul sovereigns of Delhi from Akber to
Aurungzebe, and that of the earlier Teutonic emperors in
Europe.   And the supremacy which the British Crown now
holds in India over nearly all the native potentates, is not
unlike that which mediæval theory assigned to the Emperor
among Christian princes.

NOTE D.

LINES CONTRASTING THE PAST AND PRESENT OF ROME.

Dum simulacra mihi, dum numina vana placebant,
  Militia, populo, mœnibus alta fui :
At simul effigies arasque superstitiosas
  Deiiciens, uni sum famulata Deo,
Cesserunt arces, cecidere palatia divûm,
  Servivit populus, degeneravit eques.
Vix scio quæ fuerim, vix Romæ Roma recordor ;
  Vix sinit occasus vel meminisse mei.
Gratior hæc iactura mihi successibus illis ;
  Maior sum pauper divite, stante iacens :
Plus aquilis vexilla crucis, plus Cæsare Petrus,
  Plus cinctis ducibus vulgus inerme dedit.
Stans domui terras, infernum diruta pulso,
  Corpora stans, animas fracta iacensque reggo.
Tunc miseræ plebi, modo principibus tenebrarum
  Impero : tunc urbes, nunc mea regna polus.

Written by Hildebert, bishop of Le Mans, and afterward archbishop of Tours (born A. D. 1057). Extracted from his works as printed by Migne, *Patrologiæ Cursus Completus.*

INDEX.

Lightning Source UK Ltd.
Milton Keynes UK
15 September 2010

159919UK00001B/142/P